C0-ATW-276

Proceedings of the American Catholic Philosophical Association

Analyzing Catholic Philosophy

Volume 89, 2015

Edited by:

Mirela Oliva
Center for Thomistic Studies
University of Saint Thomas

Editorial Assistants:
Maureen Bielinski, Joseph Cherny, and Andrew Grimes

Papers for the regular sessions were selected by the Program Committee:
Jeffrey Bloechl
Thomas Cavanaugh
Raymond Hain
Patrick Toner
John Zeis

Issued by the National Office of the American Catholic Philosophical Association
University of Saint Thomas
Houston, TX 77006

Since 1926 the *Proceedings of the American Catholic Philosophical Association* have published annual volumes that contain papers originally prepared for the Association's annual meeting. These volumes are available for purchase and are also distributed to members of the ACPA as a benefit of membership. For information regarding subscriptions, online access, and ACPA membership please contact:

Philosophy Documentation Center
P.O. Box 7147
Charlottesville, VA 22906-7147
Phone: 800-444-2419 (U.S. and Canada); 434-220-3300
Fax: 434-220-3301
E-mail: order@pdcnet.org
Web: www.pdcnet.org

The *Proceedings of the American Catholic Philosophical Association* are indexed in Academic Search Premier, American Humanities Index, Catholic Periodical and Literature Index, Current Abstracts, Expanded Academic ASAP, Google Scholar, Index Philosophicus, Index to Social Science & Humanities Proceedings, InfoTrac OneFile, International Bibliography of Periodical Literature (IBZ), International Philosophical Bibliography, ISI Alerting Services, Periodicals Index Online, The Philosopher's Index, PhilPapers, and Religious & Theological Abstracts.

For more information about online access options for all volumes of these Proceedings please contact the Philosophy Documentation Center at order@pdcnet.org.

ISSN: 0065-7638 (print)
ISSN: 2153-7925 (online)
ISBN-13: 978-1-63435-031-0
ISBN-10: 1-63435-031-6

Published by the Philosophy Documentation Center, Charlottesville, Virginia.

Proceedings of the American Catholic Philosophical Association

Analyzing Catholic Philosophy

Volume 89, 2015

TABLE OF CONTENTS

From Neighbor-Love to Utilitarianism, and Back: Uncovering Some Structures and Dynamics for Ethical Theory

Revised for Publication as the ACPA's 2015 Presidential Address
Spring 2017

J. L. A. Garcia

Abstract: Contrasting loving our neighbors with utilitarians' demand to maximize good reveals important metatheoretic structures and dynamics that I call virtues-basing, input drive, role centering, and patient focus. First, love (good will) is a virtue; such virtues are foundational to both moral obligations and the impersonally valuable. Second, part of loving is acting lovingly. Whether and how I act lovingly, and how loving it is, is a matter of motivation; this input-driven account contrasts with highlighting actions' outcome. Third, in regarding someone as our neighbor we view her in relation to ourselves; a role-centered perspective shows that a wide range of person-to-person role-relationships constitute moral life. Fourth, if our moral task is loving each person, the moral question is how we respond to each person's relevant welfare and needs, focusing on those toward someone acts (moral patients), not on maximizing good across persons or producing an optimal world.

C harles Larmore titled his first book *Patterns of Moral Complexity*. I hope here to identify several additional moral complexities, specifically, some largely unnoticed structural or dynamic features of morality as it can be reconstructed within ethical theory. I call these aspects of the metatheory of morals 'structural' in either of two ways. First, some of these complexities concern the hidden logical syntactical structure of some central types of moral judgment. Second, others concern which families of moral concepts and judgments (where the main families are evaluative, deontic, and aretaic) are supported by which other families. (Or which central types of moral judgment within a certain family are supported by and based on which central instances from another family.) I call these features 'dynamic' where they concern what we can call the flow or impact of moral-status-giving force, a concept similar to Robert Nozick's of the "wrong-making force" that

© 2016, *Proceedings of the ACPA*, Vol. 89
doi: 10.5840/acpaproc201742463

we think a promise packs, or Shelly Kagan's idea of the various 'factors' that different moral theories see as making right acts right.

It's probably familiar by now that Kant's ethics of imperatives from pure reason can be seen as a secularization of the divine command ethics of the late medievals and the Reformers. My concern here is with the other main approach within modernist ethics, utilitarianism. That it too can be read as a secular interpretation of Christian ethics is, perhaps, the reason why Franz Brentano in the nineteenth century, Joseph Fletcher recently, and, nowadays, Philip Pettit are among the many ethical theorists who transitioned with notable smoothness from Christian ethics to utilitarianism or something akin to it.

In the first sections, I wish to show how versions of the utility principle can be seen as closely related to and descended from Christ's command to love our neighbors as we love ourselves. Moreover, I suggest that this derivation can look like the result of sensible moves made under the pressure of, first, the Reformation's attempt to de-Hellenize Christian thought, including moral thought, and, second, the subsequent Enlightenment project of secularizing moral thought by re-packaging ideas of Christian origins in new clothes free of revelation's regalia. Utilitarianism can be made to seem a close and appealing descendent from, or even a variant of, the central tenet of Christian morality. So viewed, the strong opposition of influential Christian thinkers to utilitarianism comes to appear ignorant and unwarranted. Later, however, I will deconstruct this sunny, irenic picture and show that any such transition from Christianity's command of neighbor-love to some version of the utility principle involves distorting the former, and neglecting insights within it that, perhaps, only (or best) come into focus when we carefully analyze and follow what may be implicit in neighbor-love. My speculative history of the utility principle's derivation from Christian neighbor-love is not chiefly meant to illuminate the past—I do not mean this to be a study in intellectual history, tracing the actual influence and path of ideas—but to be a device that helps us compare the two approaches so as to enable us to see what is lost when, perhaps thinking we are taking but a small step, we shift from loving our neighbors to maximizing utility. Then the needed intellectual projects are appreciating the riches of the relinquished treasure and recovering what we've unheedingly surrendered.

Though I rely on intuitions throughout, these are mostly not narrowly moral intuitions about, e.g., which actions or types of actions are right or wrong, which states of affairs are good or bad, or which traits and responses are virtuous or vicious. Rather, they are conceptual intuitions, concerning the link between roles, on the one hand, and virtues and duties, on the other; between something's virtues and vices and its being (a) good or bad (instance) of (one of) its kind(s); between someone's doing wrong in how she treats another person and her wronging the other and impacting her welfare; between an action's being somehow virtuous or vicious and its agent's mental states; between something's being good or bad in a way that goes beyond its being good for this person while bad for that one and its being good or bad of and in us to want or value it. The importance of these intuitions is that such metaethicists as R. M. Hare accepted the importance of conceptual intuitions to ethical theory, even while they derided dependency on "received opinion." Part of where such thinkers went wrong is in overstating the distance between our normative intuitions about such moral concepts as acting rightly or viciously, on one side, and, on the other, intuitions about what can be (and what is) morally right or vicious.

My project here is programmatic, retrieving some overlooked, unexamined, and under-appreciated aspects of morality. These aspects, I hope to indicate, should attract anyone thoughtful about morality. I will also suggest that these are aspects of morality that traditional Catholic moral thought can be theorized well to express. I commend these largely new topics to the attention and consideration of thinkers striving to advance those traditions. Perhaps working together in this way, we can trigger a movement that takes Catholic moral philosophy in some new directions, where secular thought will have to catch up with us.

1. Interpreting the Scriptural Command That We Love Our Neighbor as We Love Ourselves (Mark 12:31, Matthew 22:39)[1]

It is a familiar fact that the early Reformers preached *Sola Scriptura* and advocated de-Hellenizing Christian thought in order to cleanse it of pre-Christian elements that, they worried, could only contaminate and distort it. The significance of this for moral theory has been less remarked. These two movements, however, push Christians to take moral direction directly and almost solely from the commanded neighbor-love. Proceeding thus with only limited explicit guidance from Platonic, Aristotelian, neo-Platonic, or Stoic philosophy, many Christian intellectuals and, before long, many of their post-Christian successors, still strove to understand what the Scriptural command to love neighbors as we love ourselves meant and how it enjoined us to conduct ourselves. Let us examine their task and speculatively propose a route of theoretical progression.

First, it is attractive to proceed in such a way that the 'love' in question gets interpreted as benevolence, good willing through willing what is good, and thence more directly as acting for, and so as to achieve, a result that is good. That much seems pretty straightforward, even incontrovertible, whether or not we look to St. Thomas Aquinas or others for counsel. Carrying the project forward a century or two later, and without the Reformers' explicitly Christian commitments, it became attractive for ethical theorists to give what is good for someone a secularized reading, to thin it down to her pleasure, happiness, or preference-satisfaction.

The remainder of this secularized approach to construing some version of the love-command, whether seen as theological or justified on some secular grounds, is easily discerned. Loving one's 'neighbor' will get interpreted as loving everyone, and 'as yourself' glossed as loving equally, that is, as loving others as strongly as loves oneself. Finally, since not every good, not every thing that is good for someone, can actually be brought to every person, the obligation to love everyone is appealingly read as effectively directing agents to act so as to bring the greatest good to the largest number of people (later, to the largest number of sentient beings). Eventually, it is construed as directing people simply to maximize the good or, differently, to achieve the best available state of things. We can use the term 'utility principle' broadly to include any and all of these variations. In this way, we can see ways in which Protestantism's strong Biblical emphasis, and its inclination toward literalism, can combine both with the needs of Catholicism's confessional practice and sacramentology, and also with the rapidly growing codification, bureaucratization, secularity, and scope of civil law. Together, these tendencies help shift ethical theoretic stress from the ancients' focus on virtuous character and achieving a good life for the agent herself to norms of action, including commands and rules.

2. This Post-Reformation, Secularized Reading: Its Assumptions and Discontents

This interpretation and secularization of the neighbor-love command, however, involves several crucial but largely unnoticed and undefended decision-points. These become important once we realize that they constitute significant divergences from other, and arguably more intuitive, interpretations. First, insofar as morality directs us to live lovingly in response to each of our neighbors, the questions the moral theorist must ask about actions, as forms of neighbor-response, are 'Is this action suitably loving?' and 'If so, how loving is it, and how, in what ways, is it loving?'[2] That is to say, we must inquire whether the act expresses love in a way that suits, fits, the agent's relation to the other (the patient) as neighbor. We can call this sort of account of the morality of action, including its deontic status *input driven*, since it takes what fixes an action's morality or immorality to be its motivational inputs.[3] When deontic claims are thus based on virtues and relativized to roles, they are also what Bernard Williams and other philosophers have called "thick": that is, they are expressed in terms that have substantial descriptive content (e.g., 'cruel' or 'deceitful'). Moreover, they constitute what Henry Richardson calls "transparent" norms, meaning that they say not only *that* some way of behaving is morally objectionable, even unacceptable, but also *the way* it is objectionable and *why*.[4] These features benefit our moral understanding and theorizing by helping us to *specify*, *limit*, and *ground* deontic judgments. It also draws our defense of those judgments closer to our moral intuitions, framing them in the terms in which we ordinarily conduct our moral thought and discourse.

Such an input-driven account of our actions' morality and immorality has important advantages. It avoids consequentialism's reduction of the agent to a mere mechanism for generating desirable effects, and it expresses the person-to-person relationality that is central to moral life. It also lessens the susceptibility to moral luck (at least, luck-in-results) of moral wrongness and, thus, of blameworthiness. We have called it 'input driven,' recall, to capture the fact that actions matter morally because of what, as we sometimes say, they *mean*, where an action's meaning is usually tied both to what its agent means to do in performing it, and to what that action signifies for and in that agent's relationships with the persons to whom she is connected. It can also accommodate the element of common sense in consequentialism's insistence that an action's being right and wrong be sensitive to, even dependent on, its consequences.[5] However, the account limits this dependency to effects that the agent intends (or expects, and is therein willing to cause or allow).[6]

Though it might appear that an account of wrong-making factors that includes both an action's input and outputs is more attractive, such a mixed account founders on the fact that there would be no way of combining these two radically different kinds of factor. This is a point about incommensurability, but not the incommensurability of values, as in most current literature. Rather, here the point is that the different kinds of factors in virtue of which an action is immoral in various ways, including its being morally wrong, cannot be measured against one another. Moreover, it seems that any supposed moral importance an action's output has can be traced back to a matter of its psychological input. That what I said hurts you counts towards my behaving immorally only insofar as it indicates that I acted with and from malice, callous indifference, or some similarly vicious psychological input.

Second, consider the fact that a command to love, i.e., to be loving, is a directive to have a virtue. Insofar as other virtues are modes of loving, i.e., willing goods to someone, this should help us think of morality as centered in virtuous life. How should we, then, understand moral virtues? Aristotle's most general account of virtue is as a feature that makes a thing (its bearer) and its work (that bearer's work) to be good (*N.E.*, bk. ii, chap. 6, 1106a15). I agree with Aristotle (*contra* Michael Slote and Thomas Hurka) that a moral virtue is not just any relevantly good feature, but a trait of character.[7] However, while such a trait both is needed and suffices to make someone a good person (in some way and to some extent) within some role-relationship she inhabits, to make a person's work (i.e, action) good/virtuous, such a trait is not itself needed, but only a feature/response of the sort that would make its agent good in the relevant way or respect *if* she has that response as a character trait.[8] Further, the virtues of a person are (some of) her character traits, but the virtues of her action—its being kind, etc.—are (some of) her motivations for so acting. Thus, for you to be (a) kind person, kindness must be one of your traits. However, your kind act need not be done from (your trait of) kindness; it suffices that it emerges from and expresses a, perhaps momentary, kind response.[9]

Third, many familiar moral virtues can be seen as limited or specialized forms of goodwill. Thus conceived, each of them is the willing to some person of certain goods, such as those of self-management (respect), truth (veracity), protection (confidentiality), and so on.

3. Virtues-Based Ethical Theory

We normally think that goodwill, benevolence, toward another is a moral virtue. If our moral task and calling is to be loving, whether or not that is because it is what God commands, then what we need to know about an action, in order to judge it morally, is whether it is loving and, if so, both how loving it is and how it is loving. Since a person's virtues, as Aristotle suggested, make someone good, the ways in which I'm good to you count or help toward my being good in my relevant relationship with you. However, the kind of love for you that tends to make me a good 'neighbor' (or friend, sibling, or spouse, etc.) to you must be of a sort that fits our relationship in order thus to make me good within it. Among other things, that requires my love for you to be not merely the compassion and affection that I might also have for a pet, but a practical benevolence wherein I will you the goods peculiar to your status as a human person.[10] In short, then, my love for you must be a respectful goodwill that includes my willing you the good of (duly limited) self-governance and thus willingly deferring to many of your own personal choices about how you live your life.[11]

These reflections should suggest to us an account of immoral action that is grounded in the virtues, and a more broadly virtues-based ethical theory, by which I mean an approach that analyzes both the two other families of morally central concepts—those of actions' deontic status and of states of affairs' being impersonally valuable—in terms of moral virtues. Virtues are therefore conceived as more fundamental, basal, within the structure of ethical theory. To assess someone's action toward another person morally it is crucial, as I mentioned, that we consider whether, in what ways, and to what extent, her conduct is loving, and, if she behaves in an unloving (or only marginally loving) manner, to what extent that distances her from the other person within their relationship, and therein distances her from what sort of response suits and fits that type of interpersonal connection, that is, what her relationship with that person calls for. Moral theory is thus motivated toward replacing Kant's question 'What ought I to do?' with the more insightful, 'How ought someone to conduct herself?' Thus to ask in what way we should behave is to inquire into the considerations *from* which, those *despite* which, the spirit *in* which, the goals *for* which, and the means *by* which, it is good or bad of (and in) us to act. Taking our role-relationships seriously, as central to these inquiries, helps us to see our questions about what fits and suits the relationship *within which* our agent is to act, and the role which, like it or not, she acts *as* occupying and which gives her behavior moral significance.[12]

What is desirable/valuable can be analyzed as what it is virtuous (good-making) in someone to want and value. Compare Michael Zimmerman's position that whatever has intrinsic value is that which we are required to favor. My talk of virtuous (good-making), rather than 'required,' emotions accords with Peter Geach's, Philippa Foot's, and Judith Thomson's rejection of intrinsic goodness and of twentieth-century non-naturalism. Since neighbor-love is rightly seen as benevolence, wishing and willing my neighbor well by willing her goods, the relevant goods to be willed to and for her are chiefly things good *for* the neighbor. Still, we can say your health is more than just good for you. It is a good relative to each of us. Such being valuable is best conceived as what it is virtuous of and in a person to favor for (and in relation to) some person.

This account of our value discourse is superior in several ways to analyses of value judgments in terms of Franz Brentano's *Rightigkeit*, A. C. Ewing's "fittingness," and Roderick Chisholm and Michael Zimmerman's "requiredness." One, it requires no special, unanalyzable value-feature, *pace* G. E. Moore. Two, it remains within familiar and accepted forms of good-talk, specifically, goodness-of-a-kind, being a good *F, contra* Moore, W. D. Ross, and others. Three, it allows degrees and comparatives, unlike Chisholm and Zimmerman. Four, it permits an account of betterness as what is more virtuous to want, which is superior to Brentano's own suggestion that the better is what it is correct to prefer in a special, irreducible conception of preferring.[13] Five, it captures (and reinterprets) goodness's tight connection, noticed by consequentialists, to being desirable and valuable. Six, when claims of impersonal value are virtues based and roles centered in this way, they are not only more intuitive and clearer; they are also more human and more personal. That is to say, when so conceived they then reflect the connectedness internal, even central, to anyone's life as a human person.

Such an understanding of value-judgments in terms of virtue-concepts lends an approach greater theoretic unity and systematicity. It stresses the personal and mental, like other substantive efforts in virtue ethics but, since it relies chiefly on the notion of a virtuous response—someone's being virtuous in how she feels, is inclined to behave, and what she wants—it employs virtue-concepts in a way that avoids the worry raised by John Doris and other 'situationists' about the supposed rarity of virtue-traits in people. They believe that those concerns, if validated, would undermine virtue-ethics, assuming that such an understanding of morality must assume virtuous traits to be widespread, common, or easily attained. As understood here, however, what I have loosely called virtues-basing might be more carefully framed as basing claims of impersonal value and permissible/impermissible action in concepts of virtuous response, for example, wanting this person to recover from her illness, while being disappointed that she is ill, and meaning to help her if needed. Someone in whom such responses were a deep-seated tendency and formed a trait would have a character that is at least partially virtuous. Whether many people do, however, is no part of the analysis offered here.

We have shown how to analyze something's being impersonally valuable in terms of someone's morally virtuous response to it. Similarly, we can understand what it is morally prohibited for someone to do, and therein obligatory that she omit, as that in which, within the context and her relevant role-relationships, the agent treats someone viciously.[14] We should quickly admit that motive-utilitarianism poses a complication. Such theories can be input driven on a shallow level, but the action's morality or immorality is not then deeply shaped or driven by its input. For they must hold that, even if an action's input is what makes it right or wrong, what gives that type of input value will be the general or usual results of acting on/ from its instances.

These desiderative/volitional/affective attitudes are central to virtue and vice. Cognitive attitudes become involved, take on derivative moral import, because if S1 genuinely wills S2's good, then S1 must be inclined to act toward that good as an end, and must be interested in finding out what will really help S2, and what would harm S2. Thus, S1's being 'careless,' as we say, in her treatment of S2 indicates a morally deficient (vicious) level of/in her caring about S2.

It would take us too far afield deeply to engage the common view that being virtuous is irrelevant to someone's doing her duty and fulfilling her obligations. Still, I want to suggest that the supposed gap between vicious action and the impermissible can be helpfully bridged if we attend to and employ the language of wrongdoing, and cognate terms, in striving to analyze and conceive what is morally required.

What is obligatory, we often say, is what we have to do and must do; it is what we cannot omit. What is forbidden, similarly, we also call what we cannot, mustn't, do; it is what we have to and must refrain from doing. These are modal concepts, of course, and it can be instructive for the theorist to ask in what way and *for* what the obligatory is necessary. Aristotle, of course, memorably taught that "We call 'necessary' . . . that without which . . . as a condition . . . we cannot get rid or be freed of evil" (*Metaphysics*, 1015a20–25 [trans. W. D. Ross]). A virtues-based account offers an appealing and intuitive candidate for the evil to be avoided in and by doing one's duty: it is acting viciously, which itself is internal to, even identical with acting wrongly, that is, impermissibly.

Privileging the concept of wrongdoing in thinking about morality—now conceived as what is required of us if we are to avoid acting evilly, viciously—reminds us to attend to the etymology of the term 'wrong.' Doing wrong is acting in a way that is twisted ('wrung'), awry, deformed, as vice deviates from virtue. Note how starkly the wrong, the twisted, contrasts with the good when we remember the latter term's origin in an Anglo-Saxon root meaning what fits.[15] (Think of how a puzzle piece that has become twisted and misshapen seldom fits into its space.) Also, this emphasis highlights how wrongdoing contrasts with action that is 'right,' that is, straight (which term derives from a word meaning stretched taut). The latter can be roughly understood as action that accords with virtue. Acting rightly follows directly, straightaway, from duly-informed virtuous motivation. Concentration on wrongness, rather than the impermissibility that is so often stressed today by Scanlon and others, can illuminate by drawing our attention to related locutions and syntactical forms. We can go deeper than the philosopher's familiar question: Would S's doing A be morally impermissible, forbidden? We can ask: Is it wrong *of* S to do A? Would S *wrong someone* in doing A? What is *wrong with* or *wrong in* S's doing A? The answers to these questions, I would contend, are often, even usually, best framed in terms of virtue.

We can also move toward a similar result from the opposite direction, understanding the forbidden in terms of vice. Historically, the idea of what is morally forbidden was framed and conceived in most of Europe as sin. Sins, of course, are offenses against God, acts of disobedience that, as such, express an insubordinate, defiant, truculent frame of mind. Any such attitude is ill fitted to and but poorly suits our standing as God's subordinates and creatures. So, in its original conception, the morally impermissible was closely tied to virtue and vice, specifically, to what befits a human person in her relationship with her Creator and Governor. This is a connection that need not be lost, and that, I think, we profit from recovering, even in more secular, philosophical accounts of morality.[16]

3.1. Beyond Virtues-basing to an Additional Metatheoretic Concept: Patient Focus

Neighbor-love directs your attention to the good of another as your neighbor, and thus as a person and individual who stands in a relationship with you. This is different from caring about the good of some whole, an overall situation, let alone, the goodness of a whole world. Rather, each of us is called to respond *to* her neighbor (and *as* a neighbor). This suggests a *Patient-Focused* account of moral virtues and derivative features, according to which our virtues (and derivative duties and rights) are ones we have within certain role-relationships with certain persons, in such a way that what it is virtuous/vicious of me to be and do in that relationship is shaped by what the role-respondent needs and what serves her interests.

Loving another as someone (normally) loves herself involves loving her *as a person* with her own interests and an *inner worth* that grounds a claim on love. Hence, the moral virtue here is respectful love.[17] Conceived as thus patient focused, moral norms are neither "hypothetical" in Kant's sense of being grounded in the agent's self-interest, nor "categorical" in his sense of being independent of anyone's desire and need, and instead grounded solely in pure reason. Rather, they are grounded in the needs/welfare of the agent's role-Other, i.e., the person in whose life she fills/ occupies the relevant role.[18] Patient focus contrasts both with focus on the agent, as in egoism, and with focus on the overall value comparison of worlds, conceived as maximal sets of states-of-affairs or propositions (i.e., to paraphrase Wittgenstein, as "everything that [would be] . . . the case.")

All this suits the view that any person-to-person role-relationship of the sort we deem crucial involves persons in their personhood. It's thus more than just a relationship between persons, that is, one both of whose termini/relata are persons. Each is related in her personhood in that each is involved in her (possibly) rational preferences, likes, inclinations, wants, choices, intentions, and so on, or in spite of some of these being relevantly subordinated (or blocked from being what they naturally would be).[19] The basic idea of what I here call patient focus is advanced by Plato's Socrates in dialogue with Thrasymachus (as translated below by Thomas Cavanaugh):

> [Socrates:] Your physician in the precise sense . . . Is he a money-maker, an earner of fees, or a healer of the sick? . . . [Thrasymachus:] A healer of the sick. [Socrates:] And what of the pilot—the pilot rightly so called—is he a ruler of sailors or a sailor? [Thrasymachus:] A ruler of sailors. [Socrates: Yes.] For it is not in virtue of respect of his sailing that he is called a pilot but in respect of his art and his ruling of the sailors. (*Republic* 341c–d)

He continues to widen application of this point.

> [Socrates:] Then medicine does not consider the advantage of medicine but of the body? [Thrasymachus:] Yes. [Socrates:] Nor horsemanship of horsemanship but of horses, nor does any art look out for itself . . . but [looks out] for that of which it is the art. . . . [Socrates:] Neither does

any physician in so far as he is a physician seek or enjoin the advantage of the physician but that of the patient. (*Republic* 342d)

Finally, Socrates generalizes to insist all human relationships of superordination are to serve the benefit of the subordinate.

> [Socrates: N]either does anyone in any office of rule in so far as he is a ruler consider and enjoin his own advantage but that of the one whom he rules and for whom he exercises his craft, and he keeps his eyes fixed on that and on what is advantageous and suitable to that in all that he says and does. (*Republic* 342e)

What Socrates says of positions of rule and superordination properly extends, I think, to all the principal and morally crucial person-to-person role-relationships. What makes someone, S1, to be a good R to S2 is how S1 responds to S2's welfare, and thus what counts S1 being and doing what she ought in her relationship with S2 is S1's response to, her pursuit of, S2's advantage, not S1's own. It is thus the good of the relevant other, S2, that makes S1 and her behavior good. That is patient focus.

At this point, Catholic intellectuals might well worry that what I'm calling patient focus is deeply opposed to Thomistic moral thought, according to which Thomas, thought to be following Aristotle, is seen as holding that all someone's moral features—especially, her virtues and duties—are grounded in that person's own self-fulfillment and happiness. That egoistic interpretation has, however, recently come under persuasive criticism, with an alternative advanced. According to John Cahalan, David Gallagher affirms that "the basis of [a certain subject's] ethical obligation is not the desire [in that person] for [her own] happiness/contemplation, [which is merely] a *bonum secundum quid*, which is subordinate to love of *bona simpliciter* for their own sake. [Rather, t]he duty to seek [one's own] happiness is based on the duty [that everyone has] to will the good of persons."[20] This can be seen as following from the fact that "In Aquinas happiness and desire are loved by [i.e., with, through] desire, not by love of friendship (*S. T.* Ia-IIae, q. 2, art. 7, *ad* 2; Ia-IIae, q. 25, art. 2; Ia, q. 60, art. 3, and art. 4, *ad* 3). We don't will them, as we do persons, by willing some other good for them, but [to the contrary, we will them] by willing them for another good, [viz.,] rational beings." Similarly, according to Cahalan, "Maritain knew that standard accounts of Aquinas' ethics didn't work philosophically; for he [Aquinas] says [one's own] happiness is something we are [i.e., each of us is] obligated to seek. So [it follows that my] happiness is not the source of [my] obligation."[21]

My task here is not to interpret Thomas, nor do I claim he would agree with everything I've here asserted. Still, the Catholic philosophical thinker, while not properly a slavish follower of the Angelic Doctor (or any other mortal), does well, showing intellectual humility, by limiting the extent to which she departs from her tradition and its greatest expositors. It is reassuring, then, that my concept of roles-relative patient focus can be regarded as helping ground and elucidate the link between such person-to-person modes of connection as friendship, on one side, and our moral virtues and duties on the other, a project to which Cahalan and Gallagher can be seen as opening the door.

3.2. A Virtues-based, Patient-focused Approach to Thinking Through Moral Conflicts

Above, I pointed out that, within an ethics based in neighbor-love, crucial moral questions about any action are whether, to what extent, and in which ways, it is loving or unloving. Love for individuals thus suggests, for cases where serious harms will ensue no matter what an agent does, what we might call a *minimax* second-best strategy: minimizing the maximum extent to which we distance ourselves from a truly loving response in regard to *anyone*.[22]

We should consider three kinds of conflicts between duties (and therein between virtues).

> (Scenario 1) May (Should) Aggie kill Victor, if that's needed in order to save Victoria's life?[23]

> (Scenario 2) May (Should) Aggie kill Victor if that's needed in order to save the lives of both Victoria and Vicki?

> (Scenario 3) May (Should) Aggie kill Victor if that's needed in order to save Victor from (great) suffering?

We can helpfully model our inquiry, first, by imagining that each person at risk has an advocate whose argument we will hear. In Scenario 1, Victor's side can persuasively argue that Aggie treats Victor more unlovingly (and, thus, is more nearly vicious in her relevant role-relationship to him) by targeting him for death than Aggie treats Victoria merely by failing to do everything Aggie could to save Victoria. That is because it is of the nature of loving someone to will her what is good for her, and willing her instead what is bad for her (death) is further removed from such good will(ing) than is just not willing that she have what is good for her. In Scenario 2, Victor's side can again persuasively make the similar argument that Aggie treats Victor more unlovingly by targeting him for death than she treats anyone, either Victoria or Vicki, by merely allowing that person to die as a side effect of Aggie's refusing to kill Victor. To see this, imagine that Victor's advocate first successfully makes this argument against Victoria's advocate, and then successfully makes it against Vicki's. Everyone's side, the case for Aggie's acting to help each, is duly weighed one after another. No one is left out, ignored, or treated as if he doesn't count. In Scenario 3, we can alter our hypothetical serial hearings by imagining that an advocate for sparing Victor's life persuasively argues, against an advocate for sparing Victor suffering, that Aggie's behavior toward Victor is decisively and radically against the good of Victor's life to a greater degree or extent (and hence more unloving toward him) if she kills him than Aggie's abstention is decisively and radically against the good of his peace of mind should he continue living because she refuses to kill him.

This procedure of *Serial Consideration* (that is, serializing imaginary adversarial hearings of the reasoning by counterposed advocates) to resolve conflicts keeps us theorists properly focused on what is important—how close to lovingly Aggie treats each person—and it helps us screen out such irrelevancies (unjustifiable factors) as how many persons are involved. This approach also grounds the insight toward which David Oderberg and 'the new natural lawyers' separately strain in endorsing a norm forbidding ever choosing directly against any basic human good, while tying it to the good *of* particular persons.[24] It not only captures so-called deontological constraints/prohibitions, but undermines the presumption that special exemptions are needed because we have a general duty to optimize our action's results (or, differently, to maximize the good). We don't, since such a supposed duty cannot sensibly be owed *to* anyone. Further, it better accommodates moral common sense than does so-called "sophisticated" or what Martha Nussbaum calls "sensible" consequentialism, which can explain why it is worse to cause the death of one than it is to allow five deaths, but (according to Shelly Kagan) has little explanation of why it is wrong to kill one to avoid five killings.[25]

Additionally, such an approach may suggest appealing solutions to some Trolley-style problems. In blasting someone's body out of the cave-mouth to clear a passage, for instance, or pushing someone onto a track to stop a tram, or directing a vehicle to grind to a stop in someone's flesh, an agent acts from vicious, manipulative, and demeaning attitudes toward another, whom she targets for attack and therein treats as a mere physical object when that person's very life is at stake.[26]

This serial-consideration of persons' competing interests and claims contrasts with aggregative calculation or overall commensuration/comparison. Finally, serial-consideration of competing interests well captures the Neighbor-Love Command's insight that morality is a response to *each* person, not to their aggregate or average, and, still less, to some supposed overall value of a possible world.[27]

3.3. *Roles-centering in Moral Theory*

For you to love another as neighbor is to love her as occupying a certain role-relationship to yourself, a mode of being connected.[28] This mode of regard, however, should open you to seeing persons as connected to you in a variety of ways, including seeing everyone as your neighbor. It should also open you to seeing some people as related to you in ways that others are not and that call for special forms or modes of love (esp., willing certain special goods to one's role-Other, 'role-respondent') or even for special, elevated levels of love. Each of us is to respond *as* neighbor (that is, as neighbor *to* her).

That I do well to love you as your neighbor, however, doesn't entail that I do well to love you *only* as neighbor. Rather, it allows that there may be other kinds of person-to-person relationships, also fulfilled by my loving in certain ways the one (or ones) to whom I am related, which forms of love will thus tend to make me good within the relationship, a good R to someone, and therein constitute virtues and generate duties. Indeed, by drawing attention to the role of neighbor, the neighbor-love-command's formulation may reasonably incline us to consider the moral import of other ways of being connected to a person. This suggests a *Role(-Relationship)-Centered conception* of anyone's moral life, by which I mean that anything it is virtuous or vicious of someone to be or do is what it is virtuous or vicious of her to be within one or another of certain morally-determinative role-relationships in which she stands to some person.[29] The moral virtues are character traits that tend causally or constitutively to make their bearer good in certain role-relationships (which we can therefore call 'morally determinative'). In this way, such virtues are (as in Aristotle and Aquinas) good-*making* features but not (*pace* Adams, Hurka, Slote, and some other recent writers) features that are really themselves good (let alone, intrinsically good).[30]

The role of neighbor, in its broad Scriptural sense of a fellow traveler through life (i.e., a human being like oneself), can be seen as a limit case of role-relationship, since the role-subject (role-occupant) may be very distant, emotionally and geographically, from the role-other (i.e., a moral subject's role-respondent).[31] Similarly, the self-regarding role of steward of one's own life can be seen as the limit case in the opposite direction of maximal intimacy of connection between role-occupant and role-respondent.[32] This allows that a single social role, such as that of citizen, may comprise a number of distinct role-relationships in our sense, including role-relationships to the subject's fellow citizens, to one's state, to civic officials, to members of one's community's military, to aliens, etc.[33]

Still, there is a problem: doesn't your loving each "as yourself" demand that you love each person equally? I think not, because for you to love another as you love yourself is to love her with ardent devotion, for her own sake, etc., but not necessarily to love her as much as, to the same extent that, you love anyone else.[34]

Though each such role-relationship has its own independent and irreducible significance, it may still be that some roles also incorporate others. Thus, as a creature of God, you are virtuous (obedient and cooperative) in your relationship to Him only insofar as, among other things, you treat your 'neighbors' well, as He wants and directs. Properly understood and lived, this does less to spark than to resolve and reconcile apparent conflicts among roles. Such roles-centering contrasts with views of morality as crucially, even definitively, *impartial(ist)*.

These considerations can help us see how to reply to William Godwin's infamous Fénelon scenario (from the first volume, second book of his *Enquiry Concerning Political Justice*. Godwin was correct that there is no "magic in the pronoun [*sic*] 'my'" that turns an otherwise evil action of mine into an admirable one simply because it looks to benefit my friend, or relative, or neighbor, or some such, rather than, say, yours. However, it doesn't follow from that fact that there is no moral import for how I should feel and act in the fact that this valet is or isn't my mother, father, friend, etc. Each affected person "counts for one," as Bentham affirmed, but may still count morally not merely as one sentient animal, but as related to the agent in this or that way, occupying this or that role in her life. However, it allows that morality is *universal(ist)* in that someone can be virtuous in relation to anyone, in whose life she plays a relevant role.

Morality's relativity to a variety of person-to-person role-relationships has some theoretic advantages. (1) It gives content and specificity to Aristotle's important but abstract claim that humans are essentially social animals. We don't just need society, or even social contacts, but certain somewhat specific forms of person-to-person connection, that is, what we here call role-relationships. (2) It accommodates, captures, centralizes, justifies, and explains an insight of care-ethics, specifically, its emphasis on an agent's (or, better, a subject's) different ways of being connected to various persons. (3) It similarly accommodates, captures, centralizes, justifies, and explains Christina Hoff Sommers's point that different persons exert what, adapting Nozick's terminology, she calls variant "differential ethical pull" on the agent.[35]

3.4. Some Implications of these Considerations: Revisiting the Utility Principle

In light of these investigations, the utility principle can be seen to diverge from the command of neighbor-love in several ways; moreover, a strong case can be made for the superiority of the neighbor-love side. The utility principle and, more important, modern optimizing consequentialism go astray in their accounts of what is good in the sense of being impersonally valuable, of what makes one state of affairs better, more valuable, than another, and of what makes actions morally permitted or forbidden.

First, then, what is good? Utilitarians employ an incorrect use of the term 'good,' predicatively to express a state of affairs' supposed intrinsic value, rather than adjunctively/attributively to express someone's goodness within a role (P1's being a good R to P2), and what makes for such goodness (virtue). Utilitarians incorrectly understand our sometimes calling a state of affairs, S, as good (or bad) as our therein predicating intrinsic value/disvalue directly to S, when in fact we therein predicate moral virtue/vice to persons' attitudinal responses to S.[36]

Second, what makes one state of affairs (impersonally) better than another? Complex situations are simply those situations your wanting, liking, intending, or otherwise favoring which tends to make you virtuous to some persons but perhaps vicious to others. There is little reason to assume each such state of affairs must also have some further, inclusive, overall value.

Third, what makes some actions morally right (permitted) and others morally wrong? Utilitarians go astray by looking to (the comparative intrinsic value of) actions' output instead of their motivational input. Their concern to maximize the number of people helped or the total good done can be helpfully seen as a crude but sometimes useful 'heuristic,' a shortcut to remind us that each person has a claim on us and that there is no upper limit on virtuously loving any person. Indeed, the very concept of world-optimizing is completely confused. The important ethical question is not Kant's 'What ought I to do?' but, better, 'How is it good (i.e., virtuous, good-making) or bad (vicious, bad-making) for me to behave?' Relatedly, the philosopher Garth Hallett and various proportionalist theologians go astray in thinking that Christian morality is all about securing, acting so as to achieve, the 'greater good.' Like utilitarians, they miss the promising theoretical insights extricable from the command of neighbor-love. (Likewise, in the Harry Potter books, Dumbledore's ally-turned-nemesis, the evil wizard Gelert Grindelwald, is wrong to use his slogan "For the greater good" to justify his assorted victimizations. It is only the good of each person that matters, not the overall good, nor the best world, even if there were such things.³⁷)

4. Where Lies the Appeal in Accepting a Metatheoretic Understanding of Morality as Not Only Virtues Based, but Also Roles Relative, Patient Focused, Input Driven, and Serially Considerate?

All of these features of a theory, features of the structure of some central moral judgments or about the flow of moral status from items within one category to those in another, can be seen as metatheoretic in that they indicate something of the range of the types of moral theory we can have. My claim here, for example, that morality is best theorized as based in virtue-concepts, with other moral concepts, such as those of duty and the impersonally valuable derivative therefrom, suggests an obvious contrast with a theory that takes deontic concepts or those of impersonal value as fundamental. Likewise, the position I've here taken, according anyone her moral features—her virtues, duties, and rights—only within a plurality of person-to-person relationships can be seen to contrast with alternatives in which we have some or all our duties (or our claims and rights, etc.) independently of any such relationships, maybe because we incur them simply as rational beings (or, some claim, as sentient ones), say, or simply from occupying a relationship to God, or as members of a certain society. These are theoretical alternatives.

Again, my view that my virtues and duties in relation to my parent's or neighbor's welfare are chiefly shaped by her welfare (and my attitude toward it) could be opposed by a variety of different positions according to which the agent's own welfare determines what her duties and virtues are, or that assigns that role to the interest of her society, or to God's (supposedly arbitrary) commands. In place of our input-driven account of moral obligation, we could look instead to an action's output, whether that is the comparative value of its total consequences, as in classical utilitarianism, or some special targeted effect, such as (for a certain kind of pacifist) whether it kills. Rather than serial consideration, of course, we could maximize across persons. In this way, I hope here to have illuminated for the theorist a multiplicity of overlooked and under-investigated options for various sites and types of moral theorizing.

Still, it is not enough for the ethical theorist to content herself with pointing out possibilities. We should make a case for some options over others, if we can. The justificatory questions in this section's heading are philosophically the most important, of course, but our responses must be merely cursory, indicative of paths to pursue rather than developed answers. First, suppose I have established that there can be, and neighbor-love even suggests, an ethical theory that is *virtues based* in the sense that it analyzes both judgments of state of affairs' impersonal value and judgments of duty in terms of virtue-concepts. Why go beyond accepting the possibility of such an approach to *endorsing* that kind of theory over alternatives? With regard to *basing value-judgment in virtue-discourse*, there are several attractions, but I will limit myself to sketching just two.

Basing such claims as 'Knowledge is impersonally good' in judgments that wanting and otherwise valuing people's knowing things tends to make one virtuous in relationship to them matches and improves on mainstream analyses that construe something's having value as its being fitting, appropriate, right, required, or justified for anyone to want, 'love,' favor, or bring about. It matches them because virtue-concepts are themselves evaluative, as are the special 'fittingness,' 'requirement,' and so on, that some philosophers propose. It improves on those accounts of the valuable because it eliminates the need for some such additional, technical, and irreducible value-concept as fittingness, since virtue-concepts are familiar and within the familiar realm of the moral. Unlike some of them, it also has the advantage of allowing of comparatives and degrees, enabling us to analyze the better as what it is more virtuous to value. Our analysis also humanizes and personalizes the valuable because whereas intrinsic value is supposed to be predicated of mere states of affairs, virtue-concepts apply to persons and their psychological (and therein personal) attitudes.

As for *basing our moral obligations, prohibitions, illicitness, wrongness, rights, and the like, in the virtues,* recall my earlier point that this approach, again, gives many theorists what they want by employing the 'thick,' robust moral language of vicious (and virtuous) action and by replacing thinly-formulated rules like 'Lying is wrong (or violates the moral law)' with such virtue-claims as 'Your lying to her is deceitful (or duplicitous, mendacious, etc.).' Recall, too, that this reformulation helpfully offers what Richardson called "transparent" norms, ones that partially specify what is wrong with the action it condemns. An added benefit is that it systematically construes wrongdoing as wronging someone, that is, as the agent's failing the person with whom the relevant relationship connects her. Specifically, on this view, the agent's doing wrong consists in her failing, and therein wronging, the latter person within that relationship. Morality is thus kept personalized, a step toward realizing Scheler's century-old vision of a full-blown ethical personalism.

Second, what reasons support my claim that morality is *relative to certain role-relationships?* In what ways is that appealing? An illuminating approach would look to the way in which, as social beings, this emphasis on relations between persons highlights a human, personalist conception of moral life. Improving on F. H. Bradley's famous talk of "our station and its duties," we can see the heart of morality in 'our roles and their virtues.' It is not just that, as what Aristotle called 'social animals,' we want to be around others of our kind. Rather, there are certain, more specific ways of being connected with persons that matter. It is these we consider roles, role-relationships. Note that, as Aquinas largely realized, insofar as it is a virtue, love needs to be relativized to roles anyway.[38] For the love that it is virtuous for a parent to have for her child is quite different from the love virtuous in a child for her parent, and both differ from the sorts of love a virtuous husband shows his wife and a wife her husband. These are ancient and medieval insights but, for those so inclined, such an approach should also call to mind and resonate with Heidgger's concept of *Mitsein*, that is, being-with, as definitive of the human condition.

Among today's analytic philosophers, Scheffler has started to explore "relationship-based" moral reasons as a possible way of modeling the whole of the moral

realm, and T. M. Scanlon stresses our conduct's impact on interpersonal relationships, especially in his account of what he calls "the ethics of blame," including what
it consists in and who has "standing" to do it. Somewhat earlier, in their different
ways, T. Nagel and W. D. Ross both stressed the importance of such relationships
in understanding 'deontological' (roughly, duty-based) approaches to morality. The
theologian Charles Curran's "relationality-responsibility model" of Christian ethics
can also be seen as anticipating and consonant with such an approach.[39]

Third, what of *patient focus*? What speaks in its favor, and where can we
find helpful recent antecedents for such a concept? I think Levinas's writings on
the centrality of The Other (*l'Autrui*) forms one important and influential recent
predecessor. Focus on moral patients assists us in remembering that what matters
to the morally sensitized agent, and what really matters morally, is not how much
total good exists in the world—and still less how good the world itself is—but how
loving each of us is to everyone else. Bringing good to the greater number, if it has
any moral importance at all, may be a helpful rule of thumb for someone to keep in
mind as a way of making sure that she doesn't leave anyone out of consideration.[40]
Somebody's doing good to and for a person is a sign and result of her being good,
i.e., virtuous, to the latter. It is being good (in relation) to each person, rather than
doing good overall, that animates a moral sensibility. Doing less than the most
good matters morally only when and insofar as it indicates some vicious deficiency
in the agent's love.

Fourth, what is attractive in *input drive*? Here are some answers.

(A) It helps free our moral thinking of dry and misleading legalism. Actions'
morality is shaped by what goes into them and what input means for the agent's
relationships with relevant parties, not those actions' relationship to abstract
principles, rules, or laws.

(B) Conceiving wrongness as (role-)viciousness (rather than bare "permissibility," as in Scanlon and others) also helpfully allows the theorist to exploit
the suppleness of 'wrong'-talk (wrong *of S* to V, something wrong *in* or *with*
S's Ving), and to learn from the etymology linking what's wrong to what has
gone awry, and become twisted away from what's good (etymologically, *Ghed*,
i.e., fitting).

(C) What's obligatory is therein required, necessary. Input drive leads us to
conceive what's morally required as what's necessary to avoid behaving (con-
ducting oneself) viciously, that is, behaving badly as R, in a role-relationship
with and to someone, S.[41]

(D) This approach properly understands actions as exercises of personal agency,
deriving their 'meaning' largely from what the agent does and doesn't mean to
do in them. Scanlon himself recognizes that an action's "meaning" is often its
meaning *within* its agent's personal "relationships."[42]

(E) Input drive assists us in avoiding an instrumental and mechanistic view of
agents as mere producers of effects. For that reason, it has the added theoretic

benefit of sharply limiting the moral significance and impact of luck in an action's effects. (For those who think we should acknowledge some importance of luck in moral matters, they still have the agent's good or bad luck both in the situations in which she finds herself and in the physical and mental constitution that her ancestry and environment combine to give her.)

(F) Though I won't pursue that important matter here, input drive—which highlights such matters as what an agent does and doesn't intend in acting—can help provide the theoretical rationale that Scanlon demands for double effect reasoning's view of intent's relevance to what is morally permitted.

(G) It allows us to reconceive the common (and uninteresting) objection that we can do right thing for the wrong reason, or do the wrong thing for the right reason. That is because we find the same phenomenon with respect to intellectual virtue and vice. We can similarly do a smart (or, alternatively,) stupid thing (i.e., the sort of thing that it is typically smart/stupid of someone to do) while, in fact and on this occasion, we act stupidly (or smartly), that is, in a stupid (or smart) way.

Fifth and finally, where can we find something particularly appealing in *serial consideration*? I think it lies in the way that, in such a procedure, emphasizing each person in a group as an individual, giving her a sort of turn to be considered, we show each party a respectful love and value each person separately. A vison of moral life as consisting in relationships with each person suggests that the real challenge within situations of conflict is to be loving to each person involved. Being a good (virtuous) person in one's relationship with each suggests that an agent needs to recognize a floor of good will, benevolence, beneath which she will not allow herself to sink in regard to anyone. Though she cannot be as good to each person as the virtuous agent would like, she can at least manage to avoid being bad to (vicious in her relationship with) *any*one. Beyond that, she needs to take care that each person is duly considered. Serial consideration achieves both these goals; the utilitarians' method of aggregation across persons achieves neither.[43]

In contrast, whatever rational or intuitive appeal some claim to find in aggregating across persons, we do best to understand it as what some psychologists call a "heuristic," that is, a crude reminder or rule of thumb to be used to help in our initial thought about cases, but unsuited to careful consideration of the demands of moral virtue, that is, of what is needed for an agent to avoid treating anyone viciously, in our sense of treating her badly as her R. Perhaps an inclination to maximize across persons should be seen as a useful scruple to encourage early in someone's moral education and sensitization because, if we take an interest in maximizing the good, we at least have to consider, however inadequately, every person's interest. So, caring about maximizing the number of persons helped may be a first, albeit misleading, step to insuring that we show we care about each person involved. It makes us look around, so to speak, to make sure we see everyone relevant, rather than stopping as soon we find one possible beneficiary or victim. Still, the proper way to show concern in a situation of conflicting interests is not in fact to maximize the good done—nor, what is different, the number of people helped. Rather, we proceed better in such cases when we strive to minimize the extent to which we depart from virtue in regard to anyone involved.

Let me close this section by considering an objection to serial consideration. We have reason to worry that such a procedure will systematically keep S1 from helping her friend, partner, or relative, S2, by allowing the great need of S3, a stranger, to trump S2's claim in each imaginary hearing. This is a serious matter, which could undermine the structure and insights of a virtues-based, roles-centered, patient-focused account of morality that includes an input-driven account of our actions' moral status. Perhaps the following line of reasoning can serve to rebut the objection. There is little reason to think S1 is showing adequate consideration to S2, in light of and within their role-relationship, by acting with/showing someone else, S3, a level of concern/caring that, in S1's wider situation, will clearly override showing concern for anyone else with such regularity that it marginalizes, or even eliminates, S1's frequently acting (or otherwise responding to S2) *as* S2's friend, or partner, or brother or sister, or mother or father, or husband or wife, or co-citizen, and so on.

5. Towards a Conclusion

Most of the meta-theoretic features here sketched are structural, and some of them dynamic. Virtues-basing and roles-centering are *structural* features of a moral theory, in that virtuesbasing and roles-centering reveal the structure of our judgments of virtue, the desirability of states of affairs, the wrongness of actions. Thus, for a state of affairs to be impersonally (un)desirable is for it to be virtuous (or vicious) for anyone to favor; and for an action to be immoral is for it to be somehow vicious. For someone, S1, to respond virtuously or viciously, or to have a duty or a claim-right, is always for her to be virtuous or vicious, to have a duty or right, *to* someone, S2, and within some role-relationship in which S1 stands connected to S2. Serial-consideration, for its part, indicates the constituents and order (structure) of procedures for resolving conflicts.

Input Drive and Patient Focus are *Dynamic* theoretical features. Virtues-basing and input-drive both indicate the direction of flow of moral features/status from virtuous internal attitudes to immoral action and impersonal value, i.e., whence derives forbiddenness and desirability. Patient focus indicates that the welfare of the role-respondent is the source (what, I think, Kant called the determining ground) of a morally virtuous/vicious, permissible/impermissible response to that other. Maximin (or, alternatively, satisficing) strategies indicate how and when its input make an action become vicious/wrong.

Here, I have chiefly tried to sketch each feature and to show how it can be seen as part of a richer philosophical interpretation of the command of neighbor-love than is usual. It is, especially, richer and more complex than that embodied in any version of the utility principle. I commend to others further study and broader justification of the meta-theoretic features I've here sketched, as against alternative ways of basing and centering moral concepts, of focusing theoretical attention, of sourcing moral significance, and of driving the moral status of actions, as well as further inquiry into this comparatively new field of such structural and dynamic features within moral theorizing. In doing so, I draw attention to several matters that need further determination within such an approach to ethical theory.

Boston College

Notes

I appreciate comments and suggestions from undergraduate and graduate students who participated in the 2015 inaugural Philosophy in an Inclusive Key Summer Institute at MIT, as well as those advanced by the audience at a plenary session of the American Catholic Philosophical Association's October 2015 annual meeting in Boston, and The Felician Institute of Ethics and Public Affairs 2016 Ethics Conference. I am also grateful to Ms. Carlin Menzin and to Messrs. Lucas Perry, Benjamin Rusch, Christopher Berger, and Alexander Montes for exemplary research assistance.

1. We should also note Leviticus 19:18. I claim no competence as Scriptural exegete, but do report that I have seen it argued that, for the Hebrews, one's neighbor was understood to be a member of her tribe, at least, in the extended sense that comprises the Twelve Tribes, while the parable of the Good Samaritan, among other New Testament passages, suggests a wider scope. Talk of God's command to love can be understood, not just literally, but also as indicating that such person-to-person love is appropriate, more specifically, that it is morally virtuous. Note that even God's commands derive their moral import from the fact that our disobeying them is vicious in and of us, an act stemming from an attitude that makes us bad in our capacity (what below I call a role-relationship) to the Deity as creations, workers, and Our Father's children. (Christians, of course, believe that while we are so graced as to deserve one another's love, each of us is also so corrupt that love is appropriate to us in part *in spite of* our desert.)

2. The attitudes that count toward someone's being a good R, where R is a morally determinative role-relationship in which she stands with some person, chiefly consist in wanting, willing, and liking—in general, favoring (affectively, desideratively, volitionally)—one or another aspect of the latter person's welfare. If, as we should, we think of generalized, agapic love, for moral purposes, as good will—willing that is good because it is the willing of goods—then we can see how many, even most, of these role-virtues will be forms of love. We can illustrate this with a few examples. Your confidant wills you the good of privacy and control over what you reveal, insofar as she is a good confidant. Your neighbor wills you various successes, insofar as she is a helpful caring, and therein good neighbor. Your teacher or informant wills you the good of supported and true beliefs.

3. For this reason one could talk here of normative expressivism. By that I do not mean the bankrupt metaethical idea that moral judgments state no facts but only express their maker's likes, dislikes, and preferences. Rather, I have in mind the view, anticipated by Hume and others, that actions derive their normative moral significance from the states of their agent's mind that they express, reflect, and spring from. Actions matter morally not as physical events, but as exercises of personal agency, and thus as virtuous or vicious because of the likes, preferences, choices, to which they give expression.

Since, so conceived actions are made immoral by what goes into them, it would also make sense to call this a contamination- (or infection-) model of wrongdoing. Adapting an image from T. M. Scanlon's account of value judgments, we could also call this view a 'buck-passing account' of deontic talk (Scanlon, *What We Owe*, 95–100). Again, my meaning is that, as understood here, for an action to be morally wrong/prohibited, to be what someone mustn't (is forbidden to) do, is for it to be vicious in its context, for its agent to behave viciously in performing it. That means it stems from a motivational attitude as input that, were it a stable trait of character, would count toward the one having it being bad (a bad R) in some morally determinative role. Being in conformity with or in violation of duty is thus not a separate quality an action has, but when we say it accords with or breaches duty we direct attention to other facts about the action, specifically, to the mental states in the agent that it embodies, for example, by advancing some agenda she has adopted.

4. See Williams and Richardson, *Ethics and the Limits of Philosophy*.

5. Those fixated on optimizing in ethics really should focus on which action is best. That, however, need not be the optimific action, the one that produces the largest amount of what is good, and won't be if actions are made relevantly good or bad not simply by their outputs but by other factors. The notorious Peter Singer now pushes for "effective altruism," mistakenly believing that an action's producing more good—or, differently—yielding a better outcome—makes it a morally superior, even requisite, act. Here, I make a case for an opposed, input-driven account of action's moral status. So conceived, actions matter morally as expressions of personal agency, of preferences, of wants and aversions, of likes and dislikes, and of the intentions we form and those we decide against adopting. So understood, actions engage moral factors on their input side. Even then, since actions are good (virtuous) in different ways, there will seldom be one action that is simply best. Usually, this one will be better in these ways, but that one in those, and perhaps still other options superior in still more respects.

In principle, a theorist might opt for neither an output-driven account of wrongdoing, as in major forms of consequentialism, nor an exclusively input-driven account, as here. However, there seems no way adequately to compare (let alone, to commensurate) such radically (supposed) different wrong-making factors so as to yield as determinate result. Below, I suggest that concern for optimizing sensibly gives way to avoiding actions that are presumptively vicious, especially any action that is presumptively vicious in radical ways, as when its agent intends some evil-to-will result. (Recall Thomas Nagel's insightful reminder [in his *View From Nowhere*] that it is of the nature of the bad to be that which we repudiate, so that to intend an evil is likely to be especially odious. For us, vicious.)

6. An input-driven account of actions' morality and immorality also is a natural fit for virtues-basing, since we normally think whether an action is kind, honest, respectful, and so on, or, to the contrary, cruel, deceitful, unjust, and the like depends on the spirit in which the agent performed it: what she meant to do and the considerations in the face/spite of which she chose and acted.

In contrast, Judith Thomson has sometimes suggested that an action's being virtuous or vicious is independent of its agent's mental states. Insofar as the action's being morally wrong (that is, impermissible, forbidden, and a violation of moral duty) reduces to its being vicious in the context—as it does in the theoretic approach I here advance—Thomson's position implies that an action's deontic status must similarly float free from its agent's mental state in choosing and performing it. This loses the close connection between virtuous or vicious character and virtuous/vicious action, and the grounding of both on instances of virtuous or vicious response to what is valuable, whereby a virtues-based account unites the theory of moral virtues to the theory of what is impersonally valuable. Thus, to my mind, Thomson's recent view, wherein she understands moral obligation and forbiddenness on the models, and under the rubrics, of "advice" and "directives," forsakes the unity, richness, insights, and creative innovations that virtues-based ethical theory offers.

7. See Hurka, *Virtue, Vice, and Value*, and Slote, *Morals from Motives*.

8. Samuel Scheffler has recently reminded us that Thomas Nagel stressed the moral importance of an agent's avoiding actions that would put her in an unacceptable relationship with another person (Scheffler, "Reasonable Partiality," 113–114 in Feltham and Cottingham; citing Nagel, "War and Massacre"). Scheffler rightly complains that this falls short of basing moral considerations in a moral agent's actual modes of connection to others, since it only involves bad relationships that her actions might create. Scheffler faults what Nagel says for its failure to show how the agent's abusive behavior transgresses, distorts, or undermines any pre-existent relationship between her and the victim. Yet it is on the latter basis that we are intuitively inclined to criticize the abuser.

In contrast, our roles-centered moral theorizing sees an agent as already playing a variety of roles in different people's lives. Not only is this approach in that way actualist (as we might call it) in comparison with Nagel's, but it is also attractive in being positive and comprehensive. It is positive, both because the relevant relationships are ones your having someone fulfill in your life (as a good friend, spouse, etc., to you) enhances your thriving as a human being, and because what is chiefly required in each of the role-relationships is some form of goodwill (such as your friend's discretion, devotion, encouragement), that is, loving response. (See Thomas Aquinas, *S. T.*, 2a2ae, q. 23, art. 8 on charity as the major virtues' "form" [My quotations from thomas are all from the English Dominican Fathers' 1920 revised translation.].) It is comprehensive, because it holds that *all* positive and negative moral features of our character, our actions, our mental states, and our responses to our situations and circumstances are thus relativized to role-relationships.

9. In this way, virtues-based ethical theory somewhat refocuses Bradley's famous titular dictum, "my station and its duties." This is not quite right. Rather, someone's moral life is contained in her stations—that is, certain of her role-relationships, which situate her, determining how she stands to various persons—and those roles' virtues. Relevant to this idea of someone's role-relationships and their virtues, consider also this insightful remark of Pope St. John Paul II: "[T]he social nature of man . . . is realized in various intermediate groups [i.e., in various associations, relationships below the level of the state and above that of the individual] beginning with the family . . . which [a] stem from human nature itself and [b] have their own autonomy." (*Centesimus Annus*, para. 3) The autonomy he mentions is important for ethical theory, for the moral import of my being your friend in such a way as tends to make me a good friend to you is, as understood here, internal to the structure of moral features and, in that respect, autonomous.

10. It is worth remembering that love also seems to involve privileging relieving persons from various serious ills—especially, those that injure them in their personhood—over merely bringing them positive goods. I am normally more loving to you when I spare or reduce your discomfort or suffering than when I shower you with cookies. While I use the widespread and ordinary-language terminology of benevolence, that is, willing for you that you have good things, among the more serious goods are those of relief from evils. (Both Epicurus and the negative utilitarians strove to accommodate this fact, though they were hampered by trying to do it within evaluative hedonism.)

11. Compare the theologian Margaret Farley's concept of "just love," which could be better termed respectful love. We should add, of course, this deference does not properly extend to foolhardy, self-destructive, or perversely motivated decisions. Still less does it extend from your decisions about how to live also to decisions about whether to (continue to) live at all. Though we can properly agree with the modernists in talking of 'autonomy' here, we do well also and always to bear in mind Pope John Paul II's cautionary reminder that, contra Kant and his recent epigones, anyone's due autonomy needs to be her participation in theonomy.

This close connection between justice and benevolence, while contrary to Kantianism, is in line with some recent Catholic moral thought. Thus, the Holy Father Paul VI famously asserted, justice is the "minimum measure" of charity. (See Pope Paul VI, "Address for the Day of Development" [23 August 1968].) More recently, we have this. "Charity goes beyond justice, because to love is to give, to offer what is 'mine' to the other; but it never lacks justice, which prompts us to give the other what is 'his', what is due to him by reason of his being or his acting. I cannot 'give' what is mine to the other, without first giving him what pertains to him in justice. If we love others with charity, then first of all we are just towards them. Not only is justice not extraneous to charity . . . justice is inseparable from charity. Justice is the primary way of charity . . . Charity demands justice: recognition and respect for legitimate rights" (Pope Benedict XVI, *Caritas in Veritate*, sec. 6).

12. It is not difficult by intuition to identify which person-to-person role-relationships are the ones within which we have our moral virtues and vices, duties, and rights. Certainly, we think, such modes of connections as parenthood, marriage, friendship, co-citizenship, promising, and being neighbors in both the narrow and the larger Christian sense of the term must count. The philosophical challenge is to justify such a list, what it includes and excludes and why. This is not the place to develop and defend responses to those challenges, but I will say that it is your nature as a human being whose fruition partially depends on me and others filling and fulfilling—that is, not just occupying but largely discharging and living up to—relevant ways of being connected with you. At the same time, my and their human flourishing requires that we not subject ourselves to other ways of relating to you, for example, as your slave. Those considerations help delineate what kinds of person-to-person role-relationships are, and which can't be, constitutive of an individual's moral life.

Another philosophical challenge arises from cultural relativism. Suppose we do accept such a list and that such roles as friends, parent, and neighbor are on it. Still, doesn't what constitutes being, say, a friend or parent itself vary from one society to another in such a way that the role's virtues and duties will vary too? Perhaps so, and maybe the theorist of role-centering should therefore go down the road of considering whether it is the roles as they would be conceived and be socially instantiated within an ideal community (or, maybe, some adequate approximation thereto) to which she needs to attend. Or, alternatively, it is simply the versions of friendship, parenthood, and so on, that actually exist with a given moral subject's own community that matter relative to judging her. Or, it might be some point between the ideal and the actual with which the ethical theorist should work. My own inclination, however, is rather different. Any variation across societies can only occur, and can only be intelligible, within certain fixed parameters. There is no reason to count as a form of friendship or parenthood any form of connection that demands treating the other with cruelty or contempt, after all. Those logical limits may give a theory all it needs for moral evaluation. Being a virtuous friend, parent, or neighbor, and so on, to someone S consists in the core character traits of loyalty, special concern and devotion, confidentiality, etc. Responding to S virtuously as her friend, parent, or neighbor is responding as someone with such a trait characteristically would. These virtues, and their opposed vices, cannot vary across cultures, for they constitute what any form of connectedness must incorporate in order for it even to be (i.e., to count as) a kind of friendship, parenthood, or being a neighbor, in the first place.

13. Brentano insists that there can be no upper limit to acceptably loving what deserves love, and then reasons that, since being better cannot consist in being correct to love more, it requires some different analysis, one that introduces no comparative element into his canonical form being correct to love. He chooses to define being better as being correct to prefer in a sense of 'prefer' that doesn't reduce to being loved more (for him, more intensely). However, for his own reasons, he ignored the possibility that being better could be derived from being correct to love by introducing the comparative element into the adjective rather than the verb. It might be being more correct to love. That sounds odd, because correctness doesn't normally admit of comparatives or degrees of intensity. However, as we saw, other thinkers replace Brentano's concept of correctness with alternatives—fittingness, appropriateness, etc.—many of which do allow comparatives. If we follow my suggestion here of replacing being correct with being good, in the sense of being virtuous and therein good-making, then we can say that the better is what does more to make the favorer a good R for some relevant role-relationship, R.

14. Role-relationships as understood here fall between mere logical/Humean relations, on one hand, and the robust account of interpersonal relationships as necessarily including a shared history between the parties, especially, a history of encounters, interactions, and involvements that one or both of them remember and appreciate so as to generate and sustain long-term affectional bonds. (Scheffler, "Reasonable Partiality," 115.) In my view, what matter morally are certain role-relationships, ways of being connected that tend to play a part in one or both parties living a fulfilled life that suits a human being in her humanity, in her nature as a social being.

Perhaps I should add that, in the kind of roles-centered—indeed, roles-relative—ethical theory that I here endorse, what matters to the moral subject (and to the moral judge) is the person with whom the role-relationship connects her and the way that acquitting oneself well, virtuously, in that role tends constitutively to enhance that person's welfare. Thus, my position differs from that of Scheffler, and some others, who stress and show concern for the relationship itself, even for its own sake. Of course, I allow that part of my concern for you as my friend, partner, co-citizen, even just my neighbor (in the broad Christian use of that word) is a due concern for our role-relationships themselves as constituents of your flourishing. Then, however, my concern is chiefly focused on you, not on the relationship between us. Rather, the relationship takes on importance for me only as a part of your human fulfillment, or sometimes as a mere cause of it. To be sure, if I don't care at all about our friendship, then I'm not a good friend to you. Still, since what here matters is how my being a good friend to you is part of your good, my chief concern is not, *pace* Scheffler, for our relationship, but for you.

15. This shows an important element of truth in the view of Ewing and others that positive attitudes are fitting to (i.e., they fit) what is good, especially, what is impersonally good. Rather than elaborating analyses in terms of the unanalyzed term 'fitting,' I think Ewing and his fellows would have done better to say what it is impersonally good is what it is good of us to favor. That move is no semantic improvement, since it retains the term 'good.' However, this formulation has the syntactic advantages of reminding us that 'good' needs a completing term and clarifying that of which the term is here predicated. For if something impersonally good, X, is what it is good to favor, then it is the favoring of X that is good,

and thus that someone's, S's, favoring X is a good favoring. My further suggestion is that the respect in which the favoring is called good is that it tends to make S, the favorer, good in some way, where I think the last is best glossed as S's being a good R, good, that is, in some crucial person-to-person role-relationship *vis a vis* some person S2.

16. Of course the Bible's neighbor-love inunction is formulated as a command. How can that fit what I call 'virtues-basing,' which understands deontic talk in terms of virtue-concepts? My answer has several parts. First, as to content, since what is commanded is love, obedience requires acting lovingly, and disobedience then consists in falling somehow short of the requisite love in some way by acting, say, without any love at all, from too little, or out of the wrong sort of love. Second, as to motivation, obedience to divine commands should be conceived in terms of an underlying motive and justification. Since mere fear of God's punishment cannot motivate genuine love—loving someone for her own sake rather for one's own—the obedient must act from gratitude, awed reverence, devotion, or some similarly fundamental and virtuous response to God. Third, we gain insight here by following Scheler's insight, in his *Formalism in Ethics*, that moral imperatives are important for indicating deeper values, as the prohibition on killing people points us to the value of life. If we supplement that *aperçu* with the further analysis that talk of what has value is best understood as saying it is good of us to value, and then gloss that valuing as tending to make someone good in one or another of her relevant role-relationships, then we have moved from imperative through value and the valuable to foundational virtue-concepts. Fourth, love for God, in Christian circles, is usually closely tied to love of neighbor, either emerging from it or leading to it. The divine command to us to love one another, issued at a particular time and place, is best seen as underwriting, and giving additional support and justification to, neighbor-love. That love is already and independently morally virtuous, grounded in human nature (and, thus, in God's creative Will) rather than only in His legislative Will. Similarly, the Decalogue's injunctions against dishonoring parents, homicide, theft, adultery, lying about people, and so on, all derive from the second Great Commandment, and turn what are already offenses against people, forms of morally vicious failure in our personal roles, into vicious responses also in relation to the divine Creator and Governor, to whom only loving obedience is appropriate. Such love alone tends to make anyone good in her relationship to Him.

17. Compare Margaret Farley's eponymous concept of 'just love,' and contrast Epicurus's and Bentham's ethical theories, as well as some understandings of Aristotelian and Thomistic ethics, which are egoistic, focused on the agent's own pleasure, happiness, welfare, or flourishing.

18. Sarah Harper helpfully calls this party someone's 'role-respondent.' See Harper, "Role-Centered Morality."

19. This special attention to and concern for some more than others accommodates and largely fits our natural moral sympathies, whereby we care specially for friends, close relatives, partners, and some others, even though we also care even for distant strangers. This is an important kind of "psychological realism" that should qualify any plausible approach to ethical theory. However, therein lies a problem. Imagine someone who, like Mrs. Jellyby in Dickens's *Bleak House*, has little moral sympathy for those more closely related to her, but cares deeply for people with whom she shares little beyond common humanity and prioritizes stranger's interests. Is it morally permissible for her thus to subordinate those more closely connected to her in important role-relationships? I don't see why. We may reasonably strive temporarily to tolerate her eccentricity, to accommodate it while she occupies herself with attempting to normalize, naturalize, and improve her moral sensibilities and sensitivity and

the spontaneous responses that spring from them. Still, her mind is so distorted as to be defective, and her resulting actions will display her twisted and misshapen ways of relating to persons.

20. Cahalan, citing D. Gallagher, "Person and Ethics in Aquinas," *Acta Philosophica* (Rome) v. 4 (1995): 51–71. See also Cahalan, "Natural Obligation."

21. Cahalan, "Love of Friendship."

22. Perhaps we do better construing this as a *satisficing* second-best strategy of insuring an agent respond lovingly within her role-relationship(s) to/with each person involved, at least to a certain minimal extent. Unlike minimax, satisficing is not inherently comparative and thus has wider application beyond resolving conflicts.

23. I prescind, for illustrative purposes, from various ways in which varying the kind or state of Aggie's relationship with Victor (and Victoria) might affect our imagined moral hearings and the presumptive moral case against each of Aggie's relevant alternatives.

24. Oderberg, *Moral Theory*, chaps. 2, 3.

25. Nussbaum, "Comment"; and Kagan, *Normative Ethics*, chap. 5.

26. Cass Sunstein, citing influential moral psychology work by Daniel Kahneman and others, thinks that our scruple against killing innocent people, even to protect or save other innocents, may be mistaken. He suggests, to the contrary, that this intuition of ours may be just what Kahneman calls a "heuristic," that is, not a universal truth but only a rough generalization, which our minds have developed for most situations but that philosophers misuse when they treat it as a moral truth and apply it to Trolley Problem-style cases and draw anti-consequentialist conclusions. That reasoning seems to me to stand upside down (as Marx famously said of Hegel's). Rather, unrefined talk of a moral goal to maximize the amount of good—or, what can be different, to optimize the state of things—seems more like (and more likely to be) just a rough-and-ready rule of thumb, a crude generalization, that arose in our history to help us in many situations to remind us that we should give everyone some consideration, and to use as a simplified guide when, in educating small children, for example, we don't have enough time or the right audience to get into the many complexities of moral thinking and virtuous living. It is consequentialists who misapply this crude heuristic, when they treat it as if it were an important and real moral truth, even *the* fundamental moral principle. It seems, instead, to be more of a first step toward thinking more seriously, often harmless to use in relatively easy situations free of serious and tricky conflicts between the demands of virtues internal to the morally determinative role-relationships that an agent occupies in various people's lives. (For an introduction to such 'heuristics,' see Sunstein, "How Do We Know What's Moral?" also Kahneman, "Can We Trust Our Intuitions?".)

27. There is still a consequentialist-style danger facing even this substantive roles-centered approach to moral theory, despite its justified rejection of aggregating harm across persons. That danger is that my failing to meet the needs of some stranger P1 may tend to make me worse (in one of my relevant role-relationships) to her than does my failing to do some good for my daughter, and so too for each of the strangers P2, P3, P4, and so on. In each of the serial comparisons, my doing some small kindness for my daughter appears to lose out to helping some needy stranger, by addressing her needs. The result is that my time and resources are exhausted by meeting the urgent or substantial needs of strangers, so that I never get to do kindnesses for my daughter or any of my friends, co-citizens, partners, or other relatives. That threatens to render the roles-relativity of moral features nugatory, impotent. Part of the point of serial consideration is to make sure each person is taken with

due seriousness in keeping with her role-relationship(s) with the agent, but now the worry is that those relationships get systematically subordinated. Something has gone amiss.

Perhaps we can turn this point about the point and lessons of serial consideration to our advantage in blocking this problem. The question here is whether an agent wiling to subordinate the interests of her friend, parent, spouse, partner, neighbor, and so on in order to meet the needs of a stranger is showing sufficient concern for her friend as friend (her parent as parent, and the rest), if she does this in a situation where she knows there are very many others to whom she cannot equally attend without effectively abandoning those roles altogether. When it's clear that strangers' needs will thus gobble up the agent's attention, resources, and time to the neglect of her friend (or the others), that's good reason to say the answer is negative.

Another strategy for counteracting this danger of allowing the importance of role-relationships to be smothered is to stress how important it is to be good to those with whom more intimate relationships connect us, and how bad it makes someone in her relationship to another as friend or partner consistently to fail to act out of special concern. The relevant question in our series of comparisons may quickly become 'How bad (a father or mother) am I to my daughter if I here *again* fail to act from special concern for her?' Another approach would be to say that moral life—here, each morally determinative relationship—allows, or even requires, each moral subject, in such a conflict situation, to recognize a floor below which her preserved time and energy for her more intimate relationships are not permitted to fall, despite the needs of others. It is also pertinent to note that some think there is moral significance in *how* the needs of some are subordinated, even set aside, to attend to loved ones. (See F. M. Kamm's work, such as the chapters in Section One of the volume in the bibliography.) Thus, we correctly think it normally more vicious of S1 to step over the starving S2 in order to get S1's family dinner party than we think it presumptively vicious of S3 to spend money on that party rather than send it to a relief agency that will channel it to S2 and others in similar plight. Without getting into that dispute here, we should note that virtues-based theory may be especially well suited to capture this difference and its moral significance, since S1, who steps over the starving person, appears to manifest a vicious hard-heartedness toward S2 that is not apparent in S3, and may not characterize the latter at all. It is natural for noticed proximity to another's need to trigger stronger feelings in us, and a stronger urge to help, than does need of which we are aware but from which we are, in various ways, distant. These issues of moral sensibility and sensitivity, though not ones on which I here dwell, will likely come into play in explaining and justifying this difference, and virtues-based theory provides an especially suitable context for motivating, establishing, and articulating it.

28. The image of neighbor has richness. Your neighbors are those with whom you share a common or proximate physical space, such that what you do often affects them, and what they do often affects you. In part for those reasons, we expect neighbors to consult with us about some of what they do, as they expect us to consult with them on our plans, and to do this out of mutual involvement in each other's space and even lives, but also out of concern and good will of one for the other. Scheffler sees globalism as a challenge to traditional morality's stress on relationships, but reflecting on and extending in this way what it is to be a neighbor can help us grasp how to incorporate global consciousness and responsibilities within familiar forms of moral thinking.

29. Compare the theologian Charles Curran's "relationship-responsibility" model of ethics in Curran, *Catholic Moral Tradition Today*.

30. Stroud says the main questions about the morality of relationships are (a) which relationships are morally important, (b) why these relationships so matter while some others don't, and (c) why, among the relationships that do matter morally, these relationships matter more than those do. (See Stroud, "Permissible, Partiality, Projects, and Plural Agency.")

On (a) and (b), my proposal is that they are role-relationships that give content to our nature as social animals, that is, ones that each of naturally wants or would benefit from having filled in her own life while feeling no aversion, rooted in our shared human nature, to filling in another's. The latter condition also helps set the limits to what virtue demands of anyone as occupying such a role. Beyond a certain level of sacrifice acting for the other's good goes further than what is required for being virtuous to the other in one's relationship to her. Stroud complains that no such pure permission is plausible as an "eternal moral verity." However, it stands to reason that, if my claim is correct that all morality is a matter of fulfilling certain roles in relation to persons, them there are built-in limits to how much her being a virtuous R to this or that person can demand of any moral subject. (Perhaps Stroud allows that, and wouldn't allow such permissions to go beyond a certain level of sacrifice for the sake of one's R—e.g., friend, neighbor, parent—as "pure" in his sense. Maybe he means only that it doesn't fit a morality that demands as "eternal . . . verities" that we keep our promises and help the needy also to allow, at the same theoretical level, that someone can give special consideration to her friends and family. I confess that I find that conception of morality's structure so alien, I cannot judge what does or doesn't fit it.)

On (c), I think the question less important than Stroud and others think, because the practical conflicts that its answer is supposed to solve are better approached by first looking to how well each of various courses of action available to an agent squares with the virtues internal to relevant role-relationships rather than trying to rank or compare the relationships themselves.

31. Why should we consider person S1's merely being S2's fellow human being, a (distantly) kindred traveler along life's way as S1's occupying any role in S2's life, let alone, as here required, a morally determinative role in the sense of one of the roles in (relation to) which S1 has her moral virtues, and her derivative moral duties and rights? It's a good question. One answer is that there being others with S2 (or anyone) in the world is a necessary condition—indeed, part—of S2's (or any person's) not being utterly alone, a plight contrary to any human's social nature. Another is, of course, that S2 (or anyone) needs there to be some persons who are *not yet* S2's friends, spouse, partners, co-citizens, and so on, in order for S2 ever to become friends, and so on, with anyone.

32. John Cottingham makes the interesting and appealing suggestion that care of and for oneself is not merely an indulgence that morality allows us but derived from to a duty to develop and improve oneself. (See Cottingham, "Impartiality and Ethical Formation".) Since, in virtues-based theory, duties are derivative from virtues in that duty-talk is a variant on the discourse of being vicious in a role-relationship, I think it best to reformulate Cottingham's point, affirming that being a good steward to oneself, and therein avoiding being a bad one, someone vicious to herself, is no mere indulgence that morality grandly permits us but itself a structural feature of moral life no less basic than being a good friend to this person, a good partner to that one, or a good spouse and parent to these people. Of course, Aquinas, agreeing with what Aristotle says (at *N.E.*, bk. 9, chap. 8), affirms that "the love with which a man loves himself is the form and root of friendship," so that "the origins of friendly relations with others lies in our relations to ourselves." (*S. T.*, 2a2ae, q. 25, art. 4)

Maximilian De Gaynesford wonders whether impartiality derives from a more basic moral partiality, and proposes that both derive from the same structural source. (See Gaynesford, "The Bishop, the Valet, the Wife, and the Ass," 84-97.) Without going into Gaynesford's own suggestions on why both these claims might be true, it should be clear that I think that partiality in the form of the roles-relativity of such moral features as virtues, vices, and the duties and rights derivative from them, is a fundamental structural characteristic of those features, and therein is a fundamental structural element of morality itself. Impartiality, on this view, is indeed, a derivative, occasional, and special role-virtue. A member of the state's judiciary owes its people impartiality as something she has properly promised them in order well to execute her role-function: being a virtuous judge for them. Thus, whether or not quite in the way Gaynesford envisions, her virtuous impartiality among litigants is grounded in her deeper, 'partialist' concern, specially owed to certain individuals, not to let her (normally appropriate) partiality govern her role-behavior in this special situation.

There may also be situations that themselves demand impartiality of an agent independently of any explicit promises of hers. (Some, but surely not all, trolley-problem cases may be like this.) Still, these situations demand impartiality only as a virtue within some roles that change the agent or have fallen on her. When it is A's duty to be impartial as between (not to show partiality to either) B and C, this is usually because there is someone, D, such that A's being virtuous in her role-relationship with D requires such impartiality. This impartiality is something that A owes D as D's R; it is not in the nature of morality that everyone, or even anyone, be generally impartial among persons. Indeed, the situation is quite the contrary. So, the main points remain that, contrary to what many philosophers supposed, (a) it is partiality that is universal, fundamental and normal, even within morality. In contrast, (b) impartiality is the deviation that requires special justification and, moreover, (c) such justification must itself still be rooted in some person-to-person role-relationship(s).

33. What are these role-relationships? I tentatively propose that these are relationships in that they constitute ways of a person, S, being related to some individual being in ways that engage S's personhood (understood as inherent capacity to reason in ways that can inform her action, and sometimes passions, or to develop such capacity). They are also natural in that they are both found across most cultures and are such that anyone's repudiation of, aversion to, or lack of interest in, participating in any of them properly raises questions of her normality and mental health. They are roles in that they are what J. J. Thomson's *Normativity* calls both "goodnessfixing" and "directivefixing" kinds. "Goodness-fixing" here means that what the relationship is, what it consists in, itself determines standards for evaluating someone within it. "Directive-fixing" means that it is also a relationship in which someone can be defective and thus in which there are some things she ought, and some things she ought not, to be or do. (I think these purportedly two kinds of kind are really only one, since to evaluate an occupant as a bad R is to ascribe to her some kinddefect. Thomson at least sometimes talks as if she agrees.) In this way, the subject has a kind of function within the relationship, which makes it into a role. Further, I should add that normally these are genuine relationships in that they last some considerable amount of time, rather than merely such a short-term relation as sitting to my left on the 9:47 bus this morning. There may be exceptions, however, as when you undertake to make an assertion to me and thus take on a connection that, however brief, is freighted with trust, dependency, and responsibility. Finally, intuitively, these must be relationships that some person has with some person. The person to whom I am related may have some of her personal characteristics so thwarted or stunted by immaturity, illness, or some physical or emotional trauma age that she cannot reason or respond reciprocally. Still, ours remains a person-to-person relationship.

34. This holds, whatever sense we assign to talk of S1's loving S2 'more than' she loves S3. Is the latter, for example, a matter of comparing the two loves' felt intensity? Or, quite differently, is it some sort of practical prioritization by S1 of S2's welfare over S3's?

35. See Sommers, "Filial Morality."

36. We can also ask what is in this person's interest, what advances or enhances her welfare. My abstract answer is that it is something that is good for this person, that is, something that contributes to the kind of life that fits and suits a being of her type, that is, a human person.

37. Rowling, *Harry Potter and the Deathly Hallows*, chap. 2.

38. See, for example, *S.T.*, 2a2ae, q. 26, arts. 6–12.

39. See Scheffler, "Reasonable Partiality"; Scanlon, *Moral Dimensions*, esp., chap. 4; Nagel, "War and Massacre"; Ross, *The Right and the Good*; and Curran, *Catholic Moral Tradition Today*.

40. See P. Singer, *The Most Good You Can Do*.

41. Recall Aristotle's reminder, already quoted in *Metaphysics* 1015a, 20–25, that one of the senses we assign talk of what is necessary is to designate that without which some good cannot be achieved or some evil avoided.

42. Scanlon, *Moral Dimensions*, esp. chap. 4.

43. The so-called Doctrine of Double Effect (or, better, what Thomas Cavanaugh nicely calls "double effect reasoning"), which has been developed in Catholic moral theology, holds that it is never morally acceptable to act intending someone some substantial evil. This draws some support from what we have just proposed. For if we are to recognize some limit to the extent to which we depart from benevolence in regard to anyone, where better to discern it than in a practical attitude so opposed to the love that is virtuous in us that it consists in treating some evil, understood now as what it is vicious to favor, as (if it were a) good? That, after all, is what intending a significant evil is, in that what someone intends she therein is committed to welcoming if it occurs, to wanting in preference to its contradictory, and to being (defeasibly) disposed repeatedly to strive after until she achieves it. It should be obvious that such a frame of mind takes what is by hypothesis evil, undesirable, very close to the way we should respond to what is good, valuable. This distortion of virtuous valuing, whereby we favor what it is virtuous to reject, can only be regarded as a deformation of moral sensibility, which in an input-driven account of moral action, must render any action done with such intent conclusively vicious and therein ineligible, twisted in the way we call morally wrong.

Bibliography

Adams, Robert M. *A Theory of Virtue: Excellence in Being for the Good*. New York: Oxford University Press, 2009.

Benedict XVI, Pope. *Caritatis in Veritate*. Encyclical Letter. Vatican translation, 2009.

Bentham, Jeremy. *Introduction to the Principles of Morals and Legislation*. Mineola, NY: Dover, 2007.

Brentano, Franz. *Origin of Our Knowledge of Right and Wrong*. Translated by R. Chisholm and E. Schneewind. New York: Humanities, 1969.

Cahalan, John. "Love of Friendship, Not the Desire for Happiness, is the Basis of Aquinas' Ethics." Available at www.foraristotelians.info/wp-content/uploads/2015/09/gallx3.pdf.

Cahalan, John. "Natural Obligation: How Rationally Known Truth Determines Ethical Good and Evil." *Thomist* 66 (2002): 101–132.
doi: https://doi.org/10.1353/tho.2002.0008

Chisholm, Roderick. "Ethics of Requirement." *American Philosophical Quarterly* 1 (1964): 147–153.

Cottingham, John. "Impartiality and Ethical Formation." In Feltham and Cottingham, 65–83.

Curran, Charles. *Catholic Moral Tradition Today: a Synthesis*. Washington: Georgetown University Press, 1999.

Doris, John. *Lack of Character*. Cambridge: Cambridge University Press, 2002.
doi: https://doi.org/10.1017/CBO9781139878364

Ewing, A. C. "A Suggested Non-Naturalistic Definition of 'Good.'" In *Readings in Ethical Theory*, edited by John Hospers and Wilfrid Sellars, 2nd ed. Appleton-Century-Crofts, 1970.

Farley, Margaret. *Just Love: a Framework for Christian Sexual Ethics*. New York: Continuum, 2005.

Feltham, Brian, and John Cottingham, eds. *Partiality and Impartiality*. Oxford: Oxford University Press, 2011.

Foot, Philippa. "Utilitarianism and the Virtues." *Mind* 94 (1985): 196–209.
doi: https://doi.org/10.1093/mind/XCIV.374.196

Gallagher, David. "Person and Ethics in Aquinas." *Acta Philosophica* (Rome) v. 4 (1995): 51–71.

Gaynesford, Maximilian. "The Bishop, the Valet, the Wife, and the Ass." In Feltham and Cottingham, 84–97.

Geach, P. T. "Good and Evil." In *Theories of Ethics*, edited by Philippa Foot, 64–73. Oxford: Oxford University Press, 1967.

Godwin, William. *Enquiry Concerning Political Justice*. First ed., 1793.

Hallet, Garth, S.J. *Greater Good: The Case for Proportionalism*. Washington: Georgetown University Press, 1995.

Harper, Sarah. "Role-Centered Morality." Ph. D. dissertation, Boston College, 2007.

Hurka, Thomas. *Virtue, Vice, and Value*. Oxford: Oxford University Press,

John Paul II, Pope. *Centesimus Annus*. Encyclical letter. Vatican translation, 1991.

Kagan, Shelly. *Normative Ethics*. New York: Westview, 1997.

Kahneman, Daniel. "Can We Trust Our Intuitions?" In *Conversations on Ethics*, ed. Alex Vorhoeve, 67–84. Oxford: Oxford University Press, 2009.

Kamm, Frances M. *Intricate Ethics*. Oxford: Oxford University Press, 2007.
doi: https://doi.org/10.1093/acprof:oso/9780195189698.001.0001

Levinas, Emanuel. *Basic Philosophical Writings*, edited by A. Peperzak, S. Critchley, and R. Bernasconi. Bloomington: Indiana University Press, 1996.

Nagel, Thomas. *View from Nowhere*. New York: Oxford University Press, 1989.

Nagel, Thomas. "War and Massacre." In *Consequentialism and Its Critics*, edited by Samuel Scheffler, 51–73. Oxford: Oxford University Press, 1988.

Nozick, Robert. *Philosophical Explanations*. Cambridge: Harvard University Press, 1981.

Nussbaum, Martha. "Comment." In Judith Thomson, *Goodness and Advice*, 97–125. Princeton: Princeton University Press, 2003.

Oderberg, David. *Moral Theory*. Oxford: Blackwell, 2000.

Paul VI, Pope. "Address for the Day of Development." (23 August 1968). *AAS* 60 (1968): 626-627.

Richardson, Henry. "Specifying Norms as a Way to Resolve Concrete Ethical Problems." *Philosophy and Public Affairs* 18 (1990): 279–310.

Ross, W. D. *The Right and the Good*. Oxford: Oxford University Press, 1930.

Rowling, J. K. *Harry Potter and the Deathly Hallows*. Scholastic, 2007.

Scanlon, T. M. *Moral Dimensions*. Cambridge: Harvard University Press, 2007.

Scanlon, T. M. *What We Owe to Each Other*. Harvard University Press, 1998.

Scheffler, Samuel. "Reasonable Partiality." In Feltham and Cottingham, 98–130.

Singer, Peter. *The Most Good You Can Do*. New Haven: Yale University Press, 2015.

Slote, Michael. *Morals from Motives*. Oxford: Oxford University Press, 2001. doi: https://doi.org/10.1093/0195138376.001.0001

Sommers, Christina Hoff. "Filial Morality." *Journal of Philosophy* 83 (1986): 439–456. doi: https://doi.org/10.2307/2026329

Stroud, Sarah. "Permissible Partiality, Projects, and Plural Agency." In Feltham and Cottingham, 131–149.

Sunstein, Cass. "How Do We Know What's Moral?" *New York Review of Books*, April 24, 2014, pp. 14–18.

Thomson, Judith Jarvis. *Normativity*. Chicago: Open Court, 2007.

Williams, Bernard. *Ethics and the Limits of Philosophy*. Cambridge, MA: Harvard University Press, 1986.

Zimmerman, Michael J. *Nature of Intrinsic Value*. Lanham, MD: Rowman and Littlefield, 2001.

Introduction of Rémi Brague
2015 Aquinas Medal Recipient

Thérèse-Anne Druart

Introducing Rémi Brague is not easy. There is so much one could say and still not do justice both to who he is and the significance of his works.

Let us begin with what is easier, the significance of his works. Rémi Brague began well: a book on Plato's *Meno*. Rémi Brague likes paradoxes and he found one in Plato. In the *Theaetetus*, Socrates, who did not write, presents the philosopher as a barren midwife, who helps others to deliver philosophical children but herself cannot give birth. Yet Plato, Socrates's own disciple, certainly did not follow his master in not writing. Plato wrote much and beautifully and so does Rémi Brague. Up to now, as sole author, he has given birth to thirteen books, plus translations of Leo Strauss, Themistius, Pines, Maimonides and, al-Razi, as well as to some one hundred sixty articles.

The latest of his books: *Le règne de l'homme: Genèse et échec du projet moderne* (*Man's Kingdom: Genesis and Failure of the Modern Project*) came out this year. It is the last of a trilogy dedicated to philosophical anthropology that already included *Wisdom of the World* and *God's Law*. It has already been translated into Spanish, and we are waiting with impatience for its English translation.

Plato is well known for his love of wordplay. Rémi Brague follows suit, as *Au moyen du Moyen Âge* and *Modérément Moderne* (*Moderately Modern*) attest, at times to the despair of translators. This explains why *Au moyen du Moyen Âge* in English became in more pedestrian fashion simply *The Legend of the Middle Ages*.

Rémi Brague began well with Plato and Aristotle and went on still better in broadening his interests. First, his Catholicism led him to more universality, as he learned Hebrew in order to be able to read the Old Testament in the original language. Later on, his desire to read Rabbi Moses—Maimonides in Latin—in the original language, led him to learn Arabic. His reflections on Europe, as in *Eccentric Culture: A Theory of Western Civilization*, made him aware of how European culture (which for him encompasses North America) established, *contra* Tertullian, that Jerusalem and Athens have much to do with each other and are at the root of Europe as culture. This book also pointed to Western civilization as secondary to its two sources, Greek culture and Christianity. It also made him aware of how philosophically Christianity,

©2016, *Proceedings of the ACPA*, Vol. 89
doi: 10.5840/acpaproc2015891

pp. 33–34

Judaism and Islam all interact and distinguish themselves from each other. This explains his approach, for instance, in *Eccentric Culture*, *God's Law*, *Legend of the Middle Ages*, and *On the God of the Christians (and one or two others)*, in which he reflects on the three cultures.

Brague is a voracious reader and his love for language and its subtleties in the various tongues, led him to lecture and teach not only in France, but also at Pennsylvania State University, Lausanne in Switzerland, Boston University, Ludwig-Maximilians-Universität in Munich, Universidad de Navarra in Spain, Università Vita-Salute San Rafaele in Milan, and Boston College.

Needless to say, he received many awards, such as the "grand prix de philosophie" of the French Academy and becoming member of l'Institut de France. He has also been awarded the Josef Pieper Preis, the Prix Joseph Ratzinger, the Vanenburg Prize, and a prize from the city of Poznán.

This gives you a glimpse of the significance of his works and their international impact. It still does not reveal much about the person. Rémi Brague is a proud family man and a Catholic who is not afraid to witness to his Catholicism in the very secularized milieu of French Academe. In such a milieu, to be acknowledged and respected, despite clear Catholic positions, testifies to the quality of one's work, particularly for someone who in a famous interview describes himself as "somewhat immoderately fond of provocation." Indeed, Brague is fond of provocation in the theses he defends and the manner in which he defends them. From Plato's *Symposium* he learned that one can be both deeply serious and at the same time playful. Who else than Brague would in his path-breaking *Eccentric Culture*, in a footnote to a very serious point, i.e., that Western Culture can never be said to be "mine," refer to a children's comic, Tintin, and this in a very formal way, as Hergé, *Le Lotus Bleu (The Blue Lotus)*? Even those who disagree with Brague acknowledge that he made them think by causing them to wonder.

So how could anyone doubt that Rémi Brague deserves the Aquinas Medal granted by the American Catholic Philosophical Association?

The Catholic University of America

On the Need for a Philosophy of Nature and on Aquinas's Help in Sketching One

Rémi Brague

Abstract: A philosophy of nature is an urgent need if we want to avoid falling back into the Gnostic view of the world and of man's place in it that modern science can't help fostering. The medieval idea of the world as the creation of stable natures by a rational and benevolent God should provide us with useful guidelines. In particular, Aquinas gives us valuable hints about how our scientific knowledge of nature might help us to get a correct appreciation of our own worth.

The best way for me to express my warmest thanks to the friends who awarded me this prestigious medal might be to try and show how relevant some features of Aquinas's thought could be for our present intellectual and cultural predicament.

Let me begin with a double warning: First, I won't even try to pose as an Aquinas scholar, especially in front of a bevy of people who really are. Second, I won't claim to be able to produce the philosophy of nature that I feel to be so urgently necessary. There is a great deal of extemporizing in my presentation. Yet, when menaced with drowning, we grope for the thinnest straw. This paper is a program that other people will have to fulfill.

A Philosophy of Nature, an Urgent Need

We badly need a philosophy of nature. Now, this notion has a long story behind it, and it would be apposite to sketch it, in order to distinguish its former concretizations from the kind of philosophy of nature whose existence I am wishing. Let me here sum up this story under three headings.

First, there is the Natural Philosophy such as it is still taught in Cambridge, from the chair once occupied by Isaac Newton, i.e., physics as a description of natural things, together with the writing of their laws in rigorous mathematical language.

Second, there is the inquiry into the basic concepts of natural science: to begin with, nature, motion, time, space or whatnot. This was the main subject matter of Aristotle's Physics. I wholeheartedly condone such an enterprise.

Yet, both endeavors are tasks which science either doesn't need or can't cope with very successfully on her own. Science very well can shift for herself without the aid of philosophy. She has been doing that for centuries, roughly speaking since Galileo, and she keeps developing exponentially. Philosophy could only encumber science with its help or plume itself with results which it has not toiled to get.

A third meaning is the *Naturphilosophie* that was a catch-word and a program for German idealism. Its concrete results in Schelling and Hegel were, to say the least, hardly convincing. Yet, this brings us nearer to what I dream of. For such an endeavor arose from the consciousness of a problem: how can we articulate the physical world and what singles out Man, i.e., the moral dimension and the sensitivity to values. Kant pointed towards this problem with his idea of beauty as a symbol of morality.[1] Fichte, in the wake of Kant's primacy of practical reason, endeavored to deduce the very existence of the physical world from the requirements of moral action. The underlying enigma is the possibility of those weird beings, known as "human beings" who, alone among animals, possess a feeling for the Good and for the Beautiful.

This ability was already existent among prehistoric human beings as early as one and a half million years before Christ. Paleontologists discovered objects that point towards this hypothesis, e.g., hand axes, the word of art being "bifaces," made of a beautiful kind of flint or chert, polished with great care, the production of which required a considerable amount of time. Now, some were discovered that never were used, but were put along corpses in tombs, probably as offerings fraught with a symbolic meaning.[2] Which one is anybody's guess.

The leading question of a philosophy of nature such as I wish it and, to repeat, that I could not possibly produce, would deal with our own presence in nature as human beings. It would involve, not an anthropology that would be one among other descriptions of natural things, the thing at stake being man, but a reflexive understanding of the part we play in the whole show.

Wanted: Cosmology

In a former book that hails back from more than fifteen years already, I put forward the thesis according to which we don't possess a cosmology any longer.[3] I meant thereby an intellectual pursuit different from two other ones, both belonging to science, i.e., cosmography and cosmogony. Cosmography, as the name suggests, describes the present state of affairs in the physical universe. Cosmogony endeavors to reconstruct the way in which this state of affairs became what it is now.

In the classical, late antique and medieval model, that had superseded the emergence myths, there was no room for a cosmogony. After the astronomic revolution of the sixteenth and seventeenth centuries, a new cosmography arose, that gave a description of the present structure of the world. But its genesis was shrouded in mystery and remained so in spite of various hypotheses, for instance the one of Kant, later taken up by Laplace. Those two realms, that remained separated for more than three centuries, were reunited by people like Arthur Eddington, Edwin Hubble,

Abbé Georges Lemaître, and others. We are at present in possession of a powerful model, known by the moniker of the Big Bang theory. This model becomes more and more plausible as the amount of our knowledge increases. To be sure, since scientific knowledge is essentially provisional, nobody knows how long it will last.

In contradistinction to both endeavors, I take here the word "cosmology" in the meaning that is suggested by its etymology: a *logos* about the *kosmos*. Not a description, but some sort of account, an attempt at making sense of it, at deciphering its meaning.

Here one may ask whether such an enterprise is really useful. It would not add a whit to our knowledge of nature, let alone to our technical grip on it. But the question remains whether what we have to do with nature can boil down to knowing it and taking advantage of it for our own purposes; in other words, to what extent nature is *interesting* for us.[4]

No Logos of Nature

We can write the laws of the physical universe in the precise and rigorous language of mathematics, but we don't *understand* it in the strict meaning of "understanding." Nature can be described in a very accurate way, and we can on the basis of this description perform many technical wonders. But nature can't be understood any longer.

Ancient philosophy, that comprised a rudimentary description of nature, furnished us with an understanding of nature. Heavy bodies fall and light bodies go upwards because they strive to reach their natural abodes, where they find their specific fulfilment, i.e., their good. Modern physics has gotten rid of this explanation. We are caught between an explanation that we can't accept any longer and a description that doesn't allow us to understand anything. Now, schizophrenia is a mental state that mankind can live with for a long time without pangs of conscience. It did that for centuries, e.g., when the mathematical hypotheses of Ptolemaic astronomy on the one hand and on the other hand Aristotelian physics, which refute each other, coexisted.

Understanding supposes that we introduce final causes. I understand what a person is doing when she throws a letter into a mailbox because I know that her intention is that her message be carried to her friend. Now, final causes have no place in the study of the physical world. They have been expelled since Francis Bacon's quip comparing them to consecrated virgins who remain barren.[5] Scientists are perfectly right to do without them, and even to do away with them, since their admission would let in an illegitimate kind of anthropomorphism. Attempts at reintroducing final causes are commonly frowned upon by scientists, and short-lived. Final causes can be tolerated in the study of living organisms, for want of anything better, as long as we haven't yet found the mechanism that accounts for what we want to explain. This is the prudent stand taken by Kant in his third Critique.[6] All this is not a problem for science. But it is one for us as human beings.

For, by this token, the scientific world-view makes of us *strangers* in the cosmos. It fosters the danger of a revival of the gnostic attitude. The presence of Gnosticism in modern thought was diagnosed by several thinkers already, Erich Voegelin, for instance, in his famous Walgren Lectures of 1953, later published under the title of *The New Science of Politics*.[7] Gnostic science was bogus. But real science has Gnostic consequences.

Modern man is at the same time a castaway and an upstart. Since he is the former, he has to become the latter. As a castaway, he uses makeshift implements to build a raft of sorts, floating on an ocean of chaos. As for the upstart, let us here indulge in some cheap psychology. A true-blue gentleman, convinced of his innate superiority over the rag-tag and bob-tail, can be exquisitely polite and modest towards other people. On the other hand, a person without nobility, *sine nobilitate*, short *s.nob.*, has to be a snob. Precisely because he doubts his own legitimacy, he will have to make the other ones feel his alleged superiority, he will despise them, nay lord it over them.

Modern man is such a snob. He is unsure of his legitimacy and working hard in order to be admitted into the club of which he is the only member, looking down at the other natural beings and trying to subdue them. This is what we have been doing for centuries, as a program, since Bacon's clarion call and, through technology, since the industrial revolution.

There is another aspect to that, quite practical. We are in a double double bind, a Catch 22 (or 44?) of sorts as for the way in which we understand ourselves, and the way we understand nature.

As for ourselves, on the one hand, contemporary science, or rather the ideological use made of it by the mainstream media, leads us to believe that we are hardly more than lucky monkeys, produced by the chance encounter of irrational forces. On the other hand, we harp upon the "dignity" of man, endowed with "human rights" that are supposed to provide us with the unshakable ground for our moral choices and legal rulings. Little wonder that some people propose to enlarge the notion of rights to animals, since human beings themselves are conceived of as animals that happen to be endowed, nobody knows why, with sacred and unalienable rights.

As for nature, on the one hand, we can see nature (lower case "n") as a mere fuel tank, a quarry of useful materials, at our beck and call, that we can reshape as we wish. On the other hand, we can worship Nature (capital "n") as a goddess. This was the case for the eighteenth-century *Philosophes* or again for some deep ecologists who even recycled for the Earth the Greek name Gaia. The part played by the Earth in this world-view gives us an inkling of what such worship could produce. All idols require human sacrifices. To Gaia's welfare, mankind, the trouble-maker, should be sacrificed.

Hence, we need a balanced view of nature that would steer a middle course between those two pairs of extremes.

The Helpful Medieval Outlook

Now, my claim is that what we need is something like the medieval outlook. In a book that was published two years ago, I ventured the bold thesis according to which we need intellectually to return to the Middle Ages.[8] Medieval thinkers did not experience the world as nature (*phusis*) any longer, but as creation. This feeling was so spontaneous that, most interestingly, Saint Bernard distinguished somewhere between creature in general (*creatura aliqua*) and creature of God (*creatura Dei*), parallel to the distinction between nature (*natura*) and grace (*gratia*).[9] This distinction, that at first blush sounds preposterous, might have been hardly more than a thought experiment, but it shows how deeply rooted the vision of being as created was ingrained in medieval minds.

We need the idea of creation. The trouble is that this word has been polluted by the use made of it by the so-called "creationism" that relies on a naively literal reading of the first account of creation in Genesis, a reading that was scarcely to be found among the Church Fathers. Augustine's literal commentary on Genesis, for instance, doesn't object to the idea of a progressive development of abilities sown by God on the first day.[10] By the way, Darwin toyed with this idea in the last sentence of his first masterpiece.[11]

The idea of creation doesn't tell us anything about the synchronic structure of beings, i.e., cosmography, or about the diachronic process of their unfolding, i.e., cosmogony. God has endowed us with the necessary intellectual tools for us by and by to acquire an adequate knowledge of them. But the idea of creation teaches us a basic truth about the existence of what is, i.e., that it is not out of itself (*a se*).

Aquinas could help us for several reasons. Let us group them under two headings, one general in nature, the other one peculiar to him. In other words, he could help us first because he is medieval, and second because he is himself.

Being a man of the Middle Ages, Aquinas shares the basic assumptions of the medieval world-view.[12] Being the theological and philosophical genius that he was, he sifted this world-view and recast it in conceptual terms.

One advantage of the medieval world-view and in particular of Aquinas's outlook is paradoxical in nature. I mean that his cosmography is desperately outdated and could not possibly be made up to date. It is basically Aristotle's world-view, or the framework which Ptolemy's astronomy, Galen's psychology, and other scientists filled with a more elaborate content. Hence, the temptation of trying to rejuvenate his cosmography on the scientific level can easily be staved off.

Let me give of the medieval view of nature one example only. I will borrow it from the poets, who as a rule are more adept at expressing the basic assumptions of a culture. According to them, the birds have a language of their own. The idea is a relatively common one, in Europe as well as in the Persian world and probably elsewhere. But it is interesting to point out that the language of their chirruping is not just any language. It has a name. It is Latin. For the first time, perhaps, the Provencal poet William of Aquitaine, in the second half of the twelfth century, wrote that the morning birds sing "each one in its Latin" (*chascus en lor lati*). The phrase became trite in French, Italian, and English; it is to be found as late as in the Russian poet Ossip Mandelstam, who probably borrowed it from one of the medieval poets whom he was so fond of.[13] For the poets, this probably meant that we can't understand them, and "Latin" can mean, in other contexts, language in general. But we are allowed to take this literally. The birds don't speak just any vernacular, but the dignified language of higher administration and culture, the language of the Roman Empire. This implies that they are not Barbarians. To some extent, *we* are the barbarians, because we don't understand them.

We can take the birds as a metonymy for Nature at large. Natural things have a meaning. They are not only just there, at our disposal. There is more to this idea than a naïve theory of allegory in the bestiaries: the ant as a model of assiduity at work, the pelican as a figure of Christ's sacrifice, etc. What this "more" means, Aquinas will help us to understand.

Aquinas's View of Created Nature and of the Goal of Our Knowledge of It

Aquinas as such, I contend, can help us in the formidable task of reconstructing a philosophy of nature. Let me choose two points only, one dealing with nature herself, one with our studying her.

A) Aquinas looks at creation as having as its object, not bundles of properties floating somewhere, but things that have a stable nature of their own. God is the creator of natures, an idea that is already to be found in Augustine and earlier.[14] Now, this is far from being self-evident. Whoever supports the idea of creation is not committed to conceive of the objects which are created as being full-fledged *things*.

Islam powerfully upholds the idea of creation. But Islamic thinkers of the so-called *Kalām* (*Mutakallimūn*), don't view it as dealing with things. This holds especially well for the school of al-Aš'arī, which carried the day and kept a dominant position almost to the present day. This school stood for a radical atomism, not only as for the structure of matter, but as for time, supposed to consist of instants and, more important still, for the very structure of being. Beings consist of bundles of properties. By so doing, the followers of al-Aš'arī did away with the idea of nature. They replaced it with the idea of God's "habit" (*'āda*) of creating some properties together.

The Jewish philosopher Moses Maimonides dealt this view a mortal blow in his community.[15] This did not prevent later Christian authors like Malebranche, who by the way were indirectly influenced by the Islamic Kalam, to see in Nature a pagan idea.[16] As for Aquinas, he took over Rabbi Moses's critique and summed up his own view in magnificent and famous formulas, like: "Demeaning the perfection of creatures amounts to demeaning the perfection of God's power" (*Detrahere [. . .] perfectioni creaturarum est detrahere perfectioni divinae virtutis*).[17]

Created things have stable properties, and they have their own laws, which enables us to get a scientific knowledge of their functioning. Modern science might have been made possible by the intellectual breakthroughs of late "nominalist" thinkers like Oresme or Buridan, not to mention the earlier John Philopon. This is the well-known thesis of Pierre Duhem.[18] But, earlier than that, the idea of stable natures set into being by the creative act was at least a necessary, if not a sufficient condition of natural science.

Medieval poets had a glimpse of such a view and expressed it through the basic image of nature as God's vicarious helper in shaping the variety of living beings. It is to be found for the first time in a prose part of a didactic prosimetron by Alanus ab Insulis, around 1160. He does not hesitate to call Nature "vice-God" (*prodea*). Poets like the French Jean de Meung in the late thirteenth century or the English Geoffrey Chaucer in the late fourteenth are still familiar with the idea.[19] So much for the first point, i.e., the ontological status of created things.

B) As for our study of nature, we have been plying it eagerly for centuries, but the question why we do that was seldom asked. When asked, we would off the cuff answer by pointing to the benefits of a technical control over natural phenomena, made possible by the knowledge of their mechanism.

Now, Aquinas explains why we should study nature—he says *consideratio*—, why it is useful for the instruction of the faith.[20] He adduces several reasons and even includes with a poker face a quotation by Augustine whose nose of wax he turns in his own direction, back to front. As for positive reasons, studying nature gives us an inkling of God's attributes, His wisdom and power. It even makes us somehow similar to Him. Thomas adds four negative reasons: It helps us to avoid some errors about God: to mistake Him for a body, to ascribe to the influence of creatures what God alone can do, and conversely to subtract from God's action what is His own.

A fourth reason is especially interesting for us: Aquinas insists that a sober view of nature prevents us from the temptation of lowering the level of our own being. In his time and age, this meant in particular: by submitting our freedom to astrological determinism. What is so avoided is whatever detracts from human dignity (*hominum derogant dignitati*).[21] Thomas is, strange bed-fellows, near to Epicurus, who explained that studying nature, ultimately, has no other relevance than doing away with every possible source of unease of the mind. Tranquility as absence of trouble (*ataraxia*), as the state of the mind which no wind ruffles (*galēnē*) is something that Greek wisdom strove after.

But dignity is more than peace of mind. We could even say that the consciousness of one's dignity might be the best warrant for real tranquility. And here, we are better equipped for us to meet the requirements of the modern attitude towards life and nature. I mentioned above the way in which the upstart must become a busybody, eager to compensate for his innate inferiority by working like a beaver, in contradistinction to the peaceful, somehow lackadaisical nonchalance of the authentic nobleman. If human beings were convinced of their own dignity, they would less feel the need to compensate by muscling into nature's larder and pillaging it.

Paris I/LMU Munich

Notes

1. I. Kant, *Kritik der Urteilskraft*, §59.

2. See, e.g., H. de Lumley, "Quand la culture apparaît-elle?" in *Culture et transcendance. Chemins de la création culturelle*, ed. D. Ponnau, M. Morange and J. Duchesne (Paris: Parole et Silence, 2015), 119.

3. See my *The Wisdom of the World: The Human Experience of the Universe in Western Thought*, trans. T. L. Fagan (Chicago: The University of Chicago Press 2003), 216.

4. See my "Is Physics Interesting? Some Responses from Late Antiquity and the Middle Ages," in *The Legend of the Middle Ages. Philosophical Explorations of Medieval Christianity, Judaism and Islam*, trans. L. Cochrane (Chicago: The University of Chicago Press 2009), 73–74.

5. F. Bacon, *Novum Organon*, I, §48, ed. W. Krohn (Darmstadt: Wissenschaftliche Buchgesellschaft 1990), 110 and II, ii, p. 280.

6. I. Kant, *Kritik der Urteilskraft*, §75.

7. E. Voegelin, *The New Science of Politics: An Introduction* (Chicago: The University of Chicago Press 1952), ch. IV: "Gnosticism—The Nature of Modernity," 107–132.

8. See my *Le Propre de l'homme. Sur une légitimité menacée* (Paris: Flammarion, 2013), 186–189. This book is scheduled to appear in English as *The Legitimacy of the Human*, trans. Paul Seaton (South Bend, IN: Saint Augustine's Press), in 2017.

9. S. Bernard of Clairvaux, *De gratia et libero arbitrio*, VI, 17, in *Opera* (Rome: Editiones Cistercienses 1963), t. 3, ed. J. Leclercq and H. M. Rochais, 178–179 (PL 182, 1011ab).

10. Augustine, *De Genesi ad litteram*, IV, 33, ed. J. Zycha (CSEL XXVIII-1) (Prague et al.: Tempsky, 1894), p. 132.

11. Ch. Darwin, *The Origin of Species*, ch. XV: "Conclusion" (New York: Random House, n.d.), 374.

12. See my talk "Civilization as Conservation and Conversation," Dubrovnik, Vanenburg Meeting, July 4th, 2015, to be published in *The European Conservative*.

13. William IX of Aquitaine, "Ab la dolchor del temps novel," in C. Appel, *Provenzalische Chrestomathie* (Leipzig: Reisland, 1930), 10, p. 51a (*li aucel/canton, chascus, en lor lati*); Cercamon, "Quant l'aura doussa s'amarzis," ibid., 13, p. 53a; Chrétien de Troyes, *Perceval*, v. 71–72, in Œuvres complètes, ed. D. Poirion (Paris: Gallimard 1994), p. 687; *Roman de la Rose* (Jean de Meung), v. 8378, ed. F. Lecoy (Paris: Champion 1973), t. 2, p. 6; Guido Cavalcanti, "Fresca rosa novella," 10–11, in http://ilcavalcanti.xoom.it/cavalcanti_rime.html#rimaVI; Chaucer, *Canterbury Tales*, "The Squire's Tale," v. 478 (*haukes ledene*); O. Mandelstam, "Аббат," in Камень, in Стихотворения. Проза (Moscow: EKSMO 2011), 100.

14. Augustine, *De Genesi ad Litteram*, IX, 17, 32-18, 33 loc.cit., pp. 291–292 et cf. VI, 13, 24, p. 188. See the Arabic extract from Ignatius of Antioch's Letters in *The Apostolic Fathers*, ed. J. B. Lightfoot, II-3 (London: Macmillan 1890), 301.

15. Maimonides, *Guide of the Perplexed*, I, 73, 10th proposition, ed. Y. Joel (Jerusalem: Junovitch, 1929), p. 145, 10–146, 10; trans. S. Pines (Chicago: The University of Chicago Press 1963), 207–209.

16. N. Malebranche, *De la Recherche de la Vérité*, XVe Eclaircissement, 5e preuve, in Œuvres, ed. G. Rodis-Lewis (Paris: Gallimard, 1979), t. 1, pp. 987–988.

17. Aquinas, *Summa contra Gentiles*, III, 69 (Rome: Leonina, 1934), 303b.

18. P. Duhem, *Le Système du monde. Histoire des doctrines cosmologiques de Platon à Copernic* (Paris: Hermann, 1913–1959).

19. Alanus ab Insulis, *De planctu Naturae*, 6, 3, ed. W. Wetherbee (Cambridge, MA: Harvard University Press, 2013), p. 68; 9, p. 74; 8, 30, p. 108 (*pro-dea*); 16, 25, p. 194; 18, 4, p. 204; Jean de Meung, *Le Roman de la Rose*, v. 16752 (ed. cit, t. 3, p. 3) and v. 19477 (p. 85); Chaucer, *Canterbury Tales*, "The Physician's Tale," v. 20.

20. Aquinas, *Summa contra Gentiles*, II, 2 and 3. See my *The Wisdom of the World*, 174–175.

21. Aquinas, *Summa contra Gentiles*, 3, p. 95a. See too III, 120, p. 372b.

Divine Simplicity and Divine Freedom

Brian Leftow

Abstract: I explain the doctrine of divine simplicity, and reject what is now the standard way to explicate it in analytic philosophy. I show that divine simplicity imperils the claim that God is free, and argue against a popular proposal for dealing with the problem.

The doctrine of divine simplicity (DDS) is at the core of classical theism. I now set the doctrine out and reject what has become the leading way to explicate it in analytic philosophy of religion. Having done that, I explain why theists need to affirm a robust sense of divine freedom and why there is a problem reconciling DDS with such freedom. Finally I consider and reject what has become the most popular strategy for reconciling the two.

Divine Simplicity Explained

What is simple is not complicated. If God is absolutely simple, as classical theism thinks, He is not complicated at all—not in any way complex. He has no material, spatial or temporal parts. Nor has He any metaphysical constituents—e.g., an essence or accidents. He has no constituents of any sort. Having none, He has no internal structure. These denials are common to all versions of DDS. They make DDS sound like a bit of purely negative theology—and in some writers, e.g., Plotinus, it may well be. But other authors pack further content into it. Augustine states his DDS this way: God "is what He has."[1] This is a positive claim. It says what God is, not what He is not. In the *Summa Theologiae*, Aquinas states DDS as a series of denials about God—"there is no distinction between essence and supposit," etc.[2] But this is only part of Aquinas's presentation. I do not recall Aquinas ever quoting Augustine's summary, but as we go through his DDS, we find that there are things God does not have (matter, accidents) and things He not only has but is (essence, existence). So for Aquinas too, God is what He has: there are things God has, He "is" these things, and this is part of what Thomas lays out in his treatments of DDS. The "is" claims—positive claims, identity-claims—are also part of

Aquinas's doctrine. These identity-claims tell us, for instance, that something plays the role of the divine essence, and that something is God.

As we go through Aquinas's presentations of DDS, we spot metaphysical roles God does not play—the roles of prime matter and accidents, for instance—and roles He does (essence, existence). The claims that something plays a particular role, and it's God, are as much part of Aquinas's DDS as the denials. I think we can sum up Aquinas's version of DDS this way:

1. God has no parts, constituents or internal structure,

2. Something plays the metaphysical role of God's essence, namely God,

3. Something plays the metaphysical role of God's existence, namely God,

4. Nothing plays the metaphysical role of divine matter or divine accidents.

(1)–(4) are first-order, claims about what is real, not about how what is real relates to truths about it. For metaphysical roles can be explained without bringing in relations to truths: metaphysical roles are not as such semantic roles, even if they entail semantic roles. The metaphysical role of an essence, for instance, is to settle what kinds a thing belongs to, perhaps which individual something is, the conditions under which it can be the same across time and/or the ways it could have differed while preserving its identity.

The Truthmaker Account

Over the last thirty years, analytic philosophers have debated how to make sense of DDS. Jeffrey Brower introduced a move which is now approaching canonical status: use the notion of a truthmaker. "Truthmaker" is a functional description, the way "carburetor" is: it does not say what an item is intrinsically, but simply what it does. What truthmakers do, unsurprisingly, is make propositions true. If it is true that P, some bit(s) of the world make(s) this true. Some bit(s) of the world explain this; it is true in virtue of some bit(s) of the world. The bit(s) is (are) its truthmaker. A truthmaker for <P> somehow grounds, necessitates and explains it that <P> is true. That's its function, whatever it is intrinsically.[3] According to Brower, "divine simplicity just amounts to the claim that God is the truthmaker for each of his true intrinsic predications . . . all the doctrine requires is that for every true intrinsic divine predication, there is a truthmaker, and God is identical with that truthmaker."[4] I see four problems with this.

One is that this turns DDS into a doctrine about how God relates to truths about God. It turns it into a claim about God's semantic role. That is just not what it is in Augustine, Aquinas or any other classical or medieval defender of DDS. Claims about how God relates to truths about God do not occur in their expositions of DDS. At best, claims about God and truths are consequences of DDS, not DDS itself. But—and this is the second problem—we do not need the notion of a truthmaker to express those consequences. Truthmaker theory involves a lot of contentious metaphysics: grounding, a special way truthmakers explain truth, a *sui generis* necessitation relation.[5] It would be better to express the consequences in less contentious terms. Nearly everyone believes in reference and satisfaction. We can express DDS's consequences for propositions in terms of these. For instance, we can say that any term apparently referring to something playing a metaphysical role in God either does not refer or refers only to God. As this will do, we need a particular warrant from the text to take DDS's semantic consequences in truthmaker terms. But—and this is my third problem—we do not have it.

DDS's main proponents—Augustine, Anselm, Aquinas—wrote about truth. Augustine's thinking centered around his idea that God is Truth and of the way that God illuminates our minds. This was how truth got into his thinking about God; if he ever strayed into truthmaker theorists' territory, it played no role in his theology. Anselm did give an account of how truths get to be true, thus getting into that territory. Anselm defined truth as rightness perceptible by the mind alone.[6] For him, a statement is true because it has a kind of rightness, i.e., because it is doing what it ought. If an assertion does what it ought to do, it says that what is, is. But what makes it true is not that it says that what is, is. What makes it true, for Anselm, is that it does what it ought to. It just so happens that saying that what is, is, is what it ought to do. That it says that what is, is, is important only due to that. Anselm nowhere develops the notion of saying that what is, is, in a way that could be construed as a proto-truthmaker theory. So the truthmaker notion cannot catch how Augustine or Anselm themselves thought of DDS. Aquinas does occasionally use language truthmaker theorists might use.[7] But it is at best tangential to his thinking about truth. That thinking centers on the idea that thoughts are true by their "conformity" with things.[8] What that means is not obvious, but it does not appear to be anything to do with truthmaking. So the truthmaker notion cannot catch how Augustine, Anselm or Aquinas themselves thought about DDS.

At best, then, truthmaker-talk might be a way to restate DDS in a way its formulators never thought of it—*if* DDS were partly or wholly a doctrine about God's relation to truths about God. But it is not. And if we restate it this way, we raise the problem of divine freedom with extra force, and that is my final difficulty with the truthmaker rendering. Thus I've made three points: DDS is not about the relation between God and truths, we would do well to speak of that relation without truthmaker theories' contentious metaphysics, and truthmaker theories are not close to how DDS's proponents themselves thought about that relation. I have also issued a promissory note about freedom. I now set out the need for divine freedom and the way DDS imperils it. I then show how the truthmaker rendering of DDS makes the freedom problem particularly salient.

The Need For Divine Freedom

It's orthodox Western monotheism that God acts freely, in a robust sense which implies that He could have acted otherwise. While some conceptions of freedom are compatible with inability to will otherwise, they will not do for God. For if God cannot will otherwise, nothing dependent entirely and solely on His will can *be* otherwise. If God cannot will otherwise, there had to be a universe, and this universe, and the precise natural laws and physical boundary conditions we have: it is no more possible that there have been more energy in the early universe than that $2 + 2 = 5$. If there is no contingency in God's will, there is much less than we believe there is elsewhere. Perhaps there is none at all. Perhaps if God cannot will otherwise, nothing can *be* otherwise. For if God cannot will otherwise, and wills to co-operate with me doing A, then He cannot do other than co-operate with me doing A, and so I cannot do other than A. Modal Spinozism thus looms: absolutely everything is absolutely necessary.

I take it without argument that modal Spinozism is false. If it is, there is real, objective contingency. But if God exists, there could be real contingency only in three ways:

- God necessarily intends what He does. There are no "holes" in His will: He has a will about absolutely everything, and so nothing occurs without His creation, sustaining or co-operation. Yet things can turn out differently than He wills. This is impossible in the sense of "wills" at issue, that of "executive" intentions, the ones that work like "*fiat lux.*" These by definition bring about exactly what God means them to.

- God necessarily intends what He does. But there *are* "holes" in His will. He has no will at all about some matters, and so there are "places" in the universe for things to exist or occur without divine creating, sustaining, or co-operation. Because there are things God has no will about, some things could be different even if God's will were not. Thus there is contingency even if God's will is necessarily as it is. This is at least a coherent thought. But this would be a highly non-standard version of Western monotheism.

- God has contingent intentions.

The first is impossible, the second implausible, so plausibly, if modal Spinozism is false, God could have willed otherwise. God has contingent intentions. Again, if God is robustly free, He has contingent intentions. So it seems that God must have contingent intentions.

The Simplicity/Freedom Problem

Yet DDS seems to militate against His having contingent intentions. On DDS, nothing in God is really distinct from anything else in Him. If so, then everything wholly within God—everything intrinsic to God—is identical with everything else in God. Suppose, then, that God's intentions are wholly within God. If they are, it follows that they are all identical: God has just one intention. Further, God's intention = His essence. God has His essence necessarily. So it seems to follow that He has His actual intention necessarily. But then it seems that He necessarily wills just what He does: that He could not have willed otherwise. DDS cannot be reconciled with divine freedom and contingency *if* God's intentions are intrinsic or wholly internal to God.[9]

The truthmaker rendering of DDS makes this particularly clear. On any standard version of truthmaker theory, truthmakers necessitate the truth of what they make true. Given the same truthmaker, there must be the same truth. So if DDS really is best expressed as a claim about truthmakers, and assertions that God has an intention are about how God is intrinsically, God's existence necessitates the truth of every truth about what intentions He has. God can have no contingent intentions. Thus, as I said, the truthmaker account of DDS makes the freedom problem particularly forceful. The reference/satisfaction approach to DDS's semantic consequences just does not have this implication. Some terms refer and some predicates are satisfied contingently; the mere notions of reference and satisfaction do not bring necessitation with them.

We now face the central problem: can a simple God be free?

Extrinsic Intentions

On DDS, if God's intentions are intrinsic to Him, they are necessary. So DDS's friends, and particularly those who like the truthmaker account, have sought to allow contingent divine intentions by allowing God some extrinsic intentions—i.e., saying that in some cases, what God intends is settled not solely by how things are with God, but also by how things are outside Him. This claim is not wholly bizarre. Some of what we intend is settled partly by what is outside us. For when I intend that P, my intention has that content, that P. But if externalism is correct, as I believe, the content of our mental states often is partly determined externally: when I intend to get some water, the real chemical makeup of water partly settles the content of what I intend.[10] So our intentions have content determined by external realities. However, before God creates, there are no external realities to settle His mental states' content. So if God's creative intention that P is extrinsic, it is not because it has externalist content.

Timothy O'Connor suggests a different way for God's creative intentions to be extrinsic. In us, he suggests, things go this way: I have a purpose that my wife have a happy birthday. I believe that a hand-drawn birthday card would achieve this. I therefore intend to draw a card so that my wife will have a happy birthday. That is, I generate an internal state of intention, and this internal state sets my drawing in motion. My beliefs and purpose don't cause the intention. *I* cause it- *I* intend- and I do so because the content of what I intend matches my reasons (beliefs and purposes).[11] O'Connor does not say what this matching is. I discuss this below.

On O'Connor's picture, the elements leading to my action are me, my purposes, my beliefs, and an internal intention. But if a simple God wills to create, O'Connor suggests, there is no internal intention. Instead, God's beliefs and purposes directly generate an *external* intention. They directly produce the universe and His causal relation to it, an external relation God stands in contingently. This complex—causal relation plus universe—is God's intention: "God's willing this world (is) God's creating the world."[12] For O'Connor, God's willing that the universe exist is not internal to God. It does not cause the universe's existing. Instead, it is external and includes the universe's existing.

O'Connor suggests that if God did have an internal intention to create a universe, it would be that the universe exists to fulfill purpose P. God would intend this because He had P and believed that the universe's existing would fulfill P—that is, because its existing would match His reasons to act. The intention would encode this match.[13] In the "simplified" picture O'Connor offers the friend of DDS,

> the role of matching the . . . content of . . . reasons that a state of intention plays . . . is taken over by the (universe) . . . Its nature, too, mirrors the . . . content of the explaining reasons.[14]

In other words, if God's intention is an external reality, still God has it because its content matches His reasons to act, i.e., because He is intending to do what He has reason to do. A number of defenders of DDS have adopted O'Connor's view or something close to it.[15]

O'Connor gives no sample divine purposes. I will take it that on his account there are many. I think that on any adequate account, God must have many. God has a purpose for me and a purpose for the universe. Surely they differ, for God does different things with me than He does with the universe, and He does them because of His purposes for me and for the universe. In saying that God has many purposes, I beg no questions against DDS. Aquinas, for instance, holds that God's only end in acting is His goodness, and He wills all other things as ordered to His goodness, i.e., for the sake of His goodness.[16] At one level, then, Aquinas's God has just one purpose. But Aquinas also allows a hierarchy of purposes within this purpose: for instance, while God wills the universe for the sake of His goodness, God wills various parts of the universe for the sake of the whole, and that is not the reason for which He wills the universe.[17] So even for Aquinas, God has multiple purposes in acting.

Let's consider the "match" between intention and divine purpose.

Matching

If God has an internal intention to make universe U, O'Connor tells us, its form is *that U exist to fulfill purpose P.*[18] He gives it this form to secure a "match" between intention and reason. He needs the "match" so that something in his picture will constitute its being the case that God intends what He does for some rather than others of His reasons. This *is* a fact: God has some rather than other reasons for intending what He does. So something in our picture of divine action must build that fact in, else the picture will not represent accurately. An event-causal theory of action would build this in by having some rather than others of God's reasons cause His intention: on such a view, what makes it true that God chooses for these reasons is that these reasons cause His choice. O'Connor's theory of action is agent-causal. For him, the agent, not the agent's reasons, causes the intention. So he needs something else to make it the case that God chooses for the reasons He does, and his account of the intention's form provides it. O'Connor suggests that a causal relation to U take the place of internal intentions. So for O'Connor, this must provide what an internal intention would have—i.e., constitute its being the case that God chose for some and not other reasons, that U exists for purpose P. Let's ask just what does this. There are just three options. Either it is something intrinsic to U, or it is something intrinsic to God, or it is some relation between U and God.

I do not think it can be something intrinsic to U. God makes the universe. It is His artifact. Our artifacts do not have intrinsic properties of existing for some purpose. Even their functions (a different matter) are not intrinsic properties. A clock is not for telling time because of a special intrinsic property. Clocks are for telling time because this is what clock-makers mean them to do. If something that looked and acted just like a clock appeared without cause, it would be a thing that *could* tell the time, but not a thing *for* telling time. There would be nothing to settle what it is for, and so it would not be *for* anything. Artifacts have purposes extrinsically. Their makers' intentions determine their purposes; the purposes depend on these intentions. So I submit that U does not have an intrinsic property of being for purpose P.[19]

On O'Connor's view and on DDS itself, if it is contingent that God creates for purpose P, what makes it the case that U exists for purpose P cannot be intrinsic to God, either. For if one purpose had intrinsically a "selected" status, being contingently the one for which God makes U, this would be a contingent mental intrinsic of just the sort DDS does not allow and O'Connor wants to avoid. So if it is contingent that U is for P, what makes it the case that U is for P cannot on present assumptions be intrinsic to the universe or God. Thus it must be a relation between them—the match between the universe and a divine purpose. What gives the universe its purpose, then, is that it matches some divine purpose(s). Henceforth, then, I discuss the view that M. what makes U be for divine purpose P is that it matches P.

O'Connor never says what this match consists in. Perhaps it's that the world just does contain what some purpose specifies. One of God's purposes is to save people. The universe does in fact produce people to save. Perhaps this is enough to make one purpose for the world producing people to save.

(M) raises two questions: how well U has to match P to be *for* P, and (whatever the answer to that) which divine purposes the world matches well enough to be *for* those purposes.[20] I cannot deal with either adequately here, but I can say a bit about the first. If God is perfectly rational, He will do something that best serves His purpose if any action best serves it. So if there are purposes U best serves, we should match U at least with any it would best serve. So we might say at least that U is for P if U is among the best possible universes for fulfilling P. But this is just a first pass. There may be moral constraints on how God can satisfy His purposes. These might rule out universes that satisfy God's purposes better than U, even if God has the power to make those other universes. So perhaps one "match" rule that gives (M) real content should be that U is for P if U is a best possible universe within God's constraints for fulfilling P. However, this won't do by itself. It supposes that some possible universes are "best." The Christian God, at least, has purposes no possible universe best satisfies. God wants loving relation with creatures: there could always be more creatures, better creatures, and more loving relations. God wants loving relations with *these* creatures: there could always be a more propitious setting, contingent emotional natures slightly more prone to love, etc. If I say that P is the universe's purpose, and another universe (which might be this one slightly modified) would have served P better, a reasonable response is "how can *P* be U's purpose? Surely if His purpose was P, an ideally rational God would have created this other universe instead." Unless this question has some good answer, I can't sustain the selection of P by a "pick the best" rule. No universe/purpose match is good enough to provide the universe's purpose if another universe would have matched that purpose better. But the problems I now raise for (M) would carry through to other and more complex rules, so for present purposes we can suppose that this rule is adequate to be at least one rule among many. I now raise problems for (M).

Retrospective Purpose

If the match between a universe and a divine purpose is what settles God's purpose in creating it, the character of the universe determines God's purpose in creating. It determines the reason God made it. For the character of the universe determines which purposes it matches up with, as the character of a picture determines what it most resembles. This can't be right. Surely God's reasons for creating determine which universe He makes, rather than which universe He makes determining His reasons for creating. Surely God first has some rather than other purposes for the universe, and so creates it rather than another universe for those purposes. Surely God's purposes explain His choice of universe. And this is built into O'Connor's picture, since on that, the purposes are there first, and together with God's beliefs explain the existence of the external intention which includes U. But some rather than other divine purposes cannot explain God's choice if which purposes explain it—which purposes God seeks to serve by creating—is settled by what He creates. On (M), the universe has a purpose only retrospectively, once it exists. One can't say that God created it with that purpose rather than others in mind beforehand. But then it is hard to see what point there is to purpose-talk here. Its point has to be explaining why God created what He did, but how can God's purposes explain what He creates if what He creates determines what His purposes in creating were?

The Meaning of Life

Again, motivated by the problem of evil, current theist philosophers tend overwhelmingly to be libertarians about human freedom. Given libertarianism, on (M), *we* partly determine the universe's purpose, for we help determine what purposes the universe matches, and how well it matches them, and God does not determine what we do. Moreover, on libertarianism and (M), we largely determine what purpose God made us for. For on libertarianism, we largely determine how our lives go. So we largely determine which purposes in God they best match. Given (M), when evangelists tell us that God has a wonderful purpose for our lives, they should add, "and it's largely up to you what that is." Atheist existentialists are glad

DIVINE SIMPLICITY AND DIVINE FREEDOM

to say that we largely determine the purpose of our lives. So (M) seems to jeopardize theists' advantage on meaning-of-life questions.

On (M), in a strong sense, God finds out the meaning of our lives from us. We can then learn it from Him—He knows, we do not—but theists hope that He, not we, gave it one, i.e., actively settled what it was to be before making us. To be fair, O'Connor can say that God has partly settled the purpose of our lives. For God can constrain our alternatives, allowing us choice only between certain paths of life. By doing so, God would settle the range of purposes we might have, i.e., the range of His purposes our lives would appropriately or best match. He could rule out many purposes, and by ensuring that no matter what alternative we pick, the resulting life matches some purpose P well enough, God could ensure that P is among the purposes of our lives. Perhaps God could constrain the range of purposes our lives might have very narrowly, and therefore mostly settle this. And O'Connor might perhaps wonder aloud how bad it really is to say that we have some impact on what the purpose of our lives turns out to be. He might even suggest that it is a good thing, something that makes freedom more valuable, that it can contribute to this. And as I show below, he might further argue that something like this is unavoidable on libertarianism. But still, the way O'Connor purchases this response just leads to another problem for his view. For if God can settle the purpose of our lives only by constraining our alternatives, then the more God settles our purpose, the more narrowly He constrains our alternatives, and so the less significant our freedom. On this move, there is a tradeoff between freedom and a divinely settled purpose. Intuitively, there is no such tradeoff. As a libertarian, I think that God has given me a wide range of fully open alternatives to choose among, and yet He has one settled set of purposes for my life. Why not? But on the move I've sketched out, this is just impossible: the only way to settle my purpose beforehand is to leave my life only one genuinely open path, not allowing me any open alternatives to it.[21]

What I have said so far is actually just a first pass at this argument, for I must complicate what I say to be fair to O'Connor. O'Connor is a libertarian. If we have libertarian freedom and this includes some choice among genuinely open alternatives, then God's providential plan for the world has many branches. Wherever the plan allows us a free choice, history might branch in many different directions—one direction for each alternative open to us. On each branch, God has planned what He will do, and try to get us to do, if we choose that branch. On each branch, further, God has a purpose for our lives, which dictates what He plans in response to our choice. There will be something He means to achieve with us, no matter how badly we louse up: if God's plan embodies His perfect wisdom, we can never fall so far that God has no good purpose for us at all. But our choices settle which branch of God's plan we wind up actualizing, and so which of God's branched purposes for our lives is most relevant: or, to be blunter, which purpose God has for our lives. Thus arguably any libertarian who allows us genuinely open alternatives must say that we do settle our lives' purpose to some extent, unless he/she can show somehow that exactly the same divine purpose governs all branches our lives might follow. However, this does not require me to abandon the argument. It merely complicates its exposition. Let us now grant that on libertarianism, there does turn out to be a way we at least partly settle the purpose of our lives. All this requires is that we relativize the argument to each branch in God's plan. On each branch, I now say, it *should* be the case that there is no tradeoff between the expanse of alternatives open to us on that branch and the narrowness with which God settles our lives' purpose on that branch. On each branch, it should not be the case that God finds out our lives' purpose from us. On each branch, God should have settled His purpose for our lives in advance of and independent of our actions. None of these things are true on (M).

Indeterminate Purpose

It takes the full universe's full history to serve God's full purpose for the full history of the entire universe. This seems built into talk of a purpose for the full history of the entire universe. Were part of its history all it took fully to serve God's entire purpose for the whole history, there would be no purpose for the rest of it. God's creating, sustaining etc. that rest would have no purpose—hardly what one expects of someone perfectly wise. One couldn't reply that the rest would serve His purpose by overdetermining its fulfillment. If God did not mean or want the world to satisfy His purpose (say) twice over—if that was not a purpose He had—the overdetermination does not serve His purposes. If He did mean or want this, then the later part of the universe does not in fact overdetermine the fulfillment of His purpose: His full purpose P was that part of history fulfill a different purpose P* once, and another part fulfill P* again.

It takes the universe's full history. This is so almost by definition, as I've shown, but there is a further, troubling reason for it on (M). We live in an indeterminist universe. The orthodox reading of quantum theory suggests this, and O'Connor's libertarianism requires it. On (M), given indeterminism, what purposes the full history of the whole universe serves is indeterminate at any point in time. Perhaps parts of the universe or its history serve limited purposes, and these are fully served when or where those parts end. But when only part of its history has happened, given indeterminism, history could continue in many different ways, leading (on (M)) to the universe's turning out to have had different purposes. Only the universe's full character, realized over its full history, fixes which divine purposes it "matches." Short of its full history, the universe might turn out many ways, which would "match" different divine purposes.

On (M), till history ends, it is indeterminate what at least some of God's purposes for the the full history of the universe are (though there are many purposes it determinately does not have, those ruled out by history so far). Further, on standard Western theist belief about afterlives, history will never end. There might not even be a final unending but monotonous state. Even if in the end all creatures either enjoy the Beatific Vision or are in hell, creatures in hell might well have ever-varying pains, and plausibly our grasp of the content of Beatific Vision would increase forever. If this is the truth about the afterlife, then on (M), the universe's purpose would never be fully determinate at all.[22]

Envoi

Finally, intentions are part of the mind having them. On O'Connor's picture, God's intention includes a complex material object. So then does His mind. O'Connor turns God's mind partly into an extended partly material object including the world. It is odd to defend DDS by turning an aspect of God's mind into something extended and physically infinitely complex.

I submit, then, that O'Connor's version of the extrinsic-intention strategy is not a viable way to reconcile DDS with divine freedom. Its problems stem from the model of divine action it uses. Given agent-causalism, there needs to be some link between intention and reasons *other than* the reasons themselves causing the action—since on agent-causalism, they do not. O'Connor reasonably fixed on "match" between an intention's propositional content and that of the preceding reasons, but basing the connection on "match" generated the problems of retrospective purpose I have laid out. So we might want to consider whether another theory of action provides a better setting for the extrinsic-intention strategy. The alternative libertarian view is event-causal. Rather than holding that the agent causes an intention in light of reasons, it holds that the agent's reasons themselves, or the event of the agent's considering them, causes the event of the agent's intending. There is no need for a match of propositional content: what constitutes the intention's being for those reasons is that considering those reasons causes that intention. To consider whether event-causal extrinsic intentions fare better than agent-causal ones, though, is matter for another paper.[23]

Oriel College, Oxford University

Notes

1. *Civitas Dei* XI, 10.

2. *Summa Theologiae* Ia 3.

3. Jeffrey Brower, "Simplicity and Aseity," in *The Oxford Handbook of Philosophical Theology*, ed. Thomas Flint and Michael Rea (Oxford: Oxford University Press, 2009), 110–111. See D. M. Armstrong, *Truth and Truthmakers* (Cambridge: Cambridge University Press, 2004), 17.

4. Brower, "Simplicity and Aseity," 112.

5. Ibid., 110–111. Brower's account is perfectly standard; any truthmaker theorist would say the same.

6. *De Veritate* 5.

7. Aquinas, *Commentary on Aristotle's Metaphysics*, Bk. 9, l.11, n.4 and para. 1897. See also *Quaestiones De Veritate* 1, a.2 *ad* 3. My thanks to Timothy Pawl for bringing these texts to my attention, and for the references.

8. *De Veritate* 1, 1; *ST* Ia 16, 1.

9. I say that some A has a property F intrinsically just if what settles it that A is F is nothing other than A, A's parts (if any) and Fness (if there is such an entity). If A is F intrinsically, then whether A is F is settled (so to speak) entirely within A's boundaries. How A is environed has nothing to do with it. Thus typically, if A is intrinsically F, A could be F no matter what else did or did not exist.

10. For discussion of externalism, see Andrew Pessin and Sanford Goldberg, eds., *The Twin Earth Chronicles* (London: Routledge, 1996).

11. Timothy O'Connor, "Simplicity and Creation," *Faith and Philosophy* 16 (1999): 407–408. Henceforth "O'Connor."

12. Ibid., 410.

13. Ibid., 407–408.

14. Ibid., 408.

15. See, e.g., Brower, "Simplicity and Aseity"; Alexander Pruss, "On Two Problems of Divine Simplicity," *Oxford Studies in Philosophy of Religion* 1 (2008): 150–167; W. Matthews Grant, "Divine Simplicity, Contingent Truths, and Extrinsic Models of Divine Knowing," *Faith and Philosophy* 29 (2012): 270ff.

16. E.g., *SCG* I 86–87.

17. O'Connor, 408.

18. Ibid., 407–408.

19. Thomists who believe that all natural things have ends need not jib at this. For Aquinas, a natural end is just something to which a natural agent naturally tends (see, e.g., SCG III 16, In II Phys l. 10, 240). There is a great difference between tending toward something and being *for* anything. In Aristotle's universe, everything natural had an end though nothing natural had a divine purpose, nor then any other purpose; the same would be true in an atheist Aristotelian universe. This is a coherent way for things to be, even if it is not metaphysically possible.

20. Plausibly the world has many purposes. All the same, to (slightly) simplify exposition, I will now usually speak as if it had just one—e.g., talking about *the* purpose for the world.

21. All classical and medieval defenders of DDS were strong predestinarians. For them, I have no genuinely open alternatives. So they might in principle purchase a determinate purpose for my life in just this way.

22. That is, this is so unless part of history suffices to settle what the full history's full purpose is. On (M), this is so only if part of history's matching up with some divine purpose suffices for that to be the full purpose of the full history. I hold this out as an option in principle, but I do not see how to fill it out.

23. My thanks to the audience at the 2015 meeting of the ACPA and to Alex Pruss, Tim Pawl and W. Matthews Grant for comments.

World-Maker, Mind-Maker, Revealer

Thomas D. Sullivan

Abstract: Is religion "noxious rubbish to be buried as deeply, as thoroughly, and as quickly as possible"? Philip Kitcher tells us that's the dominant idea among atheists. In this paper I take a step back from the minutiae of standard journal articles to dispute the broad atheistic claim, and in the process suggest there is in fact a great deal to be said for religious belief. I argue that: (1) It's not highly implausible that there is a cause of the universe distinct from the universe—a World-Maker; (2) Because the act of cognizing instantiables is not purely a physical action, Christian teachings on the nature and status of humans are defensible against common claims to the contrary based on neo-Darwinism, and there's reason to think the World-Maker is a Mind-Maker; (3) Kitcher's case that there is no true religion is vulnerable to myriad objections, and since it's been lauded as the best attack on the credibility of religion to date, it's entirely reasonable not to abandon all religion, and in particular Christianity: there's good reason for thinking the World-Maker and Mind-Maker is also a Revealer.

Introduction

The Prayer

While sitting on a bench reading one day, I was approached by a man clearly in need. He asked if I could spare a few dollars. I did. Then I asked in return, "Could you please sometime pray for me?" I didn't mean immediately, but he folded his hands and rolled his eyes towards heaven. Then, shaking with feeling, he prayed, "Dear Lord, make him a better man." This exquisite little prayer at first startled and then pleased me. The poor man knew what this poor man needs, and where to go for help.

Absolute Rejection of Revelation

Or so I believe. But we have all heard the incessant drumbeat of knowledgeable secular humanists marching in the opposite direction. Phillip Kitcher, the most philosophically sophisticated among them, tells us the now dominant idea among atheists is that "religion is noxious rubbish to be buried as deeply, as thoroughly, and

©2016, *Proceedings of the ACPA*, Vol. 89
doi: 10.5840/acpaproc201612754

as quickly possible."[1] Kitcher would separate himself from other former Christians turned atheist: his tone is kinder and far more understanding. Yet in substance, Kitcher is not far from the position of these so-called New Atheists, maintaining as he does that substantive teachings of all religions are "almost certainly false."[2] Like so many contemporaries, he too seems to hold that our poor man's prayer is no more effective than prayers to Zeus, Hera, or the Monkey Faced Deity of India.

In *Faith vs. Fact*, distinguished evolutionary biologist Jerry Coyne relates how at seventeen he lost his faith completely and forever because it occurred to him that he had no reason to retain his thin supernatural beliefs.[3] On initial consideration, Coyne's choice seems eminently rational and proper. Religious beliefs may appear to be a sackful of burdensome hypotheses, altogether unnecessary to understand the world illumined by the marvels of modern science.

But on second thought, it may not be best to heave the sackful of religious beliefs into time's river of oblivion. For one might think to her seventeen-year-old self, "How much do I know about reasons that can be given for my belief, and how much about the potential answers to difficulties posed to my belief, relative to the difficulties of atheism? Not all that much I must admit—I'm only seventeen." I am not suggesting that a perplexed seventeen-year-old would never be in a position to properly discard her religious belief. After all, when more mature she may conclude that her beliefs flat-out contradict massive scientific evidence, or contain ghastly precepts or, on fuller consideration over several years, simply have little going for them.

But then again she may find herself more than ever tied to her religious beliefs, for a thousand reasons, explicit and implicit. She might grow into a religion and come to love her religious community, their devout practices, the consolations received during periods of grief, joy in living, and a thousand cherished things too deeply buried in a heart's depths to explain even to herself, let alone to validate to a person fully convinced that there is no such being as God.

An assessment of revelatory claims, even to the extent that we *can* fathom their depths, is complicated for those with a philosophical disposition. Paul of Tarsus says he has no philosophic doctrine: he preaches only Christ crucified. But a philosopher qua philosopher cannot fully imitate the saint's approach to ultimate realities, even if bound to the cross. For we are also bound by our mental habits and professional commitments to investigate religion philosophically, even if at times we might prefer just to go down on our knees.

A philosophical inquiry into large questions can take many forms. Quite often, inclination or institutional requirements lead to mincing the large questions into more digestible parts, and then parts of parts, and parts of parts of parts until reaching an infinitesimal point just right to dance upon. Perhaps I should follow this path here. Yet, philosophy is about big questions and their connections, and the ties among them are lost sight of when you get down to the infinitesimal, so beloved by the journals. Moreover, as Christian philosophers, we should at least from time to time raise questions to ourselves about the soundness of the teachings of gospels, traditions, and Church. So let this be one of those times.

Nonetheless, I will offer thoughts on only a fragment of this large topic I have had the good fortune to discuss in print with co-authors Sandra Menssen and Russell Pannier, and argue in print with atheist philosopher of science Quentin Smith. Still, since I cannot here take up everything, I will basically sketch the core arguments without trying to imagine responses to my position, responses I have debated in print at some length.[4]

Section 1: World-Maker

1-A. The Basic Argument

We begin our inquiry with a "fell-swoop objection," a line of reasoning relieving us from attending to details of *any* claim by anybody to receiving a revelation from on high. There cannot be a revelation from a god unless there *is* a god. Now we have all heard many assert, often with unbounded confidence, that the probability of a god's existing is on a par with that of a mermaid's. Is such no-god confidence warranted?

Not if we are asking whether there is a god in a rather minimal sense of a being extrinsic to the universe, but making some kind of causal contribution to our world. It's crucial to recognize from the outset how different this is from asking, "Does the God of Abraham, Isaac, and Jacob exist?" Or asking the philosophers' questions about something that is omniscient, omnipotent, and wholly good. Those questions need to be taken up, but not immediately, for if you ask whether God with a capital 'G' exists, a God loaded with all the divine attributes that have appealed to religious people and philosophers, and the answer in the end is negative, then you're really not at the end. What you deny is a conjunction: It's not the case that there exists an x, such that x has attributes A through Z. For denying that the conjunction A–Z is true of any being is consistent with accepting all but one attribute, and indeed consistent, moreover, with exceedingly sublime views of the existence of a God. So if we're discussing confident atheism we had better find ourselves a meaning of 'god' with a small g. The one I propose is quite impoverished, but using it at first will help us avoid the problems with denying a conjunctive spread of divine attributes.

Let us then take the meaning of 'god' to be 'a being who is external to the universe as we know it, but causally responsible for at least some of it, if not all.' This is fair to both theists and atheists. It certainly would be dismaying to hear an atheist say: "I don't believe in a god. But of course there is some non-material being that brought this world into existence." So, we can turn to the question whether there is such a being, a god with a small g.

Now note that those who claim to *know* there is no god in our defined sense, a minimal sense, need to know that one or both of the following propositions are false—*know* at least one is false, not just conjecture: first, that the universe came to be, and second, that whatever comes to be has a cause distinct from itself. We can embed these propositions in the following argument:

(1.1) It is highly plausible that the universe[5] came to be.

(1.2) It is highly plausible that whatever comes to be has a cause distinct from itself.[6]

(1.3) If (1.1) and (1.2), then it's not highly implausible that there is a cause of the universe distinct from the universe.

Then we may continue:

(1.4) If it's not highly implausible that there is a cause of the universe distinct from the universe, then nobody *knows* that theism is false.

(1.5) If nobody knows that theism is false, then atheism (understood as believing there is no God, as distinct from not believing there is one) is unwarranted.

(1.6) Hence, atheism is unwarranted.

Now soon we will take (1.6) and run with it. However, we need to look more closely at (1.1)–(1.3). (I assume that (1.4) and (1.5) are sufficiently obvious on their face.)

1-B. Objections and Replies

It's time to look at more evidence for the constituents of (1.1) and (1.2) of the lead argument and consider objections.

As for (1.1), which of us knows something no cosmologist knows, that the world did not come to be? Theories about the beginnings of our universe abound, but the standard view is that the universe began to be, in the neighborhood of between 12 and 15 billion years ago. So, even collected doubts about particulars do not erase the plausibility of the proposition that the universe came to be.

Still, one objection deserves some thought. Many are persuaded by the Hawking-Penrose theorems of the existence of the Big Bang proceeding from an initial cosmic singularity.[7] The idea enjoys wide acceptance largely because Hawking's phenomenally successful *A Brief History of Time* (1998) urged the claim as part of the project "to know the mind of God." A natural inference is that were there no cosmic singularity, the universe would be infinitely old, as Einstein had thought. But subsequently, Hawking and Jim Hartle made the "No Boundary Proposal" (no Big Bang) that the universe is finite but with no initial singularity serving as a boundary. By itself that notion does not overturn premise (1.1), since (1.1) claims only that there is considerable plausibility to the idea that the universe came to be, *not* that it came to be from an initial singularity. Premise (1.1) in essence gives some substantial credence to the universe not being a permanent entity.

If the Hawking-Hartle Proposal fusing quantum mechanics with general relativity makes no real mischief for premise (1.1), it nonetheless generates at least two metaphysical problems for premise (1.2). In their authoritative article in the *Stanford Encyclopedia of Philosophy* Hans Halvorson and Helge Kragh state both succinctly:

[F]rom a metaphysical point of view, God's hand is not manifest even in big bang models: these models have no first state for God to create, and these models have no time for God to exist in before the big bang.[8]

Unfolded a little, the first metaphysical difficulty is this:

• God can create the universe only if there is a first state of the universe.

• There is no first state (in any current big bang models).

• So God cannot create the universe.

But both of the premises are dubious. Why can't God do what you and I can and do all the time? We set objects in motion and there is no first state of the motion. A strong wind comes my way. I raise my hand and divert it somewhat, locally. There is no first moment of the stretch I have caused. The reasons for this are complex. Spelling them out would take us from the thinking of Zeno's paradoxes, through Aristotle's critique, then Hegel's stunning proposal that motion involves a contradiction, to the use of calculus by Bertrand Russell and Michael Tooley. We could end with Graham Priest's brave defiance of the principle of non-contradiction, his dialethism (his two-truths theory), and paraconsistent logic (a logic preventing inferences to anything at all from one contradiction). There is, I insist with Aristotle, neither a contradiction in the concept of motion, nor a first instant in which it begins in the stretch from the diversion of the wind to whatever the end is. The wind blows where it wills, and you hear the sound thereof, but cannot tell from where it came, and where it goes. Does it all begin with the beating of a butterfly's wings in Africa? Will it end with the world's bang or a whisper? No matter. In the relevant segment, there is no first instant or last instant in which the diverted wind moves. It will no doubt occur to some that the position taken here is inconsistent with calculus, which allows us to ascertain the velocity of an object at a particular instant. Calculus books do commonly lapse into quite misleading statements, such as "An object is in motion at an instant if its velocity at the instant is non-zero. It is at rest if the velocity is zero." But this is impossible for the reason given by Arisotle. If an object is moving in an instant, it will be two places at one and the same instant. Hegel and Graham Priest may be happy with this. But should we be? Imagine an announcer exclaiming when Henry Aaron hit his 715th home run that Aaron not only broke Ruth's record, but also blew apart the principle of non-contradiction!

Bracketing all this, Halvorson and Kragh's doubts can be answered by appealing to ideas familiar to everyone in this audience.

To the objection that current big bang models have no first state for God to create, particularly when quantum mechanics blends with general relativity theory, a theist can simply take a cue from Aquinas and point out that since God would have infinite power from eternity, there is no conclusive reason to think a creation *couldn't* issue forth without a beginning. This is why Aquinas thought the temporal finitude of the universe was indemonstrable and had to be revealed.

As for the second problem Halvorson and Kragh raise, that these models have no time for God to exist in before the big bang, the answer is even briefer. All the theist has to do is repeat what was said endlessly in medieval cosmology—correctly, in my view: God doesn't dwell in space or time.[9]

Recently Wes Morriston has urged an old objection: that even if a universe came to be, it might not have come to be from an extrinsic source.[10] Though everything in the universe is an effect of something, the universe itself may be causeless, he suggests. Morriston's proposal is glaringly ad hoc. But that's not the end of the matter. Morriston's proposal has disturbing implications for causality within the universe, inconsistent with his supposition that everything within it needs a cause, though not the universe as a whole. For if the universe as a whole can come to be without a cause, we are back with Hume. Anything can come from anything, or nothing at all. There is nothing to demand a cause in a particular case if it's not true in general that everything that comes to be has a cause. Our explanations of things within the world will in the end turn out not to be explanations at all, but Humean correlations, decked out with mathematics.[11]

Morriston is joined by a surprising number of others in clinging to the idea that the universe might have just popped into existence. One of these, Quentin Smith, in a series of exchanges on the subject with me, began by advertising the causeless beginning of the universe, but wound up retreating to the idea that the universe created itself.[12] I will say no more about this desperate ploy here, nor Lawrence Krauss's equivocal claim that the universe could have arisen from nothing—except to note his 'nothing' is not nothing; it teems with energy.[13]

Another line of retreat I've heard insisted upon, taken with respect to the propositions embedded in (1.1) and (1.2) separately, and both together, maintains that their plausibility or probability is inscrutable. But if the propositions alone or conjunctively are inscrutable, they still could be rock-solidly true despite their inscrutability. The claim to know there is no god cannot be launched by confidently denying inscrutable propositions.

Let's pause to catch our breath.

Recall that we are entertaining a common position of contemporary atheists threatening to undermine all revelatory claims in one fell swoop by denying there is any plausibility to the belief that any god exists to produce the revelation. Putting to one side for now the entire history of natural theology—much as contemporary atheists frequently do—we have proposed that we can get things started with much, much less. As noted earlier, all we need is the plausibility of the contention that the universe came to be, and that whatever comes to be has a cause distinct from itself.

We focused on problems for (1.1–1.3), trusting that (1.4–1.5) called for no comment.

1-C. The Significance of the Argument

The result reached so far may well disappoint. A critic might comment: what you have cautiously put forward is an extremely limited conclusion: that nobody knows, or could know, that there is no such thing as god in our skinny sense of the term. We're worlds away from the robust argument sought by Aquinas, Leibniz, and some of our contemporaries, a luminously clear case making it certain or at least highly probable that God exists.

Nonetheless, while slender, our result at (1.6) is highly significant. It is no small matter to show that boldly proclaimed atheism cannot withstand an argument resting on two propositions that nobody knows to be false or even highly improbable. Furthermore, while narrow, the argument is a spear's-head-sharp tip. For it opens the way to looking to a much larger database than commonly considered in natural theology.[14]

This can be done by using the point made at (1.6) to move into the next phase of the argument with:

(1.7) If (1.6)—if atheism is unwarranted—we ought to part company with traditional natural theology narrowly construed to investigate a much larger evidential base than we would have if we stuck with the bad habit: we should consult the contents of putative revelations.

Consider a parallel: Homer.

The ancients believed that a single individual composed both the *Iliad* and the *Odyssey*, but they had no idea of when, or where, he lived. The idea that Homer existed persisted for centuries with only occasional dissent. In the nineteenth century, however, influential writers such as F. A. Wolf urged that in all likelihood, writing would be unavailable to the alleged Homer, and contended that both epics are too long to memorize. Therefore, there could not have been a Homer, and these epics must have been composed over time, by several editors. This was a standard view going into the twentieth century until Milman Parry began to explore the possibilities of oral poetry being composed by illiterates. His travels brought him to southern Serbia, where he taped poems comparable to the *Iliad* and the *Odyssey*, recited by illiterate bards. Homer thus was not a golden mountain, but a perfectly possible being who depended upon all the techniques for memorizing long poems available to him at the time. In order to ascertain whether this possibility was realized, there was no option but to turn back to the texts. Many scholars now think that Homer existed and was the primary author of the great epics, though there were additions and editorial alterations on its way to its final form.

Back to God and revelation. We have seen that the existence of a god is not highly improbable, given our argument resting on premises (1.1) and (1.2). This argument can be supplemented by all that standard natural theology has to offer, without reference to putative revelations. But the path followed in the case of Homer is a path to be followed here. Look at the texts. In the case of Homer, the discovery of the abilities of pre-literate peoples was enough to underwrite scholarly investigation into the content of the epic poems. In our case, the argument for a minimal god underwrites investigation into the content of revelation to ascertain whether its content is heavenly, i.e., such that it is redolent of wisdom beyond the human. In addition, as our understanding of who Homer was and what he could do is now considerably amplified by the investigation of the epic texts, with Homer in mind, likewise, our thin conception of a god can now be filled out by reflections on the alleged revelation. Such reflections have proved to be enormously deep and rewarding, with no end in sight.

Section 2: Mind-Maker

2-A. A Bridge from World-Maker to Mind-Maker, and Back

There are several ways to plunge into the vast revelatory database for philosophic reflection. We could begin by inquiring at a very general level into the prospects of there being a revelation. Or, we could take up a particular claim within a particular religion, and spread out to the ends of the earth. We'll start locally, with scientific and philosophical difficulties concerning a central Christian conception of human beings. Our effort will be to support the proposition earlier argued, that it's not highly implausible there's a World-Maker. Yet, there's another reason for choosing this particular problem about the origin and status of individual humans. It is that it's here one sees, sharply counterpoised to Christian revelation, an element much derided by many in an appeal to neo-Darwinian science. I'm not going to call into question the brunt of evolutionary teachings regarding natural selection and the evolution of animal bodies. But I will depart from a central dogma of neo-Darwinianism about the human mind.

2-B. Two Catechisms

The key teachings of Christianity on the nature of human beings and their relationship to a God are now widely regarded by sophisticates as obviously false, in light of modern science. Major elements of the Christian tradition are familiar to all of you. Here are extracts from the Catechism of the Roman Catholic Church just to get things going.

> [Gen. 1:27:] "God created man in his own image, in the image of God he created him, male and female he created them." (355)

> Man occupies a unique place in creation: (I) he is "in the image of God"; (II) in his own nature he unites the spiritual and material worlds; (III) he is created "male and female"; (IV) God established him in his friendship. (1700, 343)

> [H]e was created, and this is the fundamental reason for his dignity. (1703, 2258, 225, 295)

So Catholicism says, and much of Christianity agrees about the status of humankind. The Christian tradition is scarcely blind to the dark side of human beings. There is something wrong with us, each of us. But there are cures for even the worst vices, of even the worst among us.

The neo-Darwinian catechism, spread through many installments in books and journals, insists on an altogether different picture. Anathematized by neo-Darwinians is any notion that the world or ourselves can't be explained without appealing to one or more beings who affect the universe in some way, though they are extrinsic to it. As one of the high priests of the secular religion bluntly states:

> We take the side of science *in spite* of the patent absurdity of some of its constructs, *in spite* of its failure to fulfill many of its extravagant promises of health and life, *in spite* of the tolerance of the scientific community for unsubstantiated just-so stories, because we have a prior commitment, a commitment to materialism. . . . Moreover, that materialism is absolute, for we cannot allow a Divine Foot in the door.[15]

We have time to take up here only the reductive tendencies at the heart of the view. While the word 'reduction' offends pious ears in biology, philosophy, and elsewhere, it appears that it's really at the heart of biology and neuroscience in particular. For all the thumping on behalf of non-reductive physicalism despite warnings from Jaegwon Kim, Thomas Nagel, and others, the explanation of the doings of living beings in the biological community certainly looks reductive, whatever the language is for articulating it.

In *Ruthlessly Reductive Neuroscience*, John Bickle scolds philosophers and scientists for their naiveté. He describes his task as follows:

> So this book's first task is to reveal the scientific detail of some accomplished mind-to-molecules "linkages" and to evaluate the explanatory potential of this "ruthless reduction" for behavior and cognition generally. . . . I will argue for it [this explanatory potential] all the way up to consciousness. . . . If I can communicate [the factual existence of a ruthless and audacious reductionism that informs neuroscience's current cutting edge], I will at least break the popular but mistaken myth among philosophers and cognitive scientists that reduction is "dead." On the contrary: it is alive and thriving, at the very core of one of the hottest (and best funded) scientific disciplines.[16]

This reductive perspective in neuroscience is seen more generally as essential to a sound philosophical biology. Thus, for example, in an encyclopedia article entitled "Reductionism in Biology," Matthen Mohan writes:

> Until recently, physicalism could have been considered a hypothesis, or merely a metaphysical principle; now, it has acquired compelling empirical support. In Mendel's theory, for instance, genes (or 'factors', as he called them) were identified by the traits with which they were associated. They were 'hidden variables' in the inheritance of traits. But since nobody until long after Mendel knew how genes determine traits, his theory was compatible with vitalism, the doctrine that life is based on non-physical processes. Now, however, it has become clear that Mendelian inheritance is completely determined by the biochemistry of nucleic acids

and proteins. Since biochemistry is reducible to physics, it seems that Mendelian processes must be physical in character. By similar arguments, all of biology is ultimately reducible to physics.[17]

2-C. Difficulties with the Christian Catechism

The difficulties the second catechism raises for the first are evident. Why *not* just say what Mohan says, that the various spiritual factors have disappeared one by one, in favor of physical factors, and that by analogous arguments that occur in biology, we'll find that physicalism, and most prominently the reductive branch of it, is the truth about the whole world? Why not say what the world of biology is so widely taken to teach us, in direct opposition to any spiritual dimensions in humans?

2-D. Difficulties with the Neo-Darwinian Catechism

To begin with, Mohan's induction, though seemingly founded on a broad base, is actually startlingly selective. Nothing has been put forward to explain what philosophers focus upon—consciousness and its many modalities. These questions even the most thoughtful biologists largely duck.

There are questions about consciousness as such. Does it exist? If so, how is it produced? If it exists, what impact does it have in the world? And, of course, what is its ontological status—is it physical or non-physical, and in what sense of 'physical'? And, finally, what is it *for*? There are also questions about particular modalities of consciousness. At the bottom of the spectrum we have questions about sensation and so forth. At the high end, we have questions about, for instance, consciousness of the self as a self.

Some biologists and neuroscientists acknowledge what others take to be nearly obvious on its face. Michael Gazzaniga, a top researcher in neuroscience tells us:

> Right from the start we can say that science has little to say about sentience. We are clueless on how the brain creates sentience.[18]

And after trudging through the details of the neuroscience of sensation, on p. 366 of her book neuroscientist Jacqueline Ludel writes:

> I wish I could tell you how the interpretation is performed. However, with all we do know about the workings of the brain, no one is able to explain how the movements of ions across the membranes of neurons finally produce the overwhelmingly important, undeniable experience that "Yes, I exist," "yes, I perceive," "yes, I feel and think and know."[19]

Unmoved by such remarks, philosophers such as eliminativists Dennett, Patricia and Paul Churchland, and others (a good long list could be drawn up) bravely assert that there is nothing to explain. For them, contemporary science gives us our fundamental posits, and contemporary science at the bottom (physics) doesn't mention consciousness at all, or anything that can be derived from it.

For both evident and not so evident reasons, this blinkered view of consciousness and its modalities is as big a mistake as imaginable. First, you and I know that we're sometimes conscious, sometimes not, sometimes partially or intermittently, and we know this with Cartesian certitude. Or, to be fair, Augustinian and Thomistic certitude. Commenting on Aristotle's *De Anima*, Aquinas reads the great Greek thinker as asserting that the study of the soul is the noblest and most certain of inquiries.[20] Aquinas's reasoning about the certitude is what everybody now calls Cartesian.

The second reason this eliminativist position is mistaken is that science itself depends on multiple minds consciously reading results from instruments. Scientists must compare their results, which means what they consciously put forward, with those of others working at other times and sites. So, if we're mistaken about the existence of consciousness, then there is no science to support the eliminativist's position.

The third reason for the mistake is that eliminativism hastily assumes the contradictory of what distinguished quantum theorists have had to say. The position widely held in quantum mechanics, emanating from the work of Bohr, is well-expressed by distinguished physicist Eugene Wigner:

> There are several reasons for the return on the part of most physical scientists to the spirit of Descartes's "cogito ergo sum," which recognizes the thought, that is the mind, as primary.

Wigner manifestly sides with Augustine, Aquinas, and Descartes. But he adds a reason unknown to all the earlier philosophers:

> When the province of physical theory was extended to encompass microscopic phenomena through the creation of quantum mechanics, the concept of consciousness came to the fore again: it was not possible to formulate the laws of quantum mechanics in a fully consistent way without reference to consciousness. . . . It may be premature to believe that the present philosophy of quantum mechanics will remain a permanent feature of future physical theories; it will remain remarkable, in whatever way our future concepts may develop, that the very study of the external world led to the conclusion that the content of consciousness is an ultimate reality.[21]

This view that Wigner puts forward seems utterly dominant in the field. To be sure, there are other physicists who find this position dismaying. Yet, before any of us struggles against our own awareness of our consciousness on the grounds that contemporary science eliminates it, we ought to be conscious of the fact that somebody of the stature of Wigner believes consciousness is probably ineliminable from the axioms of quantum theory.

So much for consciousness as such.

Let us now turn to a specific modality at the higher end of consciousness: consciousness of instantiables, or possibilities.[22] Our terminology is somewhat non-standard. The medieval thinkers, and Aquinas in particular, preferred to discuss the mental act targeting instantiables and possibilities in the language of universals, natures, essences, and other terms from the scholastic vocabulary. The scholastic terms carry with them a trail of historical commentary that could easily sink us into a consideration of all the chief meanings they ascribe to the terms. Even worse, when Aquinas and successors discuss the cognitive side of awareness of universals, the jargon becomes overwhelming. Cryptic terms and ideas such as "impressed species," "expressed species," "intentional in-existence" in the mind, and its non-destructive assimilation of forms, abound. That language may express as well as possible to the initiated the deepest truth about cognition of the realities spoken of. But we must do with less. I will stay, so far as I can, with everyday terms. Moreover, we will shy away from sketches of computational theories of mind, arguments about wide and narrow content of thought, Meinongian objects, and the ontological status of universals. All this must wait, since these issues do not present *inaugural* questions posed by internal experience—"folk psychology," if you insist on calling it by the unflattering jargon of cognitive science. All this, I say, must wait, while we keep our eyes fixed on facts known from internal experience and the bearing they may have on sprawling efforts to naturalize the mind.

Let us look inside ourselves and see what Aquinas was getting at. To begin with, all of us are aware of instantiables or possibilities or types. (I will use these terms interchangeably.) We can know, bring to mind, an endless number of possibilities, for example, skipping down the street, or objecting to what I've been contending. If you skip, or raise an objection, you actualize the possibility of skipping or raising an objection. Yours is an instance, or a particular, or a trope. The language of contemporary literature has its own problems, not unlike those of the scholastic jargon. But I think a few examples are all one needs for getting the hang of it, whatever it's called.

Some philosophers, preferring the language of universals, believe that the whole universal is enclosed within every particular instantiation. So, if this is an apple, and that's an apple, each houses whole and entire, the abstract property of being an apple. But this immanence theory has many serious problems, including these.

If types or possibilities or universals are wholly contained within their instances, and have no independent existence, then when a particular instance leaves this world, the type identified with it is also destroyed, even as it lives on in other instantiations. Also, some possibilities are never realized, and never will be, and so cannot be identified with any instantiation. In our article "The Mind-Maker," Russ Pannier adds other reasons to his list of objections to the immanence theory of universals.[23]

What, then? Are we going to go Plato's route? Not necessarily, but it would be inappropriate here to say much more about the ontology of instantiables or possibilities or types, since extensive theorizing may well burden the entirely justified belief *that* we can bring to mind possibilities. I do, though, need to add a couple points.

First, the correct answer to the question "where is the instantiable itself located?" is: nowhere, and nowhen. The possibility does not fall within the space-time net, though of course the instances may.

Second, an instantiable like *being an apple*, if realized in every apple, before, now and after, will be located in the space-time net all over the place. To step around a quarrel about this contention, let's turn to an instantiable the instances of which manifestly are not caught in the net. Such, for example, is the property of being a *valid argument*. Or, for short, *validity*. *Validity* is not to be found under the bed or hiding in some black hole. It is meaningless to ask: "Where or when is validity?" unless by 'argument' one means only particular verbalizations rather than one or another type of valid form.

I have said that we needn't knit our brows much about the ontology of possibilities. And so too, we need not sink into a long discussion of how it is that we manage to be conscious of them. All we need to know is *that* we can be conscious of instantiables—and we all do know this—and that validity has no place in the space-time net. This will allow us to drive home the proposition that some of our cognitive states are at least partly non-physical, and go on to conjecture that considerable evidence exists for a Mindmaker.

What do we mean by 'physical' and 'non-physical'? The problems of definition are notorious. But happily, our argument will not require a precise statement of both necessary and sufficient conditions. It will be enough for our purposes to consider just three necessary conditions for things being physical. These three necessary conditions are evident from the paradigm case of a purely physical action bearing on an object. Consider a stamping machine. The operation of a stamping machine is entirely physical if any action is. Now when a stamping machine impresses an image on a metal blank, the machine, the blank, and the action are all in the space-time net.

The example may be criticized as being all too simple. Three qualifications are necessary for a general description of the conditions for a purely physical action that bears on an object. First, for obvious reasons I'll ignore the possibility that they constitute the space-time net. Secondly, if we need to fuss about it because of theories that maintain that time collapses in the earliest stages of the universe, we can drop the words 'time' and 'net' and just stick with 'space.' Third, taking into account quantum mechanics, we do not assume that *in* the space-time net means precisely determinable. The dominant theory is that particles may be nowhere precisely until the 'collapse of the wave function.'

With those qualifications, we can assert:

(2.1) Purely physical actions bearing on an object satisfy at least three necessary conditions: the agent, the act, and the object of the act are all confined to the space-time net.

(2.2) The act of cognizing instantiables fails to satisfy at least one of these three necessary conditions: validity is nowhere and nowhen.

(2.3) So, the act of cognizing instantiables is not purely a physical action, if at all.

Furthermore, if the act of cognizing universals is not purely physical, that argues to the same for the power that exercises the act: the power of cognizing possibilities must be at least streaked with immateriality.

It does not follow, however, that the act must be entirely non-physical. Were we to attempt to show that, a stronger argument would be needed, and we might have to go down the path of the medievals, with "impressed species," "expressed species," "intentional in-existence" in the mind, and non-destructive assimilation of forms, though perhaps not expressing the ideas in the scholastic language. But we don't need this stronger conclusion that the mind is entirely immaterial: we only need to show, against a physicalistic worldview, that there are actions or states that are not through and through physical.

It may help here to contrast a paradigmatically non-physical act with the physicality of the stamping machine. In 1849, a tale was told of a secret way for girls to see their future husbands walk around a room and then vanish. An unmarried girl is to sit by herself from midnight to 1:00 am, during which time she pulls many hairs from her head, and, mixing them with the herb "True Love," burns every hair separately, saying "I offer this, my sacrifice, to him most precious in my eyes. I charge thee now, come forth to me, that I may this minute see thee." And poof! There he is.[24] The girl is in the space-time net, and so are her words, though not the meaning of the words. The object of her desire is an ethereal being who pops in and out of the room. No one thinks that this would be a physical action, even if, contrary to all we know, this superstition turned out to be true.

A sign of the power of this argument we're developing is the determined effort of philosophers to dispense with or analyze away cognition of universals in favor of supposedly concrete, scientifically respectable entities. Thus for example Quine says:

> I have been inveighing against mentalistic semantics and urging in its place the study of dispositions to behavior. This move could be represented alternatively and more picturesquely as a matter not so much of substitution as of identification: let us construe *mind* as a system of disposition to behavior.[25]

And the ever-elusive Wittgenstein can be read as denying this possibility in favor of some philosophy of language that bids us not to ask for meaning but ask for use. Fodor says flat-out intentionality is inconsistent with physicalism. So it's no surprise that one of his most recent books (with Zenon Pylyshyn) is titled *Minds without Meaning*.

Faced with a choice between our internal experience and a theory, be it the strong imagist tradition in the empiricists from Hobbes on to our contemporaries, and more generally today's analytic philosophy, I for one would plump for the former without hesitancy. Wouldn't you?

What's the upshot of all this so far? If cognition of types is at least partially immaterial, then we have something quite comforting to the one who would believe in a revelation concerning the status of human beings. And the comforting result does more than validate elements of the Christian revelation. It also reaches back and supports the claim that it's not highly implausible that there is a cause of the universe distinct from the universe. And so we obtain the following argument:

> (2.1) Purely physical actions bearing on an object satisfy at least three necessary conditions: the agent, the act, and the object of the act are all confined to the space-time net.

> (2.2) The act of cognizing instantiables fails to satisfy at least one of these three necessary conditions: validity is nowhere and nowhen.

> (2.3) So, the act of cognizing instantiables is not purely a physical action, if at all.

> (2.4) Thus, Christian teachings on the nature and status of humans are defensible against common claims to the contrary based on neo-Darwinism.

But not only theists today would be comforted—so would the great but neglected nineteenth-century co-discoverer of natural selection, Alfred Russell Wallace. A few words about the history of this intriguing individual can help us see that it is possible to bring science to the aid of a mode of thinking congenial to revelation, though Wallace himself had no time for formalized religion.

Biology books typically credit Wallace with co-discovering natural selection. And they sometimes mention his prompting of Darwin to get his "big book on species" out. They seldom mention the rest of this intriguing story, and I've never come across a textbook that states the biological grounds for his break with Darwin over the sufficiency of natural selection to account for the spiritual dimension of human beings so disfavored by contemporary biologists. Few writers, even specialists, seem to know exactly what Wallace's arguments were. He had his reasons for exempting the human mind from the account elaborating natural selection, and it's anything but evident that these reasons were refuted by Darwin's terse responses, or, so far as I know, the neo-Darwinian biologists. On the rare occasions when they mention Wallace's arguments, they fail to engage them with any seriousness, preferring to fling irrelevant darts at him, ridiculing his interest in séances and left-wing social philosophy. Wallace insisted at the time that these personal attacks were simply egregious ad hominems, and that a fair-minded critic had to attend to the biological data that Wallace beautifully delineated in a series of now quite-forgotten works.

Wallace claimed that while natural selection could account for the evolution of bodies, including the human body, it could not entirely account for the evolution of mind. Two of his arguments are especially interesting.

The first turns on the fact that human beings in primitive conditions developed a brain far too large for the demands of their environment. Indeed, they developed brains quite comparable to our own. Not only that, but these over-developed brains turned out to be exceedingly useful, of course, much later in the course of human development. Wallace argued since natural selection can't account for this weird burden at the beginning (large brains require large amounts of energy), it must be accounted for by a cause extrinsic to nature. What did Darwin have to say about this in *The Descent of Man*? Not much. He denied that what we're calling "primitive conditions" were undemanding. Wallace, who lived among primitives more than Darwin, replied that Darwin had offered no evidence whatever for the claim. Which Darwin didn't. (In this connection it's much worth noting that the problem of the large brain and its rapid development in the early stages of human history continues to intrigue evolutionary biologists.[26])

Wallace's second argument of interest here drew attention to our encounter, from time to time, with colors in nature so extraordinary that it was reasonable to think the capacity for perceiving the colors was inexplicable from an evolutionary point of view. He intimated that seeing colors of whatever sort also was hard to make sense of, since this wondrous capacity could not be explained by natural selection, because we could get by with simply distinguishing one thing from another visually.

I know too little of the scientific literature on colors to tell whether Wallace's comments have met the empirical test of time or not. Remarkably, however, he's got an ally in, of all people, Jaegwon Kim, whose book *Physicalism, or Something Near Enough* acknowledges that the gift of color vision is exceedingly hard to explain, and does so for the same reasons as Wallace, perhaps unwittingly, since Wallace's work is so little known. We could compete successfully without color vision, hypothesize both Wallace and Kim.

At this juncture, we now turn to the last section of this paper and briefly consider a second "fell-swoop" objection.

Section 3: Revealer

3-A. Introduction

Recall how we distinguished between on the one hand looking to a putative revelation as God's Truth, and, on the other hand, using its content as support for taking it seriously, and perhaps committing heart and soul to its teachings. This latter endeavor means, of course, looking for evidence not just about a World-Maker or Mind-Maker but a god rich enough to be called God—a Being concerned about the world and humankind's place within it.

We want to know whether a strong enough case for a true revelation—or true revelations—can underwrite accepting the revelation mind and heart.

No one will be shocked by the disclosure that I can hardly do more in this final section than take a few steps. What Sandy Menssen and I could not complete in 350 pages of *The Agnostic Inquirer* I can't finish in 5.[27] Nor do I expect that in our future work together Sandy and I can come close to stating a full and compelling case. To produce that is the work of many scholars in a number of disciplines, and very able members of this association. But it is better to try to do a little than nothing at all.

It is imperative to realize that what we are doing here is taking revelatory claims, including Christianity's, as hypotheses. This hardly means we must uproot all our beliefs and convictions while we entertain agnostic or atheistic points of view, as Menssen and I (and Coyne, and many others) were drawn to do in our own teens, and the two of us, along with many others, for some time thereafter.

Why must religious beliefs and attachments be purged when scientists so often seem to have a death-grip on their own opinions? (Recall Lewontin's slamming the door on the "divine foot.") In any event, the demand to extinguish one's commitments before entering an inquiry places an impossible burden on any human being who is something more than a Cartesian spirit.

Now if revelatory claims are viewed as hypotheses, they can then be set against competing hypotheses, not just other revelatory claims, but also scientific and philosophical hypotheses.

3-B. Kitcher's Core Argument

In several books, including his recent work *Life After Faith*, Philip Kitcher begins by launching a critique of revelatory claims in general. This is a fell-swoop objection, our second, because if the conclusion is accepted, there's no need whatever to give close attention to any particular revelation. How are we supposed to arrive at this conclusion? I must say that here Kitcher's fairly literary presentation of his core argument makes it difficult to be sure that it is as I'm going to say it is.

Before setting out my reading of his core argument, a brief remark about a contention of Kitcher's that colors the reading of his primary argument. He thinks that an adherent to a particular faith necessarily takes his or her religion to be the sole correct religion. But while this may be true of some religions, it's not true of Catholicism, and other Christian denominations. (See Vatican II.)

So, let's move on to Kitcher' core argument itself. If it's not correct to see the argument as I will present it, then we can simply view the two propositions that appear to generate an argument as if they didn't—i.e., as if they were independently asserted. In a nutshell, Kitcher contends:

(K.1) There are massive contradictions among theistic world religions on essentials.

From this he infers:

(K.2) The faithful all follow the same radically defective method—taking for granted what is handed on by culturally bound elders.[28]

He concludes:

(K.3) No putative revelation has a shred of credibility.

What's wrong with all this, if anything? Actually, plenty.

3-C. Problems with Kitcher's First Premise

Let's start with (K.1).

The degree of disagreement in religions is arguably exaggerated, once account is taken of several well-known facts.

For one thing, the fact that many claims are prefaced by a false assumption does not automatically eliminate all truth from them. Many everyday truths are expressed with faulty prefaces. "Your neighbor's tree is gorgeous." "Thank you, but actually it's on my property." Is there no truth in the first sentence? The speaker means *that* tree. And so it is with many revelatory claims—they are introduced by faulty presuppositions. By itself that does not doom everything that follows. Cantor believed some ideas of set theory had been revealed to him from above; the great Indian mathematician Ramanujan ascribed his theorems to the consort of the Lion-god. Does prefacing a proof of a theorem with "It has been revealed to me that . . ." mean that we should automatically declare the theorem rubbish? "I see your neighbor has a gorgeous, enchanted tree over there." "Actually, it's my tree, and it's not enchanted." Once again, we see a solid truth embedded in the partially mistaken remark.

Second, Kitcher fails to acknowledge what he surely knows is the case, that propositions admit of degrees of truth. An elementary textbook teaching kids to count might say something like: "We'll teach you the numbers." They begin with *one*, and move to *two*, and so on. It never enters a six-year-old's head that there's a set called "the real numbers," let alone the hyper-reals. So, shall we say that the textbooks ought to be pitched? Of course not. The texts contain an indispensable truth, even while begging for qualification. Even in science, as philosophers of science know well, many major theories have been proposed that are only partially true. This includes theories from Galileo, Kepler, Newton, Darwin, Einstein, and Hawking.

Third, many assertions that appear to conflict aren't even talking about the same subject. The phenomenally learned master of comparative religions, R. C. Zaehner, cautions the unwary that:

> [W]hen we look at the religions of the world, we are faced with two totally different approaches to the whole subject, we are faced with two chosen peoples, not one; for whereas Europe and the Near East owe their religions directly or indirectly to the Jews, further Asia owes hers directly or indirectly to the Indians: and these two peoples see religion in an entirely different way. Perhaps they do so because they are talking of different things.[29]

Fourth, even when they're talking about the same subject, the teachings are tailored to audiences at a certain time and place. For example, it's easy to see at first blush that polytheism, if taken seriously, if taken the way we're inclined to look at it in the west, conflicts with monotheism. But consider this: The disciple asks the master: "How many gods are there?" He answers, in line with ritual prayer: 303—and, 3 and 3,000. "Yes, but the disciple continues, but how many gods are there really?" 33. "Yes, but, how many gods ARE there?" Six. "But how many gods are there?" Three. "Yes, but *really*, how many, Oh Master?" One and a half. "Yes, but really?" One. "Well, yes but who are those 303, and 3003?" They are but the powers, the greatness, of the gods.[30] And we are assured by Hindu scholar Vasudha Narayanan that most Hindus believe the supreme being takes name and form and manifests himself, or herself, to devotees.

Fifth, there's a question of degree of commitment to doctrine. While Hinduism is generally committed to doctrines of reincarnation and karma, there is little else that looks like dogma. Hinduism is often thought to be constitutionally polytheistic, but as we have just seen, this might be quite illusory.

Sixth, utterances verbally contradictory can have vague conceptual elements rendering the constituent propositions incapable of being judged as true contradictories of their denials. Familiar examples from logic include: "He is bald"; "No he's not; he's got a little hair." Who's right about the one who is *sort of* bald? (There's a movement in computer science that takes into account this vagueness—fuzzy logic.)

Seventh, even religions that seem worlds apart as Buddhism and Christianity include fundamental statements that can be accepted by both, though no doubt in a different sense. Zaehner writes:

> "There is," the Buddha says, "an unborn, not become, not made, uncompounded, and were it not . . . for this unborn, not become, not made, uncompounded, no escape could be shown here for what is born, has become, is made, is compounded. But because there is . . . an unborn, not become, not made, uncompounded, therefore an escape can be shown for what is born, has become, is made, is compounded."[31]

A Christian who believes in a maximally unified God can say: Amen!

Please don't misunderstand me to be committing myself to the wooden-headed idea that there are no contradictions at all. Of course there are. And they're often deep. My argument so far is that the line taken by Kitcher, and others, gravely exaggerates the conflicts among religions, failing to take into account much else that Zaehner, in his Gifford lectures, called "concordant discord: the interdependence of faiths."

3-D. Problems with Kitcher's Second Premise

Without exaggerating discord, proposition (K.2) gains little evidential support from (K.1). It is curious that the philosopher in Kitcher isn't alert at the moment to the embarrassing truth that philosophers themselves disagree about answering fundamental questions. Shall we say that methods in philosophy are *all* hopelessly defective?

In any event, proposition (K.2) is extremely dubious. That proposition, again, was:

(K.2) The faithful all follow the same radically defective method—taking for granted what is handed on by culturally bound elders.

Here are some reasons to reject it.

First, Kitcher's claim that all religions employ the same radically defective method is way over-stated. It's true enough that most adherents of a religion take the content that was handed on to them, and get on with life. But some religions, at least, have a history of critical reflection on these doctrines. To pick a name out of a hat, Thomas Aquinas from time to time gave a thought to objections to Christian doctrine, and to the proper wording of its substantive claims, and what can be inferred from those claims. In other words, he was a theologian.

But it's not only critical development of the theology that separates some faiths from others, but also their grounding in the facts. Christian creeds include the substantive claim that Jesus of Nazareth suffered under Pontius Pilate and was crucified and buried. Atheists can agree with these substantive historical claims. The historical claims underpin much of the theology about Christ's conquest over sin through death on the cross, and his rising three days later. The historical claims stand in stark contrast to the ancient myths of dying and rising gods. When Hercules voluntarily immolated himself on Mount Oeta, it's lost in the darkest and most distant past, and narrated in questionable myths.[32] Where and when, exactly, did the immolation occur? This is an unanswerable question, and probably a foolish one. Christ suffered under Pontius Pilate. When and where did that take place? We know. And so do atheists.

Second, Kitcher contends that the method used by people who accept and then transmit a religion to their children is across the board radically defective. This is all too quick. It ignores the fact that in some religions, including Christianity, the doctrines have been scrutinized over the course of centuries for their meaning and truth. And it's open to people to abandon their beliefs, as did Kitcher, if it comes to look to them like the case against is much stronger than the case for.

Third, it places in the shadows departures from, and conversions to, the transmitted revelation. Kitcher himself says he relinquished his beliefs because of rational considerations. And Edith Stein, Ph.D. in philosophy under Husserl, came to accept Catholicism at high personal cost. Shall we say she went to her death at Auschwitz clinging to her new religion uncritically?

Fourth, if accepting at the outset what is given to you is somehow a big misstep, what *should* we start with? Imagine a child of six—and it is hard to imagine this—who believes that there are problems with the teacher's assertion that there exists a number *one*, *two*, etc. Where, he asks, *is* the number *one*? Should the child go on, if possible, to do the philosophy of mathematics without knowing how to count? Of course it's not possible. Another case: not long ago, two psychologists decided—for lord knows what reasons—to teach their daughter the wrong names of colors. What was the daughter supposed to do? Not believe the instruction until she had gotten confirmation of the names from her classmates? Or believe it, and then when she learned the truth about how color-words are used in English, adjust her confidence in the package of beliefs handed on by her parents?

Psychologists have pointed out that we can hardly do without *anchoring* belief to belief. If you are asked to guess what the result would be if you multiply one times two, and continue up to ten, you will in all likelihood come up with a number extremely smaller than if you are asked to do it by multiplying ten times nine and carrying it down to one. *Anchoring* can cause us trouble in complex situations. Yet without this heuristic we evidently would be epistemically paralyzed.

Fifth, our vision is an exquisite instrument for perceiving the world around us. Yet, it's subject to illusion. That's not enough, surely, to conclude that it's entirely unreliable. Of course it's not. So, too, with other ways of seeing the world. Not only do we retain a cautious confidence in vision, but we can make certain inferences about ourselves and the world by recognizing why it is vision can be misleading at times.

For a more exotic example, consider the illusion produced by gravitational lensing. In 1979 two quasar images only five arc-seconds apart showed identical spectral characteristics. It's possible that this was mere chance, but probably not. The hypothesis was proposed that the twin spectra were double images of just one quasar. In all probability, a gravitational field somewhere between the earth and the quasar bent the radiation flowing from the object and produced two images instead of one. This prompted a successful search for galaxies properly positioned to account for the relativistic bending. The image's doubling is called "gravitational lensing."[33] In this example we come to realize that there's a good explanation for the double images. We do not call into question the value of our instruments. In the case of doublings of images and the like, in certain communities the bending also can be accounted for by the pull of the social environment of the believers. This, we conjecture, explains the possibility of their being behind the multiplication of images of God. How many gods are there? 303—and, 3 and 3,000. But really, just one.

3-E. Problems with Kitcher's Positive Program

After his negative arguments purporting to show that no putative revelation has a shred of plausibility, Kitcher carries forward a more positive program. I have not yet gone through his several books to analyze with any confidence his humanistic replacement for life lived in accord with any supposed supernatural revelation. I am confident that what he develops on the back of evolutionary biology is rich and in its own way rewarding. But having seen several such attempts by capable scholars, I have reason to believe prospects of arriving at any system even remotely satisfying are bleak. Thus I hold:

(3.1) Kitcher's argument is vulnerable to objections at every point.

(3.2) His positive case for a competing atheistic humanism is also unattractive, and far less appealing epistemically and practically than the Christian account.

(3.3) Kitcher's argument has been lauded as the best attack on the credibility of religion to date.

(3.4) If (3.1)–(3.3) are true, then it is entirely reasonable not to abandon all religion, and in particular Christianity.

(3.5) It is entirely reasonable not to abandon all religion, and in particular Christianity.

3-F. Conclusion: Comparing Two Hypotheses

I find myself lost in a cave with several worried explorers. Afraid of dying in this black pit, I eagerly look for light and listen for rescue voices. Some of my companions do the same but others counsel stoic resignation. Our duty now is to face reality squarely and not fill our heads with delusions of escape. Lie down and die like a man, a being born to death. But I do see a light, seemingly strong, and I do hear voices from above. I will not lie down and die. I will follow the light and the voices as far as they will take me. Foolish? I don't think so.

Kitcher himself senses the inadequacy of what he or any atheistic humanist has to offer. In *Life After Faith* he prefaces his account with an apology for humanism's current state of development, noting that while world religions have had thousands of years to refine their offerings, atheistic humanism is just now making a start. There is good reason to doubt, therefore, no-god humanism satisfies here and now. This already concedes a huge advantage to revelatory claims, particularly the more enlightened ones. Moreover, given this advantage, it is not a priori evident that anything effectively rivaling one or another revelation will be spirited into existence at any time in the foreseeable future.

What will a less bleak atheistic humanism look like? An intriguing passage from a nineteenth-century novelist writing to a friend gestures, I think, in the right direction. George Eliot deftly fingers something worth expanding upon. Reflecting here thoughts from her youth and disillusioned maturity, thoughts projected onto the characters in her novels, particularly *Middlemarch*'s Dorothea, Eliot writes:

> The first impulse of a young and ingenuous mind is to withhold the slightest sanction from all that contains even a mixture of supposed error. When the soul is just liberated from the wretched giant's bed of dogmas on which it has been racked and stretched ever since it began to think there is a feeling of exultation and strong hope. We think we shall run well when we have the full use of our limbs and the bracing air of independence, and we believe that we shall soon obtain something positive which will not only more than compensate to us for what we have renounced, but will be so well worth offering to others that we may venture to proselyte as fast as our zeal for truth may prompt us. But a year or two of reflection and the experience of our own miserable weakness which will ill afford to part even with the crutches of superstition must, I think, effect a change. Speculative truth begins to appear but a shadow of individual minds, agreement between intellects seems unattainable, and we turn to the *truth of feeling* as the only universal bond of union. We find that the intellectual errors which we once fancied were a mere incrustation have grown into the living body and that we cannot in the majority of cases,[34] wrench them away without destroying vitality. We begin to find that with individuals, as with nations, the only safe revolution is one arising out of the wants which their *own progress* has generated. It is the quackery of infidelity to suppose that it has a nostrum for all mankind, and to say to all and singular, "Swallow my opinions and you shall be whole."[35]

Eliot's incapacity to shake off entirely early beliefs points up the need to find a philosophy of life adequate to the most noble conceptions handed on to her as a youth. This appears entirely realistic to me. We anchor in what is noble in what was handed on. It is extremely difficult even for the most determined atheists to break cleanly with what was inscribed in the heart. But, in the end it may be deemed best to follow, say, a Nietzschean plan for dominance rather than an atheistic philosophy of life concocted with a view to producing a rational counterpart to the "superstitions" of Christianity—universal love and all that.

Philosophers in our time have struggled mightily to give an adequate account of moral precepts planted deep within the consciousness of liberal democracies. Despite his absurd claim that they are "self-evident," we want to believe Thomas Jefferson's "we hold these truths." Though now endlessly repeated without a blink, Lincoln seems to have known that equality and fundamental rights are not "self-evident," except perhaps to the angels. A cataclysmic civil war proved that the propositions are not self-evident *to us*. In his Gettysburg Address and elsewhere Lincoln moved silently past Jefferson's claim of self-evidence, saying only—though majestically: "Four score and seven years ago our fathers brought forth on this continent, a new nation, conceived in Liberty, and dedicated to the proposition that all men are created equal."

If the grand commitments are not self-evident, how are they to be grounded philosophically? A reading of the philosophic literature aimed at providing adequate warrant for the beliefs in equality and inalienable rights can readily lead to despair. Where are these justifications to be found? From what axioms are they inferred? And how are the axioms to be known?[36] Eliot draws a moral in the passage earlier cited:

> Speculative truth begins to appear but a shadow of individual minds, agreement between intellects seems unattainable, and we turn to the *truth of feeling* as the only universal bond of union.

Has philosophy managed to explain why Eliot's benevolent attachment to the underlings is obligatory, or best, rather than Nietzsche's alternative or a consequentialism that devours the innocent?

It is not just desire to construct a philosophy moving in the direction of our anchored superstitions that we carry into a comparison between particular philosophic and revelatory offerings, but a desire as well for transcendence of our own inherent limitations. In discussions of the problem of evil, it is common to dilate on the hideous evils in the world not of our own making. But at least from the time when the psalmists bewailed their own state, individuals alive to their own wickedness and flaws, past and present, have joined in praying:

> Have mercy upon me, O God, according to thy lovingkindness: according unto the multitude of thy tender mercies blot out my transgressions. Wash me thoroughly from mine iniquity, and cleanse me from my sin. For I acknowledge my transgressions: and my sin is ever before me. . . . Make me to hear joy and gladness; that the bones which thou hast broken may rejoice. . . . Create in me a clean heart, O God; and renew a right

spirit within me. Restore unto me the joy of thy salvation; and uphold me with thy free spirit.[37]

Or most simply, Lord, make me a better man.

Nor is it only forgiveness of our sins we long for, but for repair of gashes we have inflicted on others and cannot remedy. Yes, even God cannot change the past. But revelations—and Christian revelation in particular—teach that God is so good that he can bring good out of evil. And the divine gift God's love bestows on earthlings is redemption through the crucifixion of his only Son.

Nothing like this is to be expected in god-scorning humanism, and it is inconceivable how it could be. The promised abundant rivers of God's grace help us on the way to living in accord with noble ideals nowhere to be found in speculation's parched deserts.

Many other desires exceed philosophy's power to satisfy—the list is unbounded, as is the strength of the desire. We die ultimately unfulfilled. The desire for complete and eternal happiness is inextinguishable from the human heart. And so, too, our temporal blessings—friendship and the bond of love with supportive community.

All this atheistic humanism may blithely concede. It will no doubt be objected, however, that while the satisfactions of all such desires cannot be realized by enacting the precepts of the human disciplines, the desire is no mark of the truth. We must not deceive ourselves by clinging to vain fantasies, but live our lives in accordance with what the rational mind understands of the available evidence, even if it leaves us with a terrifying world.

But is it really the case that desires provide no evidence for truth? Much that we desire has a corresponding truth. You desire to see a sunset, and there are sunsets. You desire love and affection, and these can be had. C. S. Lewis somewhere remarks that it would be a strange world indeed that contained not even the possibility of bread, and yet we craved bread daily. It would be a strange world if it were impossible, ultimately, to satisfy our craving for endless bliss.

I shall not complain that I live in a world where morning never breaks with a blackbird singing like the first bird. Delights of family, friends, and nature, philosophy, theology, science, literature, art, and music often fill my mornings, and entire days, with joy.

There are times, however, when the singling birds fly off. Instead, drawn by the stench of corrupting flesh, a vulture circles under menacing black clouds. The contrast between Edenic moments and pangs of loss and riot of sin sharply reminds that this is not our permanent home.

I am not suffocating in a dark, freezing cave. But I do walk with all of you through a valley of the shadow of death. Still, I think I have seen and heard a voice from above. I mean to follow the light and the voice where they lead, in the hope of finding again my loves in the infinite love of God.

University of St. Thomas (St. Paul)

Notes

1. Philip Kitcher, *Life After Faith: The Case for Secular Humanism* (New Haven and London: Yale University Press, 2014), xii.

2. Ibid., 105.

3. Jerry A. Coyne, *Faith vs. Fact: Why Science and Religion are Incompatible* (New York: Viking, 2015), xiii.

4. I want to publicly thank dear and ever helpful colleagues Sandra Menssen and Russell Pannier for continuing discussions of issues relating to this paper, and Sandy more particularly for her extraordinary efforts to help get this version of the paper into final form.

5. Cosmologists use 'universe' in both a broad and narrow sense. In the broader and more common sense the 'universe' refers to what is described in Big-Bang cosmology, as the material that expanded from a hot, dense initial state. This is how 'universe' is used in these pages. In a more restricted state, 'universe' refers to the observable portion of the entire universe. See "Universe" in Andrew Liddle and Jon Loveday, *Oxford Companion to Cosmology* (Oxford: Oxford University Press, 2009), 314–15, for explanation of the difference it makes.

6. Here 'cause' does not mean 'sufficient condition'; 'necessary condition' will do. With this we can avoid problems generated by quantum mechanical considerations that in many standard expositions identify 'cause' with 'sufficient cause.' Of course there's a vast literature on the subject of causality. But of particular note is the discussion of G. E. M. Anscombe in her inaugural lecture at Cambridge, *Causality and Determination* (Cambridge: Cambridge University Press, 1971).

7. See Peter Coles's *Critical Dictionary of the New Cosmology* (New York: Routledge, 1999), "Big Bang Theory" for a summary treatment of difficulties with the notion of a singularity, particularly given the forced marriage between quantum mechanics and general relativity theory. For a deeper and more technical discussion, see John Earman's *Bangs, Crunches, Whimpers, and Shrieks: Singularities and Acausalities in Relativistic Spacetimes* (Oxford: Oxford University Press, 1995), 28–40.

8. Hans Halvorson and Helge Kragh, "Cosmology and Theology," *Stanford Encyclopedia of Philosophy*, 2011.

9. See Thomas D. Sullivan, "Omniscience, Omnipotence, and the Divine Mode of Knowing," *Faith and Philosophy* 8.1 (1991): 21–35.

10. Wes Morriston, "Doubts About the Kalam Argument," in *Debating Christian Theism*, ed. J. P. Moreland, Chad Meister, and Khaldoun A. Sweis (Oxford: Oxford University Press, 2013), 20–32. Cf. Quentin Smith, "Can Everything Come to Be Without a Cause?" *Dialogue* 33.2 (1994): 313–324. See also Thomas D. Sullivan, "On the Alleged Causeless Beginning of the Universe: A Reply to Quentin Smith," *Dialogue* 33 (1994): 325–336.

11. See Thomas D. Sullivan, "Coming to Be Without a Cause," *Philosophy: The Journal of the Royal Institute of Philosophy* (Cambridge) 65, no. 253 (July 1990): 261–270.

12. See the four-part exchange between Thomas D. Sullivan and Quentin Smith, which includes: (1) Quentin Smith, "The Uncaused Beginning of the Universe," *Philosophy of Science* 55.1 (1988): 39–57; (2) Sullivan, "Coming to Be Without a Cause"; (3) Quentin Smith, "Can Everything Come to Be Without a Cause?"; (4) Thomas D. Sullivan, "On the Alleged Causeless Beginning of the Universe.

13. Lawrence M. Krauss, *A Universe from Nothing* (New York: Free Press, 2012); see esp. ch. 9, "Nothing is Something."

14. For traditional descriptions of natural theology, see William Alston, *Perceiving God: The Epistemology of Religious Experience* (Ithaca, NY: Cornell University Press, 1991), 289, and Norman Kretzmann, *The Metaphysics of Creation: Aquinas's Natural Theology in "Summa congra gentiles II"* (New York: Oxford University Press, 1999), 3.

15. Richard Lewontin, "Billions and Billions of Demons," *The New York Review of Books* 44.1 (Jan. 9, 1997): 31.

16. John Bickle, *Philosophy and Neuroscience: A Ruthlessly Reductive Account* (Dordrecht; Boston: Kluwer Academic Publishers, 2003), 5.

17. Matthen, Mohan, "Causation and laws in biology," in *Routledge Encyclopedia of Philosophy*, ed. E. Craig (London: Rutledge). Retrieved November 14, 2011 from http://www.rep.routledge.com/article/Q129SECT1.

18. Michael S. Gazzaniga, Richard B. Ivry, George R. Mangun, *Cognitive Neuroscience: The Biology of the Mind*, 2d ed. (New York: W. W. Norton & Company, 2002), 659–660. In the next edition of the textbook, by the way, he deletes this comment, without explaining why.

19. Jacqueline Ludel, *Introduction to Sensory Processes* (San Francisco: W. H. Freeman, 1978), 366.

20. Thomas Aquinas, *Opera Omnia* Bk. I., L. 1.

21. John Archibald Wheeler and Wojciech Hubert Zured, eds., *Quantum Theory and Measurement* (Princeton: Princeton University Press, 1983), 169.

22. Russell Pannier has well spelled out the surprising proposal that the target of our intellectual acts is possibility.

23. Russell Pannier and Thomas D. Sullivan, "The Mind-Maker," in *Theos, Anthropos, Christos: A Compendium of Modern Philosophical Theology*, ed. R. A. Varghese (New York: Peter Lang, 2000), 88–89.

24. Iona Opie and Moira Tatem, eds., *A Dictionary of Superstitions* (Oxford: Oxford University Press, 1992), 185.

25. W. V. Quine, "Mind and Verbal Dispositions," in *Meaning and Reference*, ed. A. W. Moore (Oxford: Oxford University Press, 1993), 88.

26. See a famous chapter in Loren Eisley's *The Immense Journey* (New York: Vintage Books, 1959), "The Dream Animal," 107–127, esp. 111–12.

27. Sandra Menssen and Thomas D. Sullivan, *The Agnostic Inquirer: Revelation from a Philosophical Standpoint* (Grand Rapids, MI: Eerdmans, 2007).

28. For instance, Kitcher writes in *Life After Faith* (13): "The conclusions often taken to be grounded in religious experience are thoroughly soaked in the brew of doctrines prevalent in the surrounding society and typically passed on in early enculturation. . . . [T]he processes through which those doctrines have come to be adopted are all of the same general type."

29. R. C. Zaehner, *At Sundry Times* (Westport, Connecticut: Greenwood Press, 1958), 16.

30. See Vasudha Narayanan, *Hinduism* (Oxford: Oxford University Press, 2004), 34–35.

31. Zaehner, *At Sundry Times*, 18.

32. See Martin Hengel, *Crucifixion in the Ancient World and the Folly of the Message of the Cross*, trans trans. John Bowden (London: SCM Press, 1977).

33. This account based on Timothy McGrew's fine essay "Confirmation, Heuristics, and Explanatory Reasoning," *British Journal for the Philosophy of Science* 54.4 (2003): 553–567.

34. The definitive Norton text has 'causes' instead of 'cases.'

35. George Eliot, *Middlemarch*, ed. Bert G. Hornback (New York: W. W. Norton & Company, 2000), 519.

36. See Menssen and Sullivan, *The Agnostic Inquirer*, 251–271.

37. Psalm 51, KJV.

Molinist Divine Complicity: A Response to Neal Judisch

Robert A. Elisher

Abstract: I argue here that God, as Molinism conceives Him, is complicit in moral evil. This is of course a problem because complicity in evil undermines divine perfection. I argue, however, that it is a problem that Open Theism, as a theory of "general" (as opposed to "meticulous") providence, avoids. This claim opposes that of Neal Judisch, who has recently (2012) argued that theories of general providence (e.g., Open Theism) are in no better position to answer the problem of gratuitous evil (i.e., the evidential problem of evil) than theories of meticulous providence (e.g., Molinism or Calvinism). Here, Judisch draws on important insights about just what these theories involve in terms of gratuitous evil to diffuse what he calls "the argument for divine complicity." In response, I offer a reformulation of this argument that is immaterial to the question of gratuitous evil. I then explain why my argument does not convict an Open Theist God and, in the course of doing so, I consider whether an application of the doctrine of double effect exonerates a Molinist God as well.

Religious believers often speak of God's "ordaining" significant life events. When it seems wholly unreasonable to call some event a "coincidence," they prefer to invoke God. But locutions like "God-ordained" are usually confined to extraordinary events. It sounds somehow strange to extend the phraseology to *every* event, much less *evil* events along with the good. If God is understood to be completely sovereign over the created order, however, it seems right to admit that God ordains even those events that we call moral evils. This is a problem. Even if humans are ultimately responsible for bringing about moral evils, a God exercising a strong degree of providential control would seem a bit too intimately connected with such events to uphold His moral perfection. In a recent article (chiefly dedicated to the discussion of a different but related problem known as the problem of gratuitous evil), Neal Judisch (2012) assesses whether one theory with a particularly *meticulous* view of divine providence—Molinism—falls victim to this problem. He argues that Molinism circumvents what he refers to as *the argument for divine complicity*. The present paper is partly a criticism of Judisch's explanation of how Molinism eludes the problem and partly an independent argument for a

© 2016, *Proceedings of the ACPA*, Vol. 89
doi: 10.5840/acpaproc201612552

Molinist God's complicity in evil. Further, because I largely rely on Judisch's framing of the discussion as a contest between Molinism and Open Theism, I shall dedicate a section to assessing an Open Theist response to the complicity problem. I argue that in virtue of the way Open Theism limits God's providential control, it overcomes the snares of the problem that convict a Molinist God of complicity. I therefore argue that, other things equal, Open Theism is to be preferred to Molinism.[1]

I. Divine Complicity and Gratuitous Evil

The literature uses the term "gratuitous" to refer to instances of evil which appear to be pointless or purposeless, which appear unnecessary to contribute to further good or to prevent further evil. It seems that an upright, omni-competent God would prevent such evils. It would seem therefore that such a God does not exist. This is what is known as the argument from gratuitous evil.

One promising answer to this problem comes from proponents of Open Theism.[2] They insist that God is not as meticulous in presiding over his creation as is traditionally supposed—that not every event is stamped with a divine purpose. If not every event is divinely orchestrated, there is logical room for purposeless or gratuitous evils. Open Theists have no problem admitting that some evils resulting from free human actions are gratuitous because, for them, there are no settled facts about free choices that God could foreknow and factor into His plan. So if moral evil occurs, God does not bear direct responsibility. At worst, He bears indirect responsibility for creating creatures capable of doing evil. God could not have foreseen what horrendous evils might result from granting creatures the capacity for free will, but He decided in His creative act that the value of freedom and the meaningful relationships it makes possible were worth the risk.

Contrast this theory of *general providence* with a theory of "no-risk," *meticulous providence*. Let us say, with Alan Rhoda, that God exercises meticulous providence over creation just in case God ordains all events. God may be said to ordain an event if He is either the ultimate sufficient cause of the event or if He is the ultimate sufficient cause of conditions that He knows for certain will lead to an event, without those conditions being causally sufficient for it (Rhoda 2010, 283). Molinists espouse this weaker view of event actualization.

According to Molinism, "in between" God's knowledge of necessary truths and all the possible worlds He might create (natural knowledge) and His knowledge of contingent truths of the actual world (free knowledge), lies His middle knowledge (Craig 2001, 121). Middle knowledge, like free knowledge, is of future contingents, but whereas free knowledge is of what *is* because of the nature of the actual world God willed to create, middle knowledge is of what *would* be. Prior to God's creative act, God knows via middle knowledge every counterfactual of human freedom with a sufficiently precise antecedent—what certain free creatures would choose, if they were in certain circumstances. Molinists insist that if God knew the outcome of human actions in the way He knows those facts about the actual world that are determined by His own will, then God's will would, as it were, transfer to human actions, abrogating human freedom in the libertarian sense. So, in order to preserve the contingency of human actions, Molinists contend that God only knows free actions in counterfactual form: "If person S were in circumstances C, then S would freely choose action A."

God employs his knowledge of such "counterfactuals of creaturely freedom" (CCFs) in his deliberation about which world to create. CCFs are pieces of "prevolitional" knowledge in that they are known by God prior to his creative act and enter into his deliberation in the creation situation (Laing 2005 [2004]). The range of possible worlds that God can actualize without undermining human freedom is limited to what are called *feasible* worlds. Possible worlds are restricted to feasible worlds by true CCFs. For example, if it is eternally true that "if the Apostle Peter were in circumstances C, then Peter would freely deny Christ three times," then the world where circumstances C obtain but Peter *affirms* Christ is not feasible for God to create, for Peter would not be acting freely. By placing particular persons in particular circumstances, God is able to carry out His ultimate purposes *through* creaturely decisions, planning the world down to the final detail (Craig 2001, 122).

But if so, it looks like He effectively exercises intentional control over every event. And if *every* event is specifically and intentionally planned for, then God would seem to be implicated in moral evils. Even if God does not Himself perform moral evils, surely He is complicit in them for intending them. Judisch (2012) refers to this worry as *the argument for divine complicity*. An important upshot of the argument is that it seems to disallow the Molinist to draw a coherent distinction between God's permitting and his intending evil, which compromises God's moral perfection.

Open Theism seems to avoid these consequences, inasmuch as they think of God as adopting only "general strategies" to govern the world, the detailed consequences of which are neither foreseen nor intended by Him prior to His decision to adopt them (Hasker 1992, 102). He *merely permits* the evil consequences because He could not adopt the worthwhile general strategies without risking them. There is no trace in Open Theism of the kind of involvement with evil that gets Molinism into trouble.

By way of an offhand response, the Molinist might be tempted to emphasize that God does not will evil for its own sake but in order to achieve some greater good or prevent some evil equally bad or worse. A worry remains, however, inasmuch as it seems wrong intentionally to will evil, whether for its own sake or for the sake of some other good. Hence we find instrumental justifications of evil condemned in Scripture. So Molinism seems faced with a real problem here, if indeed, as a theory of meticulous providence, it is committed to the claim that God intends every instance of evil with a justifying end in mind. In fact, several critics of Molinism have assumed this is so. That is, they assume that if God exercises meticulous providence, then there is no gratuitous evil.[3] Judisch (2012, 69) rightly points out, however, that meticulous providence does not entail that there is no gratuitous evil. That God chose to bring about this particular world, with full knowledge of everything that would happen if He did, is a separate consideration from the idea that there is a purpose behind everything that happens—that everything is ordained as a means toward some end. Even if God ordains some instance of evil, by determining the conditions that He knows for certain will lead to it, the evil might just be an unhappy byproduct of a larger-scale sub-plan in the creation plot. For suppose that the only *feasible* means of God's achieving some purposes is the creation of an agent who, incidentally, will also commit a heinous crime. In this case, the heinous crime is not the means of achieving His purpose. It may have no discernable purpose whatever. It is just an unfortunate outcome of the counterfactuals of *this* creature's freedom.

Nevertheless, that Molinism is a "no risk" theory means that once God has decided which world He will create among a range of worlds, everything will proceed precisely as expected, according to God's knowledge of counterfactuals. It would seem to follow that God has complete control over everything that occurs in this world, that God specifically intends each event, and that he is therefore complicit in every moral evil. But Judisch (2012, 81) rejects this line of argument too, since even critics of Molinism insist on the important sense in which the Molinist God is subject to *luck*. Whereas luck confronts the Open Theist God in the actual making of choices by human beings, it confronts the Molinist God in the CCFs encountered in the creation situation. God chooses among feasible worlds on the basis of *contingent* facts about how creatures would use their freedom, facts whose truth does not itself depend on God's choice. So it is false, Judisch argues, that God has complete control over, and specifically intends, every event: if there is a sense in which he has control, it is shared by the creatures whose choices he must take into account.

II. An Argument for Divine Complicity

I don't think Judisch's criticism of the argument for divine complicity is decisive. I will now show that the Molinist God is complicit in evil regardless of whether or not there is gratuitous evil and hence regardless of whether God specifically intends evil as a means to certain goods:

(1) God as conceived by Molinism causes circumstances in which human beings perform evil while knowing of any such circumstances that they will result in some particular evil E and while knowing how He can act otherwise so that E doesn't occur. (premise)

(2) If agent S causes a certain something X, which S foreknows will result in a particular something Y, while S knows how S can act otherwise so that Y wouldn't occur, then S has *significant* (though not necessarily complete) *control* over Y, even if S does not approve of Y. (premise—Principle C)

(3) God has significant control over evil human decisions. (1 & 2)

(4) If God has significant control over evil human decisions, then God is complicit in evil. (premise)

(5) God is complicit in evil. (3 & 4)

The argument is simple but, depending on what is meant by "significant," the premises are not obviously true and will take some arguing for. Premise (1) is simply a statement of standard Molinist doctrine. According to Molinism, the various conditions of human action are the facts about the actual world that generally depend directly on God's will. It is uncontroversial to say that God is often the ultimate sufficient cause of these. Moreover, whatever circumstances He opts for, God knows with certainty the exact decision that would result. And, finally, with respect to any event in the creation scheme (including human decisions), God can elect to actualize circumstances that would issue in different results,[4] and knows just what circumstances would do so. Alternatively, God can always elect not to create at all. So, to sum up, (3) follows validly from premise (1) and premise (2) (which I've labeled "Principle C" for "control") because a Molinist God meets all the conditions necessary for a degree of control I'm calling "significant."

Molinists maintain that God's tight control of history does nothing to impinge human freedom. Thus because God knows what creatures will *freely* choose, their actions are said to be contingent and controlled by the agents. These claims are generally considered contentious. Yet I am granting them here for the sake of argument. Nonetheless, even if agents are in control of what they bring about, it can't be quite right to say that agents are in *complete* control, since nothing actual would be actual were it not for God's ideally informed and rational choice of the circumstances. The sort of control this choice implies, I am arguing, is *significant* enough to render God complicit in the evil creatures freely do.

Just as (on the Molinist view) God's control does not preclude that of agents, neither does agents' control preclude God's. Thus the "not necessarily in complete control" qualification in Principle C is included to capture the obvious fact that not all foreknown effects of actions are entirely up to agents who foreknow them. Consider how we apportion blame to such agents. According to the doctrine of double effect, we may blame people when the foreseen bad effect of their actions outweighs the intended good effects.[5] But even when we blame them for the foreseen effects of their actions, we don't always blame them and them alone. Suppose an agent undertakes some moderately worthwhile project that she foresees will have deleterious effects. She sees that it will cause a handful of people to riot in the street. Suppose that although the riot was not the primary point of her project, she held it as a subordinate goal. In this case, her action would clearly warrant blame. But blaming her would not preclude blaming the rioters as well: no one is forcing them to riot. Thus even if she intended for them to riot, they too intended the same. So it is, I would suggest, with regard to free human decisions to act in an evil manner, if Molinism is true. Humans decide to *do* particular moral evils, but God decides *that particular moral evils happen*, or at least He decides to refrain from acting so that they wouldn't.

Judisch assumes that a Molinist God is complicit in evil only if He completely controls every event. He argues that, because of the way God is also subject to luck—because he does not control the truth of the CCFs he encounters in the creation situation—He effectively shares control of events with free creatures and thus lacks the complete control required to convict him. My argument grants the sort of control that Judisch insists on but it contends that such control is nevertheless sufficient for complicity. For the term "accomplice" is not, after all, used to refer to someone exercising complete, intentional control over an evil's occurrence. Rather, an accomplice, as described by the *Catholic Encyclopedia*, refers to someone who merely "*cooperates* in some way in the wrongful activity of another who is accounted the *principal*."[6] So an argument charging God with complicity already presupposes a principal or primary agent of evil in whose wrongdoing God in some way cooperates and in whose responsibility God to some limited degree shares. Therefore, the requirements for complicity are looser than Judisch presumes. And I can admit without difficulty a sense in which God conceived by Molinism has less control than God conceived by, say, Calvinism. Because a Molinist God's creative decision is informed by luck, God alone does not make contingent facts about human decisions true. Creatures and God make certain counterfactuals factual in different ways: God takes care of the antecedent while creatures take care of the consequent. The set of CCFs God settles on are chosen by creatures and are not in a similar manner chosen by God. We can grant all this. There nevertheless remains a sense in which God chooses their choices by opting for a world he knows would contain them.

But why think the control implied by such activity is significant enough to render God complicit (see premise [4])? I promised to present an argument that makes the consideration of evil's gratuitousness, and thus the consideration whether God specifically intends evil as a means to certain goods, irrelevant to God's complicity. Yet this might not seem irrelevant. Suppose the Molinist claimed that most or all evils are gratuitous—mere by-products of some overarching divine purpose. At least with regard to these evils, God would seem not to be complicit, for it is not as if He conspires in the committing of *these* crimes, specifically intending them, approving of them as means to His desired good.

I have three responses to this objection. First, it may well be inappropriate to view God as a sort of conspirator in the case of gratuitous evil, but it seems the same cannot be said for non-gratuitous evils. For these He specifically intends, if only as means to His desired ends. And I doubt any Molinist would be so bold as to suggest that all evil is gratuitous, that God never factors evil into His plan to promote good: the sheer pervasiveness of evil is enough to make this stance implausible. But unless they bite this bullet, God comes out less than perfect because conspiratorially liable (and thus clearly complicit).

Second, suppose the Molinist bites this bullet, maintaining that God does not intend any evil as a means to good. It wouldn't follow from this that He doesn't intend evil at all. Certainly He would in no sense approve of or desire evils, as He would in a sense if they were means to His desired ends. But one can intend an end without approving of it or wanting it to occur. That is, one can act intentionally though reluctantly, and this would likely be the case for God if indeed He does intend every event. I think it can be shown that a Molinist God does intend every event even if He doesn't desire some or all of them. But for now, I want only to emphasize that just as God's *control* of an event is compatible with creaturely control (as I demonstrated above), God's intending an event is compatible with creaturely intention.

Third, it seems that one can deny the claim that God intends evils in the sense relevant for complicity and still be forced to accept the conclusion of my argument. For complicity does not just entail intentional, conspiratorial liability; it incorporates "accessorial liability" as well.[7] Thus one may be complicit in a crime by conspiring in a criminal plot; though one may also be complicit by deliberately aiding or abetting a criminal or simply by failing to make an effort to prevent a crime when it is within one's power to do so. But with respect to every criminal event it is within God's power to act in such a way that the crime doesn't happen. According to Molinism, God knows prior to His creative deed that if He does not choose to create some other feasible world (or if He does not choose to create at all), a certain crime will happen. Because He refrains from doing so, He is aptly identified as an accessory to said crime.[8]

But we should not simply think of a Molinist God as sitting idly by while knowing certain evils will occur. This picture does not fully capture the level of His involvement with evil that makes him an accessory. To say He "aids" or "abets" evil doers would be putting it too lightly: He actually brings it about that the evils that occur are such as they are. Now consider the Catholic principle of immediate material cooperation with evil:

> Immediate material cooperation occurs when the cooperator does not share the intentions of the principal agent but participates in circumstances that are essential to the commission of an act, such that the act could not occur without this participation.[9]

The principle further substantiates my point above that participation in intrinsically evil acts is morally illicit regardless of whether the participant intends the evil.[10] Moreover, the Molinist God does not merely participate in or contribute to the "circumstances essential to the commission" of evil acts; He is the ultimate sufficient cause of the particular circumstances in the absence of which agents would not commit the particular evil acts they do.

III. Why an Open Theist God is not Complicit

If there is no chance of the Molinist's escaping these untoward consequences, why think the Open Theist fares any better? Suppose God simply actualized the conditions for human freedom, seeing that freedom was a great good, but did so without antecedent knowledge that so much evil would occur. Certainly we wouldn't hold such a God morally accountable for evil, but this seems a far cry from the all-wise God of the theistic faiths. Open Theist God or not, it is plausible that He knew at least to a very high degree of probability that creating free creatures would result in large amounts of horrendous evils. Why, therefore, is He not complicit in the evils that occur?

The first thing to highlight in response is the differences in the Molinist and Open Theist creation situations. Recall that, on Open Theism, God does not actualize one world from among an infinite range of possible worlds; rather, He actualizes one world from among a set of possible worlds delimited by the free choices of creatures. Therefore, God foreknows no specific evil. While it's reasonable to think that God knows probabilistically that huge amounts of evil would result from creation, there is a morally salient difference between this variety of knowledge and that of a Molinist God. There is oftentimes a difference between doing something one knows will result in a *specific* evil and doing something that one knows will result in *some* evil. Principle C implicates the former sort of action in evil, but not the latter. According to principle C, "an agent S causes a *certain something* X, which S foreknows will result in a *certain something* Y." Thus, the principle convicts a Molinist God who foresees the occurrence of specific evils, though it will not convict an Open Theist God. It is important to note that it is not the specificity of a crime per se that makes the person involved morally accountable. However, specificity usually signals a higher level of involvement, and *this* is what is morally salient.

An example will make this more evident. Consider someone deciding whether to have a child. She knows that if she does, the child will inevitably sin at some point. So she knows that if she were to have a child, she would indirectly cause evil. Still, having the child would not make her complicit in whatever evils the child commits. Now imagine that she has the child and that she somehow knows that, placed in certain circumstances, her child will commit a particular sin. Let's say that she knows the child's tendencies and aims with such precision that she is certain of the counterfactual "if I place my child in this sandbox, he will throw sand in the eyes of another child." No one is forcing her to fix the circumstances so that the child throws the sand. But suppose she fixes them anyway. We would clearly be within our rights to reproach her for the evil (even if she didn't approve of it), unless, it seems, we lacked pertinent information concerning her reasons for fixing the circumstances. The reason we would probably blame her in this second, and not the first, scenario is that she is more directly involved in her child's crime.

The obvious problem with this example is that it is not as clear that we would hold the mother accountable if she had good reason for fixing the circumstances. Perhaps her intention was to give her child the opportunity to improve upon his social skills and the sand-throwing was a mere foreseen effect. According to the doctrine of double effect, it is sometimes permissible to cause harm (e.g., sand-throwing) as a side effect of bringing about a good result (e.g., a valuable social experience) when the harm is foreseen but not intended and when the intended good outweighs the foreseen harm (McIntyre 2014 [2004]). Applying the doctrine to Molinism, it would seem that God circumvents blame if His purpose for allowing any gratuitous evil[11] is to bring about the better feasible world.

This position is, unfortunately, untenable. I mentioned earlier how I think it can be shown that a Molinist God intends every event in whatever world He actualizes. If this is right, then the application to Molinism of the doctrine of double effect fails, for it depends on the possibility of a coherent distinction between foreseen and intended actions. The doctrine affords the mother in our example with an exonerating excuse because she did not intend, but only foresaw, the harm that resulted from her action. If, as I will now argue, a Molinist God intends *every* event, then He is not similarly exonerated.

God, in the creation situation, is faced with a choice between feasible *worlds*. That is, in making his decision, God is considering worlds as a whole, not specific events or states of affairs. But no doubt God also intends that the world of His choosing be a certain way. And what else could this mean except that, down to the finest detail, God intends that the world be characterized by its particular events—i.e., that God intends every event in that world? Of course, the way God intends events is different from the way free creatures intend them. I would suggest that the way a Molinist God intends the particular events in the world of his choosing is analogous to the way human beings, in intending some state of affairs, intend every aspect of that state (of which they're aware). Nor is it any help to the Molinist to say that He intends the events He likes (desires, approves of, etc.) and merely foresees the ones He hates. For this begs the question by conflating intention and desire, and I've already explained that these two concepts come apart. If a Molinist God intends the world down to the last detail, He does not get to intend the good and merely foresee the bad, just as a doctor (e.g.), in intending to perform an abortion, does not get to intend to vindicate the woman's autonomy and merely foresee the termination of a human being (assuming this is what is at stake). So, in conclusion, because the Molinist cannot coherently distinguish between events God intends and those He merely foresees and permits, a Molinist God remains blameworthy for the harm he indirectly brings about.

IV. Conclusion

I have been concerned in the foregoing with the status of divine goodness on the Molinist account. I have argued that Molinism has, while Open Theism lacks, a sufficient condition for divine complicity in evil—namely, middle knowledge of creaturely freedom. By virtue of His middle knowledge, the Molinist God possesses significant control over good and evil events alike, a control that does not compete with creaturely control. With respect to every occurrence of evil, He can act in such a way that it doesn't occur. He knows both how to do so and the consequences of His actions. Yet He refrains from acting in the requisite way and this makes Him complicit. This conclusion holds regardless of what is said about the gratuitousness of evil. If there is no gratuitous evil, or even some non-gratuitous evil, then God wills evil as a means to the good (divine goodness is compromised). If all evil is gratuitous—a highly implausible thesis—then God is nevertheless an accessory, if not a conspirator, in the crimes of humanity. I therefore conclude that Open Theism is superior to Molinism in respect of its response to the argument for divine complicity.

Baylor University

Notes

1. I want to emphasize that the point I am defending regarding Open Theism is a very narrow one. I make no claims about the superiority of Open Theism "all things considered," but grant for the sake of argument that it has satisfactory answers, for instance, to questions about how it accords with orthodox Christian teaching and the Biblical witness.

2. See Hasker 1992; Hasker 2008, 204–205; and Rhoda 2010, 296–297.

3. See Hasker 1992, 99 and Rhoda 2010, 295–296.

4. This is true even if there are reasons why God would not want to opt for different circumstances—if, say, given God's purposes, there is no other feasible option that would as effectively promote the good. More on this later.

5. The central claim of the doctrine is that it is sometimes permissible to cause harm as a side effect of bringing about a good result, when the harm is foreseen but not intended (McIntyre, 2014 [2004]). Proponents of double effect have always acknowledged a proportionality condition if actions are to count as instances of the principle. The condition requires that the good effect outweigh the foreseen bad effect or that there be sufficient reason for causing the bad effect (ibid.).

6. "Accomplice," in *Catholic Encyclopedia*. Accessed January 8, 2016.

7. "Complicity Law and Legal Definition," in *Legal Definitions*. Accessed November 25, 2013.

8. Such inaction is also condemned by Scripture: "So whoever knows the right thing to do and fails to do it, for him it is sin" (James 4:17).

9. My thanks to Jared Brandt for drawing my attention to this. The National Catholic Bioethics Center, "What is the Principle of Cooperation in Evil?" Accessed January 8, 2016.

10. It is a little strange that Judisch would make complicity entail *complete*, intentional control, inasmuch as we normally don't even use the term "complicit" for someone who completely controls an evil's occurrence. Complicity tends to be somewhat less morally serious and so the requirements for complicity are looser.

11. We are assuming, as I've argued the Molinist must, that all evils are gratuitous. Consequently, no evils have a purpose in the strict sense of being a means to an end. It is rather that even the most optimific set of true CCFs forces God to permit them.

Bibliography

Catholic Encyclopedia. n.d. "Accomplice." http://www.catholic.org/encyclopedia/view.php?id=113.

Craig, William Lane. 2001. "The Middle-Knowledge View." In *Divine Foreknowledge: Four Views*, ed. J. Beilby and P. Eddy, 119–143. Downers Grove, IL: Intervarsity Press.

Hasker, William. 1992. "Providence and Evil: Three Theories." *Religious Studies* 28.1: 91–105. doi: https://doi.org/10.1017/S0034412500021405

Hasker, William. 2008. *The Triumph of God over Evil: Theodicy for a World of Suffering.* Downers Grove, IL: Intervarsity Press.

Judisch, Neal. 2012. "Meticulous Providence and Gratuitous Evil." In *Oxford Studies in Philosophy of Religion, Volume 4*, ed. J. Kvanvig, 65–83. Oxford: Oxford University Press.
   doi: https://doi.org/10.1093/acprof:oso/9780199656417.003.0004

Laing, John. 2005 [2004]. "Middle Knowledge." *Internet Encyclopedia of Philosophy.* http://www.iep.utm.edu/middlekn/.

Legal Definitions. n.d. "Complicity Law and Legal Definition." http://definitions.uslegal.com/c/complicity/.

McIntyre, Alison. 2014 [2004]. "Doctrine of Double Effect." *Stanford Encyclopedia of Philosophy.* http://plato.stanford.edu/entries/double-effect/.

National Catholic Bioethics Center. n.d. "What is the Principle of Cooperation in Evil?" http://ncbcenter.org/document.doc?id=139.

Rhoda, Alan. 2010. "Gratuitous Evil and Divine Providence." *Religious Studies* 46.3: 281–302. doi: https://doi.org/10.1017/S0034412509990503

Aquinas on Believing God

Matthew Kent Siebert

Abstract: Aquinas says that faith is belief about things one does not "see" for oneself. But if you do not see it for yourself, what makes your belief reasonable? Recent interpreters have missed a key part of Aquinas's answer, namely, that faith is believing God (*credere Deo*). In other words, they have not given sufficient attention to the formal object of faith. As a result, they overemphasize other parts of his answer. Drawing partly on recent epistemology of testimony, I explain how the formal object of faith contributes to the justification of one's faith.

Let's start by seeing where three recent readings of Aquinas on faith go wrong.

I. Three Readings

First, one might take Aquinas to be an evidentialist, saying that faith is reasonable only to the degree it is based on one's own evidence. Alvin Plantinga, for example, focuses on one of the passages where Aquinas says Christians "do not believe lightly" (*Summa Contra Gentiles*, henceforth *SCG*, I.6). There Aquinas gives Augustine's argument that the conversion of the world to Christianity on the word of uneducated fishermen was either based on miracles, or if not, was itself a miracle. And such miracles confirm that their message was from God. In contrast, "those who give faith to [Mohammed's] sayings believe lightly" he says, because Mohammed does not provide such supernatural evidence. Plantinga comments:

> What [Aquinas] means to say, I think, is that to believe in the mysteries of faith is not foolish or to believe with undue levity, because we have *evidence for* the conclusion that God has proposed them for our belief. . . . I think he means to suggest, furthermore, that if we did *not* have this evidence, or some other evidence, we would be foolish or irrational to believe. It is just because we have evidence for these things that we are not irrational in accepting them.[1]

Here Plantinga implies that Aquinas's "credibility arguments" or "supports of the faith" (*adminicula fidei*) provide all of faith's epistemic justification.[2] In support of this view, one could point to passages where Aquinas says that the Christian "would not believe [the articles of faith] without seeing that they should be believed, on account of the evidence [*evidentia*] of signs or on account of something similar" (*Summa Theologiae*, henceforth *ST*, II-II.1.4 ad 2).

The problem for the evidentialist interpretation that I want to focus on is that Aquinas distinguishes faith from belief based solely on evidence.[3] He does this, first, by distinguishing faith from his three evidentialist intellectual cognitive habits (three of his various propositional attitudes): intellection, science, and opinion.[4] Intellection and science are ways of "seeing" that something is true. Intellection is a matter of seeing that a proposition is self-evidently true, as with the first principles of science;[5] while science (that is, *scientia*) is a way of seeing that a proposition is evidently demonstrated from those first principles (*ST* II-II.1.5c). But faith is only required for truths that remain "unseen"; if one already sees that something is true, faith has nothing to contribute to the justification of one's belief (*ST* II-II.1.4c). Opinion, on the other hand, when it is "strong opinion," is a way of giving assent to something unseen.[6] Opinion is, for Aquinas, purely evidentialist: it is the product of inductive or "probable" inference based on "signs," "verisimilitudes," or "probable" (i.e., non-demonstrative) syllogisms.[7] But Aquinas points out that opinion does not have the certainty of "adhesion" that faith does,[8] and does not involve the will the way faith does.[9] Between the three of them, intellection, science, and opinion seem to exhaust the deductive and inductive ways Aquinas recognizes of having a purely evidentially based belief. And they exclude faith.

Aquinas confirms that faith is excluded from this group when he says that assent is not faith when the proposition is believed

> by some human reasons and natural signs . . . but only when one believes from this reason [*ratione*], that it is said by God, which is designated by calling it *credere Deo*. And this specifies faith, the way any cognoscitive habit has its species from the reason [*ratione*] by which it assents to anything. (*Commentary on Romans* 4.1)

Not all assent is the product of reasoning, but each kind of assent has a *ratio* or distinctive character distinguishing it from other kinds.[10] The unique way of believing required by faith, called "*credere Deo*," or "believing God," is distinguished from other kinds of assent by the formal object of faith (*ST* II-II.2.2c), discussed in section II below.

At the opposite extreme from the evidentialist interpretation are two views on which evidence plays little or no role in the reasonableness of faith. One is what I will call the "voluntarist reliabilist" position, which overemphasizes the role of the will. The idea is that the willing involved in faith is purely prudential, based on self-interest. Eleonore Stump has argued for such a position by starting from passages like this, where Aquinas contrasts faith with opinion and science by pointing to the role of the will:

> Sometimes the intellect . . . is determined by the will, which chooses to assent to one part [of a contradiction, i.e., to *p* rather than to not-*p*] determinately and precisely on account of something which is sufficient for moving the will, but not for moving the intellect, such as that it seems good or fitting [*conveniens*] to assent to that part. And that is the disposition of one believing, as when someone believes the sayings of some man, because it seems either suitable [*decens*] or useful [*utile*]. And so also we are moved to believe the sayings of God, inasmuch as the reward of eternal life is promised to us if we believe. And this reward moves the will to assent to what is said, although the intellect is not moved by something understood [*intellectum*]. (*Quaestiones Disputatae de Veritate*, henceforth *QDV*, 14.1c)

Stump then explains how believing one of the articles of faith (that God exists), when willed in such a way, might be justified because the method of attaining one's beliefs is reliable (in producing true beliefs). Here is a rough summary of her argument: Aquinas says God is perfect goodness, and perfect being. God also "is" our happiness in the sense that human happiness consists in the beatific vision of God's essence. Thus, willing to believe that a perfect being (God) exists, on the basis of willing to believe that one's perfect happiness (God) exists, happens to be a reliable method of acquiring true beliefs, and so is justified.[11]

There are several problems with this second approach.[12] But the problem I want to focus on is that this account does not restrict faith to cases of belief *on divine authority*. Nothing in Stump's account makes it relevant *who it is* that tells you what propositions to believe. But of course it *is* relevant for Aquinas:

> Since whoever believes assents to the word of someone, it seems that the principal thing in any believing, like an end, is the person to whose word one assents [*ille cuius dicto assentitur*], while the items one believes in order to assent to that person are secondary. (*ST* II-II.11.1c)

Aquinas explains this further by saying that God is the "formal object" of faith.

> Every cognoscitive habit has two objects: that which it knows materially . . . and that through which it knows, which is the formal aspect of the object [*formalis ratio obiecti*]. For example, in the science of geometry the conclusions are known materially, but the formal aspect of knowing is the means [*media*] of demonstration, by which the conclusions are known. Thus in faith, the formal aspect of the object is nothing but the First Truth [i.e., God], for the faith I am talking about does not assent to anything except because revealed by God; hence it holds to the Divine Truth as to a means.(*ST* II-II.1.1c)

Elsewhere, Aquinas explains the idea of a formal object with the example of light: the material object of sight is color, but color is made visible only by means of light.[13] Similarly, faith is assent to propositions, but only by means of God's revelation. These passages show that faith is a matter of believing *a person*, by means of which one believes what the person says. So it requires an awareness of who the speaker is.

The third view I will consider, the "basic belief" view, makes the reasonableness of faith independent of evidence by saying that a belief can be reasonable even if the believer is not aware of how he acquired it. John Jenkins, for example, says that faith is warranted in an entirely externalist way by divine grace. He says the warrant "is *externalist*, for the individual has no privileged access to whether his cognitive faculties have the appropriate design and were operating properly in producing his assent" (Jenkins 197). This warrant is "basic in the sense that the propositions are believed, but are not believed on the basis of any other beliefs" (200). Believing that a message is from God is only a necessary "background condition," and not something from which one infers that the message is true, or in any other way gets justification for believing it (201). This view downplays the role of evidence from credibility arguments and confirmatory miracles, while recognizing the epistemic justification provided by a divine infusion of grace. However, this view also downplays the role of the speaker as the formal object of faith.[14] Even if you believe that God has said something, and you meritoriously choose to believe God on that matter, the "basic belief" view says that arriving at your belief in this way is not what contributes to your faith being reasonable, but rather the divine infusion of grace alone.

II. The Formal Object of Faith

In short, all three views seem to either ignore or misunderstand the role of the formal object of faith. How then should we understand it? As I see it, each of these views rightly recognizes one aspect of Aquinas's account of faith, but overemphasizes it. On Aquinas's account, faith *is* supported by arguments, by the will, *and* by externalist justification. But none of these factors on its own fully explains the reasonableness of faith. Rather, they all contribute to the way faith, unlike evidential inference, pragmatic acceptance, or basic belief, essentially involves believing God (*credere Deo*). In the rest of this paper, I will try to explain what is required for this unique way of arriving at a belief.

It is important from the beginning to draw a distinction that Elizabeth Anscombe (1979) does between *believing what a speaker says*, and *believing a speaker*. Suppose I do not trust my neighbor, so when he tells me he is leaving town for the weekend, I do not *believe him*. But then I overhear him tell his close friend that he is leaving town for the weekend, and infer from that evidence that he is. Then I *believe what the speaker said*, even though I had not *believed him*.[15] Part of the problem with the evidentialist reading is that belief on evidence is not enough for believing the speaker. When discussing what it is to believe God (*credere Deo*), Aquinas seems interested in what it is to believe the speaker.

Aquinas explains this feature of faith by saying that the speaker is the formal object of one's faith. As I mentioned before, Aquinas says that every power (or act or habit) has both material objects—the items at which it is directed—and a formal object, that is, the formal aspect of those items that allows that power to be directed at them.[16] For example, my will is right now directed at a ripe mango as material object, but according to Aquinas it can be directed at that mango only insofar as I apprehend the mango as good.[17] And that same mango can be a material object for various other powers, under its other formal aspects, by being visible, liftable, etc. It can also be a material object for different kinds of willing, more specific than willing in general, as distinguished by different formal aspects under which the mango is good (e.g., good as tasty, as opposed to good as nourishing).

Similarly, the intellect is a cognitive power aimed at the truth, but different ways of grasping the truth make for different formal objects. My geometer friend Joe believes the theorems of geometry as self-evidently following from self-evidently seen first principles. But when I take those same theorems on faith from Joe, I believe them as said by Joe. I don't just believe that they are true; I believe *him*, the speaker. So the "material objects" of faith are propositions believed, while the "formal object" is a particular aspect under which that proposition is considered believable, the aspect "told to me by Joe." When I believe what Joe says under this aspect of "told to me by Joe," then, according to Aquinas, I am "adhering" to the speaker.

> On the part of the intellect, there are two ways to take the object of faith. One is the material object of faith. . . . Another is the formal object, which is like a means [*medium*] on account of which one assents to such a credible [proposition]. In this way the act of faith is called *credere Deo*, because, as said above, the formal object is the First Truth [i.e., God], to which a man *adheres* so as, on account of it, to assent to what he believes.[18] (*ST* II-II.2.2c)

I mentioned that the same mango can be the material object of different kinds of willing. Likewise, the same proposition can be the object of different cognitive powers, acts, or habits (and so, of different propositional attitudes) such as suspecting that *p*, knowing that *p*, trusting that *p*, and so on, depending on how those cognitive acts or habits treat that proposition.[19] Opinion and faith are both cognitive habits of assent to a proposition, but the assent of opinion is brought about by inductive inference from one's evidence, while the assent of faith is brought about by "adhering" to the speaker.[20]

Aquinas explains such adherence by analogy to means and ends: assent to a proposition stated by a speaker is like a means to the end of adhering to that speaker.

> Since whoever believes assents to the word of someone, it seems that the principal thing in any believing, like an end, is the person to whose word one assents, while the items one believes in order to assent to that person are secondary.[21] (*ST* II-II.11.1c)

Aquinas's talk of "adherence" seems to combine our intuitive notions that faith is a matter of both trusting and loyalty. Aquinas treats faith as trusting belief out of loyalty to the speaker. By contrast, opinion is just a matter of taking something to be probable on one's own evidence, without regard for whether one is adhering to the speaker. The loyalty and trust of faith are ways of depending more extensively on a speaker for the truth than the dependence of opinion. For example, faith is incompatible with taking certain precautions against the speaker being wrong, whereas opinion is not.[22] Thus, the attempt to establish one's opinion on some matter of faith by considering all the evidence (or at least enough evidence to judge the matter for oneself) is in effect an attempt to replace faith with either "seeing" or opinion.

Nevertheless, even when Aquinas says that "faith does not assent to or dissent from something because of evidence [*argumenta*], but because of the First Truth [i.e., God]," he still admits that "some evidence supporting faith [*adminiculantia fidei argumenta*] can be used [*possint induci*]" (*Commentary on the Sentences*, henceforth *Sent.*, III.21.2.3 ad 1). There are at least three ways to use such evidence without making faith evidential. One is to undermine arguments *against* the faith, by showing that the claims of faith are at least possibly true (*ST* I.32.1c). Another is to see how what one already believes on faith fits well with other truths (*ST* I.32.1 ad 2), for the sake of understanding. The most interesting for our purposes is the way evidence can be used to indirectly support faith by putting one in a position to have faith.

For example, to believe God on some topic, one must believe that God really is the author of the message one is entertaining on that topic. When a prophet performs miracles that only God could perform, that helps confirm that the message really is from God, the way a signature or royal seal does (*ST* III.43.1c). There are also many ways that an act of communication depends on other evidence, about, for example, what the meaning of the communication is.[23] But these uses of evidence do not bear directly on the epistemic justification of one's faith.

One consideration that bears more closely on such justification is evidence about what kind of speaker is worth having faith in. And one reason Aquinas gives for thinking a speaker worth having faith in is that the speaker is truthful.

Aquinas says that a good reason for believing a human speaker is the speaker's conscientious veracity (*Sent.* III.23.3.4.3expos.), and that when we consider whether to have faith in God, even miracles "do not prove [the propositions of] faith directly, but prove the truthfulness of those announcing the [propositions of] faith" (*Sent.* III.24.1.2.2 ad 4). God is the ideal speaker in this regard, since God is perfectly truthful, and so cannot lie.[24] Truthfulness, for Aquinas, is not just a matter of reliability; truthfulness is a virtue. The Aristotelian virtue of truthfulness (*veritas* or *veracitas*) is a moral virtue of accurate self-representation (avoiding the extremes of boasting and self-deprecation). It is motivated by a love of truth, and falls under the virtue of justice, because it is oriented toward giving others the truth.[25] Aquinas notes that as a virtue of accurate self-representation, truthfulness concerns the particular case of accurately representing one's knowledge.[26] Thus, the truthfulness of a speaker contributes to the rationality of one's faith by putting one in touch with a speaker's knowledge.

Unlike opinion, which restricts one to one's own evidence, faith in a truthful speaker allows one to "share" and be "joined" to the knowledge of the speaker. Faith, Aquinas says, joins us to God's knowledge.[27] Faith makes one's belief more sensitive to the speaker's evidence, and less sensitive to one's own evidence.[28] So when presented with a knowledgeable and truthful speaker's statement, the audience that restricts itself to inferring from its own evidence will be less certain and have worse epistemic standing than an audience that has faith.

Here's an example from the analogous case of human faith. Suppose both Fay and Opie are told by their friend Knox that the fastest way to the CN tower is to take the second highway exit after the tower. They both assent, but Fay has faith while Opie has opinion. As they separately drive there, they each see what looks like a much more direct route. Opie might either change his mind, or at least be more ready to change his mind than Fay. So if Knox does know the way, Fay is in a better epistemic position than Opie.

But now suppose that Knox is wrong and doesn't know the way. Then Opie can blame only himself for his mistaken inference, whereas Fay can also blame Knox for breaking faith with her by not being truthful. Faith has the drawback of making one dependent on the speaker, but it also has the benefit of linking one's justification to that of the speaker in a way that inductive inference does not. Thus faith is not merely a very strong inferential belief that p, supported by a premise about the truthfulness of the speaker (or any other "credibility arguments").

To conclude, the formal object of faith (*credere Deo*/"believing God") has been missed by evidentialist, voluntarist reliabilist, and basic belief readings of Aquinas on faith. This is a pity, since the formal object of faith plays an interesting and important role in the epistemic justification of faith, and deserves further investigation.[29]

University of Toronto

Notes

1. Plantinga, "Reason and Belief in God," 46.

2. Penelhum similarly argues that Aquinas ought to be an evidentialist. He poses a dilemma for Aquinas: either credibility arguments give the intellect conclusive reason for belief, and so yield the rational certainty of *scientia*, or they do not, with the result that the certainty of faith is irrational ("The Analysis of Faith in St. Thomas Aquinas," 146, 152). Penelhum seems unaware of Aquinas's distinction between the certitude of evidentness and the certitude of adhesion (see note 7 below). Below I will argue that credibility arguments put one in a position to rationally have faith, but on their own do not give the believer the epistemic status she acquires through faith.

3. Here are three further problems. First, Aquinas says that miracles do not sufficiently confirm a divine message (*Commentary on Romans* 10.2), and for that reason divine grace is necessary for the certainty of faith (*ST* II-II.6.1c). Second, Aquinas says it is the will rather than evidence that brings about the belief of faith (*Quaestiones Disputatae de Veritate*, henceforth *QDV*, 14.2 ad 14) and gives the will an important role in the assent of faith (*ST* II-II.1.1c,

1.4c, 2.1 ad 3, 2.9 ad 2). Such an act of will should be unnecessary on an evidentialist view. On my reading, the act of will is an act of "adhering" to the speaker, believing the speaker out of loyalty to the speaker as a truthful or epistemically authoritative speaker. That act of will provides a unique connection to the knowledge of the speaker not available through the other cognitive habits that Aquinas recognizes and thinks of as evidentialist—intellection, science, and opinion. I say more on this and on the differences between faith and opinion in Siebert, "Aquinas on Testimonial Justification."

4. Aquinas recognizes other intellectual cognitive habits based on reasoning or evidence, such as wisdom, prudence, and art (*ST* I-II.57). But he thinks of wisdom as a kind of science. And he thinks of prudence and art as non-evidentialist in their dependence on connatural knowledge. But he would still say that, unlike faith, they are concerned solely with things to be done or made (*ST* I-II.57.2–3) and are not infused with divine grace. Aquinas also distinguishes faith from the infused intellectual gifts (of understanding and knowledge) that support faith (*ST* II-II.8.2c, 9.1c). On connatural knowledge in Aquinas, see Suto. I do not mean to imply in this paper that connatural knowledge is not an important component in Aquinas's account of faith. I simply have not discussed it. See Niederbacher.

5. Intellection (*intellectus*) is sometimes translated "understanding." In addition to this kind of *intellectus*, Aquinas recognizes a non-propositional kind of intellection, the immediate grasp of terms or natures.

6. *Sent.* III.23.3.4.3 expos., *Commentary on Boethius's De Trinitate*, henceforth *In BDT*, 3.1 ad 4, *Sent.* I prol. 1.3.3 ad 1. Aquinas's terminology can be confusing on this point, since he accepts from Cicero (via Boethius) the use of the term "faith" (*fides*) for the conviction produced by an ordinary inductive or deductive argument. I suspect that is what he means by "faith or opinion" in his *Commentary on the Posterior Analytics* (henceforth *In PA*), I.1.

7. *In PA* I.1.6 is Aquinas's fullest discussion of the way *opinio* is justified, but see also *ST* I-II.51.3c, *Sent.* III.17.1.2.1c, and *In BDT* 3.1 ad 4. Aquinas contrasts opinion with cognitive habits (or propositional attitudes) that have lower credence than opinion: suspicion is a slight inclination to assent to p, and doubt is an equal inclination to assent to p and to not-p (*ST* II-II.2.1). Further, opinion that p makes space for the possibility that not-p is true (*ST* I-II.67.3c, II-II.1.5 ad 4; cf. *In PA* I.1—but on this passage see the previous note). So opinion that p is roughly taking p to be probable by inductive inference.

8. *Sent.* III.23.2.2.3 ad 1, ad 2; *QDV* 14.1c and ad 7; *ST* II-II.4.8c and ad 1.

9. *QDV* 14.1c, *ST* II-II.2.9 ad 2.

10. Hence "reason" ("*ratione*") should not be taken to imply that every cognoscitive habit involves reasoning. The intellection of first principles, for example, is direct and preceded by no syllogistic reasoning. "*Ratio*" here is used in a more general sense sometimes translated as "notion," "nature," or "character." In light of my explanation of the "formal object" of faith below, we can paraphrase this quote thus: assent is Christian faith "only when one believes *in light of this*, that it is said by God . . . the way any cognoscitive habit has its species from the *aspect under which* it assents to anything." The aspect under which opinion assents to anything is as made probable by arguments or evidence. The aspect under which faith assents is different.

11. Stump, *Aquinas*, 367–369.

12. First, this account does not explain why Aquinas would think that faith is an intellectual virtue directed only at the truth (*ST* II-II.1.3 ad 1). Second, it is hard to see how this

approach can be extended to account for the justification of belief in other articles of faith, for example, that Jesus Christ was resurrected, or that God is a Trinity of persons. Third, this approach leaves out the infused grace that, according to Aquinas, makes faith its own intellectual "light."

13. *Sent.* III.24.1.1.1c: "[I]n the object of some potency three things are to be considered: what is formal in the object, and what is material, and what is accidental. This is clear in the object of sight, since the formal in itself is light, which makes colour visible in act, but the material is the colour itself, which is visible in potency; while the accidental, like quantity and other such things, are concomitant with the colour. . . . And these three are found in the object of faith. For since [divine] faith does not assent to something but because of the believable First Truth [i.e., God], that [proposition] is not credible in act except from the First Truth, as colour is visible from light. Thus the First Truth is formal in the object of faith, and that from which is the whole notion of the object. But whatever is believed from God, such as that the Passion happened, or some such thing, this is material in the object of faith; while those things which follow from such credible [propositions] are accidentally [the object of faith]."

14. Another serious problem for this view is that Aquinas says that when you have faith, you know that you have faith (*QDV* 10.9 ad 8, *ST* I-II.112.5 ad 2, *ST* III.30.1 ad 3).

15. For other interesting cases (involving hypnotism and double-bluffing) that illustrate the difference between believing a speaker and believing what the speaker said, see Anscombe, "What Is It to Believe Someone?"; Coady, *Testimony*, 45; and Moran, "Getting Told and Being Believed."

16. *Sent.* III.27.2.4.1 ad 3: "Material diversity of objects suffices for distinguishing acts numerically, but they are not distinguished according to species except by diversity of formal objects. But the diversity of formal objects is according to the notion which a habit or power principally attends to . . . ." *ST* I.59.2 ad 2: "Powers are not distinguished by a distinction of material objects, but by a formal distinction, following the notion of the object. And thus a notional diversity of good and true suffices for distinguishing intellect from will." A vice like incest, even if materially the same as other sexual acts, has a different formal object (*Sent.* IV.41.1.4.1 ad 1). Similarly, the vice of lying is defined by the "formal falsity" of the speaker's intent to speak falsely (*ST* I-II.110.1c). See also *Sent.* III.23.1.4.1c, *SCG* I.76.2, *ST* I.59.4c, *ST* I-II.1.3, *ST* I-II.62.2c. See also Boyle, "Toward Understanding the Principle of Double Effect," 530 on Aquinas on the formal objects of virtuous and vicious acts.

17. *ST* I.59.4c, I-II.8.1c, I-II.9.1–2.

18. The term "credible" here just means "believable" or "believable by faith." Some other passages where Aquinas highlights the difference between the material and formal objects of faith are *Sent.* III.24.1.1.1c, *QDV* 14.8 obj 9 and ad 9, *Quaestiones Disputatae de Virtutibus*, henceforth *QDVC*, 4.1c and ad 4, *Commentary on 2 Timothy*, henceforth *In 2 Tim*, 1.4, and *ST* II-II.129.6c, where Aquinas says "it pertains to faith to believe something and someone." See also *ST* II-II.17.6c.

19. In *ST* I-II.67.3c Aquinas similarly distinguishes the cognitive habits of faith, opinion, and *scientia* with regard to their means (*media*). Note that many cognitive habits do or can have an affective or conative component (e.g., hoping that p, doubting whether p, trusting that p).

20. Aquinas also recognizes that one's assent can be overdetermined. For example, one could have both inductive and demonstrative reasons to assent to p. However, if one attitude

requires "seeing" that *p* (as does *scientia*) while another requires not seeing that *p* (as do opinion and faith), then one cannot have both the seeing and the not-seeing attitude at the same time toward the same proposition (*ST* I-II.67.3c). In such a case there is a conflict of formal objects.

21. Note that in this context "believes" refers specifically to the act of faith in a narrow sense (*ST* II-II.2.1ff.), not to the assent that can also be found in other cognitive habits like knowledge from demonstration or opinion from inductive inference.

22. See Keren for an account of testimonial trust on which trust requires seeing oneself as having a reason not to take precautions against the speaker's testimony being false.

23. The gifts of understanding and knowledge support faith by ensuring in various ways that one gets the right message (*ST* II-II.9.1c). A well-known account of the reasoning behind ordinary acts of communication ("utterances") can be found in Grice, *Studies in the Way of Words*.

24. *In 2 Tim* 1.4; *Commentary on Galatians* 6.2; *ST* II-II.2.4c, 5.2c, 89.1c. Aquinas emphasizes this aspect of God in his discussion of faith by referring to God as First Truth (e.g., throughout *QDV* 14 and *ST* II-II qq. 1 and 2). Note also how *QDV* 14.8 ad 9 does not deny the "truthfulness" part of *QDV* 14.8 obj 9.

25. For Aquinas on truthfulness, see *Commentary on the Nicomachean Ethics* 4.15, *ST* I.16.4 ad 3, *ST* II-II.109.

26. *ST* II-II.109.3 ad 3: "But since knowable truths, inasmuch as they are known by us, are about us and pertain to us, in this way the truthfulness [*veritas*] of teaching can pertain to this virtue, and whatever other truthfulness [*veritas*] by which one manifests by word or deed what one knows."

27. *QDV* 14.8c, *SCG* I.4, *ST* I.1.1c.

28. *ST* II-II.4.8 ad 2. See Keren, "Trust and Belief," 20–21 for an account of how trust makes one "less sensitive to evidence available to one" but "more sensitive to evidence available to the speaker."

29. See Camelot, "Credere Deo, credere Deum, credere in Deum" and Siebert, "Aquinas on Testimonial Justification."

Bibliography

Anscombe, Elizabeth. "What Is It to Believe Someone?" *Rationality and Religious Belief*, ed. C. F. Delaney. 41–151. Notre Dame: Notre Dame University Press, 1979.

Boyle, Joseph. "Toward Understanding the Principle of Double Effect." *Ethics* 90.4 (1980): 527–538. doi: https://doi.org/10.1086/292183

Camelot, Pierre-Thomas. "Credere Deo, credere Deum, credere in Deum. Pour l'histoire d'une formule traditionnelle." *Revue des sciences philosophiques et théologiques* 30 (1941/2): 149–155.

Coady, C. A. J. *Testimony: A Philosophical Study*. Oxford: Clarendon Press, 1992.

Grice, H. Paul. *Studies in the Way of Words*. Cambridge, MA: Harvard University Press, 1989.

Jenkins, John. *Knowledge and Faith in Thomas Aquinas*. New York: Cambridge University Press, 1997.

Keren, Arnon. "Trust and Belief: a Preemptive Reasons Account." *Synthese* 191 (2014): 2593–2615. doi: https://doi.org/10.1007/s11229-014-0416-3

Moran, Richard. "Getting Told and Being Believed." *Philosopher's Imprint* 5.5 (2005): 1–29.

Niederbacher, Bruno. "Die eingegossene Tugend des Glaubens bei Thomas von Aquin." *Das Mittelalter* 20.2 (2015): 266–278.
doi: https://doi.org/10.1515/mial-2015-0017

Penelhum, Terence. "The Analysis of Faith in St. Thomas Aquinas." *Religious Studies* 13.2 (1977): 133–154. doi: https://doi.org/10.1017/S0034412500009938

Pickavé, Martin. "Human Knowledge." In *The Oxford Handbook of Aquinas*, ed. Eleonore Stump and Brian Davies, 311–326. New York: Oxford University Press, 2012. doi: https://doi.org/10.1093/oxfordhb/9780195326093.003.0024

Plantinga, Alvin. "Reason and Belief in God." In *Faith and Rationality: Reason and Belief in God*, ed. Alvin Plantinga and Nicholas Wolterstorff, 16–93. Notre Dame: University of Notre Dame Press, 1983.

Siebert, Matthew. "Aquinas on Testimonial Justification: Faith and Opinion." *Review of Metaphysics* 69 (2016): 555–582.

Stump, Eleonore. *Aquinas*. New York: Routledge, 2003.

Suto, Taki. "Virtue and Knowledge: Connatural Knowledge According to Aquinas." *Review of Metaphysics* 58.1 (2004): 61–79.

Tyrell, Francis Martin. *The Role of Assent in Judgment: A Thomistic Study*. Washington: Catholic University of America Press, 1948.

Transcendental Multitude in Thomas Aquinas

Joshua Lee Harris

Abstract: In this study, I consider the viability of what is perhaps one of the more "obscure" transcendentals in Aquinas's work—that is, the concept of *multitudo transcendens*. This strange notion is mentioned explicitly (as a member of the *transcendentia*, that is) on four occasions in Aquinas's *oeuvre*. Despite its apparent difficulties, i.e., the clear difficulties associated with claiming that *ens* is really convertible with both *unum* and *multitudo*, I suggest that Aquinas's affirmation of *multitudo* as a transcendental is a conceptually coherent way of providing a compelling answer to a perennial problem in both ancient and modern philosophy: namely, the logical and metaphysical problem of doing justice to the seemingly equiprimordial notions of "the one" and "the many"—as *harmonious* perfections rather than *competitive* notions.

I n his magisterial work on the subject, Jan Aertsen notes that the development of the doctrine of the "transcendentals"—i.e., the "most common notions" or "first conceptions of the intellect"—is the project that most properly characterizes medieval philosophy in general.[1] As one of the preeminent figures in medieval philosophy, then, it should come as no surprise that the "convertibility" of transcendental concepts such as *unum*, *verum*, and *bonum* with *ens* plays a crucial role in the thought of Thomas Aquinas.

In this study, I consider the viability of what is perhaps one of the more "obscure" transcendentals in Aquinas—that is, the concept of *multitudo transcendens*. This strange notion is mentioned explicitly (i.e., as a member of the *transcendentia*) on four occasions in Aquinas's *oeuvre*, twice in the *Prima Pars* of the *Summa theologiae*,[2] once in the third book of his *Commentaria physicorum*,[3] and finally once in the eighth article of his *Questiones disputatae de spiritualibus creaturis*.[4] Despite its apparent absurdity, i.e., the absurdity of claiming that *ens* is really convertible with both *unum* and *multitudo*, I suggest that Aquinas's affirmation of *multitudo* as a transcendental is a conceptually coherent way of providing a compelling answer to a perennial problem in both ancient and modern philosophy: namely, the logical and metaphysical problem of doing justice to the seemingly equiprimordial notions of "the one and the many"—as *harmonious* perfections rather than *competitive* notions.

© 2016, *Proceedings of the ACPA*, Vol. 89
doi: 10.5840/acpaproc20171558

This is especially true for Aquinas, since for him all transcendentals are also divine *perfections* in which created beings participate.[5] This point is not some inessential, theological "add-on" to the more properly philosophical development of the transcendentals; on the contrary, it is crucial in that it motivates Aquinas's desire to account for the *multitudo* that is properly predicated of the triune God as a name for a perfection of both himself (in a preeminent manner) and the created order which participates according to its finite and limited capacity. Indeed, as Aertsen has already claimed, the development of the concept of *multitudo transcendens* is one of the clearest examples of a decidedly *theological* commitment which clearly motivates what is otherwise a properly *philosophical* point in Aquinas.[6]

Now because *multitudo* is the "opposite" of *unum*,[7] an understanding of the latter, more familiar transcendental notion is crucial for any attempt to understand the former. In his *Metaphysics*, Aristotle argues that unity is "the first measure of a kind, and above all of quantity; for it is from this that it has been extended to the other categories."[8] This extension to other categories is already a sign of unity's transcendental status. Because unity properly understood is merely the negation of division—and because part of what it means to have being at all is to be undivided—it follows that unity is "convertible" or "co-extensive" with being. Put simply, a being has unity *precisely to the extent that it has being*. For Aquinas, this sort of implication is precisely what it means to be a transcendental perfection. He affirms the distinction between (1) the aforementioned unity that is convertible with being (being undivided), and (2) the unity that belongs properly to the category of quantity, i.e., "numerical" unity.[9] Because the category of quantity only admits of accidental being (as opposed to substantial being), any numerical or quantitative unity must be predicated of a "unit" of measure as an accident is predicated of a substance. What this ultimately means is that numerical unity presupposes or assumes an already *undivided* subject of predication. This so-called "transcendental unity," then, serves as a condition of possibility for numerical unity, and so the two unities are distinct. Whereas transcendental unity can be predicated of all beings as beings, numerical or quantitative unity can only be predicated of beings that are subject to quantitative determination (i.e., material substances).

If *multitudo* is to be coherently understood as a transcendental notion, i.e., as convertible with *ens*, then Aquinas's careful development of *unum* is necessary. The distinction between transcendental and numerical unity is especially important, since an analogous distinction is also present in *multitudo*.

Aliquid in *De Veritate* Q. 1

Before moving on to the texts in which Aquinas explicitly discusses *multitudo transcendens*, there is one final "pre-condition" to be discussed in his derivation of *aliquid* as a transcendental in *De Veritate*, Q. 1. Since this is the only place in Aquinas's *oeuvre* (to my knowledge) in which *aliquid* is explicitly granted a place amongst the *transcendentia*, neither its purpose nor its lasting significance for later texts is very clear. Building upon what Ed Houser and Jan Aertsen have already suggested in passing,[10] however, here I aim to develop the idea that *aliquid* is best understood as an early expression of what will ultimately be refined further in the notion of *multitudo transcendens*.

The order of derivation in *De Veritate* 1.1 differs slightly from an otherwise similar schema of transcendentals developed in *De Potentia* 9.7. In the former, *aliquid* comes fourth in the order of primary notions—after *ens per se*, *res*, and *unum*, and before *bonum* and *verum*.[11] *Ens per se*, Aquinas notes, is being considered absolutely, i.e., being considered "in itself." Its logical distinction from *res* has to do with the so-called "real distinction" between *esse* and essence in Aquinas. Whereas the sheer *esse* of any being is its pure "that-ness," the essence or quiddity of a being is its "what-ness." In the context of these two transcendentals here in *De Veritate* 1.1—namely, *ens per se* and *res*—the former is a name for being as considered in light of its sheer *esse*, whereas the latter is a name for being as considered in light of its essence or quiddity.

This brings us to *unum*, which Aquinas barely considers in the body of his response. In what almost feels like an afterthought, he merely says that *ens per se* implies a negation of division. Thus, he argues, being considered in light of this undividedness is precisely the meaning of *unum*. Yet what really interests Aquinas here in *De Veritate* 1.1 is the possibility of the so-called "relational transcendentals," i.e., notions that are convertible with being while still implying a relation "to another" being. This comes as no surprise, since the disputed question at issue here has to do with the nature of truth, which implies a *relation* between intellect and *res*. The relationality that is needed here is precisely what is expressed by *aliquid*, i.e., "division from another [unity]."[12]

Immediately this begs the question of how *aliquid*, as transcendental, can be convertible with *ens per se*—especially since the latter has already been affirmed as convertible with its *in*division from itself (*unum*). Although this sort of question is answered more explicitly in later work on *multitudo*, Aquinas offers an important reason for thinking that *aliquid* deserves a place alongside the other *transcendentia*: namely, that there is a being for whom it is proper *convenire cum omni ente*, i.e., "to agree with every being."[13] This being, for Aquinas following Aristotle, is the soul. Thus, Aquinas establishes *aliquid* as a transcendental by noting that *all* beings, to the extent that they are beings, "agree" with the soul. *Bonum* and *verum* are also vindicated as transcendentals by *aliquid*, since they name different agreements between the soul and other beings. *Bonum* names the agreement of the appetitive power with beings, whereas *verum* names the agreement of the intellectual power with beings. In effect, then, *aliquid* is the relational "bridge" that Aquinas needs for establishing relational transcendentals such as *bonum* and *verum*.

Aliquid is instructive for *multitudo* because it paves the way for a notion of relation "one-to-another" as co-extensive with being. Such a relation is important not only because *multitudo* is itself a relational transcendental, but also because it seems to beg the question of the possible varieties of *division*. This brings us to the next conceptual innovation in Aquinas: the distinction between material and formal *division*.

Multitudo in Its Material and Formal Varieties

It was already said that both *unum* and *multitudo* are each meant in at least two different ways: (1) numerical or material; and (2) transcendental or formal. Since this is perhaps the most important distinction for understanding the notion of *multitudo transcendens*, it behooves us to explore it in greater detail in the context of *multitudo*.

Aquinas notes that, in quantitative divisibility, "both or one of these constituents is by nature 'a one,' that is, something which is pointed out." The important thing here is that quantitative divisibility requires a logically prior unity that is not contained in the category of quantity: namely, "something which is pointed out" or "something that is shown." (*hoc est aliquid demonstratum*).[14] Insofar as this logically prior unity serves as a necessary condition for numerical unity, then, we already have a basis from which to distinguish the two.

In *III Physicorum*, lect. 8 (one of four aforementioned texts in which he explicitly mentions *multitudo transcendens*), Aquinas mentions *multitudo* in the context of a commentary on the subject of whether or not there can be such a thing as a "sensible infinite," i.e., an infinite that is material or "bodily" in nature.[15] Aquinas considers two points from Aristotle that make such an idea impossible to conceive, since they are mutually exclusive by definition.

The first of these two reasons is the apparent incoherence between the definitions of "body" and "infinite." Whereas a body by definition is *determined* by an extended "plane" or "surface," the very meaning of "infinite" implies a resistance to any such determination. Thus, for Aquinas following Aristotle, it is incoherent to suggest that there is such a thing as a sensible or bodily infinite. However, for the same reason, neither can there be a quantitative or mathematical infinite; for even mathematical objects such as line segments are likewise *determined* by the points in which they terminate.[16] Thus, for Aquinas and Aristotle, mathematical objects cannot be infinite for the very same reason that sensible matter cannot be infinite: namely, that both kinds of object contain the concept of determination in their definitions.

The second reason that a sensible infinite is impossible by definition builds upon the first. It has to do with Aquinas and Aristotle's views on what is implied by something being "countable" (*numerabile*). If everything countable is determined by number, then it seems for Aquinas that (in principle, at least) that which is countable can be "passed through" (*transiri*) by the act of counting. Again, though, this is impossible—precisely because that which is infinite cannot be "arrived upon" or "passed through."

With these two arguments against a "sensible infinite" in mind, Aquinas is now in a position to clarify the notion of *multitudo transcendens*; for he remarks that these arguments "do not conclude of necessity," since the notion of an "infinite body" may not imply the sort of determination (material or numerical) assumed by each of them. Recalling Aristotle's definition of number as "multitude *measured* by unity" (*multitudo mensurata per unum*), Aquinas suggests that *multitudo* does not necessarily imply the notion of "measure." On the contrary, although all that is "numerable" is a *multitudo*, not every *multitudo* is numerable. In short, *multitudo* has a greater extension than discreet quantity or number. Indeed, as Aquinas feels free to say here without further argument, *multitudo* extends beyond the categories altogether as a member of the *transcendentia*.[17]

Later in the commentary, Aquinas makes some remarks about the two kinds of division—"one is formal, *which is through opposites*; the other is according to quantity. Now the first division causes that multitude which is a transcendental, accordingly as being is divided into 'one' and 'many.'"[18] The key point here is that formal division does not require the aforementioned "measure" that is characteristic of number; rather, Aquinas affirms a sort of irreducible presence of *unum* and *multitudo* that lies at the heart of what is implicitly expressed by "being." In order to clarify this rather abstract and difficult notion, Aquinas resources his metaphysics of angelic being.

Multitudo as a Perfection: The Case of Angelic Being

Even if it has been shown that *multitudo* is predicable of any and all categories, it remains to be seen how *multitudo* could be considered a "perfection," especially one that admits of even divine, preeminent proportion. In order to do so, it is important to note the sense in which Aquinas says that multitude can be predicated of the angelic host and ultimately even God himself. For this we turn to the *De spritualibus creaturis* and the *Summa theologiae*—the other texts (besides the *Physics* commentary) in which *multitudo transcendens* is explicitly mentioned.

Although the question of *De spiritualibus creaturis*, A. 8 (in which *multitudo transcendens* is invoked) considers whether angels differ in species from one another, it is important to grasp the trajectory of prior questions leading up to it—all of which deal with the relationship of spiritual substances with respect to bodies. While of course it is quite possible for spiritual substances to be united with a body, as evidenced by the soul-body composite constituting the human being, perhaps the most notable property of the angelic host is its pure immateriality. In the fifth article, after considering three perspectives of the philosophers (i.e., Anaxagorous, Plato and Aristotle) on the subject of immaterial substances, Aquinas devises three of his own reasons for thinking that angels are not united to any determinate body—all of which have to do with the notion of perfection in the created order.

The first reason for thinking that angels are immaterial substances wholly separate from bodies is that the perfection of the universe seems to imply "that [the universe] does not lack any nature which can possibly exist."[19] Now since in the genus of substance there exist both strictly material bodies (animals and inanimate objects) and soul-body composites (human beings), it is fitting for there to be a third kind: namely, a kind consisting of strictly *im*material bodies. Of course, this species of substance is comprised of the angelic host.

The second reason for thinking that angels are immaterial substances wholly separate from bodies has to do with the hierarchical order of being. Whereas the supremely simple God who exists outside of any genus resides preeminently as the first principle of this hierarchy, Aquinas says that it is "not possible" for human beings as body-soul composites to come next; for this would "skip," as it were, an important *intermediary* class of beings, which resides between absolute simplicity and body-soul composite substances.[20] If strictly immaterial substances were to exist, they would be located "in-between" both absolute simple being and body-soul composites in terms of their own relative simplicity. Again, then, the perfection of the created order demands a certain elegance that cannot omit such obvious intermediaries. Thus, angels must occupy this intermediary place between divine and human being.

Finally, there is also a similar order of perfection with respect to intellectual activity, for Aquinas. Whereas God *just is* the pure act of intellect itself, human intellects must abstract from imagined phantasms as a means towards the end of knowledge. But this properly material operation that is proper to human intellectual activity is entirely *accidental* to intellectual activity *as such*. Therefore, Aquinas concludes, there seems to be yet another intermediary class between divine and human—this time with respect to intellectual activity rather than being. Angels again occupy this intermediary stage, since although they are not the pure act of intellect itself, neither is their act of knowing hindered by the properly material powers of sense or imagination. Again, because there is an elegance that seems to be characteristic of the created order, Aquinas feels at liberty to assign the bodiless angelic host to what would otherwise be a puzzling lacuna in being.

Having established the strict immateriality of angelic being in this fifth article and others, Aquinas then moves on to the question of individuation in the context of angelic being. Quantitative determination is only possible in material things, since the determinacy proper to number demands a concomitant determinacy that is proper to material beings in time and space. Yet the angelic *host* does indeed imply that there are a multitude of angels. How then is this plurality to be made intelligible? This predicament motivates objectors in both this article from the *De spiritualibus creaturis* and the *Summa theologiae* Ia, Q. 50, A. 1: "number is a species of quantity, which is not apart from matter. If, then, there were no matter in the angels, there would be no number in them, which is false."[21]

Aquinas answers this apparent *reductio ad absurdum* employed by the objector by appealing the notion of *multitudo transcendens*: "But in immaterial substances there is a multitude which derives from the transcendentals, inasmuch as 'one' and 'many' are divisions of being; and this multitude is the result of a formal distinction."[22] The case of the angelic host, since it is both plural and immaterial, immediately demands a kind of division that is not subject to the material determination implied by quantitative division.

Fittingly, then, this is precisely the conceptual work that *multitudo transcendens* is designed to perform. By exemplifying a *multitudo* that is characterized by formal opposition rather than material division, the plurality of the angelic host is preserved conceptually. There is even a sense in which the angelic host is "more" diversified than the numerical quantity of material beings, since their *multitudo* is characterized by a division which is not even limited by the accidental unity bestowed by the category of quantity. Instead, their *multitudo* is divided by a formal opposition that cuts to the core of being *qua* being. Thus, to the extent that angels enjoy a more perfect state of being than material creatures, so do they exemplify the perfection that is *multitudo transcendens* more eminently than do the numerically quantified aggregate of material creatures.

Yet it remains to be seen how *multitudo* can be predicated of God, especially since the divine being is marked most notably by his absolute simplicity. On this topic, we consider *Summa theologiae* Ia, Q. 30, in which Aquinas treats the nature of the plurality that is proper to the Persons of the triune God.

Multitudo as a Divine Perfection

The challenge that Aquinas takes up in his treatise on the trinitarian life of God in the *Summa theologiae* is to provide a means of avoiding heresy and illuminating the mystery that is the content of the doctrine of the Trinity: namely, that God is absolutely simple and identical with himself in his undivided essence, *yet* simultaneously constituted by the really distinct Persons of the Father, Son and Holy Spirit. As Gilles Emery has recently suggested, the task is to view these two commitments as a "counterpart" with respect to the other.[23] Now obviously an appropriate discussion of Aquinas's doctrine of the Trinity goes far beyond the comparatively meager scope of this more properly philosophical investigation. However, since it is also that case that the fullness of *multitudo transcendens* is ultimately realized in the multitude implied in the divine Persons, a cursory treatment of this *quaestio* is required insofar as it helps to illuminate the meaning of *multitudo* as a perfection of being—especially one that is harmonious with *unum*.

Aquinas quotes Augustine saying that there is both substance and relation in God, but immediately this begs an obvious question. In the schema of the Aristotelian categories, relation has only accidental being, and there are no accidents in God.[24] If there were accidents in God, this would imply composition, and it is crucial to the aforementioned doctrine of divine simplicity that there be no composition in God. Aquinas's solution, then, comes in the form of his understanding of the relations in the Trinity (e.g., "paternity" and "filiation") as "real" or "subsistent" relations. Often designated by the formulation *se habere* rather than the more pedestrian *relatio*, Aquinas argues that these relations of the Trinity are *constitutive* (i.e., God "has himself" in them) rather than accidental. As John Deely has recently put it, relation in this sense is "equiprimordial" with respect to substance.[25]

Yet this distinction between the formulations of accidental *relatio* and substantial *se habere* may seem rather *ad hoc*; for how is it possible to give a principled rationale for what is ultimately a rather incomprehensible doctrine? Aquinas's answer to this implicit question in Q. 28 is important for *multitudo transcendens*: "when something proceeds from a principle of the same nature, then both the one proceeding and the source of procession, agree in the same order; and then they have real relations to each other."[26] If the terms of a given relation are identical in nature, then it is impossible to assign the respective positions of "substance" and "accident" accordingly. But this is precisely what is implied in the Trinity. Therefore, Aquinas concludes, the relations in God are "subsistent" or "real" rather than accidental.

Now since everything that exists in creatures accidentally, exists in God substantially,[27] it follows that these substantial, real relations also exist in creatures accidentally. Once again, then, we have the distinction between formal and material division as the main (quasi-)*differentia* here. The multitude found in material creatures is designated, and therefore it is measured and quantitative. As we have already seen in the case of angels, however, the multitude that is properly predicated of God implies both indivision of and formal opposition between members of the multitude. Insofar as it implies indivision of its members, *multitudo transcendens* is not mutually exclusive with *unum*. Insofar as it implies formal opposition rather than measured opposition, *multitudo transcendens* does not imply composition of substance and accident. Thus, nothing prevents it from being predicated of God.[28]

Yet there seems to be at least one question that is left unanswered at this point: namely, if *multitudo* is predicated of both the angelic host and God, how is the latter's *multitudo* more perfect than the former's? Although Aquinas does not answer this question explicitly anywhere in his *oeuvre* (to my knowledge), it seems to follow that God's *multitudo* is more perfect even than angels, since unlike angels his essence is not even divided by a composition of those most fundamental metaphysical principles, *esse* and *essentia*. Although simpler than material creatures in this way, an angel's essence is not the same as its sheer *esse*, which is given gratuitously from *ipsum esse subsistens*, i.e., the most proper philosophical name for God. Further, because *multitudo transcendens* names the extent to which *undivided* members of a multitude are formally distinct from one another, any division of individual members of a multitude is not just a diminished in terms of *unum*, but also *multitudo*. Perhaps paradoxically, the intensity of *multitudo* is indexed proportionately to the intensity of *unum*—each perfection is complementary of the other. Hence, just to the extent that God is absolutely "one," he is also absolutely "many." In other words, he *just is* both *unum* and *multitudo*.

Aquinas is quite clear that the arguments for this understanding of unity and multitude "do not sufficiently prove the point advanced";[29] for this doctrine of subsistent relations in God is only available by means of revelation.[30] Despite this fact, though, there is little doubt that Aquinas's development of *multitudo* as a transcendental notion is a properly philosophical innovation—even if it is unimaginable outside of Aquinas's specifically Christian dogmatic commitments. For this reason and others, then, the notion of *multitudo transcendens* makes for one of the more powerful demonstrations of Aquinas's imagination as both a "philosophical theologian" *and* what we might call a "theological philosopher."

Institute for Christian Studies

Notes

1. See Jan Aertsen, *Medieval Philosophy and the Transcendentals: The Case of Thomas Aquinas* (Leiden: Brill, 1996), 17–24.

2. Thomas Aquinas, *The Summa Theologica* (hereafter *Summa Theologiae*), trans. Fathers of the Dominican Province (New York: Benziger Bros., 1947), Ia, q. 30, a. 3; Ia, q. 50, a. 1, *ad* 1.

3. Thomas Aquinas, *Commentaria in octo libros Physicorum*, trans. Pierre H. Conway, O.P. (Columbus, OH: College of St. Mary of the Springs, 1962), III, lect. 8.

4. Thomas Aquinas, *De spiritualibus creaturis*, trans. Mary C. Fitzpatrick and John J. Wellmuth (Milwaukee, WI: Marquette University Press, 1949), a. 8, *ad* 15.

5. For a systematic development of this particular point about the ontological purchase of the transcendentals in Aquinas, see Jason A. Mitchell, L.C., "Aquinas on the Ontological and Theological Foundation of the Transcendentals," *Alpha Omega* 16.1 (2013): 39–78.

6. See Aertsen, *Medieval Philosophy and the Transcendentals*, 224.

7. Aquinas, *Summa Theologiae*, Ia, q. 11, a. 2, *responsio*.

8. Aristotle, *Metaphysics*, 1052a.

9. On this point, see R. E. Houser, *Thomas Aquinas on Transcendental Unity: Scholastic and Aristotelian Predecessors* (Toronto: University of Toronto, 1980), 14–15 [dissertation].

10. See Houser, *Transcendental Unity*, 9 and Aertsen, *Medieval Philosophy and the Transcendentals*, 110.

11. Thomas Aquinas, *Questiones disputatae de veritate*, trans. Robert W. Mulligan, S.J. (Chicago: Henry Regnery Company, 1952), q. 1, a. 1, *responsio*.

12. Ibid.

13. Ibid.

14. Thomas Aquinas, *Expositio in libros metaphysicorum Aristotelis*, trans. John P. Rowan as *Commentary on the Metaphysics of Aristotle*, 2 vols. (Chicago: Regnery, 1964), l. 15, 977.

15. Aquinas, *Commentaria in octo libros Physicorum*, III, lect. 8, 350.

16. Ibid., III, lect. 8, 351.

17. Ibid., III, lect. 8, 352.

18. Ibid., III, lect. 12, 394.

19. Aquinas, *De spiritualibus creaturis*, a. 5, *responsio*.

20. Ibid.

21. Aquinas, *Summa Theologiae*, Ia, q. 50, a. 1, *obj.* 1.

22. Ibid., Ia., a. 1, *ad* 1.

23. Gilles Emery, O.P., *The Trinitarian Theology of Saint Thomas Aquinas*, trans. Francesca Aran Murphy (Oxford: Oxford University Press, 2007), 141.

24. See Aquinas, *Summa Theologiae*, Ia, q. 3, a. 6, *responsio*.

25. Deely develops this point with the help of John of St. Thomas's commentary. See John Deely, "The Role of Thomas Aquinas in the Development of Semiotic Consciousness," *Semiotica* 152.1–4 (2004): 85.

26. Aquinas, *Summa Theologiae*, Ia, q. 28, a. 1, *responsio*.

27. Ibid., Ia, q. 28, a. 2, *responsio*.

28. Ibid., Ia, q. 30, a. 3, *ad* 3.

29. Ibid.

30. Ibid., Ia, q. 32, a. 1, *responsio*.

A New Argument for the Incompatibility of Hylomorphism and Metaphysical Naturalism

Travis Dumsday

Abstract: Within the substance ontology literature in recent analytic metaphysics, four principal theories are in competition: substratum theory, bundle theory, primitive substance theory, and hylomorphism. This paper is part of a larger project attempting to show that each of these four theories is incompatible with metaphysical naturalism (which of course creates a problem for that view, if indeed these four theories are the only potentially workable options). To that end, I explicate and defend the following argument:

> **Premise 1**: Prime matter either can exist on its own (unactualized by substantial form) or it cannot.
>
> **Premise 2**: If prime matter can exist on its own (unactualized by substantial form) then metaphysical naturalism is false.
>
> **Premise 3**: If prime matter cannot exist on its own (unactualized by substantial form) then metaphysical naturalism is false.
>
> **Conclusion:** Therefore, either way, metaphysical naturalism is false.

Introduction

The four principal competing substance ontologies in the current metaphysics literature are substratum theory, bundle theory, primitive substance theory, and hylomorphism. I expect that for most readers these theories are familiar territory; nevertheless some may profit from a quick refresher:

- Substratum theory is typically formulated as the idea that a substance/object (I'll take those terms as synonymous) is a compound of properties[1] (whether conceived as universals or tropes) and a substratum (or 'bare particular,' or 'thin particular') in which those properties inhere. By that inherence in one and the same substratum the attributes are grouped together such that we get an object that is both unified and internally complex. The substratum is

© 2016, *Proceedings of the ACPA*, Vol. 89
doi: 10.5840/acpaproc20171357

also that by which a substance is individuated, such that in theory two numerically distinct substances could share all the same kinds of traits, making them qualitatively identical, while yet remaining distinct objects. It is also that which preserves continuity through radical change. It is worth noting that among substratum theorists it is a matter of dispute as to whether a substratum can ever exist on its own, wholly devoid of any properties. Most recent substratum theorists favour the view that substrata can only exist when instantiating properties (though which *specific* properties they instantiate is always merely contingent).[2]

- According to bundle theorists, what we think of as a substance actually consists of a property or compresent (or collocated or co-instantiated or mereologically fused) group of properties, with some viewing the properties as universals and others as tropes.[3]

- Advocates of primitive substance theory deny that a substance is made up out of metaphysical *constituents*, whether attributes or substrata. Instead, 'substance' is a basic ontological category, and an individual substance is the instantiation of a substance-universal or what E. J. Lowe calls a *kind*. Thus a particular electron is just an instantiation of the substance-universal 'electron' or 'electronhood,' where that universal is seen as irreducible to any property-universal or group of property-universals associated with it and as being in a way ontologically prior to such properties. At least, that is the most common formulation of the view; John Heil's work is a relatively rare example of a primitive substance theory formulated in nominalist terms. On his view, a substance is just an individual object possessed of assorted tropes.[4]

- Hylomorphism, like primitive substance theory, is the view that an individual substance is the instantiation of a substance-universal/kind (usually known in hylomorphism as a *substantial form*), but with the added claim that in the case of *material* substances this instantiated substance-universal is ordered to a basic potency for the reception of new substantial forms and thus for substantial change, a basic power to be transformed into an object belonging to another natural kind. This potency is viewed not as a property but as a substantial principle, traditionally known as 'prime matter.' Prime matter also shares certain commonalities of explanatory role with the substratum, insofar as it is invoked as part of the explanation of individuation (though in a manner rather different from that supposed by substratum theorists) and of persistence through radical change. In another parallel with substratum theorists, there is a dispute among hylomorphists on the question of whether prime matter can ever exist on its own, without being actualized by some substantial form or other. Most self-identified hylomorphists today are Thomists who, in accordance with St. Thomas Aquinas's view of the issue, affirm that prime matter can only exist while actualized by substantial form. Still, some continue to defend the view (very commonly held in mediaeval and early modern Scholastic circles, including by such notables as Scotus and Suarez) that prime matter can exist on its own, independently of any substantial form.[5]

Having reviewed the basic idea behind hylomorphism and the context in which it is debated, I should now clarify the meaning of the next theory referenced in the paper's title. Metaphysical naturalism (also often called 'physicalism' or 'materialism') can be taken as involving a commitment to *at least* the following propositions: (1) the only objects in existence (past and present) are physical objects;[6] and (2) all those physical objects are *essentially* (rather than merely *contingently*) physical.[7] Thus if one is a metaphysical naturalist/physicalist/materialist, one rejects the existence of paradigmatic irreducibly immaterial entities like God, angels, souls, Cartesian egos, etc.[8]

With the general contours of these two theories now on the table, we can turn to their relationship. Both historically and in the recent literature, it has been argued that hylomorphism is incompatible with metaphysical naturalism. I wish to add to that fund of arguments the following:

Premise 1: Prime matter either can exist on its own (unactualized by substantial form) or it cannot.

Premise 2: If prime matter can exist on its own (unactualized by substantial form) then metaphysical naturalism is false.

Premise 3: If prime matter cannot exist on its own (unactualized by substantial form) then metaphysical naturalism is false.

Conclusion: Therefore, either way, metaphysical naturalism is false.

Note that for the remainder of the paper I will be taking hylomorphism on board as an assumption, and one which I will not attempt to defend. There are two reasons I will not make that attempt: first, for those readers unfamiliar with the existing case for hylomorphism, a diversity of important arguments can easily be accessed via the authors cited above. I cannot make the case as ably as they do, and given space constraints it would be imprudent to try. Second, the present paper is part of a broader project aimed at undermining metaphysical naturalism. In the context of that broader project, I do not need to argue for the truth of hylomorphism.[9]

The rest of the paper is structured as follows: in the next section I defend premise 2 of this argument, while the succeeding section sees a defence of premise 3. I conclude with a brief recap. (I take it that premise 1 needs no defence, so I will say no more about it.)

Defending Premise 2

At this point I must ask the reader to indulge me in a temporary terminological shift. For the next little while, in place of 'prime matter' I am going to use the Greek 'hyle' (from which, of course, 'hylomorphism' partially derives). The reasons for this will shortly be made clear.

It is worth expanding a bit further on how hylomorphists think of hyle. (Again, this will be familiar ground for many readers, but it may be helpful for some, especially any non-Scholastics.) Hyle is inherently devoid of characterizing properties, whether essential or accidental. And yet, unlike bare substrata, it would be incorrect to say that hyle is characterless, a wholly de-natured blank slate; while devoid of all properties, it still makes sense to think of hyle as being a certain sort of thing, namely a *potency*. It is after all, of itself, a capacity for the reception of substantial form—or, in other words, it is a power to become a complete substance belonging to some natural kind. This is admittedly a difficult notion to wrap one's head around, as we are used to thinking of potencies as being properties of a substance (e.g., negative charge is a power to attract positively charged particles and to repel negatively charged particles, physical strength in a human being is a power to lift heavy objects and do other comparable tasks etc.). Hyle is importantly different insofar as it is not a property of a substance, but rather what is sometimes termed a *substantial potency* or *substantial principle*. Hyle may be devoid of properties, but it remains an entity of a definite sort, namely a substantial potency, a power for the reception of substantial form, and thus a certain kind of incomplete substance.

Premise 2 focuses on the version of hylomorphism according to which hyle can exist on its own, independent of any substantial form. Given the further character-ization of hyle just provided, that version may seem to involve a counter-intuitive claim. A mere capacity, even a capacity for receiving a natural kind/substantial form, may seem too ephemeral to be the subject of independent existence. And in fact even those who affirm that hyle can exist on its own have generally been reluctant to refer to it as a substance; rather, hyle is at best an *incomplete* substance. Scholastics have traditionally distinguished between complete and incomplete substance, where the latter does not necessarily imply an incapacity for autonomous existence. Another classic example of an incomplete substance would be one of the fingers on your hand. Your finger is capable of existence on its own, in a sense; it could after all be chopped off, and when thus detached it would not immediately pop out of existence. But so long as it remains a part of your hand (which is in its own turn a part of your body) it is not a complete substance, since by definition a finger is a part of a larger substance; it is naturally ordered to that larger substance and properly understood only in the context of that whole. Hyle is likewise an incomplete substance: yes it can exist on its own, but if and when it does it will not be a complete substance, since it is inherently defined by its natural ordering to the reception of substantial form and is missing something when deprived of form.

I will not review the assorted arguments provided historically for the possibility of independently existent hyle; it was a topic debated over the course of centuries and too involved to be delved into here. Moreover, among those who advocated the independence of hyle there was considerable variety in how exactly this was cashed out, and I cannot get into these specifics.[10] Plus, it is clearly not something that requires defence in the present context, given the nature of the larger argument we are considering.

What is crucial to emphasize here is that hyle is, of itself, devoid of intrinsic properties. That includes of course geometrical properties like spatial extension, and all the properties entailed by spatial extension, including such further intrinsic properties as shape and size, and such relational properties as occupancy of a particular spatial region. With that in mind, try the following experiment on some of your students, students not previously exposed to hylomorphism. Explain the basic tenets of the theory, being careful to use 'hyle' in place of 'prime matter' and defining it simply in terms of its explanatory role. Stress again its ability to exist on its own, and that when it is thus existent it is devoid of properties, most especially the geometrical properties just named. Then ask them: would you say that independently existent hyle counts as a material object? Don't try to get them to specify first what exactly the necessary conditions for being a material object are, which properties are required to constitute something as physical rather than non-physical. Just ask them whether, intuitively, it makes sense to them to think of hyle as a physical thing, an inhabitant of our spatio-temporal universe. I am willing to bet that you will get a resounding 'no' from nearly everyone, if not everyone. Why? Because it makes intuitive sense to think that (1) being physical demands the possession of some properties, whatever they might prove to be exactly, and that (2) most likely those properties will have to include spatial extension. An object devoid of all intrinsic and relational geometrical properties (including of course the relational property of spatial occupancy/location) seems not to be an inhabitant of our physical, spatio-temporal universe at all. The fact that it has the *ability* to become such an inhabitant (by becoming actualized by an inherently immaterial substantial form and thus being able to receive properties like determinate shape etc.) is unlikely to sway them into thinking that it is physical even *prior* to taking up residence (especially if they've any knowledge of the doctrine of the Incarnation). Their commonsense intuitions on this score are both reasonable and supported to a degree in the recent literature.[11]

There is some reason then to think that hyle is not material, not according to the commonsensical meaning of 'material.' You can see now why I requested the temporary terminological shift; it would look very odd to say that prime matter is not material. But that is a case where one's metaphysics is liable to be tripped up by one's semantics. For in fact it is true that prime matter, as hylomorphists understand it, is not material, and independently existent prime matter, while a sort of object (an incomplete substance) would not be a *material* object, not by a long shot.

To relate this back to our larger argument: if prime matter can exist on its own, and prime matter in that state does not count as a physical object, then non-physical entities can exist. Indeed, any object currently composed in part out of prime matter (which, for hylomorphists, encompasses all physical objects) could in principle become non-physical, namely by losing its substantial form (and with it the geometrical properties that come via form) and not having that form replaced by any other form. And this possibility clearly violates the commitment of meta-physical naturalists to the idea that all existent objects are not only physical but *essentially* physical.

With that the justification for premise 2 is complete. Naturally it is vulnerable to some potential objections. Perhaps most obvious is the worry whether independently existent prime matter, even if lacking spatial extension and spatial location, would really make metaphysical naturalists squirm. After all, it's not as if the prime matter would be conscious, and prima facie one might think it is immaterial minds that metaphysical naturalists are most keen to exclude from ontology. Perhaps they could stomach independently existent, non-spatial prime matter so long as it can't think.

In reply, it can be noted that both historically and in the recent literature there are all manner of non-mental/unconscious but still paradigmatically non-physical entities that most metaphysical naturalists refuse to countenance, and refuse to countenance precisely because of their obvious non-physical status. Consider for instance the widespread rejection of Platonic abstracta: metaphysical naturalists are often severely uncomfortable with Platonism in the philosophy of mathematics (with this discomfort being a major prompt for the rise of mathematical fictionalism), and likewise Platonism in meta-ethics (hence the popularity of the so-called 'queerness argument' for moral anti-realism made famous by J. L. Mackie[12]). Why? Because Platonic abstracta are clearly not material objects, and cannot easily be accommodated (if accommodated at all) within a physicalist paradigm. (For instance, as Platonists have long noted, mathematical and moral truths, among others, would remain true even if all material objects were wiped out, or never existed in the first place. Not being grounded in material realities, i.e., not finding their truthmakers in any material realities, mathematical and moral truths must be grounded in non-material realities, in this case abstract objects, Platonic forms.) Platonic abstracta are not material objects, and they're not minds. The former fact is quite sufficient to turn many physicalists against Platonism. For the same reason, they will turn against independently existent prime matter.

Or if the example of Platonic forms does not convince, consider David Chalmers's version of neutral monism in the philosophy of mind. According to the theory he's entertained, matter and mind are neither of them fundamental in nature; rather they are both manifestations or aspects of a third, deeper kind of reality that is neither physical nor mental in nature. His candidate for this third kind of reality is *information*. He proposes that information theory might be at the basis of ontology.[13] (Arguably this could be developed into a very Platonic proposal, though Chalmers doesn't seem to think of information as a Platonic abstract object or set of abstract objects: after all, concrete realities are its manifestations/aspects.) As one might expect, this variety of neutral monism has found few if any takers among self-identified physicalists. They object to taking information as a standalone, fundamental reality, not because it is mental (for Chalmers clearly it isn't) but because it is so clearly non-physical.

I could go on with other examples of supposed phenomena that are clearly not conscious but just as clearly rejected by physicalists as inconsistent with physicalism (e.g., vitalistic forces, magic, impersonal gods like the Hindu Brahman . . .). The point is simply that the reality of such entities is incompatible with physicalism because they are all clearly non-physical. It is not always specified why they are non-physical, but if pressed I expect most of those who object to Platonic forms and to neutral monism would at some point appeal to the fact that these entities lack spatial extension and/or do not inhabit the spatial realm in the way paradigm physical objects do. And of course the same can be said for independently existent hyle (or, at the risk again of semantic impropriety, 'prime matter').

Defending Premise 3

We come now to that version of hylomorphism (the most commonly held today) committed to the claim that prime matter can only exist as actualized by some substantial form or other, though of course it is not dependent on any *particular sort* of form and can receive any substantial form naturally ordered to prime matter. On this view, prime matter is existentially dependent on actualization by substantial form.

Hylomorphists of this stripe have a number of strategies available to them to argue that this substance ontology is incompatible with metaphysical naturalism. I will consider only two, with the first of them familiar from the existing literature,[14] and the second not.

The first strategy argues from hylomorphism to theism (and thus, by obvious implication, to the falsity of metaphysical naturalism) and involves a line of reasoning comparable in general outline to a number of other standard cosmological arguments for theism. Basically, because prime matter cannot exist on its own, an external cause must be referenced to bring it into being and keep it in being. That external cause will of course be whatever is bestowing substantial form upon it, which actualization of matter through inputting of the form just is the bringing-into-being of a material object, a substance that is compounded out of matter and form. Thus, for every material object, the hylomorphist automatically knows that it must have an external cause. It cannot be self-existent or uncaused or some sort of primitive brute fact. (Relatedly, because prime matter is inherently open to all substantial forms, an external cause must be referenced to explain why it is being actualized by *this* form rather than some other. So there are at least two reasons why this version of hylomorphism needs to make reference to an external cause or causes to explain the reality of any material object.) Now, if the cause of the inputting of form is itself another material object, it too will of course be a compound of matter and form and be in need of the same sort of causal explanation, and if we want to avoid circular causal dependence and infinite regress we must eventually reference some external cause that is not itself a material object, not itself in need of an external cause to explain the conjunction of its form and matter. And that external cause will have to be immaterial—since on this version of hylomorphism there is no independently real prime matter, the only non-compound sort of external cause left will be one wholly lacking in prime matter, i.e., a wholly immaterial causal actor. Whether or not that external cause is immediately identified with the God of traditional theism (and clearly more argumentative steps would be needed to conclude to further divine attributes besides just immateriality and causal power), it is certainly a non-physical entity (or entities), and thus an entity whose reality would disprove metaphysical naturalism.

Naturally this sort of route from hylomorphism to the rejection of metaphysical naturalism is vulnerable to an assortment of objections, but as the most notable of these are common to a wide range of other cosmological arguments for theism (e.g., concerns about whether circular explanations and infinite explanatory regresses are really inadmissible), I will not take them up here.

The second sort of strategy for concluding to the rejection of metaphysical naturalism from the present version of hylomorphism is not evident in the recent literature, and is in fact similar in important respects to the argument seen in the previous section. Consider that those hylomorphists who maintain that prime matter cannot exist independently of substantial form also affirm that properties are ontologically posterior to substantial form. That is, once the substantial form has actualized the prime matter and we have a genuine, complete substance on our hands, in theory it is still possible that that complete substance lack a wide range of actual properties. It must of course have the *potentialities* for receiving those properties (unlike prime matter, which cannot take on properties directly but can only receive substantial form), which potentialities are of course themselves necessary properties ('propria' to use the traditional terminology) immediately rooted in the substance because entailed by the nature that is the substantial form. Thus the substantial form 'gold' (for instance) entails that the object compounded out of that substantial form and prime matter must possess the ability to have assorted geometrical properties (like spatial extension and occupancy of a spatial location). Still, the substantial form does not entail the *determinate value* of those properties. Their determinate value must be set down to an external cause—and ultimately to an external cause devoid of any properties needing to have their determinate value specified, and thus devoid of all geometrical properties and thus non-physical, which (once circular causal explanation and infinite regress are rejected) would get us an argument akin to that just considered. However, rather than pursuing that line of reasoning, I want to draw attention to a more foundational point: a real substance that has no determinate geometrical properties, and instead just has the potency for taking on such properties, is not itself a *physical* substance, because again it will lack spatial extension and all the intrinsic and relational properties entailed by extension. Thus our second version of hylomorphism can be shown to be incompatible with metaphysical naturalism for a similar reason to that already canvassed with respect to our first version. Namely, the substance that is open to receiving a diverse array of determinate geometrical properties does not of itself possess any determinate geometrical properties.

But do hylomorphists of this second variety really affirm that real physical substances (prime matter actualized by substantial form) could, at least in theory, exist without having these determinate geometrical values specified, and thus could exist in an unextended, non-spatial state of being? Some Thomists openly do so. For on the standard Thomistic account, the substance (the composite of prime matter and substantial form) is ontologically prior to all of its associated characteristics/traits/accidents, whether these be possessed contingently or necessarily. Moreover the standard account holds that determinate spatial extension (the accident of *quantity*) is not even among the *necessary* accidents (*propria*). Rather, the *potentiality* for receiving determinate spatial extension, the power-to-be-extended, is the necessary accident, entailed by prime matter's actualization by certain sorts of substantial form. Thus Owens writes:

> A corporeal nature just in itself, therefore, is not extended. But it is a nature that is *capable* of extension in the three dimensions. The capability or potency to extension belongs to its very essence, and distinguishes it radically from supersensible substance. A material nature is necessarily composed of the two physical principles, matter and form. The matter allows the formal principle to be spread through parts outside parts without any formal increase[15] whatsoever. In this way it renders the nature itself potentially extended. But that potentiality can be actuated only through an accident, the accident of quantity. Not even the matter, just in itself, is extended. The matter is only the substantial basis of extension.[16] (Emphasis in original)

The standard Thomistic line then is that determinate extension is an accident that is not essential to the compound substance, not entailed by its mere existence. Determinate extension comes to be possessed upon the substance receiving some external causal influence that causes in it determinate extension. Of course, Owens and other Thomists would readily affirm that in the normal state of things, objects compounded out of prime matter and substantial form only exist qua extended/shaped/with some determinate size etc. Nevertheless they also affirm that in theory, they don't have to; they could exist without these determinate accidents being specified, and thus devoid of actual geometrical properties (as opposed to the mere potential for them, which would count as a necessary property grounded directly by the substantial form). In theory at least, actual geometrical accidents could be removed and the substance remain in existence. For reasons already laid out in the previous section, that alone suffices to render this substance ontology incompatible with metaphysical naturalism.

A potential complication: the example of gold might not be the best one to use here, since gold, of its nature, is what older Thomists would have called a 'mixtum,' a substance compounded from the mixture of other, lower-level substances, and ultimately the elements. Consequently, gold might be a poor candidate for a substance that could exist in unextended form, insofar as, by its very definition, it is a composite of smaller substances and thus, presumably, essentially extended. The best (only?) example of a substance that could exist in unextended form may well be the elements—for early Thomists that meant earth, air, fire, and water, for today's Thomists it would mean perhaps electrons, quarks, or strings, or fields, or whatever the genuinely fundamental physical entities are supposed to be in physics.

Conclusion

With justifications of premises 2 and 3 having now been offered, and premise 1 in need of no supporting argument, we seem to have at least some decent reasons for affirming our conclusion: whatever version of hylomorphism one is working with (whether one on which prime matter can exist independently or one in which it cannot), hylomorphism will come out incompatible with metaphysical naturalism.

As noted earlier, there are still other strategies one might employ to argue that hylomorphism is incompatible with metaphysical naturalism, strategies not considered here. For instance, some believe that any kind of realism about universals (even the immanent, Aristotelian realism of the Scholastics) is incompatible with metaphysical naturalism, and in fact the desire to buttress physicalism has historically been a motivation for nominalism (though of course nominalism is itself arguably compatible with theism and other forms of metaphysical nonnaturalism, as the many nominalist theists in philosophical history would attest). Or consider the work of Peterson, who provides still another distinct route to the incompatibility conclusion.[17] Still, hopefully the argument made here can be seen as at least a promising original strategy to that same conclusion, even if a far from decisive one.[18]

Concordia University of Edmonton

Notes

Versions of this paper were presented at the Dominican Colloquium (at the Berkeley DSPT) in summer 2014, the 2015 conference of the American Maritain Association, and of course the 2015 ACPA. I'd like to thank all three audiences for constructive feedback, most especially my ACPA commentator, Erin Stackle. Work on this project was completed thanks in part to generous funding from the Canada Research Chairs program, for which I am grateful to the government and taxpayers of Canada.

1. For Scholastic readers: take 'properties' here as neutral between necessary accidents ('propria') and contingent accidents.

2. Recent advocates include David Armstrong, *A World of States of Affairs* (Cambridge: Cambridge University Press, 1997); C. B. Martin, "Substance Substantiated," *Australasian Journal of Philosophy* 58 (1980): 3–10; J. P. Moreland, "Theories of Individuation: A Reconsideration of Bare Particulars," *Pacific Philosophical Quarterly* 79 (1998): 251–263; and Timothy Pickavance, "Bare Particulars and Exemplification," *American Philosophical Quarterly* 51 (2014): 95–108.

3. See for instance Keith Campbell, *Abstract Particulars* (Oxford: Blackwell, 1990); Peter Simons, "Particulars in Particular Clothing: Three Trope Theories of Substance," *Philosophy and Phenomenological Research* 54 (1994): 553–575; and David Robb, "Qualitative Unity and the Bundle Theory," *Monist* 88 (2005): 466–492.

4. Consult for instance Brian Ellis, *Scientific Essentialism* (Cambridge: Cambridge University Press, 2001); John Heil, *From an Ontological Point of View* (Oxford: Oxford University Press, 2003); Michael Loux, *Metaphysics: A Contemporary Introduction*, 2nd ed. (London: Routledge, 2002); and E. J. Lowe, *The Four-Category Ontology: A Metaphysical Foundation for Natural Science* (Oxford: Oxford University Press, 2006).

5. Recent proponents of hylomorphism include W. Norris Clarke S.J., *The One and the Many: A Contemporary Thomistic Metaphysics* (Notre Dame: University of Notre Dame Press, 2001); Edward Feser, *Scholastic Metaphysics: A Contemporary Introduction* (Editiones

Scholasticae, 2014); James Madden, *Mind, Matter, and Nature: A Thomistic Proposal for the Philosophy of Mind* (Washington, DC: Catholic University of America Press, 2013); and David Oderberg, *Real Essentialism* (London: Routledge, 2007). They are all advocates of Thomistic hylomorphism, the version most commonly defended today. However, historically there have been other important versions of the theory within the Scholastic tradition; further, a number of newer alternate versions of hylomorphism have appeared in the analytic metaphysics and philosophy of mind literatures, such as those of Peter Forrest, "The Operator Theory of Instantiation," *Australasian Journal of Philosophy* 84 (2006): 213–228, and William Jaworski, *Philosophy of Mind A Comprehensive Introduction* (New York: Blackwell, 2011).

6. This is best stated in terms of objects rather than properties, as there are some self-identified physicalists who attempt to argue that physicalism is compatible with the existence of some non-physical properties; this is evident in some of the recent literature in philosophy of mind, specifically assorted versions of non-reductive 'materialism' and emergentism. While I would be inclined to dispute the claim that these are legitimately physicalist theories (hence the scare quotes in the last sentence), I do not wish to take up this issue here, and so will define metaphysical naturalism in a less controversial manner, as a thesis about the unreality of immaterial/spiritual objects. That is at least an uncontroversial 'common denominator' affirmation amongst self-identified physicalists.

7. This modal proposition is required in order to rule out certain scenarios that the truth of metaphysical naturalism is intuitively supposed to rule out. If one claims to be a metaphysical naturalist in good standing since one affirms that all real objects past and present are physical, and yet also believes that it is entirely possible for a rock to be transformed into a ghost, then one's bona fides as a metaphysical naturalist would properly be questioned.

8. For detailed discussion of how exactly to formulate metaphysical naturalism (the precise contours of which are, predictably, a matter of dispute), see for instance Michael Rea *World Without Design: The Ontological Consequences of Naturalism* (Oxford: Oxford University Press, 2002); and Stewart Goetz and Charles Taliaferro, *Naturalism* (Grand Rapids, MI: Eerdmans, 2008).

9. The broader project consists in trying to explicate and defend the following argument:

> **Premise 1**: Substances are real, and the four principal substance ontologies (substratum theory, bundle theory, primitive substance theory, and hylomorphism) are the only potentially workable substance ontologies.
>
> **Premise 2**: Each of those four principal substance ontologies is incompatible with metaphysical naturalism.
>
> **Conclusion**: Therefore metaphysical naturalism is false.

The present paper is thus a stab at providing part of the justification of premise 2 of *this* argument.

10. For a helpful summary of some of these debates and a look at the variety of specific proposals involved see especially Robet Pasnau, *Metaphysical Themes: 1274–1671* (Oxford: Oxford University Press, 2011), esp. pages 35–76. I will just note that there were a few Scholastics (among them Ockham) who attributed to hyle inherent properties, in his case spatial extension. In doing so he departed quite far from his predecessors, who stressed the nature of hyle as tied up with potency and as devoid of properties (however else it is characterized or understood). He also departed from hylomorphism as it has here been defined,

and Pasnau rightly recognizes Ockham's view as a bridge to the very different ontology of material substance seen among the early modern corpuscularians.

11. For a recent, compelling argument to the effect that spatial location is required for materiality see Ned Markosian, "What are Physical Objects?" *Philosophy and Phenomenological Research* 61 (2000): 375–396. See also E. J. Lowe, "Primitive Substances," *Philosophy and Phenomenological Research* 54 (1994): 531–552, and Travis Dumsday, "Why Pan-Dispositionalism is Incompatible with Metaphysical Naturalism," *International Journal for Philosophy of Religion* 78 (2015): 107–122, who argue that extension is a precondition for location (in line with Aristotle, who presses the same point in *On Generation and Corruption*, bk. 1, ch. 2, 316b5–7).

12. J. L. Mackie, *Ethics: Inventing Right and Wrong* (Harmondsworth: Penguin, 1977).

13. See David Chalmers, "The Puzzle of Conscious Experience," *Scientific American* (1995): 80–86.

14. See for instance the clear presentation provided of this strategy in Edward Feser, "Existential Inertia and the Five Ways," *American Catholic Philosophical Quarterly* 85 (2011): 237–267.

15. By 'formal increase' he just means a substantial change, a shift to membership in some higher natural kind. Thus I can gain weight (expanding the girth of my *corpus*) without thereby becoming a member of a different, higher species.

16. Joseph Owens, *An Elementary Christian Metaphysics* (Houston: Center for Thomistic Studies, 1985), 167.

17. John Peterson, "The Dilemma of Materialism," *International Philosophical Quarterly* 39 (1999): 429–437.

18. And if the present argument is sound, we will have made some progress in the gradual support of the larger case against metaphysical naturalism noted in the Introduction. I will not attempt to preview in any detail how other elements of that larger case are to proceed; I will just observe briefly that the arguments employed in this paper with respect to hylomorphism are in fact broadly applicable (with suitable adjustments) to substratum theory. E.g., independently existent substrata would likewise not fit into a physicalistic paradigm, while substrata co-dependent on properties will require an external cause to input those properties and to account for why those specific properties were inputted rather than others.

Robert Spaemann's Approach to Ethical Analysis

Alexander Schimpf

Abstract: The essay identifies and explains four prominent features of Robert Spaemann's approach to applied ethical analysis: recollection of the origins of ethical dilemmas, assignment of the burden of proof, appeals to shared ethical intuitions, and references to the reality of the human person. The article concludes with a brief assessment of the potential merits and demerits of Spaemann's approach.

Introduction

In this essay, we will discuss some important features of Robert Spaemann's approach to the ethical analysis of specific moral dilemmas. As Holger Zaborowski has written, Spaemann's philosophy tends to have, on the whole, a "discursive and investigative character."[1] We agree with Zaborowski, yet we think more can be said about the particular form that "discursive and investigative character" takes in Spaemann's large body of work in applied ethics. Specifically, we would like to draw attention to four hallmarks of Spaemann's mode of ethical assessment: his attention to the origins of ethical dilemmas, his formulations of the burden of proof, his argumentation drawing upon common ethical intuitions, and his references to the reality of the human person. After examining each of these characteristics, we will conclude with a brief consideration of the possible advantages and disadvantages of this approach to ethical analysis.

The Origins of Ethical Dilemmas

One of Spaemann's signature moves in his ethical assessments is to explore what we might call the genealogy of moral problems. The character of the investigation varies to some degree. Sometimes Spaemann traces what we might call the "philosophical genealogy" of ethical dilemmas, those currents of thought that give rise to new ethical challenges.[2] For example, in a 1974 article on abortion, Spaemann sees the position of his opponent, Giselher Rüpke, as emblematic of modernity's larger quest to rid itself of the constraints of nature.[3] Spaemann makes a similar move in his more recent 2012 piece in *Die Zeit* on the issue of infant circumcision. He suggests that the real motivation behind the decision of a regional court in Cologne to treat

©2016, *Proceedings of the ACPA*, Vol. 89
doi: 10.5840/acpaproc201612553

circumcision as a punishable offense was not any concern about physical injury to children.[4] Rather, the decision reflects a powerful trend in the Western world, a quest for absolute self-determination—or as the piece's title puts it, "fatelessness" (*Schicksallosigkeit*).[5]

However, in Spaemann's applied ethics, this method of "genealogical investigation" sometimes has a different, more practical character. Spaemann identifies concrete historical circumstances—not merely currents of thought—that contribute to the formation of particular ethical dilemmas. For example, in a 2011 interview about nuclear power, when asked by an interviewer why the generation of energy from nuclear fission could be considered morally problematic, Spaemann does not immediately respond with an analytic-style philosophical argument. Instead, he offers a genealogical consideration: "Nuclear power had a military beginning: the nuclear bomb."[6] In a 1988 piece about abortion, Spaemann points out that the initial attempts to legalize abortion in America and Germany were aided by the deliberate spread of false information concerning abortion rates and damage to women's health: "Fraud stood at the beginning of the matter."[7] In his discussions of the neurological criteria for determining human death (i.e., "brain death"), Spaemann says that the criteria's acceptance in Germany owed a great deal to the influence of transplantation surgeons—that is, to those with a vested interest in the use of the criteria.[8] On that same topic, Spaemann also finds something problematic in the motivations of the Ad Hoc Committee of the Harvard Medical School, whose 1968 formulation of the neurological criteria for death has since met with wide acceptance.[9] As Spaemann says, the Committee seems interested in securing legal immunity for discontinuing life-prolonging measures and facilitating the collection of organs for transplantation—yet the Committee seems strangely uninterested in the welfare of the patients in question.[10]

It might be objected that such historical considerations should have little place in ethical analysis. This technique of Spaemann's could be seen as a failure to achieve the sort of *epochē* that ought to characterize philosophy.[11] That is, instead of thinking through the issues themselves in due abstraction, Spaemann's references to the sordid origins of many debatable ethical practices could seem like philosophical "cheap shots." These genealogical considerations could be seen as a variant of the fallacy of guilt by association: "Because nuclear weapons are associated with war and death, nuclear power is morally evil."

However, we should note that Spaemann does not draw substantive conclusions about the moral character of ethical problems from these genealogical considerations. His recollection of the origins of ethical problems typically has a more modest aim: the assignment of the burden of proof in regard to these difficult matters. As he says in the context of his discussion of the neurological criteria of death: "The fact that a certain hypothesis regarding the death of a human being is in the interest of other people who would benefit from the verification of this hypothesis does not prove its falsity. It should cause us, however, to be extremely critical, and it requires setting the burden of proof for the hypothesis very high."[12]

In fact, we might even recommend Spaemann's approach as a welcome corrective to the temptations of "fact-adverse" moral philosophy. Logical analysis is important, but it helps to remember what it is we are analyzing. In ethics, we are thinking about the actions of human beings—embodied beings, material beings. Since matter always remains a bit recalcitrant, our actions and technologies will sometimes fail to fully transcend the historical circumstances that give rise to them. There is no philosophical failure in a cautious recognition of that fact.[13]

The Burden of Proof

Another hallmark of Spaemann's approach to ethical analysis is his formulation of the burden of proof.[14] Although he admits that philosophical debate is a sort of "pleasant anarchy" in which "every monstrosity must be allowed to be brought forward," Spaemann does not seem to believe that every monstrous argument actually has an equal chance of success.[15] Argumentative success or failure typically depends on the initial distribution of the duty to give reasons—i.e., the burden of proof.[16]

Spaemann typically places the burden of proof upon those who would challenge the legal status quo, that which is "normal."[17] For example, in a 1988 article on abortion, Spaemann draws attention to the decision of the German Federal Court that unborn children are human beings. While by no means infallible, the Court's decision nevertheless places the burden of proof on those parties in the German abortion debate who would wish to deny the humanity or personhood of the fetus.[18] In a similar way, Spaemann claims in a 2006 article on nuclear power that those who wish to undo the Germany government's decision to withdraw from nuclear fission as a method of energy production have the greater argumentative obligation. Those who wish to support the status quo need only point out the problems with the opposing arguments.[19]

However, Spaemann does not grant absolute status to this presumption on behalf of the status quo. We have already seen that Spaemann is willing to reassign the burden of proof in regard to "brain death." In that particular case, the possibility that third party interests unduly influenced the debate about the issue calls the moral rightness of the status quo into question. Moreover, Spaemann seems especially willing to ignore the presumption in favor of the status quo when great goods are at stake. For example, in two of Spaemann's assessments of nuclear power, one from 1979 and another from 2011, the legal standing of nuclear power in Germany is not important to his analysis. What is important is the potential of radioactive nuclear waste to make entire habitats uninhabitable for millennia.[20] In the face of such great risks to our descendants, Spaemann assigns the argumentative burden to the proponents of nuclear power. The danger of nuclear power should be presumed, while its innocuousness must be proven.[21]

One might argue that this technique of formulating the burden of proof violates the otherwise "open-ended" character of Spaemann's philosophy. As Spaemann says, philosophy is a continuous conversation about ultimate questions.[22] However, at least in regard to applied ethics—a practical portion of philosophy—the conversation is often limited by the burden of proof. Not all questions need to be explored and not all options need to be weighed. The limitations imposed by the burden of proof sometimes even prompt Spaemann to claim that the conversation about a particular moral problem has come to an end. As he says in the first line of "Responsibility for the Unborn," his 1988 article on abortion: "The discussion about the problem that occupies us here has actually long been finished."[23]

Nevertheless, we propose a different interpretation of this technique of Spaemann's. In a paradoxical way, this attention to the burden of proof actually helps give his ethical analyses an "investigative," exploratory quality. By formulating the burden of proof, Spaemann is typically enabled to arrive more quickly at a decision about the moral character of issues. He does not have to "start from scratch," explaining and weighing all the possible arguments and counterarguments. As a result, Spaemann is free to turn his attention to other important matters related to the moral problems being examined.

Spaemann's ethical analyses of abortion are a case in point. Having placed the burden of proof on the proponents of abortion (or at least those among them who would assign some date later than conception as the beginning of human personhood), Spaemann is quickly able to reach a moral conclusion.[24] The evidence for the continuity of the development of the embryo is too strong; there is no plausible point, post-conception, to say that "something" becomes "someone."[25] Abortion must therefore be held to be morally wrong. Yet reaching this conclusion does not bring to a close Spaemann's philosophical consideration of the issue. Instead, he considers and criticizes opposing arguments.[26] He explores the various sophistries that are employed in the public debate about abortion.[27] He clarifies the teaching of St. Thomas Aquinas on the situation of a mistaken conscience.[28] He even challenges the involvement of Catholic counselors in legally mandatory pre-abortion counseling in Germany—a practice that the Church has since discontinued.[29] In short, Spaemann's ethical analyses of abortion address a host of important issues surrounding the practice. The same holds true for Spaemann's analyses of nuclear power, genetic manipulation, and brain death (to name but a few issues). We contend that Spaemann has the time and space to explore ancillary issues in his ethical assessments precisely because of the "intellectually economizing" effect of formulating the burden of proof.

Argumentation Based on Shared Moral Intuition

A third hallmark of Spaemann's approach to ethical analysis is his frequent recourse to moral intuition. However, the intuitions upon which Spaemann draws are not merely his own idiosyncratic responses to reality; rather, Spaemann likes to anchor his argumentation in intuitions that are more widespread and enduring, moral intuitions that he believes are common to humanity.[30] As Richard Schenk says, "In these and many other public debates, Spaemann demonstrates an uncommon ability to argue with clarity from often overlooked, common convictions and shared ethical intuitions for the superiority of what are often minority positions."[31]

What are some examples of these "shared ethical convictions" that figure so prominently in Spaemann's ethical analyses? As our space here is limited, we must be content only to point out a few of the main thematic groups into which they fall. There is, first of all, an intuitive preference for human life. For example, Spaemann argues that there is no such thing as a "pressure-free" situation with regard to abortion. "What is worse, the pressure of an environment for the killing of children, or the pressure of laws in support of life?"[32] As Spaemann goes on to say, "The question answers itself as soon as it is asked."[33] Though life is not the highest value—i.e., Spaemann is not a "vitalist"—it is nevertheless the case that for human beings, Spaemann believes that life must generally "trump" death. One finds a similar consideration in the closing paragraph of Spaemann's essay on "brain death" in *Love and the Dignity of Human Life*: in cases of doubt, we ought to give preference to life (*in dubio pro vita*).[34] Here, and in some of his assessments of nuclear power, Spaemann expresses not only a preference for life over death, but also for life over human action, the exercise of freedom. As he explains elsewhere, life is the essential precondition of every action, every exercise of self-determination.[35] As such, we cannot rationally justify actions that would intentionally destroy life: "All our justifying reasons ultimately presuppose life."[36]

Other shared ethical intuitions invoked by Spaemann concern the moral necessity of recognizing limits. For example, one of Spaemann's arguments against "ameliorative" genetic manipulation, genetic interventions aimed at improving the human race, is that the betterment of the human species is entrusted to a particular (*bestimmten*) group of human scientists. Expecting good to come from such an arrangement is, as Spaemann says, absurd (*abwegig*); that is, it should strike us as intuitively incorrect.[37] The scientists have obviously taken upon themselves too large of a task.[38] One finds another example of the intuitive necessity of recognizing limits in Spaemann's assessments of abortion. Spaemann objects to the way in which legalized abortion places a mother "on the spot," making her morally responsible for the life or the death of her child. Asking a mother to accept such responsibility is, as Spaemann says, a violation of her dignity, a "degradation" (*Erniedrigung*).[39] The legal possibility of abortion degrades the mother by placing her in a situation that neither she, nor any other human person, is equipped to deal with: "To make the human being into the lord of life and death fundamentally overtaxes him."[40]

A third group of common ethical intuitions has to do with our perception of an *ordo amoris*, an objective order of love that prevails among human beings (and even extends to non-living objects, to some degree).[41] As Zaborowski explains this point, "According to Spaemann, philosophy properly serves to recall an immediate and self-evident knowledge whenever social practice ceases to be aware of it, . . . the (self-evident) *ordo amoris*—the order of particular responsibilities, for instance."[42] While the order of love is a way of explaining why our primary obligations are to our families and friends, the moral thought of mankind has recognized that situations of dependency also create moral claims. Dependency establishes a place for the needy person within the order of love that ought to guide our actions. One finds a clear example of this latter sense of the order of love in Spaemann's assessment of the destructive use of embryos: "We cannot justify to any human being that we tried to kill him when he was still dependent on us."[43] The fact that the embryo in vitro has no hope of survival without help from other humans gives the embryo more of a claim on us, not less. Intuitive appeals to the order of love also help Spaemann show why neither a favorable calculus of probability nor current energy requirements can fully justify the use of nuclear fission to produce energy. As he says, "When a man in a life-threatening emergency wagers the life of his child, he acts irresponsibly even if the chance of winning the wager is 99:1 in his favor."[44]

The Being of the Human Person

A fourth—and in our opinion, most important—characteristic of Spaemann's approach to ethical analysis is his technique of evaluating issues in light of the being of the human person.[45] One wishes to avoid absolute statements in regard to writers as prolific as Spaemann; however, we can say there are few moral issues Spaemann treats at any significant length without some reference to the reality of the person. The being of person serves as the ultimate theoretic basis for his applied ethics. The person is the touchstone of his applied ethical thought, the standard according to which practices are ultimately judged.

Spaemann does not understand the human person as some sort of disembodied consciousness that is created by memory or by societal recognition. The human person is instead a natural, embodied being—yet a being who relates freely to his own finite nature: he "has" his nature.[46] This idea of the person as a free relation to a nature may be seen in one of Spaemann's criticisms of suicide and voluntary euthanasia. One reason such practices are wrong is that they undo the harmony of nature and freedom in the human person. Freedom gets turned against nature, creating a sort of ontological contradiction in the person: "[Suicide] splits the human being into an acting part, i.e., the killing part, and a passive part which gets eliminated and drags the one acting along with it into this extinction. . . . it is the extreme form of the non-identity of human beings."[47] Human freedom is also important to some of Spaemann's critiques of genetic manipulation. Interventions into the human genetic code, especially any interventions that would aim at "improving" the human being, would preemptively and arbitrarily curtail the freedom of the person. As Spaemann asks, "What is a desirable human being? Should he be more intelligent or happier? Or more warm-hearted, creative, easily satisfied, robust, sensitive? One only has to pose the questions to recognize their absurdity."[48] A similar offense against freedom would occur in human cloning, along with an additional problem: the clone's freedom would be restricted by having the openness of his future taken from him. The life of the "original" person, the one who was cloned, would place unjust pressures and expectations on the clone.[49]

With regard to the issue of abortion, it is not freedom that is important, but rather the nature that is freely possessed: personhood is located in human nature, and the continuous development of the embryo offers clear evidence that human nature begins at conception.[50] Spaemann admits that this same sense of a union between human person and human nature motivates his critique of Edward Furton's defense of the neurological criteria of human death: "Furton's primarily philosophical arguments in favor of "brain death" convinced me more than anything else of the opposite of his position. . . . Furton is only able to sustain his thesis of "brain death" as the death of the human being by distinguishing between the death of the human being as a person and the death of the human being as a living being."[51]

Relating freely to their natures makes persons self-transcendent, intersubjective beings. As Spaemann says often, "Persons exist only in the plural."[52] It is this intersubjective nature of the human person that is important to Spaemann's criticism of the destructive use of embryos. As rationally intersubjective, we are capable of recognizing certain actions as being in the interest of an embryo, or as violating that interest, even though the embryo cannot speak for itself. As Spaemann says, "What matters is whether the perspective of a being should count, wherever a being exists, and whether or not it also belongs to the community of persons."[53] The intersubjectivity of persons also provides the theoretic basis for Spaemann's criticisms of nuclear power. After all, one might grant Spaemann's particular criticisms of nuclear power, yet still ask why one should care about the danger posed to one's descendants by radioactive nuclear waste. Spaemann grounds the obligation in what we are as persons. We are not atomized individuals. Instead, the community of persons is spread across time: "Unless every generation considers itself a member in a generational community of solidarity—with obligations to those before and to those after—there can be no life on earth."[54]

Conclusion

In this paper we have identified four important aspects of Spaemann's approach to ethical analysis: his attention to the philosophical and historical origins of ethical dilemmas, his formulation of the burden of proof, his appeal to common ethical intuitions as part of his argumentation, and finally his grounding of ethical analysis in the reality of the person. It seems appropriate to end our exposition with two brief points of evaluation. What is a possible advantage of Spaemann's method of ethical analysis, and what is a possible disadvantage?

We would suggest that this method of ethical analysis is well-suited to "public intellectuals" such as Spaemann, those philosophers who wish to take part in the contemporary debates concerning moral dilemmas. Contributions to newspapers and other popular periodicals must often be severely limited in size, and the readership may lack philosophical sophistication. Spaemann's approach to ethical analysis successfully addresses both of these problems to some degree. As we have argued, Spaemann's technique of formulating the burden of proof allows him to reduce complex moral problems to more manageable sizes, and his recollection of the origins of ethical dilemmas often provides crucial evidence that he has not arbitrarily placed the burden of proof upon his opponents. His appeal to commonly-held ethical intuitions helps his readers to see what goods are at stake in the various ethical dilemmas, and his appeal to the reality of the person imparts a measure of depth to the analysis: Spaemann's ethical assessments are not simply "op-eds," for they are grounded in an unchanging truth, the reality of the human person.

However, Spaemann's approach to ethical analysis might not contribute as successfully to the contemporary philosophical discussion of these issues. Since Spaemann typically understands his opponents to bear the burden of proof, he allows his own argumentation to become condensed in some spots. As Spaemann's translators Guido de Graaff and James Mumford say, "There are moments when Spaemann's dance is hard to follow."[55] An even more obvious and serious problem occurs in Spaemann's appeals to commonly-held intuitions, whether ethical or ontological in nature (i.e., the being of the person): namely, not all philosophers hold such intuitions in high esteem, philosophically speaking.[56] It may be that agreement with Spaemann's conclusions in applied ethics will ultimately depend on some shared understanding of how philosophy itself ought to proceed—and consensus on that question is notoriously difficult to achieve.

St. Gregory's University

Notes

1. Holger Zaborowski, *Robert Spaemann's Philosophy of the Human Person: Nature, Freedom, and the Critique of Modernity* (New York: Oxford University Press, 2010), 28.

2. Richard Schenk identifies such investigation as a characteristic of Spaemann's philosophy as a whole: "Spaemann begins a program of historical pathology, not altogether unlike Heidegger's deconstruction of the history of philosophy, tracing back counterproductive developments to their origins." Richard Schenk, "The Ethics of Robert Spaemann in the Context of Recent Philosophy," in *One Hundred Years of Philosophy*, ed. Brian Shanley, O.P. (Washington, DC: The Catholic University of America Press, 2001), 160.

3. "Die Richtung dieser Veränderung heißt 'Emanzipation des Menschen von den Zwängen der Natur.'" Robert Spaemann, *Grenzen: Zur ethischen Dimension des Handelns* (Stuttgart: Klett-Cotta, 2001), 364.

4. "Es steckt aber hinter dem Urteil und vor allem hinter der Argumentation seiner öffentlichen Verteidiger noch ein anderes Motiv, das meines Erachtens sogar das eigentliche ist, denn man kann einfach dem Gericht nicht unterstellen, die folgenlose Körperverletzung ernsthaft für so gravierend zu halten." Robert Spaeman, "Der Traum von der Schicksallosigkeit," *Die Zeit*, May 7, 2012, available at http://www.zeit.de/2012/28/Beschneidung/seite-2.

5. "Das eigentliche, das Hintergrundargument scheint mir zu sein, dass religiöse Erziehung von Kindern überhaupt verschwinden müsse, weil sie die spätere religiöse Selbstbestimmung präjudiziere und beeinträchtige." Spaemann, "Der Traum," http://www.zeit.de/2012/28/Beschneidung/seite-2.

6. "Es hat mit der Atomkraft ja militärisch begonnen: mit der Atombombe." Robert Spaemann, *Nach uns die Kernschmelze: Hybris im atomaren Zeitalter* (Stuttgart: Klett-Cotta, 2011), 101.

7. "Am Anfang der Sache stand Betrug." Spaemann, *Grenzen*, 369.

8. Robert Spaemann, "Ars Longa, Vita Brevis," in *Ethics of Biomedical Research in a Christian Vision*, ed. Juan De Dios Vial Correa and Elio Sgreccia, 109, available at http://www. academiavita.org/_pdf/assemblies/09/ethics_of_biomedical_research_in_a_christian_vision. pdf.

9. Ad Hoc Committee of the Harvard Medical School, "A Definition of Irreversible Coma: Report of the Ad Hoc Committee of the Harvard Medical School to Examine the Definition of Brain Death," *Journal of the American Medical Association* 205 (1968): 85–88.

10. See Robert Spaemann, *Love and the Dignity of Human Life: On Nature and Natural Law* (Grand Rapids, MI: William B. Eerdmanns, 2012), 49–50.

11. For a brief discussion of how the shift into philosophical analysis involves a sort of *epochē*, a "bracketing" of our natural intentionality, see Robert Sokolowski, *Introduction to Phenomenology* (New York: Cambridge University Press, 2000), 49–50.

12. Robert Spaemann, *Love and the Dignity of Human Life*, 50.

13. Inasmuch as "grace builds on nature," attention to the origins of ethical dilemmas could also be useful to moral theology. A good example of this may be found in Spaemann's recent article on "Divorce and Remarriage" for *First Things*. Spaemann suggests that it is not deeper insight into the truths of the faith that is motivating the new interest in readmitting divorced Catholics to Holy Communion. Instead, he sees the interest in regularizing so-called "second marriages" as arising from the high Catholic divorce rate and the weakness of some Catholic prelates. See Robert Spaemann, "Divorce and Remarriage," *First Things* (August 2014), available at http://www.firstthings.com/article/2014/08/divorce-and-remarriage.

14. As Spaemann says in *Philosophische Essays*, the distribution of the burden of proof is the most decisive factor in regard to nearly all philosophical questions. However, we find that Spaemann is especially attentive to assigning the burden of proof in the most practical part of his philosophy, his applied ethical assessments. See Robert Spaemann, *Philosophische Essays: Erweiterte Ausgabe* (Stuttgart: Reclam, 1994), 49.

15. Robert Spaemann, "Begotten, Not Made," trans. Michelle K. Borras, *Communio* 33 (Summer 2006): 294–295.

16. See Spaemann, "Der Traum," http://www.zeit.de/2012/28/Beschneidung; Spaemann, *Nach uns*, 86; and Robert Spaemann, "About Normality," in *Close by the Incurable Sick Person and the Dying: Scientific and Ethical Aspects*, ed. Elio Sgreccia and Jean Laffitte, 217, available at http://www.academiavita.org/_pdf/assemblies/14/close_by_the_incur-able_sick_person_and_the_dying.pdf.

17. Spaemann's preferential option for established normality seems to have a practical motivation: life would be made impossible if we had to constantly prove and re-prove the rightness of the status quo. See Spaemann, "Der Traum," http://www.zeit.de/2012/28/Beschneidung.

18. Spaemann, *Grenzen*, 368.

19. Spaemann, *Nach uns*, 86. Spaemann's sense of the burden of proof helps to explain the defensive and somewhat "skeptical" character of many of his arguments in applied ethics. He does not feel a need to make a positive case for his position.

20. See Spaemann, *Nach uns*, 104.

21. "Nicht die Schädlichkeit, sondern die Unschädlichkeit muss glaubhaft gemacht werden." Spaemann, *Nach uns*, 46.

22. See Spaemann, *Philosophische Essays*, 106.

23. "Die Diskussion um das Problem, das uns hier beschäftigt, ist eigentlich seit langem beendet." Spaemann, *Grenzen*, 367. In our interpretation, Spaemann does not mean that people no longer debate abortion. Rather, he means that the "debate" is intellectually sterile. It is difficult to say anything original in regard to abortion: the important philosophical options have already been identified.

24. "Jeder, der glaubt, eine zeitliche Grenze für den Anfang der personalen Existenz des Menschen angeben zu können, eine Grenze, die später liegt als der Augenblick der Zeugung, trägt dafür die Beweislast." Spaemann, *Grenzen*, 368.

25. "Aber dieser Beweislast kann er nicht genügen. Denn angesichts der strikten Kontinuität der Entwicklung menschlichen Lebens können wir einen Anfang des Personseins überhaupt nicht fixieren." Spaemann, *Grenzen*, 368.

26. See Spaemann, *Grenzen*, 355–359.

27. One such sophistry involves a failure to distinguish an action about which the conscience is silent from an action commanded by the conscience. See Spaemann, *Grenzen*, 378. Another sophistry consists in claiming that one bears no moral culpability for the misuse of the "Schein," the certificate indicating the requirement of pre-abortion counseling has been fulfilled. As Spaemann points out, the certificate has only one possible use—the procurement of abortion. See Spaemann, *Grenzen*, 386.

28. See Spaemann, *Grenzen*, 389.

29. See Spaemann, *Grenzen*, 377–380 and 386–387. In 1998 Pope John Paul II asked the German clergy to stop issuing the certificate showing pre-abortion counseling had taken place. Furthermore, in 2007 the Congregation for the Doctrine of the Faith also asked the German bishops to distance themselves from a group called Donum Vitae that operated abortion counseling centers associated, to some extent, with the Catholic Church.

30. One finds, in Spaemann's writings, an attentiveness to what G. K. Chesterton calls the "democracy of the dead," the moral tradition of humanity spread across time. See G. K. Chesterton, *Orthodoxy*, available at http://www.leaderu.com/cyber/books/orthodoxy/ch4.html.

31. Richard Schenk, "Encomium to Robert Spaemann," *Nova et Vetera* 7, no. 4 (2009): 765.

32. "Was ist aber schlimmer: der Druck der Umgebung zur Tötung des Kindes oder der Druck des Gesetzes zugunsten des Lebens? Spaemann, *Grenzen*, 359. In our interpretation, Spaemann's point is that the existential challenges of parenthood create a pressure towards abortion, wherever abortion is legal.

33. "Die Frage stellen heißt sie beantworten." Spaemann, *Grenzen*, 359.

34. Spaemann, *Love and the Dignity of Human Life*, 69.

35. See Robert Spaemann, "Death—Suicide—Euthanasia," in *The Dignity of the Dying Person: Proceedings of the Fifth Assembly of the Pontifical Academy for Life (Vatican City, February 24–27, 1999)*, ed. Juan de Dios Vial Correa and Elio Sgreccia, 123–131 (Città del Vaticano: Libreria Editrice Vaticana, 2000), 127.

36. Spaemann, "Death—Suicide—Euthanasia," 128.

37. "Daß es zu etwas Gutem führen könne, wenn einer bestimmten lebenden Generationen von Wissenschaftlern und ihrer Vorstellung von dem, was ein wünschenswerter Mensch ist, die weitere Evolution der Gattung anvertraut würde, ist eine abwegige Idee." Spaemann, *Grenzen*, 409.

38. Spaemann explains the problem through an economic analogy: entrusting the progress of human nature to a select group of scientists is akin to preferring a planned economy to a market economy. In both cases, there is a culpable blindness to the obvious fact that human intelligence and action is limited, especially in comparison to the nearly countless interactions and adjustments that take place in a free market and in nature. See Spaemann, *Grenzen*, 408–409, and Spaemann, "Begotten, Not Made," 290–291.

39. Spaemann, *Grenzen*, 374.

40. "Den Menschen zum Herrn über Leben und Tod machen heißt ihn prinzipiell überfordern." Spaemann, *Grenzen*, 374.

41. See Robert Spaemann, *Happiness and Benevolence*, trans. Jeremiah Alberg, S.J. (Notre Dame, IN: University of Notre Dame Press, 2000), 118.

42. Zaborowski, *Robert Spaemann's Philosophy of the Human Person*, 54.

43. "Keinem Menschen gegenüber aber können wir es rechtfertigen, dass wir versucht haben, ihn, als er noch von uns abhängig war, umzubringen." Robert Spaemann, "Freiheit der Forschung oder Schutz des Embryos?" *Die Zeit*, November 20, 2003, http://www.zeit.de/2003/48/Retortenbabies/.

44. "Wenn ein Mensch in einer existenzbedrohenden Not das Leben seines Kindes verwettet, handelt er auch unverantwortlich, selbst wenn die Gewinnschancen bei dieser Wette für ihn 99:1 stehen." Spaemann, foreword to *Nach uns*, 8.

45. "Parallel to the common language school, Spaemann's is a philosophy of the common ontology of the person and the common moral intuition." Schenk, "Encomium to Robert Spaemann," 765.

46. See Robert Spaemann, *Persons: The Difference between 'Someone' and 'Something,'* trans. Oliver O'Donovan (New York: Oxford University Press, 2006), 31.

47. Spaemann, "Death—Suicide—Euthanasia," 124.

48. Spaemann, "Begotten, Not Made," 291.

49. Spaemann, "Begotten, Not Made," 292. Spaemann credits Hans Jonas with first noticing the problem of the lack of an open future for clones.

50. See Spaemann, *Grenzen*, 354, 368.

51. Spaemann, *Love and the Dignity of Human Life*, 62.

52. Spaemann, *Persons*, 232.

53. "Worauf es ankommt, ist, ob dort, wo es um die Existenz eines Wesens geht, die Perspektive dieses Wesens selbst zählt, ob es also zur Gemeinschaft der Personen gehört oder nicht." Spaemann, "Freiheit der Forschung."

54. "Ohne dass sich jede Generation als Glied in einer solidarischen Gemeinschaft der Generationen betrachtet—mit Schuldigkeiten nach hinten und nach vorn—, gibt es gar kein menschliches Leben auf der Erde." Spaemann, *Nach uns*, 25.

55. Guido de Graaff and James Mumford, introduction to Robert Spaemann, *Essays in Anthropology: Variations on a Theme* (Eugene, OR: Cascade Books, 2010), xii.

56. See, for example, Derek Parfit's treatment of the human person in *Reasons and Persons*. The title of ch. 11 of Parfit's book suggests a rejection of our common ontological intuitions: "How We Are Not What We Believe." Derek Parfit, *Reasons and Persons* (Oxford: Clarendon Press, 1984).

The Limits of Double Effect

Heidi M. Giebel

Abstract. In the decades since Anscombe re-introduced the distinction between intention and foresight into philosophical ethics, supporters and critics of the related principle of double effect (PDE) have displayed disagreement and confusion about its application and scope. The key to correct interpretation and application of PDE, I argue, is recognition of its limits: (1) the principle does not include an account of the goodness or badness of effects; (2) it does not include an account of intention; (3) PDE does not specify a particular action as right or obligatory; and (4) the privacy of intention limits its application in interpersonal and legal contexts. While all four of these features are "limits" in the sense that they are things PDE does not do, I argue that (a) only the fourth is a real limitation or disadvantage of the principle—and (b) none of the limits implies that the principle should be rejected.

I. Introduction

In a perfectly just world, all and only good acts performed with good intentions would produce good (and only good) results. But as we all have experienced, and as creative philosophers have demonstrated with stories of treacherous trolleys, stuck spelunkers, and even liquefied legs,[1] our world is far from perfectly just. Sometimes we can't help but cause harm even with the best of intentions—as when we redirect a runaway trolley from a track with five trapped innocents to a track with only one. Sometimes intentionally causing harm leads to a good that seems to outweigh it—as when we liquefy a bystander's leg to cause a chemical reaction deactivating a bomb. And sometimes even a malicious act accidentally brings good results—as when we give a hated spouse medicine that we mistakenly believe to be poison.[2]

In the Catholic intellectual tradition, ethicists have long analyzed acts, intentions, and effects in our less-than-perfectly-just world via appeal to the principle of double effect (PDE). As its name suggests, PDE is used to evaluate acts having at least two morally significant effects: one good and one bad. Commonly-cited examples include military operations that accomplish legitimate objectives but result

©2016, *Proceedings of the ACPA*, Vol. 89
doi: 10.5840/acpaproc201692946

in civilian casualties, surgical procedures that save the lives of pregnant women but cause fetuses' deaths, and end-of-life care that relieves patients' pain but hastens their deaths. As traditionally understood, PDE consists of four conditions, all of which must be met for morally permissibility:[3]

    (1) Acceptable-end condition: The bad effect must not be intended as the end or goal of the act.

    (2) Acceptable-act condition: The act must not be bad in itself (independently of its causing the bad effect).

    (3) Acceptable-means condition: The bad effect must not be intended as a means to the good effect.

    (4) Proportionate-reason condition: The agent must have a proportionately serious moral reason for performing the act (i.e., at least as serious a reason to pursue the good act and/or effect as to avoid the bad effect).[4]

Although similar reasoning is found much earlier, PDE is usually thought to originate with Aquinas's discussion of killing in self-defense.[5] Although moral theologians further developed and applied the principle over the following centuries, it was largely absent from philosophical ethics until Anscombe re-introduced the distinction between intention and foresight to philosophical ethics half a century ago.[6] Since that time, moral philosophers—non-Catholic as well as Catholic—have published dozens of articles supporting and criticizing the distinction and PDE.[7] As is perhaps to be expected, these display much disagreement and a fair amount of confusion about the application and scope of PDE: e.g., some argue that the principle is unjustifiable apart from its original role in natural-law ethics;[8] others use it in a broader range of theoretical contexts.[9] While most appear inclined to apply PDE only to ethical dilemmas with especially dire consequences, a few use it more widely: as a colleague says, "Some people need the principle of double effect to get out of bed in the morning. Good effect: I get to work on time. Bad effect: I don't get to sleep in."[10] Knauer even refers to PDE as *the* basic principle of ethics.[11]

The purpose of this paper is to analyze some puzzles that have come with PDE's varying interpretations, applications, and theoretical contexts. The key to correct interpretation and application of PDE, I argue, is recognition of four main features that limit its proper use. First, PDE does not itself determine the badness of effects or the seriousness of reasons. Second, PDE does not include an account of intention. Third, it does not specify that an act is the right one—it simply determines whether an act is morally permissible. Fourth, its focus on a private aspect of human acts—intention—limits the applicability of PDE in interpersonal evaluation and especially in matters of law and policy.[12]

II. PDE and Determining Badness

One obvious limit to the principle of double effect is that while it provides guidelines for evaluating an act that brings about a bad effect, it gives no criteria for determining whether an effect is to count as bad. In fact, PDE gives no account of goodness or badness at all. The principle's user must first determine whether the effects in question are good or bad, whether her act is bad in itself, and whether her reason for acting is sufficiently good in order to determine whether her act accords with PDE.

Although PDE's lack of an account of goodness may appear to be a serious limitation, the principle's purpose is to apply an *independently-defended* account of goodness to concrete and difficult cases. In a classic example, a pilot in a just war must decide whether to help shorten the war by dropping a bomb that will almost certainly kill civilians. Given an account of goodness and badness specifying that the death of civilians is a bad effect and that shortening the war is a worthy goal, one can use PDE to determine the permissibility of dropping the bomb based on the bad effect's role (or lack thereof) in the pilot's plan. Similarly, when a physician can relieve her patient's pain only by administering a drug strong enough to hasten his death, PDE is useful for analyzing the physician's act—provided that the principle's user applies an adequate account of the ethical significance of the effects in question (causing an innocent person's death and ending his pain). The user of PDE considers not only the value of the effects themselves, but also the agent's intending (or foreseeing) them and the circumstances that provide (or fail to provide) justification for the agent's act. As these examples suggest, PDE's user must supplement it with a defensible account of the goodness or badness of various effects, acts, and ethical reasons. However, as the examples also show, given such an account, PDE has an important role to play in evaluating difficult cases, facilitating consideration of several factors relevant to act assessment.

Although I called this first limit of PDE "obvious," some philosophers appear to believe that it includes an account of the badness of certain effects. For example, Thomson apparently assumes PDE includes or entails the view that the death of an innocent person is always a bad effect and thus that intending it is always wrong.[13] She offers an example in which a doctor (Alice) has two drugs, either of which could be injected to relieve her patient's pain (call him "Bob"). Drug D could relieve Bob's pain by causing his death immediately.[14] Drug C could relieve Bob's pain by inducing a coma, which would persist until his eventual death. Thomson objects, "If PDE is correct, then Alice must choose C. But do the patient's wishes not matter? By hypothesis, if the patient is injected with C he will live longer than if he is injected with D. By hypothesis also, however, that stretch of additional life will be unconscious life, and the patient might prefer not to live it. Does morality, and should law, require him to?"[15]

Thomson appears to interpret PDE to include an analysis of the relative badness of effects according to which coma until natural death—unlike immediately-induced death—is not a bad effect. She then suggests that this may not be the case, depending upon the patient's preferences. In fact, however, none of PDE's conditions contains stipulations regarding the badness of various effects. Thus PDE does not require a particular stand on the badness of coma until natural death versus immediately-induced death—although of course it can and should be applied within a broader ethical theory that *does* require such a stand. So depending upon her account of the goodness or badness of various effects, a proponent of PDE might agree with Thomson that coma until natural death may be worse. Further, if the PDE proponent considers coma until natural death to be a significantly bad effect, whether or not it is worse than immediate death, he will not, *contra* Thomson, claim that Alice must choose to induce a coma as a means to relieving Bob's pain: Alice must *avoid* intending a bad effect as a means to a good one.

Interestingly, Thomson, along with Beauchamp and Childress,[16] argues that in some circumstances (such as the last stages of a terminal illness) death may not be a bad effect at all but may be good for an individual who is suffering. This position makes the topic of physician-assisted suicide an odd vehicle for Thomson's attempt to refute PDE: if there is no bad effect of the physician's action, the principle isn't refuted—it simply doesn't apply. On the other hand, Catholic philosopher John Finnis argues that life is a basic human good and therefore that death is always bad.[17] A fuller moral theory is needed to determine the badness of a particular effect; PDE cannot act alone. One applying PDE to her situation must already possess a defensible account of what makes an effect bad.

If PDE is in fact limited in its lack of an account of the goodness and badness of effects, acts, and reasons, an objector might claim, perhaps it should be rejected: this limitation renders it too vague to be of significant help in ethical analysis. Such a suggestion, however, fails to recognize both the mitigation of that limitation that comes with a more comprehensive theory in which to apply PDE and the utility of having a systematic decision scheme like PDE, with several conditions, as a vehicle for ethical analysis. Such a scheme clarifies the problem at hand, reveals unacceptable actions, shows constraints on acceptable actions, and provides a systematic, non-arbitrary procedure for assisting in ethical decision-making.[18] For example, in the case of the pilot with the bomb, even one who has determined both that shortening the war is good and that the death of civilians is bad needs a clear and principled strategy for evaluating the pilot's options when she realizes that the pilot cannot accomplish the former without also bringing about the latter. The principle of double effect can help her analyze the pilot's options by considering his intentions in dropping the bomb as well as the importance of shortening the war and the badness of killing civilians. Although it is true that PDE is abstract, it is not vague when considered in the context of a comprehensive ethical theory. After all, any principle must be abstract enough to have wide applicability—but this abstractness is not a defect: it is necessary to the principle's utility.

III. PDE and Accounts of Intention

In addition to its not providing an account of goodness and badness, the principle of double effect is limited by its not including an account of intention. Although PDE specifies that the agent must not intend the bad effect of her act, the principle does not give criteria for determining what she in fact intends. One must develop a defensible account of intention *before* applying PDE to concrete acts.[19]

This limit is not as problematic as one may suppose for reasons similar to those discussed in section II: PDE is not a comprehensive moral theory (or action theory); but when used in the context of a more comprehensive theory it can be of significant help in ethical analysis. Take, for example, the classic case of two bombers in a just war. The tactical bomber drops his bombs on a munitions factory, foreseeing but not intending that some nearby civilians will be killed; the terror bomber deliberately drops his bombs on civilians to terrorize the enemy and thereby shorten the war.[20] Once we have determined independently of PDE that the terror-bombing pilot intends to bring about civilians' deaths and the tactical-bombing pilot does not, we can apply PDE to show that the terror bomber acts impermissibly even if he succeeds in shortening the war—and even if he and the tactical bomber kill the same number of innocent people. Similarly, in the often-discussed case of obstetric craniotomy, a nearly-born but too-big fetus's skull is crushed in an effort to end a difficult labor and thereby save the mother from heart failure. Once we have determined whether the physician intends to harm the fetus (and whether such harm is an ethically significant bad effect) we can apply PDE to discover whether she acts permissibly.

Interestingly, despite the lack of an imbedded account of intention within PDE, there is widespread agreement among the principle's proponents and detractors (including Ford, Bratman, Thomson, and possibly Bennett[21]) that according to PDE tactical bombing is permissible and terror bombing is not. Why? There are a couple of natural interpretations of this apparent consensus: perhaps philosophers not referring to a specific account of intention are simply using a commonsense approach—and, in some cases, are mistakenly attributing their common sense to PDE. Or it may be that PDE's two intention-related conditions do give some account of intention: they specify that anything that is an agent's end or means is intended. If so, all one must do is provide definitions of "end" and "means" to show that the principle of double effect includes—or entails—an account of intention.

Although the suggestion that PDE entails an account of intention—and thus is not limited by the lack thereof—seems promising, it is less helpful than it appears. First, the terms "end" and "means" are likely no easier to define and defend than "intention" is—and the relevant account of these terms may in fact depend upon a definition of "intention." So it may not be possible to derive an account of intention from widely-accepted and non-question-begging definitions of "end" and "means." Second, PDE does not specify that *all* ends and means are intended: it says that a bad effect must not be intended *as* an end or a means. The wording of the conditions leaves open the possibility that an effect could be an agent's end or (more plausibly) a means to her end but not be intended as such. Bennett gives an example in which an effect is a means—a causal contributor—to the agent's goal but appears not to be intended: agent A wants to keep X (who is brilliant) happy in his job, so she promotes him instead of Y (who is competent). As A foresaw but did not intend, her act infuriates Y so much that he leaves the profession altogether, which further contributes to X's job satisfaction.[22] Similarly, Bratman gives a modified description of a tactical bomber: civilian casualties resulting from his strategic bombing have a (nonintended) terrorizing effect on the enemy, further contributing to the end of shortening of the war.[23] The possibility of something's being a causal means to a legitimate end, although that means does not in fact motivate the agent, shows that not all means need be intended—which, in turn, shows that PDE need not be understood to include or entail an account of intention according to which all causal means *are* intended. However, the principle's conditions regarding intention do place some restriction on the accounts of intention that can be used with PDE: e.g., it would seem incompatible with an account of intention that specified that an agent's means were *never* intended.[24]

As was the case with accounts of goodness and badness, PDE can function well despite its lack of an imbedded account of intention when applied in the context of a broader theory of action and ethics that *does* include such an account. For example, on Finnis's account, an effect is intended if it plays a role in the agent's plan of action.[25] Boyle gives a similar interpretation,[26] according to which an effect is intended if the agent's goal commits him to bringing it about and if it, "strictly speaking," serves his purposes. Both argue that in the case of obstetric craniotomy to save the mother's life, the physician need not intend to kill the fetus: the changed shape of the fetus's head rather than its death plays a role in her plan and serves her purpose of saving the mother. Bratman argues that an effect is intended if (1) it presents an occasion for deliberation, (2) it constrains other intentions, and (3) the agent endeavors to bring it about.[27] Under these criteria, the tactical bomber does not intend to bring about civilians' deaths. So while PDE does not itself define "intention," it is usefully applicable once one provides the missing definition.

Finally, the limit that a lack of an account of intention imposes on PDE is mitigated by the fact that an appeal to our common intuitions about intention—which, as noted above, seems to occur implicitly among many defenders and detractors—is often sufficient to determine whether an effect is intended. A detailed account of intention is needed primarily in especially difficult cases such as obstetric craniotomy. Thus, although not including an account of intention in PDE limits the principle in theory, it is not nearly as limiting in practice.

IV. PDE and Doing the Right Thing

A third limit of the principle of double effect is that, although it provides a useful and systematic method for determining whether a given act is *permissible*, it does not typically indicate which act is the *right* one to perform. For example, it does not tell the potential tactical bomber whether he *must* or even *should* drop his bomb on the military target; it only tells him whether he *may*. Thus the principle may prove disappointing to one looking for more guidance regarding his positive obligations.

As was the case with the first two limits discussed in this article, there are two general types of objection to my account of this limit: those suggesting that PDE is not really limited in this way and those claiming that the limit is serious enough to render PDE unhelpful. The first sort of objector might point to apparent consensus among PDE's proponents to argue that the principle often *does* specify a right act. For example, one might suggest that PDE tells a physician she must provide enough palliative medication to relieve her patient's pain even if the medication hastens his death, or that it tells a bystander at a trolley switch that he must direct a runaway trolley away from a track with five innocent (and stuck) people and onto a track with only one. In fact, Thomson seems to expect PDE to indicate the right act to perform even in a case that does not enjoy fame and consensus among PDE's proponents: as I noted in section II, she thinks PDE tells us that Alice *must* inject drug C (inducing coma) to relieve Bob's pain.[28] She also suggests that PDE plays such a role when a malicious person refuses to aid those in need because he wants them to suffer. Thomson says, "No doubt a man's refusing to aid others in order that they suffer marks him as a bad person; the refusal itself, however, may be permissible—he is not required to give aid just on the ground that his intention in refusing would be a bad one."[29] Here Thomson appears to think that PDE *does* declare giving aid to be the uniquely right thing to do, given that the man's intention in refusing would be that others suffer.

However, although acts such as administering morphine, diverting the trolley, aiding others, and perhaps even inducing coma may be the best for the agent to perform under the circumstances, PDE indicates only that they are permissible—not that they are required. Although PDE alone does not specify a right act in Thomson's cases, her conclusions are understandable: PDE may indirectly "specify" the right act by eliminating the obvious alternatives. However, specifying a unique right act is not the principle's primary role in ethics; and in fact in many cases to which PDE is applicable it does not (even indirectly) indicate that a particular act is required of an agent. As noted earlier, in the case of the tactical bomber, PDE can be used to show that dropping the bomb is permissible, but not to show that the pilot *must* drop it. Similarly, in the popular example of a hysterectomy performed on a pregnant woman with aggressive uterine cancer, PDE does not show the surgery to be required but simply indicates that the woman may undergo it: it may be permissible or even supererogatory to forgo the hysterectomy for the sake of sparing the fetus although the mother's death will result (and indeed choosing to forgo the surgery might also require PDE for justification). Even in Thomson's case of doctor Alice and patient Bob, PDE tells Alice that she *must* inject C only if:

(1) Alice would not be intending anything significantly bad in injecting C (either because she would not be intending to induce coma or because coma is not significantly bad);

(2) Alice is not doing anything that is bad in itself (independently of causing coma);

(3) Alice has a sufficiently serious moral reason for injecting C;

(4) Alice would fail to meet one or more of the above three criteria if she injected D;

(5) No other methods are available to relieve Bob's pain adequately, or Alice would fail to meet one or more of the first three criteria by using the other methods; and

(6) Alice would fail to meet one or more of the first three criteria if she did not relieve Bob's pain.

Perhaps less obviously than in the case of Alice and Bob, PDE does not necessarily dictate the right act even in the case of a man's malicious refusal to aid others (call the man "Bill"). In the case of Bill and others, it is clear that Bill's refusing to aid so that others suffer is ruled out by PDE—Bill intends the bad effect. Since aiding and not aiding seem to be exhaustive of Bill's options, Thomson concludes that PDE says Bill must aid others. However, it may be the case that Bill's aiding others is also ruled out by PDE: there may be sufficiently serious moral reasons for not aiding them. For example, Bill may need to use all of his resources to support his family, or the others may be likely to cause serious harm to Bill if aided. Does PDE then determine that Bill must act wrongly no matter what he does? Not really: Bill is responsible for his own bad intentions. If he intended simply to support his family or to avoid harm, his failure to aid others would be permissible according to PDE. Bill's seemingly tragic moral dilemma arises from his bad character. If PDE were to prescribe a right course of action, I suppose it would tell Bill to improve his attitude and keep his money.[30]

An objector (perhaps a consequentialist) might claim that given PDE's limited guidance regarding what act is morally required of an agent, the principle should be replaced with a principle that *does* tell an agent which act to perform. Ethical analysis, the objector might argue, requires principles that give more moral guidance than PDE can offer.

Although PDE typically does not dictate the right act for an agent to perform, that fact is not sufficient reason for the principle's rejection. In fact, almost no ethical principle claims to determine the right act for an agent to perform in every situation. This state of ethics seems desirable: the ethical life is likely complex enough to merit more analysis than a single principle can provide. While its not determining the right act in most situations may be considered a *limit* to the principle—something it does not do—it need not be thought of as a *limitation*. PDE's ability to determine permissibility but not (typically) to require a particular act simply may reflect the way life is. In most circumstances, even those involving significantly bad effects, we may not be morally obligated to perform one specific action. PDE allows room for multiple options and supererogation; these seem attractive in a moral theory.

A persistent objector might argue: if multiple options and supererogation are valuable in ethics, PDE's failure to distinguish among permissible options must be a disadvantage. It does not determine whether one permissible act is better than another (or whether one impermissible act is worse than another), nor does it give any indication that a permissible act may be supererogatory. Surely, my objector may continue, we can expect an ethical principle to help in making such a determination, and one that does not has a serious limitation; thus, PDE should be rejected.

The objection correctly points out PDE's incompleteness; however, although it is true that PDE does not itself determine the relative merits of acts except insofar as it determines that one act is permissible and another is not, a broader ethical theory of which PDE is a part should be able to determine the acts' relative merits or demerits. A virtue-based ethical theory may determine that although two acts both conform to PDE, one is more virtuous than the other, and hence is the better act to perform. For example, in the hysterectomy case it is permissible to undergo surgery to save one's life, but it may be more in accordance with charity or generosity to carry the pregnancy to term and save one's child instead. A deontological theory may determine that one permissible option is most in accordance with important human rights. While PDE must be supplemented with a theory that has the resources necessary to assess the relative merits of various permissible acts, this is not a reason to eliminate the principle from ethical analysis. A principle that performs some ethical tasks—especially tasks that few others can handle—should not be rejected on the grounds that it does not perform *all* ethical tasks. Besides, as already mentioned, it is far from obvious that any single principle successfully performs all ethical tasks.

V. PDE and the Law

A fourth limit of the principle of double effect is that it involves something private: the agent's intention. Thus while the principle may be highly useful in evaluation of one's own act or of hypothetical acts in which the agent's intention is stipulated, it is less helpful when one must evaluate another's act and cannot be sure of the agent's intention. This sort of difficulty may arise especially in cases of legal liability, in which one must determine whether and to what extent another person should be punished for his act. For example, it may be difficult to discover whether Bob's killing Susie was nonintentional (manslaughter), intentional but not premeditated (second-degree murder), or intentional and premeditated (first-degree murder). Although the privacy of intention creates a significant limitation for applying the principle, it is not an insurmountable obstacle in most cases. In this section I argue that despite this limit, PDE as suitably applied has significant usefulness in interpersonal and legal analysis.

PDE's defenders may argue that the privacy problem is not as limiting as I have suggested: perhaps we can usually draw reasonable conclusions regarding an agent's intentions by observing his actions. However, it is not always easy to tell what act another agent is performing. Suppose I find a colleague crouched under his desk, muttering in a language I do not understand. It is reasonable for me to ask what he is doing even though I can see and hear him. The possibilities are many: he may be searching for his lost contact lens while reciting Latvian poetry, trying to repair his computer using a manual written in Korean, or hiding from his students and attempting to cast an invisibility spell on himself. Sometimes observable behavior is insufficient for determining the agent's action: if my colleague answers my question by saying, "As you can see and hear, I've been crouching under my desk and muttering in a language you don't understand," I will not be any closer to knowing what he is doing. His unobservable intention may play a significant role in determining which of the many possible acts he is performing.

As a critic of PDE might object at this point, my response to the previous objection seems to show PDE's untenability. If intentions are both unobservable and vital for the application of PDE, he might protest, the principle is useless in evaluation of other agents. That sort of objection, however, shows excessive pessimism about the knowability of intentions. Although we cannot *always* tell what another agent intends, we need not go so far as to claim that we (almost) *never* know. We can frequently tell what another agent intends with a reasonable degree of certainty through testimony or other evidence regarding the intention in question or his related intentions. That is, an agent often (but not always) provides enough evidence to allow others to draw reasonable conclusions about his plans.[31]

Many lawmakers as well as ethicists, it seems, have drawn conclusions similar to mine regarding the knowability of others' intentions.[32] While the privacy of intention may create some difficulty for those attempting to determine culpability partly on the basis of what the agent intended in acting, the law in many countries does in fact take account of intention. As Hart points out,[33] the intent of the accused is often considered relevant both in conviction (or acquittal) and at sentencing. For example, as I noted in the example of Bob's killing Susie, we distinguish between murder and manslaughter on the basis of the criminal's intentions. Because ethical and legal assessment based at least partly upon evaluation of the agent's intention is so common, we may reasonably suppose that the privacy problem can be overcome at least to some extent. How? Easiest would be the agent's disclosure of his own intention; but of course, if we suspect him of criminal behavior we may have no reason to believe his claim that he intended no harm. Also fairly easy would be (reliable) testimony of others: e.g., accomplices or friends aware of his plans. Given reliable testimony, applying PDE to criminal cases may not be especially problematic.[34]

Of course, matters are not always so simple. Often a court must rely on less direct evidence of the agent's intentions. Previous malicious behavior may be indirect evidence, as may items found among the agent's possessions (e.g., corporate memos, threatening letters, browsing history, or a collection of deadly weapons). In especially difficult cases, with little or no evidence of the agent's intention, PDE's acceptable-end and acceptable-means conditions are not very helpful unless we make questionable assumptions—which we want to avoid doing when things like lives and freedom are at stake.

Of the paradigmatic acts taken to be forbidden by PDE, however, only active euthanasia presents a significant problem regarding privacy of the agent's intention: a physician administering a drug may appear to intend only to relieve her patient's pain, although she actually intends to kill him. But this problem arises only if (a) the physician is using a painkiller and (b) she is not giving the patient a higher dose than needed to relieve his pain. Such a case will look to observers just like the morphine-for-pain relief case that PDE is generally considered to approve.[35] A law forbidding the physician's intention of her patient's death would be unenforceable in such a case. However, a law requiring, in effect, that it be *plausible* to suppose that the physician does not intend her patient's death—i.e., that she provide no death-hastening "treatment" or dose that doesn't serve a clear medical purpose—*would* be enforceable. Even were a PDE-based law to address intention more directly, however, limits on enforceability of such a law seem to be an insufficient reason to reject it—especially given that all laws have similar limits: they can be enforced only when there is sufficient evidence of someone's breaking them.

Further, it seems unlikely that there are alternate ethical principles that would fill PDE's role but be unproblematic in interpersonal evaluation. Any principle taking account of the agent's intentions would also be limited by the privacy of intention, and any principle dismissing intention would be incomplete. In any case, an alternate principle would have to be defended independently of an analysis of the merits and demerits of PDE; it could have additional theoretical or practical problems of its own.

VI. Concluding Remarks on the Limits of PDE

In this article I have discussed four features of PDE that I have described as "limits": (1) PDE does not include an account of what makes an effect good or bad; (2) it does not include an account of intention; (3) PDE does not normally tell its user whether a particular act is the right one; and (4) its applicability to legal and policy matters is limited by the privacy of intention. While all four features can be called "limits" in the sense that they indicate things PDE does not do, only the fourth is a real *limitation* of the principle. The first three merely describe the boundaries of PDE within a more comprehensive moral outlook: these must be recognized for its correct interpretation and application.

The first two limits of PDE point to the need for a richer moral context in which the application of the principle must be situated. As I have argued, PDE is not a comprehensive ethical theory and should not be expected to behave like one. One wishing to apply PDE must already possess accounts of intention and of goodness and badness of effects and of intention; both accounts must be compatible with a morally significant distinction between intention and foresight.

The third limit of PDE is not unique to the principle: it is, I think, a limit of ethics itself. As most ethicists (possibly excepting strict consequentialists) acknowledge, usually there is not one right act required of an agent. Often there is a variety of acceptable acts, ranging from the barely permissible to the truly heroic. PDE serves only to determine whether a particular act is acceptable or unacceptable. It does not tell the agent how ethically good an acceptable act is, and it does not tell her that she is required to perform one particular act—except by default should the principle rule out all other options.

While the fourth limit of PDE is a concern for those wishing to use it (or intention more generally) as a basis for legal liability, the privacy problem does not affect PDE's theoretical tenability in ethics: it is solely a practical problem. And although this practical problem is genuine, it is less severe than it may seem. As I argued in section V, in many cases it is sufficiently obvious that the agent must have intended to bring about harm. Where the agent's intent is not so obvious, the judge or jury applying a law based on PDE must proceed as usual: presume the accused is innocent until proved guilty.

University of St. Thomas
St. Paul, Minnesota

Notes

1. For interesting discussions of runaway trolleys, see Judith Jarvis Thomson, "Killing, Letting Die, and the Trolley Problem," *The Monist* 59 (1976): 204–217 and Peter Unger, *Living High and Letting Die* (New York: Oxford University Press, 1996); Unger's book is also the source of the case involving liquefied legs. Regarding the spelunkers, see Philippa Foot, "The Problem of Abortion and the Doctrine of Double Effect," *Oxford Review* 5 (1967): 5–15.

2. See Judith Jarvis Thomson, "Self-defense," *Philosophy & Public Affairs* 20 (1991): 283–310. I include Thomson's example because it aptly demonstrates the potential disconnect between intentions and results, although it does not have an obvious "double effect"—the only relevant effect of the attempted poisoning is the (presumably good) effect of curing the ailing spouse.

3. PDE was first explicitly formulated in terms of four necessary conditions by J. P. Gury in *Compendium Theologiae Moralis* v. 1 (Ratisbonae: Georgii Josephi Manz, 1874). As Stuchlik explains, it was originally formulated in terms of liceity rather than permissibility; while permissibility addresses the act more abstractly, liceity addresses whether the agent acts well or badly in performing the act—intention is especially relevant to the latter. He proposes the following principle regarding the relationship between liceity and permissibility: "It is permissible for S to do A in C just in case A could licitly be performed in C in light of reasonable beliefs about the circumstances." (Joshua Stuchlik, "A Critique of Scanlon on Double Effect," *Journal of Moral Philosophy* 9 [2012], 178–199, at 194.)

4. I borrow this statement of PDE's conditions from an earlier paper: H. M. Giebel, "Ends, Means, and Character: Recent Critiques of the Intended-Versus-Foreseen Distinction and the Principle of Double Effect," *American Catholic Philosophical Quarterly* 81.3 (2007): 447–468.

5. See Thomas Aquinas, *Summa Theologiae* II-II q. 64 a. 7. While Thomas doesn't appear to see himself as developing a new ethical principle, his discussion of self-defense is generally thought to be the *locus classicus* of PDE. For an interesting argument disputing this common interpretation, see Bernard G. Prusak, "Aquinas, Double Effect, and the Pauline Principle," *American Catholic Philosophical Quarterly* 89 (2015): 505–520.

6. G. E. M. Anscombe, "Modern Moral Philosophy," *Philosophy* 33 (1958): 26–42; cf. Anscombe, *Intention*, 2nd ed. (Cambridge MA: Harvard University Press, 1963).

7. See, for example, Jonathan F. Bennett, *The Act Itself* (Oxford: Clarendon Press, 1995); Joseph Boyle, "Toward Understanding the Principle of Double Effect," *Ethics* 90

(1980): 527–538; H. L. A. Hart, "Intention and Punishment," *Oxford Review* 4 (1966): 5–22; Thomas Nagel, *The View from Nowhere* (New York: Oxford University Press, 1986); Warren Quinn, *Morality and Action* (New York: Cambridge University Press, 1993); Thomson, "Killing, Letting Die, and the Trolley Problem"; and Peter Unger, *Living High and Letting Die.*

8. See especially Joseph Boyle, "Who is Entitled to Double Effect?" *Journal of Medicine and Philosophy* 16 (1991): 475–494. Boyle argues that PDE is justified only within a deontological system of ethics (such as the Thomistic natural law tradition in which it originated) as a specification of the scope of absolute moral prohibitions: certain acts are absolutely forbidden *when performed intentionally.* The restriction is needed for cases (like those already mentioned) in which one will inflict a prohibited harm no matter what she does.

9. For philosophical applications, see Nagel, *The View from Nowhere* and Quinn, *Morality and Action.* For philosophical discussion of legal applications, see Hart, "Intention and Punishment"; Raymond Lyons, "Intention and Foresight in Law," *Mind* 85 (1976): 84–89; and Leo Katz, *Bad Acts and Guilty Minds: Conundrums of Criminal Law* (Chicago: University of Chicago Press, 1987).

10. Steven Long, personal communication.

11. Peter Knauer, "The Hermeneutic Function of the Principle of Double Effect," *Natural Law Forum* 12 (1967): 132–162.

12. Since most recent discussion of PDE assumes (*contra* Boyle 1991) that PDE can be interpreted and applied in contexts differing at least to some extent from its original role in Thomistic natural-law ethics, I take that as my working assumption as well. The first two limits of PDE become trivial if one assumes that PDE is to be applied only within the context of Thomas's theory of ethics (and action).

13. In "Physician-Assisted Suicide: Two Moral Arguments," *Ethics* 109 (1999): 497–518. Or perhaps one could interpret Thomson as applying PDE in the context of a theory that includes or entails this view (such as a Thomistic natural-law theory), although she doesn't say that she is doing so and doesn't endorse any such theory herself.

14. Some argue that death does not, strictly speaking, relieve the patient's pain but merely ends it: see, e.g., T. A. Cavanaugh, "DER and Policy: The Recommendation of a Topic," *American Catholic Philosophical Quarterly* 89 (2015) 539–556, at n26: "Ceasing to exist ends pain but it does not relieve it. (By contrast, as is the case in [terminal sedation], an analgesic relieves pain.)"

15. Thomson, "Physician-Assisted Suicide," 513–514.

16. See ibid., 511 and Tom Beauchamp and James Childress, *Principles of Biomedical Ethics*, 5th edition (New York: Oxford University Press, 2001), 132.

17. John Finnis, *Natural Law and Natural Rights* (Oxford: Oxford University Press, 1980), especially 86–87. Like Joseph Boyle, Finnis strives to defend an ethical theory similar to the one in which PDE had its original application.

18. Of course, I would argue that PDE is not *just* a handy decision scheme: it is a correct ethical principle when included in a more comprehensive theory.

19. This second limit, like the first one, was of particular interest only once people began applying PDE in contexts other than the original Thomistic one. Thomas Aquinas's

theory of intention—the traditional account applied in PDE—can be found in his *Treatise on Action*, questions 6–20 of part I-II of the *Summa Theologiae*.

20. This case was first developed in the ethics literature by John Ford. See his "The Morality of Obliteration Bombing," *Theological Studies* 5 (1944): 261–309.

21. See ibid.; Bennett, *The Act Itself*; Michael Bratman, *Intentions, Plans, and Practical Reason* (Cambridge, MA: Harvard University Press, 1987); and Thomson, "Self-Defense." Bennett's analysis is a bit more complex than the others: he argues that there could be a case in which the terror bomber doesn't intend civilians' deaths (or, perhaps, even serious harms) but only the *appearance* of death and destruction—such a "sophisticated" terror bomber might meet PDE's conditions. For a helpful discussion of that sort of case, see Philip Reed, "How to Gerrymander Intention," *American Catholic Philosophical Quarterly* 89 (2015): 441–460.

22. In *The Act Itself*, 199.

23. Bratman, *Intention, Plans, and Practical Reason*, 156.

24. Technically, such an account could be compatible with PDE but would render the acceptable-means condition trivial. I assume that that result would be unacceptable to a proponent of PDE.

25. See his "Intention and Side-Effects" in *Liability and Responsibility*, ed. R. G. Frey and Christopher W. Morris (Cambridge: Cambridge University Press, 1991), 32–64.

26. In "Toward Understanding the Principle of Double Effect," 527–538.

27. Bratman, *Intentions, Plans, and Practical Reason*. See also T. A. Cavanaugh, *Double-Effect Reasoning: Doing Good and Avoiding Evil* (Oxford: Oxford University Press, 2006), ch. 3.

28. "Physician-Assisted Suicide," 513.

29. Ibid., 517.

30. Of course, Bill may not be able to improve his attitude immediately. His intent to allow unnecessary suffering may be the result of a deep character flaw that would take years to correct. As unfortunate as this may be, it is the result of Bill's choices and is not a reflection of the tenability of PDE. As I noted earlier (n3), Thomistically speaking, Bill's refusal to aid with bad intentions is *illicit* rather than *impermissible*, a distinction that seems lost on many contemporary secular ethicists. Thomson is correct that the refusal itself may be permissible—i.e., a morally acceptable sort of act. It is not licit as performed here and now by Bill in light of his bad intention. See Stuchlik, "A Critique of Scanlon on Double Effect."

31. E.g., if we see Bob glancing around furtively and quickly slipping Susie's gold watch into his pocket, then running out the door, we could reasonably (but defeasibly) conclude that his act was one of stealing rather than mistaking the watch for his own or attempting to return it to its rightful owner. For comments on evidence of intention, see Lyons, "Intention and Foresight in Law"; and Anthony Kenny, "Intention and Purpose," *Journal of Philosophy* 63 (1966): 642–651. See also Errol Bedford's remarks on Kenny's article on pages 654–655 of the same issue.

32. E.g., US Supreme Court Justice William Rehnquist endorses the acceptable-means and side-effect propositions. See his opinions in *Washington v. Glucksberg*, 521 U.S. 702 (1997) and *Vacco v. Quill*, 521 U.S. 793 (1997).

33. Hart, "Intention and Punishment."

34. For general comments on intention and law, see Hart, "Intention and Punishment," and Katz, *Bad Acts and Guilty Minds*. For a helpful analysis of PDE as applied to laws themselves (as opposed to individuals' actions under the law), see Cavanaugh, "DER and Policy."

35. As before, I assume that the patient's death counts as a significant bad effect. Thomson argues that a similar problem (namely, the difficulty of determining the physician's intention) exists for laws against physician-assisted suicide through the prescription of lethal drugs. She contends that doctors who prescribe such drugs may do so "intending only to provide the patient with the comfort of knowing that if his condition becomes unbearable, so that he wishes to end his life, he will be able to do so" ("Physician-Assisted Suicide," 510). She suggests that to be consistent, proponents of PDE must advocate laws that allow doctors to prescribe lethal drugs if they do so with such an intention. The PDE proponent, however, will not be convinced by Thomson's reasoning. After all, the physician who intends to provide psychological comfort clearly intends to do so by giving her patient the means to kill himself, which is the very thing to which opponents of physician-assisted suicide object. However, there could be another difficult case for PDE parallel to the one discussed with respect to euthanasia. If her patient is suffering from pain or anxiety (or says that he is), a doctor may prescribe painkillers or sedatives with the intention that her patient be able to kill himself by taking them in high doses. Although such a case will really be one of physician-assisted suicide, forbidden by PDE (again, assuming that the patient's death would be a bad effect), it will look like an ordinary case of a physician prescribing needed medication for her patient.

Catholics and Hugo Grotius's Definition of Lying: A Critique

John Skalko

Abstract: Among Catholic philosophers, Saint Augustine was the first boldly to propose and defend the absolute view that all lies are wrong. Under no circumstances can a lie be licit. This absolute view held sway among Catholics until the sixteenth century with the introduction of the doctrine of mental reservation. In the seventeenth century, Hugo Grotius introduced another way to uphold the absolute view by changing the definition of lying: If the right of another is not violated, then there is no lie. One could thus tell the murderer at the door "Nobody is home" without lying, as he has no right to know the whereabouts of his potential victim. By the late nineteenth century, Grotius's definition of lying began gaining a following among Catholic philosophers and theologians, and continues to be held today by some Catholic philosophers. This article argues that adopting the Grotian definition of lying is a mistake.

Most people hold that lying is morally wrong. When confronted with difficult situations, however, many are willing to grant that in such cases lying ceases to be wrong. If a murderer comes to your door asking if your friend is at home, many would say you should just lie to him. Tell him your friend is not there. Tell him she ran away. Just go ahead and lie. Among certain philosophers this view is morally problematic. Aristotle,[1] Augustine, Aquinas, virtually every major medieval theologian,[2] and Immanuel Kant held lying is wrong in all circumstances. The view that lying is always wrong has echoes in Scripture[3] and even in the most recent edition of the *Catechism of the Catholic Church* 2485: "By its very nature, lying is to be condemned." The view that lying is always wrong will be called the "absolute view" for the purposes of this paper. The view that lying is not always wrong will be called the "non-absolutist view."

The arguments of Augustine that lying is always wrong held sway among most Catholics until the sixteenth century.[4] During the persecution of Catholics in Elizabethan England, however, a difficulty arose. In 1559, the Act of Uniformity ordered that all Catholics attend Anglican services on a weekly basis and take communion monthly.[5] One could be killed for being a priest. This persecution put stress

© 2016, *Proceedings of the ACPA*, Vol. 89
doi: 10.5840/acpaproc20172260

on the traditional doctrine that lying is always immoral. As a result of the persecution, there was pressure to uphold the traditional absolute view on lying while still giving leeway to say things allowing one to escape from danger. The Jesuits developed ways in which one could deceive persecutors without lying.[6] For example, if a Catholic in hiding were asked whether he was a Catholic, he could say "I worship God just like you" while mentally reserving "like you insofar as we are generically Christian." This is called the doctrine of mental reservation. Mental reservation had a certain appeal to Catholics at the time. It allowed one to uphold the absolutist view on lying, while also allowing for broad acts of deception. Mental reservation largely focused on explaining what the definition of lying truly is.

Years later, another view came to the fore in Catholic circles. Like the doctrine of mental reservation, it allowed one to uphold the absolute view, while also allowing for broader acts of deception that were not normally morally allowed. According to this new view, one needs to take into account the hearer's right to know the truth. The murderer at the door has no right to the truth that you are hiding his victim in your home. You do not owe him this truth and so you should not tell him it. Silence would likely not save the victim in this scenario as it would be taken as indication that you are indeed hiding the potential victim at home. Since silence would not work, and since the murderer has no right to know, it follows that one should be able to tell the murderer "Nobody is at home except me" without doing anything morally wrong. Lying must take into account the demands of justice and justice demands that you save the innocent life from the murderer. The only way the absolute view can accommodate for these demands is to change the definition of lying. Lying only counts as lying if the recipient of the speech act has a right to know the truth. Since the murderer has no right to know the truth, you are not lying if you tell him "I am not hiding anyone."

This "right to know" view was not in use by persecuted Catholics in Elizabethan England. The earliest recorded entry of it in Catholic circles is by Benedikt Stattler in the late eighteenth century.[7] After him the record remains silent for several decades among Catholic authors until 1834. From 1834 through 1957 the view grew rapidly in popularity, with at least thirty-five Catholic writers adopting the view.[8] Prominent among them was Dubois, Tanquerey, Gerard Kelly, S.J., social ethicist Msgr. John A. Ryan,[9] and Dorszynski.[10] Two, more contemporary Catholic authors, who hold a similar definition of lying are Charles Curran[11] and Martin Rhonheimer.[12] With such a list of authors who held the "right to know" view, it is not possible to detail all of their arguments. What I hope to do here though is to give a decent sampling of their arguments and definitions.[13]

I will begin with Walter H. Hill, S.J. In his 1879 book *Ethics*, Hill defines a lie as "a privation of truth that is due, or, which is a positive concealment of a truth that ought to be manifested."[14] Abbé F. Dubois in an article in *La Science Catholique* in 1897/1898 wrote:

> The definition of lying, adopted by Mr. Dignant, therefore seems insuf-
> ficient. It must be added: *the violation of a right*, which constitutes the

formal element of a lie and *specifies* it morally. Thus, the saying of a falsity with the intention to deceive is the material element of a lie, analogous to the material act of killing, indifferent like it, that is to say good or evil according to the circumstances and the condition determining the morality of the act.[15]

About a decade later, an anonymous author in *The Casuist* makes a similar claim:

> In the face of this unsurmountable difficulty many moralists think that the definition of a lie, as commonly given in the textbook ought to be revised; that is to say, it ought to be made to read something like this: A lie consists in speaking contrary to one's mind, with the intention of deceiving one *who has a right to the truth.* If the person has no right to the truth it ought not to be called a lie if the truth is concealed from him by saying the thing that is not in one's mind.[16]

In the first edition of the *Catechism of the Catholic Church* in French (1992)[17] and in English (1994)[18] the "right to know" view makes a more official entrance. There in CCC no. 2483 it is written, "To lie is to speak or act against the truth in order to lead someone into error who has the right to know the truth."[19] Yet, in the most recent edition, the *editio typica*, the qualifier "someone who has the right to know the truth" is dropped.[20] Today Janet Smith[21] prominently holds the "right to know" view. Hadley Arkes also holds a similar view. Arkes says,

> A "lie" is an unjustified act of speaking falsely, as a murder is an unjustified act of killing.[22]

Arkes, however, is more of a political scientist than a philosopher. Thus, among Catholic philosophers today that means Janet Smith is the only one who publicly holds the "right to know" definition of lying. Peter Kreeft just outright defends lying.[23] Non-Catholics typically do not care about the "right to know" view as they typically say one should just go ahead and lie in Nazi-at-the-door-scenarios.

The "right to know" view has its origins in the Protestant Hugo Grotius,[24] one of the fathers of international law.[25] Other Protestant writers like Alberico Gentili, Samuel Pufendorf, Jeremy Taylor, and William Paley followed Grotius in this view.[26] In Book III, Chapter I, Section XI of his book *De Jure Belli ac Pacis*, Grotius puts forth his new definition of lying as follows:

> But a lie, in this stricter acceptation . . . *is a violation of the existing and permanent rights of the person, to whom a discourse, or particular signs, are directed* [emphasis added].[27]

On this Grotian definition, it follows that if the listener has no right to the truth, you can speak falsehood to him without lying. What I wish to address in the rest of this paper is this: Is this a correct definition of a lie? Is the "right to know" qualifier really part of the true definition of lying? This paper shall argue that it is not. This paper shall be divided into three parts. Part One will explicate more of the context of the Grotian view and show why it is wrong in principle. Part Two will argue that accepting the Grotian definition is particularly troublesome for any Thomist who accepts other aspects of Aquinas's moral theory. Part Three will point out that ironically on the Grotian definition lying ends up becoming a much graver sin than it is held to be on the traditional Augustinian-Thomistic definition of lying.

A few disclaimers must be noted first. This paper is not discussing the morality of lying. It is not arguing that lying is intrinsically evil, nor that it is evil, but defeasibly so. I am bracketing the debate about the morality of lying for the purposes of this paper. I am merely focusing upon the question of the Grotian or "right to know" definition of lying. Is this definition a good definition? I argue that it is not.

Part One: The Grotian Context and Its Problems

Hugo Grotius (1583–1645),[28] a seventeenth-century Protestant lawyer, published *De Jure Belli ac Pacis* (*The Law of War and Peace*) in 1625.[29] The work is divided into three books. Book I treats of the nature of war, rights, and the false opinion that all wars are wrong. Book II treats what constitutes the just causes of war, that is justice in going to war (*ius ad bellum*). Book III treats of justice in war (*ius in bello*). In Book III, Chapter 1, Grotius treats of justice in war from the perspective of the law of nature, whether one may consider a supplier of the enemy an enemy, and in Section VI whether stratagems may be morally used in war. It is in this context of stratagems that Grotius discusses the morality of lying. Before discussing the morality of lying itself, Grotius makes a distinction between two types of stratagems: negative stratagems and positive stratagems.[30] Negative stratagems are actions that have nothing criminal in them, but are calculated to deceive.[31] Concealment or dissimulation falls under the category of negative stratagems. An example of this is when Abraham called Sarah, his wife, his sister, as she was truly a blood relation in some sense. Abraham did not lie. A positive stratagem "practised in actions, is called a feint, and when used in conversation it receives the name of a lie or falsehood."[32] Some of these positive stratagems are morally acceptable as in the case of the feigned retreat of Joshua in the Old Testament[33] or of Christ on the road to Emmaus pretending he would go farther when he did not.[34] Lies, however, are different. Grotius says here, "All stratagems of this kind are so direct a violation of all moral principle, both in their nature and consequences, that almost every page of the revealed will of God declares their condemnation."[35] Grotius then goes on to cite that the poets, philosophers, and Aristotle agree with his position. Yet, Grotius says there are also great authorities on the other side, who hold that at times lying is allowed, as in the case of a physician helping a patient.[36] In order to reconcile such opposing opinions, Grotius then proceeds to examine the nature of lying. Merely speaking an untruth is not a lie. Rather "the known and deliberate utterance of any thing contrary to our real conviction, intention, and understanding" is a lie.[37] Thus, it is no lie for a man to utter something that he believes to be true, even though his belief happens to be false.[38] There must be an intention to deceive in order for it to be a lie in the proper and common sense of the word.[39] Speaking ambiguously or equivocating does not count as a lie so long as at least one sense of the words used is true.[40] This ambiguity may be acceptable in some situations, though not all. Such ambiguity may be not only censurable, but even wicked where the honor of God or the welfare of mankind is concerned or where explicit avowals are needed as in the case of making contracts.[41]

So far, most of what Grotius has said is rather straightforward. In the next sentences, however, he makes an interesting distinction by introducing a new definition of lying:

> The common notion of a lie therefore is something spoken, written, marked, or intimated, which cannot be understood, but in a sense different from the real meaning of the speaker. But a lie, in this stricter acceptation, having some thing unlawful in its very nature, necessarily requires that a distinction be made. . . . And if this acceptation be properly considered, at least according to the opinion prevailing in all nations, it seems, that no other explanation of it is necessary to be given, except that *it is a violation of the existing and permanent rights of the person, to whom a discourse or particular signs, are directed. It is a violation of the rights of another* [emphasis added].[42]

Here lie the beginnings of the "right to know" definition of lying. Grotius then explains certain things that follow from his definition of lying:

1. This right may pass away if circumstances change. If the right existed previously, but now has become obsolete due to the rise of some new right, then it is not a lie to state a falsehood.[43] Grotius gives no example here, but presumably an instance of this would be where an employer has a right to know his employee's criminal history, but if the employee ceases being employed with them, then their right to know his criminal history no longer holds.

2. "To constitute a violation of this right . . . the ensuing injury should immediately affect the person addressed."[44]

3. Speaking the truth thus falls under justice.[45]

4. This right to know may be "relinquished by the express consent of the persons." If beforehand two parties agree not to reveal certain points, they may do so without lying. Tacit consent also suffices for something not to count as a lie.[46]

5. One may utter what one believes to be false to madmen or children without lying. Children and madmen possess no perfect power of judging, and so no injury can be done to their rights by telling them falsehoods.[47]

6. If the deception is done upon someone whom it would benefit and who would not feel a grievance at it, then it does not count as a lie. Just like taking something on the presumed consent of the owner for his benefit does not constitute theft, neither does deception on the presumed consent of the recipient for his benefit count as a lie.[48] Thus, uttering falsehoods that you believe to be false to console a friend in distress are not lies.[49]

7. If the deception is done by some preeminent authority conducive to the individual or the public welfare, then it is not a lie. Presumably, on this account the noble lie of Plato's Republic is not a lie. Nonetheless, this authority to tell falsehoods for the public welfare does not apply to God. God cannot tell falsehoods, as such would convey an imperfection in him.[50] So though other human authorities may tell falsehoods without them being lies to someone who has no right to know, this does not apply to God, because he cannot speak falsely.

8. If the only means of saving the life of an innocent person is to utter a falsehood that one believes is false, then it is not a lie. The same logic applies if the only means of obtaining some object of equal importance is to speak falsely, then doing so is not a lie.

9. It may not be a lie to speak falsely to a public enemy on this account. Grotius, however, is hesitant to affirm this point.[51]

Grotius adds that keeping promises is an issue distinct from lying, and not all that he said about lying applies to keeping or breaking promises. Grotius also says that his views on lying do not apply to affirmative or promissory oaths, where God is called upon as a witness: "Such an appeal to the supreme being demands the performance of an oath, even if it gave the individual no right to the same."[52] One may not hold to any mental reservation or appeal to the right to know in speaking falsely in any kind of oath.[53] Rather one must speak the truth clearly.[54]

As mentioned earlier, this Grotian definition of a lie is echoed centuries later in the first printing of the *Catechism of the Catholic Church* and in the writings of Janet Smith, as "To lie is to speak or act against the truth in order to lead someone into error who has the right to know the truth."[55] Although the wording of these definitions slightly differ from that of Grotius, I do not see any significant difference between them that will substantially affect my analysis of such definitions.

Problems

Grotius introduces his new definition of lying in the context of Book III about justice in war. Wartime is a difficult situation that often entails difficult moral decisions. Similar to Grotius, Smith and Arkes put forth their definition of lying in the context of a difficult situation: saving the lives of unborn babies from abortion by deceptive undercover sting operations. The remote intentions of Smith and Arkes are praiseworthy and noble in wishing to save the lives of the unborn. Nevertheless, as can be seen from Grotius's own explication of his definition of lying, what began as allowing one small exception to lying, namely when human lives are in danger, seems to have grown to allow a whole host of other exceptions. This leads to the first set of objections to the Grotian definition. The Grotian definition claims that certain statements are not lies when I think intuitively most people would hold that they are lies.

The first objection to the "right to know view" is as follows: Nobody has any right to know how much money is in my pocket. Much less does any random person at the grocery store have any right to know how much money is in my pocket. If I walked around the grocery store and randomly went up to strangers telling them "I have no money in my pocket" I would surely be lying. Yet, it follows on the "right to know" view that this is no lie.[56] This seems a bit strange. Intuitively most would recognize that I told a lie in the grocery store. The Grotian definition is counter-intuitive here. As Edward Feser says,

> In this connection, it is not the Scholastic, but rather those who propose redefinitions of lying like "A lie is a falsehood told to someone who has a right to the truth," who are at odds with common sense, at least where the definition of *what a lie is* is concerned.[57]

A second objection may be raised against the "right to know" view. Nobody in the waiting room of the doctor's office has any right to know my life story. But if I went around telling them fanciful stories about my childhood, surely this would be a lie. However, on the "right to know" view not only is this not a lie, but even if I went to the doctor's office everyday and told wild, fantastically false stories about my childhood, I would not only be not telling any lies at all, I would not even rightly be called a pathological liar.[58]

This leads to the third objection. If the Nazi at the door has no right to know whether I am hiding Jews in my home, then not only would telling him "I am hiding no Jews" not be lying, but it would also not be a dishonest action. For on the "right to know" definition, one can fabricate false stories in doctor's offices, tell random customers falsehoods about how much money is in one's pocket, and tell people falsehoods about what one had for breakfast without lying.[59] Yet, not only is one not lying in such scenarios on the "right to know" definition, one is also speaking honestly. For the one who spoke falsely in such cases did not lie. If he did not lie, but still spoke, then he must have been speaking honestly. This, however, is counterintuitive. Whatever one may say about the morality of lying to the Nazi, it surely seems strange to call the one who utters a falsehood honest.

To press the point even further, say one actually truthfully told the Nazi at the door that one is hiding Jews. Though this would be stupid, one cannot say such a man is not honest. But is this man who speaks truly more honest than the one who tells a falsehood? On the "right to know" definition, both the speaker of truth and the speaker of falsity are speaking honestly. But acts of honesty lead the agent to possession of the habit corresponding to the act. Ergo, it follows that since the act of intentionally speaking falsely to the Nazi at the door is an act of honesty, one would grow in the virtue of honesty by telling the Nazi "There are no Jews here." Is that not in the least bit counterintuitive?

Further, if one wishes to redefine lying in terms of the "right to know," then so too must one redefine perjury. As Aquinas says, quoting from Hugh of Saint Victor, in ST II-II, Q98, A1 perjury is "a lie confirmed by an oath."[60] An oath is to call upon God as witness that what one says is in fact true.[61] Now, on the Thomistic definition of a lie, a lie is asserting as true what one believes to be false.[62] So perjury is asserting as true what one believes to be false by calling upon God as a witness. On the Grotian definition of lying, however, perjury would be "a violation of the existing and permanent rights of the person, to whom a discourse or particular signs, are directed by calling upon God as a witness." If someone has no right to know, then not only is it not a lie, it is not perjury. Thus, if a Nazi came to your door and you said, "I swear by God, I am hiding no Jews" when in fact you are, you are not only not lying, you are also not perjuring yourself on the Grotian definition. But are you really not perjuring yourself? It seems not. The Grotian view runs into absurdity here. Would you really be willing to look the Nazi in the eye and tell him you swear by God there are no Jews there?

Now, as mentioned earlier, Grotius claims his definition of lying does not pertain to the taking of oaths. His claim, however, is *ad hoc*. The existing or permanent rights of the Nazi are in no sense violated if you call upon God as a witness to your statement. The Nazi's rights are not being violated in telling him there are no Jews at home even if you invoke God's name as a witness. You are telling a lie, but you are not violating his rights.

Perhaps, upon Smith's definition of lying, the Nazi now has a "right to know" if God is called upon as a witness. The difficulty here is that Smith's definition is not nearly as clear as Grotius's definition. Grotius elaborates upon his understanding of rights. Smith does not. As Christopher Tollefsen points out, the "right to know" view "raises more questions than it answers. What, in particular, does it mean to have a right to the truth, and under what conditions is that right lost or waived? Are the conditions easy to meet or strict? Frequently met or only rarely? Are they well known?"[63]

A sixth objection is raised by Tollefsen:

> The Grotian view also leads to paradox, if not outright contradiction. Consider the following scenario: I spend $500 of family money on gambling. My wife has a right to know what happened to this money; my ten-year old son does not. The 'right to know' view would have it that I lie only to my wife when I assert to both that I gave the money to charity. This seems clearly wrong, if not absurd.[64]

Tollefsen's point is that where there is a case of genuine collusion of rights on the part of the recipients of the speech act, it follows that one is both lying and not lying.[65]

A seventh difficulty is that on the Grotian definition it would follow that if the martyrs had not born witness to Christ, but instead had denied that they were follower of Jesus Christ in order to save their own lives, they would not have been liars. Telling their persecutors that they were not followers of Christ would have been no violation of the "existing and permanent rights" of the persecutors.[66] Ergo, the martyrs would not have lied if they had denied their faith. They would have still burned in hell for doing wrong, but not because what they told was a lie. They would have burned only because they did not obey Christ's words: "whoever denies me before others, I will deny before my heavenly Father."[67] This, however, is absurd, as what they did would be more accurately called a lie as opposed to just an act of disobedience.

Further, on the Grotian definition it follows that lying under duress is a contradiction in terms.[68] If one's life is in danger and someone points a gun at you and says, "Tell me a lie or I'll kill you," it is literally impossible for you to tell him a lie in such a scenario. Why? Because a person who is threatening to harm you and is morally speaking a murderer has no right to anything that you know. Ironically, the implications are that whatever you tell him, it is not a lie. The problem here is that in such a case if the murderer is smart enough and knows that it is impossible for you to lie to him in such case he will have to kill you anyway if he wishes to carry through on his threat: "Tell me a lie or I'll kill you."

Further, on the "right to know" definition, it follows not only that telling the Nazi at the door "I am hiding no Jews" is not lying, but also that no matter what one says to the Nazi about the Jews' whereabouts it is not a lie. In other words, imagine this scenario: You are hiding a family of Jews at your home. The Nazi comes to the door and asks, "Are you hiding any Jews?" The Nazi has no right to know you are hiding them. On the "right to know" definition, it follows that one could tell him "I am hiding no Jews" or "There are no Jews at my home" without lying. It also follows that on the "right to know" definition it is absolutely impossible for you to lie to the Nazi about the whereabouts of those Jews. You can tell him any wild manner of stories about those Jews, but it really does not matter because whatever you say about their whereabouts is not a lie. This is a bit strange. As James Mahon says, "surely . . . it is *possible* to lie to a would-be murderer, whether it is impermissible . . . or permissible."[69] The Grotian definition leads to some strange logical consequences.

Finally, if one accepts the Grotian or Smith's definition, then since lying violates the rights of another, this means that all lies are contrary to justice. Injustice is thus included in the very definition of lying. Ergo, to say "lying is unjust" would be a tautology.[70] It would thus be impossible for one to give a demonstration that lying is unjust and nearly pointless in arguing with someone whether lying is unjust. One who does not see that lying is unjust would not understand the meaning of the terms. That "lying is unjust" is a tautology becomes particularly clear on Arkes definition of lying as "an unjustified act of speaking falsely." This poses a problem for the "right to know" view. Whatever one may hold about the morality of lying surely it is possible for one to understand what a lie is and yet hold that lying is not always unjust without contradiction.

This leads to an interesting paradox within Grotius's work, *The Law of War in Peace*. At the beginning of the work, Grotius says that justice is not included in the definition of war, for the very point to be decided is whether any war is just.[71] But can the same not be said about lying? Is not the point to be decided whether lying is just or not, right or not?

Part Two: Acceptance of "Right to Know" Upsets Aquinas's Moral Theory

The previous list of problems alone should be enough to reject the Grotian definition of lying. Nevertheless, I hold that for Thomists there are additional compelling reasons why the Grotian definition of lying should be rejected. Aquinas, of course, does not accept the Grotian definition. What I wish to point out in this next section of the paper is that one cannot accept the Grotian definition of lying without seriously upsetting other aspects of Aquinas's moral theory.

First, on Grotius's definition injustice is included in the very definition of lying. Lying is "a violation of the existing and permanent rights of the person, to whom a discourse or particular signs, are directed." Grotius later in the same chapter makes various claims that indicate by "rights" here he means claims of justice.[72] Now, the opposite of the vice of lying for Aquinas is the virtue of truthfulness. If injustice is included in the very definition of lying, then it would follow that justice should be included in the very definition of truthfulness. If justice were included in the very definition of truthfulness, then truthfulness would be a species of justice. This, however, is not the case for Aquinas. Truthfulness is the virtue by which one says what is true.[73] Justice is not included in the definition of truthfulness. Truthfulness is a part of justice for Aquinas, but as a potential and not a subjective part. Potential parts are those that share in the *ratio* of justice, but fail in the full *ratio* of justice.[74] Subjective parts are the species of justice.[75] The virtue of truthfulness is not a species of justice. Truthfulness is a potential part of justice, as it shares in the *ratio* of justice insofar as it is involves another and equality, but it fails in the full *ratio* of justice with regards to the notion of due.[76] Truthfulness regards not a legal due as justice does, but rather a moral due.[77] In other words, one does not strictly speaking owe another the truth; nobody strictly speaking has a right to know. Rather, others are owed the truth insofar as it is honest to do so.[78] Thus, if one wishes to accept the Grotian definition of lying, not only must one reject Aquinas's definition of lying, one must also reject his definition of truthfulness, and his claim that truthfulness is only a potential part of justice.[79] According to the Grotian definition, truthfulness must be a subjective part or a species of justice, which is contrary to Aquinas's schema.

The Grotian definition also has the authority of Aristotle explicitly against it. On the Grotian view, one must not only reject Aquinas's definition of truthfulness, but also Aristotle's definition of truthfulness (which Aquinas accepts[80]). In the *Nicomachean Ethics* IV.7 1127a33–1127b3, Aristotle explicitly says that justice is not included in the definition of truthfulness:

> For we do not mean someone who is truthful in agreements in matters of justice and injustice, since these concern a different virtue, but someone

who is truthful both in what he says and in how he lives, *when nothing about justice is at stake*, simply because this is his state of character.[81]

This points to a further objection to the Grotian definition: if truthfulness is really only about matters of justice, then by what virtue do we regulate or speak the truth in our daily conversation with others? On the Grotian definition, it is not truthfulness whereby we are honest with others in matters where there is no justice or "right to know" at stake. This is a major difficulty: What exactly do you wish to call a virtue that regulates speaking the truth where no justice is at stake? It cannot be called truthfulness, as that has already been taken for cases where there is justice at stake in speaking. And if one wishes to call this virtue Small Truthfulness, or some new name of that sort, then what is its opposing vice? Lying cannot be its opposing vice as lying has already been taken as the vice opposed to Truthfulness (in the Grotian sense). In short, the Grotian definition of lying logically leads to an incoherent account of the virtue of truthfulness.

Further, if one accepts the Grotian definition of lying, one must also reject Aquinas's argument against lying. In ST II-II, Q110, A3, Aquinas argues thus:

> Now a lie is evil in respect of its genus, since it is an action bearing on undue matter. For as words are naturally signs of intellectual acts, it is unnatural and undue for anyone to signify by words something that is not in his mind. . . . Therefore every lie is a sin.[82]

The very purpose of words is to indicate what is in one's mind—that is why words were created. Lying is contrary to the very purpose for which words were created. What this or that word means is up to the custom of the country, but what words in general are for is not up to the customs of the country. Lying is contrary to the very purpose for which language was instituted.

Notice how Aquinas's argument works perfectly well given Aquinas's definition of lying as asserting as true what one does not believe.[83] Thus, even if the Grotian definition of lying is true, this argument still shows that all assertions of formal falsehood are wrong (even if the recipient of the speech act has no "right to know"). The difficulty here is that the whole reason in the first place why the Grotian definition was instituted was to allow one to speak more than is normally allowed without doing anything morally wrong. On the Grotian definition you can tell the Nazi "I am not hiding any Jews," but on Aquinas's definition you cannot. The problem is that even if you reject Aquinas's definition, if you still accept his account of the purposes of language, then Aquinas's conclusion still follows. Ergo, one must reject Aquinas's account of the wrongfulness of lying. This is in fact what Janet Smith does.[84]

Part Three: The "Right to Know" Definition Makes Lying Grievously Evil

A third major set of objections to the "right to know" view is that it makes lying overly sinful. A major motivation for accepting the Grotian definition is that the traditional absolute view that all lying is wrong seems overly harsh. Ironically, however, it is not the traditional absolute view that ends up being overly harsh, but the Grotian view. In order to make this point clear, let us begin with Augustine's eightfold division of lying:[85]

1. Lies in matters of religious doctrine (a mischievous lie[86]),

2. Lies against man that profit nobody, but injure someone (a mischievous lie),

3. Lies against man that injure someone but profit another (a mischievous lie),

4. Lies for the mere sake of lying and deceiving,

5. Lies for the sake of pleasing (jocose lies),

6. Lies for the sake of profiting someone in saving money (an officious lie),

7. Lies for the sake of saving a man from death (an officious lie),

8. Lies for the sake of saving one from unlawful defilement of the body (an officious lie).

The Grotian definition of lying states that a lie is only a lie if it is "a violation of the existing and permanent rights of the person, to whom a discourse or particular signs, are directed." There may be some overlap between these categories, but if one is merely telling an officious lie that harms nobody then one is not violating the rights of another. In fact, this is what Augustine here means by the last 3 kinds of lying, lies that harm nobody else but benefit someone. Such is why Aquinas categorizes the last three kinds of lies on the list as officious lies. Now since these officious lies violate no rights of another, then based upon the Grotian definition these last three kinds of lies do not exist. Further, Augustine's fifth kind of lying seems to be lies that not only are for the sake of a joke, but also those that harm nobody else. But if jocose lies do not violate the rights of another, then based upon the Grotian definition such lies do not exist. This means that the only kinds of lies that exist are the first four kinds of lies. The first three of these all injure another and so Aquinas groups them together as mischievous lies. All mischievous lies are mortal sins. The fourth kind of lie is that which is told out of the mere enjoyment of lying, by one who is a pathological vicious liar. Such lies are also mortal. Thus, it follows that the only kind of lies that exist on the Grotian definition are those that are grievously evil and mortal sins.[87] The paradox here is that on the "right to know" view there is no such thing as a "little white lie,"[88] and "it is also not possible to tell an intentionally benevolent lie."[89]

Conclusion

In conclusion, the Grotian and "right to know" definition of lying suffer from a host of difficulties. It is understandable why one would wish to adopt such definitions in the first place. The Grotian definition gives one an easy way out in wartime or in cases of hiding the Jews. As much as we might wish the demands of morality were easy, difficult circumstances require heroic acts. The truth must not conform to our desires, rather our desires must conform with the truth—and the Grotian definition is just not true.

UST—Houston, The Center for Thomistic Studies

Acknowledgements

Many thanks to those attending the 2015 ACPA Conference for helpful feedback on my paper, especially to Daniel Shields for his insightful commentary and to Fr. Kevin Flannery, S.J. I would also like to thank all those at the Center for Thomistic Studies for graciously allowing me to give a colloquium on an earlier version of this paper in January of 2015.

Notes

1. Aristotle, *Nicomachean Ethics*, Book IV, Chapter 7, 1127a, trans. Terence Irwin, Second ed. (Indianapolis/Cambridge: Hackett Publishing Company, 1999): "Now in itself [when no ulterior purpose is involved], falsehood is base and blameworthy, and truth is fine and praiseworthy." The Greek text is as follows: καθ' αὑτὸ δὲ τὸ μὲν ψεῦδος φαῦλον καὶ ψεκτόν, τὸ δ' ἀληθὲς καλὸν καὶ ἐπαινετόν (*Nicomachean Ethics* IV.VII 1127a, Loeb Classical Library [London/Cambridge: Harvard University Press, 1934], p. 240).

2. Christopher Tollefsen and Alexander Pruss, "The Case Against False Assertions," *First Things*, September 22, 2011, accessed October 7, 2014, http://www.firstthings.com/web-exclusives/2011/09/the-case-against-false-assertions.

Cf. Julius A. Dorzynski, *Catholic Teaching About the Morality of Falsehood*, PhD diss., The Catholic University of America, 1948 (Washington, D.C.: Catholic University of America Press, 1948), 22–27. Dorzynski's magisterial dissertation on the topic cites Gregory the Great, Saint Gregory VII, Hugh of Saint Victor, Pope Alexander III, Saint Raymond of Pennafort, and Duns Scotus.

3. Sirach 7:13: "Refuse to tell lie after lie, for it never results in good"; Leviticus 19:11: You shall not steal. You shall not deceive or speak falsely to one another"; Proverbs 12:22: "Lying lips are an abomination to the Lord, but those who are truthful, his delight"; Colossians 3:9: "Stop lying to one another, since you have taken off the old self with its practices"; Revelation 22:15: "Outside are the dogs, the sorcerers, the unchaste, the murderers, the idol-worshipers, and all who love and practice deceit" (NAB).

4. Dorzynski, *Catholic Teaching About the Morality of Falsehood*, 22.

5. Christopher O. Tollefsen, *Lying and Christian Ethics* (New York: Cambridge University Press, 2014), 159.

6. Ibid., 160.

7. Gregor Müller, OSB, *Die Wahrhaftigkeitspflicht Und Die Problematik Der Lüge* (Freiburg, Basel, Wien: Herder, 1962), 212; also footnote 9.

8. Ibid., 326–327.

9. John A. Ryan, *The Norm of Morality: Defined and Applied to Particular Actions* (Washington, D.C.: National Catholic Welfare Conference, 1944), 42–43. To be precise here, Ryan does not redefine lying so as to make asserting falsely to the murderer at the door to be not a lie. Rather his position is that since the purpose of speech is the social good of justice, when this end no longer holds lying is justified. In this respect he differs from many of the other authors listed, as they do not defend lying, but rather redefine it.

10. Dorszynski, *Catholic Teaching About the Morality of Falsehood*, 94–101.

11. Charles E. Curran, "Absolute Norms and Medical Ethics," in *Absolutes in Moral Theology?* (Washington, D.C.: Corpus Books, 1968), 123–124. Curran adopts this definition in order to reject the perverted faculty argument.

12. Martin Rhonheimer, *The Perspective of the Acting Person: Essays in the Renewal of Thomistic Moral Philosophy*, ed. William F. Murphy, Jr. (Washington, D.C.: Catholic University of America Press, 2008), 230: "The most important point, however, and one that is often ignored, seems to me to be that for St. Thomas, lying by its nature is not only contrary to the nature of linguistic acts and to the truth, but it is also a *violation of justice*. To say what is false so as to mislead is *unjust*, because it violates another's right, that is, that of living in community with one's fellow men on the basis of a mutual trust." In reply to Rhonheimer, it must be noted that nowhere does Aquinas assert lying is in its nature contrary to justice in the strict sense. It is only contrary to it as being contrary to a virtue annexed to justice; but it is not in its nature contrary to justice in the sense in which theft is contrary to justice as being opposed to a strict species of justice. Lying in its nature is no more opposed to justice than pride in its nature is opposed to temperance. For lying is only directly opposed to a virtue annexed to justice, and pride is only directed opposed to a virtue annexed to temperance.

13. Special thanks to Ali Kremer and Joseph Arias for finding some of the late nineteenth- and early twentieth-century Catholic sources that hold the "right to know" view.

14. Walter H. Hill, S.J., *Ethics: Or, Moral Philosophy*, 2nd Revised ed. (Baltimore: John Murphy, 1879), 220–221.

15. Abbé F. Dubois, "Une Théorie Du Mensonge Replique (1)," ed. M. L' Abbé Duflot, *La Science Catholique* 12 (December 1897–December 1898): 168. The translation is my own.

The original French is as follows: La définition du mensonge, adoptée par M. Dignant, nous parait donc insuffisante (1). Il faut y ajouter : *la violation d'un droit* qui constitue l'élément *formel* du mensonge et le *spécific* moralement.

Ainsi, l'énonciation du faux avec intention de tromper est l'élément matériel du mensonge, analogue à l'acte matériel de tuer, indifférent comme lui, c'est-à-dire bon ou mauvais selon les circonstances et la condition déterminant la moralité de cet acte, c'est comme pour l'acte de tuer, la violation d'un droit, du droit à la vie dans le premier cas, du droit à la véritè dans le second.

16. *The Casuist: A Collection of Cases in Moral and Pastoral Theology*, vol. III (New York: Joseph F. Wagner, 1910), 48.

17. *Catéchisme De L'Église Catholique* (Paris: Mame-Libraire Editrice Vaticane, 1992), no. 2483: "Mentir, c'est parler ou agir contre la vérité pour induire en erreur celui quo a le droit de la connaître."

18. *Catechism of the Catholic Church* (Rome: Ubi Et Orbi Communications, 1994), no. 2483: "To lie is to speak or act against the truth in order to lead into error someone who has the right to know the truth."

19. Ibid.

20. *Catechism of the Catholic Church*, 2nd ed. (Citta del Vaticano: Libreria Editrice Vaticana, 1997), no. 2483: "To lie is to speak or act against the truth in order to lead someone into error."

Tollefsen makes some interesting observations on this point; see *Lying and Christian Ethics*, 25.

21. Janet E. Smith, "Fig Leaves and Falsehoods, Pace Thomas Aquinas, Sometimes We Need to Deceive," *First Things*, June 2011, accessed October 7, 2014, http://www.firstthings.com/article/2011/06/fig-leaves-and-falsehoods.

22. Hadley Arkes, "When Speaking Falsely Is Right," *Public Discourse*, February 19, 2011, accessed November 17, 2014, http://www.thepublicdiscourse.com/2011/02/2631/.

23. Peter Kreeft, "Why Live Action Did Right and Why We All Should Know That," CatholicVote.org, accessed November 06, 2014, http://www.catholicvote.org/why-live-action-did-right-and-why-we-all-should-know-that/comment-page-18/.

24. Tollefsen, *Lying and Christian Ethics*, 27; Dorszynski, *Catholic Teaching About the Morality of Falsehood*, 30.

Technically Dorszynski does not say this view was first invented by Grotius, but Grotius is the first one that Dorszynski mentions as holding this view. Apparently he is not aware of anyone before Grotius who held such a view, nor am I.

25. J. D. Forde, *Routledge Encyclopedia of Philosophy*, vol. 4 (London, New York: Routledge, 1998), s.v. "Grotius, Hugo."

26. Dorszynski, *Catholic Teaching About the Morality of Falsehood*, 30.

27. Hugo Grotius, *On the Law of War and Peace*, trans. A. C. Campbell, A.M., vol. III (Kitchener: Batoche Books, 2001), 260.

> Si recte res inspiciatur . . . Nulla videtur alia dari posse praeter repugnantiam cum jure existente ac manente ejus ad quem sermo aut nota dirigitur (Hugonis Grotii, *De Jure Belli Et Pacis: Libri Tres*, trans. William Whewell, D.D., ed. Jean Barbeyrac and William E. Butler, vol. III, Chapter 1, Section XI.1 (Clark, NJ: Lawbook Exchange, 2011), 26). All further Latin citations of Hugo Grotius are from this work unless otherwise indicated.

28. Jon Miller, *Stanford Encyclopedia of Philosophy*, s.v. "Hugo Grotius," July 28, 2011, accessed January 29, 2015, http://plato.stanford.edu/entries/grotius/.

29. Ibid.

30. Hugo Grotius, *On the Law of War and Peace*, trans. A. C. Campbell, A.M., vol. III (Kitchener: Batoche Books, 2001), 255.

31. Ibid.

32. Ibid., 255.

33. Ibid., 257.

34. Ibid., 256.

35. Ibid., 257–258.

36. Ibid., 258.

37. Ibid., 258, Section X.

38. Ibid.

39. Ibid.

40. Ibid., 258–259.

41. Ibid., 259.

42. Ibid., Section XI, 260–261; Ad communem ergo mendacii notionem requiritur, ut quod dicitur, scribitur, notatur, innuitur, intelligi aliter nequeat, quam in eum sensum, qui a mente proferentis discrepet. Huic autem notioni laxiori strictior mendacii, qua naturaliter illicitum est, significatio differentiam aliquam propriam adjiciat necesse est, quae, si recte res inspiciatur, saltem secundem communem gentium existimationem, nulla videtur alia dari posse praeter repugnantiam cum jure existente ac manente ejus ad quem sermo aut nota dirigitur: nam sibi neminem mentiri, ut maxime falsum proferat, satis constat (Hugonis Grotii, Book III, Chapter 1, Section XI.1, p. 26).

43. Geach brings this up as an objection to the "right to know" view. Unfortunately Geach does not seem to realize that the very founder of the "right to know" view has already bitten the bullet on this one.

Cf. Peter T. Geach, *The Virtues* (Cambridge: Cambridge University Press, 1977), 112–113.

44. Grotius, *On the Law of War and Peace*, 260.

45. Ibid.

46. Ibid., 260–261.

47. Ibid., Section XII, 261. Grotius had mentioned earlier (Section XI) that the rights he was speaking of imply liberty of judgment. Since children and the insane have no free judgment, it logically follows on his position that their rights in this regard cannot be violated.

48. Ibid., Section XIV, 262.

49. Ibid.

50. Ibid., Section XV, 262.

51. Ibid., Section XVII, 263.

52. Ibid., Section XIX, 264.

53. Ibid.

54. Ibid.

55. *Catechism of the Catholic Church* (1994), no. 2483; Janet E. Smith, "Fig Leaves and Falsehoods, Pace Thomas Aquinas, Sometimes We Need to Deceive," *First Things*, June 2011, accessed October 7, 2014, http://www.firstthings.com/article/2011/06/fig-leaves-and-falsehoods.

56. Daniel Shields, in his commentary on this paper at the 2015 meeting of the ACPA, pointed out that perhaps on the Grotian definition the rights of another are being violated in such a case. Perhaps the Grotian sense of "right" is a *prima facie* right not to be deceived. This right is based on the human need to find other people trustworthy. So if a false assertion denigrates trust, then it violates this *prima facie* right. The difficulty here, as Shields points out, is that this qualification does not accomplish what the Grotian proponents wish it would accomplish, namely allowing one to assert falsely to the Nazi. For asserting falsely

to the Nazi *per se* renders one untrustworthy to the Nazi, even though *per accidens* it renders one more trustworthy to the Jews one is hiding. Shields is absolutely right to point out that there seems to be no reasonable way in which one can weaken the notion of "right" as used in the Grotian definition that both allows for one *not* to be lying to the Nazi, but also to be *in fact* lying to the those in the grocery store (not to mention the other examples I list further in this article).

57. Edward Feser, "What Counts as a Lie?," *Edwardfeser.blogspot.com* November 15, 2010, accessed January 29, 2015, http://edwardfeser.blogspot.com/2010/11/what-counts-as-lie.html.

58. One may object that in the grocery store and in the doctor's office people do have a right to know the truth. I am violating their rights by knowingly uttering falsehoods to them. Ergo, I am lying. To this objection, I reply as follows: if these random people really have a right to know, then it follows that you owe the truth to them. Whatever one has a right to is due to that person. Since that person has a right to the truth, it follows that he is due the truth. But denying another what is his due is wrong. Ergo, it follows that not telling him the truth is wrong. Silence is not telling him the truth. Thus, it follows that being silent to random people about these random facts is morally wrong. Ergo, if it is claimed that those in the grocery store and in the doctor's office have a right to know in this sense, then it logically follows that one is morally obligated to go around telling random people random truths that you know.

59. Christopher O. Tollefsen, *Lying and Christian Ethics*, 29.

60. Sed contra est quod periurium definitur esse *mendacium iuramento firmatum.* Latin from hereon, unless otherwise indicated, is from the Pauline edition.

61. ST II-II, Q89, A1.

62. A fuller account of Thomas's definition will be given in a later footnote in this article, but for now I refer my reader to the following passages: *Super Sent.* III, d. 38, q. 1, a. 3: quandocumque aliquis loquitur quod in corde non habet . . . Hoc autem contingit in omni mendacio. Latin is from Moos.

Quaestiones de Quolibets VIII, q. 6, a. 4: et ideo quando aliquis voce enuntiat quod non habet in mente, quod importatur in nomine mendacii. Latin is from the Leonine, vol. 12.

ST II-II, Q110, A1: Sed tamen ratio mendacii sumitur a formali falsitate, ex hoc scilicet quod aliquis habet voluntatem falsum enuntiandi. Unde et mendacium nominatur ex eo quod contra mentem dicitur. Latin is from the Pauline.

63. Tollefsen, *Lying and Christian Ethics*, 29.

64. Ibid., 29.

65. Christopher Kaczor replies to this objection by saying, "It is indeed possible that one communication can be intrinsically evil with respect to one person, but not with respect to another. Consider, for example, a lawyer speaking to both his own client and a stranger about privileged information, a doctor speaking both to her patient and to a stranger about privileged medical matters" (Christopher Kaczor, "Can It Be Morally Permissible to Assert a Falsehood in Service of a Good Cause?," *American Catholic Philosophical Quarterly* 86, no. 1 [2012]: 105). Kaczor raises a good point here, but a difference remains between his cases and the gambling husband case. Intuitively, it seems the lawyer is not lying to either party, nor is the doctor. One party just misunderstands what the doctor is saying; likewise one party just misunderstands what the lawyer is saying. Thus, I think intuitively most people would say

neither the lawyer nor the doctor lied. But in the gambling husband scenario it just seems counterintuitive to say that the husband is not lying to *both* parties when he asserts *to both* "I gave the money to charity."

66. One may object here that the truth is due to them as God's command has made it so. This, however, is not supported by the Biblical texts. God never said that the truth is owed to others in justice, or that others have a right to know the truth about our religion. We ought to preach the Gospel, but out of charity, not out of justice.

Further, if the truth is really due to others in strict justice, then it follows that being silent is also an injustice. Ergo, one ought to go around telling everyone one meets that one is a follower of Jesus Christ. This is quite impractical in many situations. I am not doing any injustice in not speaking to every person I pass by on my morning run through the park.

67. Mt. 10:33 (NAB); cf. Luke 12:8–9: "I tell you, everyone who acknowledges me before others the Son of Man will acknowledge before the angels of God. But whoever denies me before others will be denied before the angels of God" (NAB).

68. This view is expressed as an objection to a similar definition of lying in Edwin Mahon, *Stanford Encyclopedia of Philosophy*, s.v. "The Definition of Lying and Deception," February 21, 2008, Section 1.6, accessed November 7, 2014, http://plato.stanford.edu/entries/lying-definition/.

69. Mahon, *Stanford Encyclopedia of Philosophy*, s.v. "The Definition of Lying and Deception," Section 1.6, http://plato.stanford.edu/entries/lying-definition/.

70. Cf. Mahon, *Stanford*, s.v. "The Definition of Lying and Deception."

71. Hugo Grotius, *On the Law of War and Peace*, Book I, Chapter 1, II, p. 7.

72. Ibid., Book III, Chapter 1, Section XI: "It is further requisite, to constitute a violation of this *right*, that the ensuing injury should immediately affect the person addressed: *as in contracts, there can be no injustice,* but what affects one of the parties, or persons concerned" (emphasis added). Same place: "And perhaps under the head of this *right*, it may not be improper to assign a place to that true speaking, which Plato, following Simonides, classes *with justice,* in order to form a more striking contrast with falsehood. . . . Cicero also in his offices *lays down truth, as the basis of justice*" (emphasis added). He then says that if consent is given, then the right to know ceases. This, however, is exactly the case with justice, as it is impossible to do injustice to another with that other's consent.

73. ST II-II, Q109, A1.

74. Cf. ST II-II, Q48, A1; Q109, A3.

75. Cf. ST II-II, Q48, A1.

76. ST II-II, Q109, A3.

77. Ibid.

78. Ibid: sed potius debitum morale, inquantum scilicet ex honestate unus homo alteri debet veritatis manifestationem. Latin is from the Pauline.

79. Interestingly in spite of defining lying in terms of rights, Dubois still claims that "veracity is a virtue annexed to justice (cf. Saint Thomas)" (171). Whether Dubois properly understands the meaning of an annexed virtue in Aquinas is unclear. Perhaps, what Dubois means is that there is a broad right of your neighbor to know the truth, but that this right is not indefeasible and can be superseded by a higher right (171–172). This, however, only

further complicates the issue. What then is the difference for Dubois between a broad right and a strict right? Is it only possible to lie if the broad rights of the person are violated? Or is it only if the strict rights of the person are violated that your utterance counts as lying? How does one tell if one's audience has a broad or a strict right? Is this broad right only defeasible by another broad right? Or is it defeasible only by other strict rights?

80. In his commentary Aquinas explicates Aristotle's word without any disagreement here: *Sententiae Quarti Libri Ethicorum*, IV.7, *Lectio* 15, 100–120, pp. 252–253. Latin is from the Leonine, *Tomus* XLVII, Vol. II.

81. Irwin translation. The Greek text is as follows: οὐ γὰρ περὶ τοῦ ἐν ταῖς ὁμολογίαις ἀληθεύοντος λέγομεν, οὐδ' ὅσα εἰς ἀδικίαν ἢ δικαιοσύνην συντείνει (ἄλλης γὰρ ἂν εἴη ταῦτ' ἀρετῆς), ἀλλ' ἐν οἷς μηδενὸς τοιούτου διαφέροντος καὶ ἐν λόγῳ καὶ ἐν βίῳ ἀληθεύει τῷ τὴν ἕξιν τοιοῦτος εἶναι (*Nicomachean Ethics* IV.VII 1127a33–1127b3, Loeb Classical Library [London/Cambridge: Harvard University Press, 1934], p. 240).

82. Translations of the Summa are all from newadvent.org unless otherwise indicated. The Latin is as follows: Mendacium autem est malum ex genere. Est enim actus cadens super indebitam materiam: cum enim voces sint signa naturaliter intellectuum, innaturale est et indebitum quod aliquis voce significet id quod non habet in mente. Unde Philosophus dicit, in IV *Ethic.*, quod *mendacium est per se pravum et fugiendum: verum autem et bonum laudabile.* Unde omne mendacium est peccatum: sicut etiam Augustinus asserit, in libro *contra Mendacium.*

83. Unfortunately, there is no single text where Aquinas gives his precise definition of lying. So what his precise definition is must be gathered from an examination of the various texts. In ST II-II, Q110, A3, he describes lying as *voce significet id quod habet in mente*, in his *Commentary on the Nicomachean Ethics* Book IV.7, Lecture 15, he describes it as *repraesentat rem aliter quam sit mentiendo*; in his *Quaestiones de Quolibets*, VIII, Q6, A4, he describes lying as *quando aliquis voce enuntiat quod non habet in mente*; and in his *Super Sent.* III, D38, A3, he describes lying as *quandocumque aliquis loquitur quod in corde non habet.* None of those passages though are precise definitions of lying. For in speaking a lie one is in a sense speaking what one has in one's mind, namely the words that one will speak in telling the lie. This indicates that Aquinas's descriptions of lying as *contra mentem* needs some nuancing. Thus, one needs to also take into consideration that in ST II-II, Q110, A1 Aquinas adds the requirement of formal falsity. Further, in ST II-II, Q110, A1, ad 3 Aquinas mentions that the intention to deceive is not essential to lying. Likewise, one needs to take into account the fact that in various passages Aquinas takes assertions as being essential to his definition: ST II-II, Q110, A1, "Whether lying is always opposed to truth?," s.c.: Sed contra est quod Augustinus dicit, in libro *contra Mendacium*: Nemo dubitet mentiri eum qui falsum *enuntiat* causa fallendi. Quapropter *enuntiationem* falsi cum voluntate ad fallendum prolatam, manifestum est esse mendacium;

ST II-II, Q110, A1, co: Respondeo dicendum quod actus moralis ex duobus speciem sortitur: scilicet ex obiecto, et ex fine. Nam finis est obiectum voluntatis, quae est primum movens in moralibus actibus . . . Quae quidem manifestatio, sive *enuntiatio*, est rationis actus conferentis signum ad signatum . . . Inquantum tamen huiusmodi manifestatio sive *enuntiatio* est actus moralis, oportet quod sit voluntarius ex intentione voluntatis dependens. Obiectum autem proprium manifestationis sive *enuntiationis* est verum vel falsum. Intentio vero voluntatis inordinatae potest ad duo ferri: quorum unum est ut falsum *enuntietur*; aliud quidem est effectus proprius falsae *enuntiationis,* ut scilicet aliquis fallatur. Si ergo ista tria concurrant, scilicet quod falsum sit id quod *enuntiatur*, et quod adsit voluntas falsum *enuntiandi*, et iterum intentio fallendi, tunc est falsitas materialiter, quia falsum dicitur; et formaliter, propter voluntatem falsum dicendi; et effective, propter voluntatem falsitatem imprimendi. Sed tamen ratio mendacii sumitur a formali falsitate: ex hoc scilicet quod aliquis habet voluntatem falsum *enuntiandi*. Unde et mendacium nominatur ex eo quod *contra mentem* dicitur. Et ideo si quis falsum *enuntiet* credens illud verum esse, est quidem falsum materialiter, sed non formaliter . . . Sic ergo patet quod mendacium directe et formaliter opponitur virtuti veritatis;

ST II-II, Q110, A3, ad 6: sicut Augustinus dicit, in libro *contra Mendacium*, quidquid figurate fit aut dicitur, non est mendacium. Omnis enim *enuntiatio* ad id quod *enuntiat* referenda est: omne autem figurate aut factum aut dictum hoc *enuntiat* quod significat eis quibus intelligendum prolatum est. Emphasis added. Latin is from the Pauline. Note that Aquinas uses *enuntiatio* or *enuntiat*, which I take to be practically the same as an assertion.

Lest it seem that I am reading too much into Aquinas's account, it must be noted that Rockcastle (S. Austen Rockcastle, "St. Thomas Aquinas On The Nature And Morality Of Lying" [PhD diss., University of St. Thomas—Houston, 1993], Chapter 9.), Boyle ("The Absolute Prohibition of Lying and the Origins of the Casuistry of Mental Reservation: Augustinian Arguments and Thomistic Developments," *The American Journal of Jurisprudence* 44, no. 1 [1999]: 59), and probably Sorenson (Roy Sorensen, "Bald-Faced Lies! Lying Without The Intent To Deceive," *Pacific Philosophical Quarterly* 88, no. 2 [2007]: 254) all think assertions are fundamental to Aquinas's definition.

Further evidence of the importance of assertions in Aquinas's account can be found in the following passages: a) ST II-II, Q110, A3, ad 1: Ad primum ergo dicendum quod nec in Evangelio, nec in aliqua Scriptura canonica fas est opinari aliquod falsum *asseri*, nec quod scriptores earum mendacium dixerunt; b) *Super Sent.* III, d. 38, a. 5, ad 1: Ad primum ergo dicendum quod ille qui disputando falsum loquitur, quamvis scienter, non mentitur, nisi *asserendo* dicat: quia non ex sua persona falsum illud *enuntiat*, sed gerens personem veritatem negantis (Latin is from Moos, p. 1275); c) ST II-II, Q111, A1, ad 1: Et subiungit exemplum de figurativis locutionibus, in quibus fingitur quaedam res non ut *asseratur* ita esse, sed eam proponimus ut figuram alterius quod *assere* volumus. Emphasis added.

84. Janet E. Smith, "Fig Leaves and Falsehoods, Pace Thomas Aquinas, Sometimes We Need to Deceive," *First Things*, June 2011, accessed October 7, 2014, http://www.firstthings.com/article/2011/06/fig-leaves-and-falsehoods.

Janet E. Smith, "Why Tollefsen and Pruss Are Wrong about Lying," *First Things*, December 15, 2011, accessed October 7, 2014, http://www.firstthings.com/web-exclusives/2011/12/why-tollefsen-and-pruss-are-wrong-about-lying.

85. Augustine, *De Mendacio (On Lying)*, trans. H. Brown, ed. Kevin Knight, vol. 3, Nicene and Post-Nicene Fathers, First Series (Buffalo: Christian Literature Publishing Co, 1887), accessed January 29, 2015, http://www.newadvent.org/fathers/1312.htm.

86. Augustine's eightfold taxonomy is organized by Aquinas in ST II-II, Q110, A2 into the mischievous, jocose, officious, and pathological lies.

87. Daniel Shields has pointed out that "proponents of the right to know definition could simply say that violations of someone's right to know in insignificant matters are venial sins." In reply, I must say Shields raises an interesting point, but the difficulty is finding what a concrete example of this would look like. If I go around a grocery store telling people lies about what I ate for breakfast, am I really violating their rights? It seems not, not even in some insignificant sense. Perhaps then a better concrete example would be thus: my high school was a rather difficult maze to get around for the new freshmen. The incoming

freshmen would occasionally ask the upperclassmen where the gym was. As a joke, a senior would say, "by the pool," knowingly fully that there was no pool in the entire school. In this scenario it seems that the right to know of the freshman was violated, but perhaps in only an insignificant sense. So a lie was, in fact, told on the Grotian definition. This seems correct. Nevertheless, I must point out that everyone whom I have encountered who supports the Grotian definition also wants to hold that jocose lies do not exist.

At the very least, if jocose lies do exist under the Grotian definition, cases like this would be the only cases where lying is merely a venial sin. The Grotian definition effectively eliminates all officious lies, as by definition the officious lie does not harm anybody, nor does it violate the rights of another.

88. Mahon, *Stanford Encyclopedia of Philosophy*, s.v. "The Definition of Lying and Deception," Section 1.6.

89. Ibid.

Truthmaking and Christian Theology

Timothy Pawl

Abstract: This paper analyzes Catholic philosophy by investigating the parameters that Catholic dogmatic claims set for theories of truthmaking. First I argue that two well-known truthmaker views—the view that properties alone are the truthmakers for contingent predications, and the view that all truths need truthmakers—are precluded by Catholic dogma. In particular, the doctrine of transubstantiation precludes the first, and the doctrines of divine causality and divine freedom together preclude the second. Next, I argue that the doctrine of the Incarnation, together with an admittedly-contested theological premise, requires a vast and sweeping revision to the standard view of truthmakers for predicative truths.

The teachings of the Catholic faith preclude certain philosophical views. For instance, Lateran V, the Ecumenical Council summoned by Pope Julius II and held from 1512–1517, in its "Condemnation of every proposition contrary to the truth of the enlightened [C]hristian faith," (Tanner 1990, 605) claimed that the mortality of the soul and the unicity of the soul among all humans are theses contrary to the faith. In fact, they went so far as to address *you* about this matter, my fellow philosophers. They wrote:

> We strictly enjoin on each and every philosopher who teaches publicly in the universities or elsewhere, that when they explain or address to their audience the principles or conclusions of philosophers, where these are known to deviate from the true faith—as in the assertion of the soul's mortality or of there being only one soul or of the eternity of the world and other topics of this kind—they are obliged to devote their every effort to clarify for their listeners the truth of the [C]hristian religion, to teach it by convincing arguments, so far as this is possible, and to apply themselves to the full extent of their energies to refuting and disposing of the philosophers' opposing arguments, since all the solutions are available. (Tanner 1990, 606)

A daunting task, no doubt, even if all the answers are available somewhere. It is said—I do not know whether it is true, and one finds differing accounts—that once

©2016, *Proceedings of the ACPA*, Vol. 89
doi: 10.5840/acpaproc201610548

a fellow traveler to Paris was struck by the beauty of the city. Aquinas's response to the star-struck sojourner was that he would rather have a copy of Chrysostom's commentaries on Matthew than the whole of the city. I imagine that we all feel the same about the comparative value of Paris and the treasure trove of solutions the conciliar fathers mention here.

In this article, I intend to analyze the implications of the Christian faith on a metaphysical enterprise with a deep history, but also a recent resurgence: truthmaker theory. By focusing on three central dogmas of the faith, I will show how these dogmas preclude certain well-known theories of truthmaking in the contemporary discussion.

To accomplish this, I will first say a bit about truthmaker theory. Then I will present the two live possibilities that Catholic dogma precludes in the truthmaker debates. After presenting those possibilities, I will show how the doctrines of transubstantiation and the attributes of God preclude them. I then go on to show that the doctrine of the Incarnation, along with a contested theological premise, requires a sweeping revision to the standard accounts of truthmakers for predications.

Truthmaking

Contemporary philosophers use the term *truthmaker* to designate that part or those parts of the world in virtue of which a proposition is true. For instance, each individual elephant is a truthmaker for the proposition, *there are elephants*. Truthmakers are the bits or portions of reality that make propositions true; they set the truth-value of at least some propositions. The medievals had the notion of a truthmaker as well. Though Aquinas does not employ the word, his contemporaries and later scholastics used the word *verificativum* (in English, quite literally, truthmaker). For instance, Ramon Llull (1232–1315) employs the term in no fewer than four of his works.[1] Later medieval thinkers—especially Jesuits in the seventeenth century—spilt much ink over truthmakers.[2] While Aquinas himself did not use the term, he was no stranger to the concept.[3] On occasion, Aquinas talks of truth being caused by something outside the mind. He says in his commentary on the Metaphysics:

> When I say *Socrates is a man*, the truth of this statement is caused [*causatur*] by the composition of the human form with the individual matter by which Socrates is this man. And when I say *the man is white*, the cause of this truth is the composition of whiteness with the subject. And it is similar in other cases.[4]

The point to recognize here is that Aquinas is giving an account of how reality has to be in order for certain types of predications to be true. And again, in the same work, he writes:

> [Y]ou are not white because we think truly that you are white; but conversely we think you are white because you are white. Hence it has been shown that the way in which a thing is disposed is the cause of truth both in thought and in speech.[5]

Here again Aquinas maintains that the foundation of truth in our assertions is reality.[6] Reality grounds what propositions are true. As the contemporary metaphysician David Lewis said (Lewis 1992, 218):

> [N]o two possibilities can differ about what's true unless they also differ in what things there are, or in how they are. . . . [T]ruths are about things, they don't float in a void.

One necessary condition for an object, call it T, to be a truthmaker for a proposition, call it p, is that, were both T and p to exist, p would be true. For instance, if the truthmaker for *Bob exists* is this particular guy, Bob, then whenever Bob and the relevant proposition exist, that proposition will be true. And likewise, were T to exist but p nevertheless to be false, that would give reason to think that T really isn't a truthmaker for p—after all, in such a case, here T is, existing its heart out, and there p is, as false as can be; T isn't making p true. With these examples in mind, we can present a necessary condition for a viable theory of the dependence of truth on reality, which we can call *Necessitation*:

> *Necessitation*: If a thing, T, is a truthmaker for a proposition, p, then, whenever both T and p exist, p is true.[7]

For the remainder of this article, I will assume that the propositions exist at the relevant times, and so only focus on the existence or non-existence of T. I will also assume, as is standard in the truthmaker literature, the truth of Necessitation.

T's necessitating the truth of p is commonly accepted as a necessary condition for truthmaker theory. Even more commonly accepted, though, is the fact that T's necessitating the truth of p is not a sufficient condition for T's being a truthmaker for p. To see why, suppose, for argument's sake, that necessitation is sufficient for truthmaking. Consider the proposition *that God exists*, or *that the Son is begotten*, or *that two plus two equals four*. Provided that those propositions are necessarily true, they are true whenever they exist. Thus, they are true whenever T happens to exist, too. But then, T fulfills the conditions for necessitating the truth of those propositions. Thus, on the supposition that necessitation is sufficient for truthmaking, T is a truthmaker for *that the Son is begotten*. But T could be anything! Look at your left shoe. It might be a mighty handsome shoe. But it isn't so fine as to make necessary theological and mathematical truths true. It is not the ground in being, the *fundamentum in re*, for the truth about the inner relations of the persons of the Godhead.

Here I won't give sufficient conditions for truthmaking. I needn't for my project. For we will see that Necessitation as stated is enough to show that the Catholic dogmas of transubstantiation and the attributes of God foreclose certain live possibilities in the contemporary philosophical discussion.

Two Live Possibilities in the Contemporary Truthmaker Debate

One live possibility in the contemporary truthmaker debate is the view that the truthmaker for contingent, intrinsic predicative truths is the individual property of the subject, and that individual property alone. This view is discussed by Ross Cameron (2008, 416), and affirmed by both E. J. Lowe (2012) and Gonzalo Rodriguez-Pereyra (2006b). Lowe writes of Dobbin the horse,

> Dobbin is white in virtue of being characterised by a certain whiteness *mode*, call it *W*. Now, it is part of the essence of *W* that it characterises Dobbin, since *W* depends for its identity on Dobbin. Equally, it is part of the essence of *W* that it instantiates the attribute *whiteness*. Hence, in any possible world in which *W* exists, *W* instantiates whiteness and characterises Dobbin, whence it follows that in any such world it is true that *Dobbin is white*, since he is characterised by a whiteness mode in that world. Thus *W* is a truthmaker of the proposition that Dobbin is white, as indeed would be *any* whiteness mode of Dobbin. (2012, 101–102)

Here Lowe claims that modes (which he elsewhere says are the same as tropes) are truthmakers for contingent predicative truths.

Similarly, Rodriguez-Pereyra writes,

> If one postulates tropes (or modes, or particularised properties, as they are sometimes called) one can account for the truthmakers for contingent propositions provided the tropes in question are non-transferable, that is, provided that any trope that characterises a certain particular cannot characterise another particular. In that case tropes can be the truthmakers for the relevant propositions (Lowe 2006, 205–7). For instance the rose's redness is the truthmaker for the proposition that the rose is red, and there is no conflict with Truthmaker Necessitarianism since it is impossible for the rose's redness to exist and the proposition that the rose is red not to be true. (Rodriguez-Pereyra 2006b, 192)

Here again we see a philosopher asserting that the mode, or trope, is the truthmaker for a contingent predicative truth. Henceforth, I will follow Lowe and Rodriguez-Pereyra in taking "mode," "trope," and "particularized property" to name the same entities. I will add another synonym to the list: "accident," in the medieval sense of the term.

Many in the Catholic Intellectual Tradition will agree with Rodriguez-Pereyra's claim that tropes (or accidents, as they may refer to them) are non-transferrable. Aquinas, for instance, writes in the *Summa* (*ST* III q.77 a.1 *resp*), "accidents do not pass from subject to subject, so that the same identical accident which was first in one subject be afterwards in another."[8] But these same thinkers will need to deny the implication that Rodriguez-Pereyra draws from non-transferability, given the doctrine of transubstantiation. In fact, we see Thomas deny it earlier when he says that the truthmaker for *the man is white* isn't merely the man's whiteness accident, but is that accident in composition with the man himself. Later I will argue, though, that even this Thomistic view may be in tension with an understanding of the doctrine of the Incarnation.

A second live possibility in the contemporary truthmaker debate is the thesis called *Truthmaker Maximalism*, or *Maximalism* for short. A natural question for truthmaker theorists is, "Which truths require truthmakers?" The maximalist is one who answers, "All of them." According to the maximalist, every truth requires a truthmaker. David Armstrong (2004, 5–6), Ross Cameron (2008), and Rodriguez-Pereyra (2006a) defend Truthmaker Maximalism in print, while Trenton Merricks (2009, 24–26) argues that truthmaker theorists have good reason to be Maximalists, and Mark Jago (2012) argues that the best reason on offer for being a non-maximalist truthmaker theorist fails. We shall see, though, that the Catholic doctrine of the attributes of God will entail the falsity of Truthmaker Maximalism.

Dead on Dogma

Begin with the first live possibility, the possibility of properties alone (modes, tropes, or accidents) playing the role of truthmaker for predications. Why must this view be precluded, given Catholic dogma? The answer is that the doctrine of transubstantiation allows the very possibility that Rodriguez-Pereyra claims impossible in his last above-quoted sentence, if we change the example from red roses to white bread. Recall that Rodriguez-Pereyra writes: "[I]t is impossible for the rose's redness to exist and the proposition that the rose is red not to be true." In what follows I will show why the doctrine of transubstantiation requires this possibility.

According to the doctrine of transubstantiation, what was once bread is transformed, whole and entire, into the body of Jesus Christ. On Aquinas's understanding of the ontology of the sacrament (*ST* III q.77 a.2), the accidental forms of the bread remain in existence where they were, though all the accidents but the dimensive quantity now inhere in that dimensive quantity. John Wyclif denied this metaphysical view, claiming that the accidents do not continue existing without the bread on the altar.[9] In response, the Ecumenical Council of Constance (1414–1418) condemned the following proposition from Wyclif's works: "The accidents [*Accidentia*] of bread do not remain without their subject in the said sacrament" (Tanner 1990, 411). The council went on to say it "forbids each and every Catholic henceforth, under pain of anathema, to preach, teach or affirm in public the said articles or any one of them in particular" (Tanner 1990, 414–415). Given this condemnation, along with the context from the other condemnations, we can see that the church is committed here to the accidents remaining without their subject in transubstantiation.

On Lowe and Rodriguez-Pereyra's view, the accident alone is the truthmaker for the predication *the bread is white*. Consider this view, though, in conjunction with the doctrine of transubstantiation as described. At consecration, the bread ceases to exist. Since the bread is not, it is not white (something has to *exist* to be colored). Thus, the predication *the bread is white* cannot be true.[10] However, if Lowe is right, then the proposition is true, since a truthmaker for that proposition, the whiteness accident, exists at that time. Now, however, we have derived a contradiction. The proposition is both true (given necessitation) and false (given the dogma).[11] Thus, the first live possibility is dead on dogma.

Consider now the second live possibility, Truthmaker Maximalism. What in Catholic Dogma precludes Maximalism? Here the connection is less apparent, though it is still there. The problem for Maximalism arises from the teachings that God creates freely, and that anything aside from God that exists is created by God.

According to the Catholic teaching concerning God's creative power, God is the creator of all things, visible and invisible, as many creeds of the church say. Moreover, the Catholic manualists, for instance, Ludwig Ott (1960, 79), claim that it is a *De Fide* truth of the Catholic Faith that "All that exists outside God was, in its whole substance, produced out of nothing by God." The manualist, Joseph Pohle (1911, 371), claims similarly that God is the creator of all that exists that is not God. Moreover, God created freely. As the First Vatican Council taught:

> If anyone does not confess that the world and all things which are contained in it, both spiritual and material, were produced, according to their whole substance, out of nothing by God; or holds that God did not create by his will free from all necessity, but [says instead that God created] as necessarily as he necessarily loves himself . . . let him be anathema. (Tanner 1990, 810)

Since God creates of his own free will, free from all necessity to create, it is possible that he not create anything. And if he doesn't create anything, there would be nothing in such a possible world but God alone, given that God creates everything that is not God. Now, in such a world, there are no dogs. God, being omniscient, would know that truth. What could make that truth true?

By hypothesis, the only thing there to make anything true is God. So, given Truthmaker Maximalism, God would need to be the truthmaker for the truth. But God is not a truthmaker for the truth *that there are no dogs*. We know this because both God and dogs exist in our actual world. If God were a truthmaker for the proposition *that there are no dogs*, and dogs are truthmakers for the proposition *that there are dogs*, a contradiction would be true, given Necessitation. For by Necessitation, both the propositions *that there are dogs* and *that there are no dogs* would be true, given the existence of God and dogs. So the conjunction of Truthmaker Maximalism and the dogmas in question are inconsistent. Thus, if the Catholic view of the attributes of God is true, then Truthmaker Maximalism is false.[12]

It might be objected to this argument that, were God to create nothing at all, not even dogs, there would be no proposition *that there are no dogs* there to be known. And so it is false that the proposition *that there are no dogs* would be true in that situation. Bread needs to exist to be white; likewise, propositions need to exist to be true.

I dealt with this objection in detail in a previous article (Pawl 2012a, 209–212). Since God is necessarily omniscient, he must know in worlds without dogs that there are no dogs there. And knowledge implies truth—God couldn't, in the same world, know the falsehood that there are some dogs. So something is true in that world. But there are open questions about the ontology of that true thing. I will consider three options.

Perhaps God doesn't know truths by there being something that is true, as we know by there being a proposition known. That is, God doesn't know by being acquainted in a certain way to a proposition that is true. In such a case, then, God knows, but there is nothing there that is known, and there is no truthmaker for that truth that is known. Such a theory would need fleshing out, but note that on it there is truth without a truthmaker, and so Maximalism is false.

Perhaps there is a thing that is known (call it a proposition) and it is necessarily existent. In such a case, the dogma that God is the creator of all things might be understood as saying that anything *contingent* is freely created by God, and so not require that God freely create these propositions. In such a case, there would be the proposition, *that there are no dogs*, there to be known. And since it is there to be known, and true, it would require a truthmaker, on Truthmaker Maximalism. The truth *that there are no dogs* is a contingent truth, so given the necessary existence of the propositions (as we assume in this paragraph), the truthmaker for the truth could not itself be necessarily existent. For if both the proposition and the truthmaker were necessarily existent, the truth would be true in every world, which is contrary to its being contingently true. So neither God nor the necessary things that he does not create (on this assumption) could be the truthmaker for *that there are no dogs*. Again, we find that Maximalism is false, given the dogma and the assumption of necessarily existing truthbearers.

Perhaps, finally, there is a thing known, *that there are no dogs*, and it is contingently created freely by God. Consider the possible creation where God creates all and only the propositions that he knows. In such a world, there would be no dogs. So the freely created proposition, *that there are no dogs*, would be true. But no proposition is a truthmaker for *that there are no dogs*. For any proposition can co-exist with a dog. I am not claiming here that any proposition can be *true* while a dog exists; I am claiming that any proposition, independent of its truth-value, can co-exist with a dog. But given Necessitation, no truthmaker, T1, for a proposition, p, can co-exist with the truthmaker, T2, for the proposition $\sim p$, provided that those propositions exist. For in such a case both p and $\sim p$ would be true. But then it follows that, since a dog can co-exist with any proposition, no proposition is a truthmaker for the proposition *that there are no dogs*. And so in a world in which God contingently, freely creates only propositions (it doesn't matter which propositions, perhaps all, provided that *that there are no dogs* is included), *that there are no dogs* is true and lacks a truthmaker. Thus, Maximalism is false.

I conclude this section with the assertion that Catholic dogma precludes both the possibility that contingent truths are made true by contingent properties alone and the possibility that all truths require truthmakers. In the next and final section of this article I will discuss a broader worry for truthmaker theories that arises from Christology.

Christology and Truthmaking

Consider the doctrine of the Incarnation. According to that doctrine, the Son of God became flesh and dwelt among us. He did this, as the doctrine words it, by assuming a human nature. And that human nature is not itself something abstract or platonic or shared among all humans, according to the conciliar documents. That nature is rather something that can be hung, pierced, and weep, as St. Leo says in his Tome, which was accepted and ratified at multiple early Ecumenical Councils starting with Chalcedon:

> It does not belong to the same nature [*non eiusdem naturae est*] to weep out of deep-felt pity for a dead friend, and to call him back to life again at the word of command . . . or to hang on the cross and . . . to make the elements tremble; or to be pierced by nails and to open the gates of paradise for the believing thief. Likewise, it does not belong to the same nature to say *I and the Father are one*, and to say *The Father is greater than I.* (Tanner 1990, 80)

And again:

> [I]f he accepts the Christian faith and does not turn a deaf ear to the preaching of the gospel, let him consider what nature it was that hung, pierced with nails, on the wood of the cross [*quae natura transfixa clavis pependerit in crucis ligno*]. With the side of the crucified one laid open by the soldier's spear, let him identify the source from which blood and water flowed, to bathe the church of God with both font and cup. (Tanner 1990, 81)

In these examples we see Leo predicating of the nature that it calls, that it hangs, that it is pierced, that it is the source of the blood and water that flowed. And when St. Cyril, in the conciliar documents from the Council of Ephesus (431) speaks of the nature Christ assumed by way of paraphrase, he does it with terms such as "flesh enlivened by a rational soul," or a "holy body rationally ensouled" (Tanner 1990, 41, 44). Again, none of these paraphrases is apt of an abstract nature.[13]

So Christ assumed a flesh and blood composite of body and soul. Later councils, starting with the 3rd Council of Constantinople (681) claim that this assumed nature had its own will, so that dyothelitism, the view that Christ had two wills, one human and one divine, becomes dogma. In the remainder of this article, when I refer to a human nature, whether assumed or not, I am referring to a flesh and blood composite of body and soul; something Cyril would call "flesh enlivened by a rational soul" and something that could rightly be said to be able to hang on a cross or bleed, as Leo says.

Suppose, as is disputed, that some actual, but not assumed human nature is possibly assumable. For instance, while Socrates's human nature was not assumed, it is within the divine power, absolutely considered, to assume that nature. Or suppose that the human nature that the Second Person actually assumed could have existed unassumed. Aquinas grants the possibility of Christ's human nature existing unassumed, at least for the sake of argument, in his *Disputed Questions on the Union of the Incarnate Word*, a.2, ad.10, where he says:

> As long as the human nature is united to the Word of God, it does not have its own suppositum or hypostasis beyond the person of the Word, because it does not exist in itself. But if it were separated from the Word, it would have, not only its own hypostasis or suppositum, but also its own person; because it would now exist per se. (Aquinas 1953, a2 ad10)

Either supposition will work for the following argument, since in either case there will be some nature or other such that in some possible worlds it is assumed and in others it is not.

Stick with Socrates's human nature for now. Earlier I quoted Aquinas as saying that the truthmaker for *Socrates is human* is the form of humanity that inheres in Socrates, in composition with the particular matter in which that form inheres. Aquinas looks to be saying that the truthmaker is the composition of that particular substantial form and prime matter. However, this cannot be right on the suppositions that Socrates's human nature is possibly assumable and that "Socrates" names a person, as I will go on to show.

Consider a world in which Socrates's human nature is assumed. In such a world, Socrates, the person, does not exist. For if he did exist, then there would be two persons there in the Incarnation in question, which is a condemned view. It might be that the Son could enter into some relation or other with Socrates's human nature so that both persons exist, but that relation is not the relation of assumption, and the human and divine natures would be united in some way otherwise than a hypostatic union, given the definitive pronouncements of the Church concerning the hypostatic union.

In such a world, Socrates's human nature would exist, composed of the same form and matter, though Socrates would not exist. It follows from this that the purported truthmaker would exist, while the proposition, *Socrates is human*, is false. That, though, is impossible, given the truth of Necessitation. Thus, given Necessitation, the doctrine of the Incarnation, and the possibility that at least one nature could exist either assumed or unassumed, it follows that the composition of Socrates's substantial form and prime matter is insufficient for making true the proposition *Socrates is human*.

The difficulty here is isomorphic to the difficulty raised by transubstantiation, but instead of being a change across time, as when the thing on the altar goes from being bread to being Christ's body, it is a change across worlds. The very same entity, Socrates's human nature, can exist and the proposition be false that *Socrates is human*, owing to the non-existence of the person named "Socrates."

Something similar can be shown for contingent predications as well. Suppose that the truthmaker for *Socrates is white* is the composition of his human nature and the whiteness that inheres in him, as Aquinas said. Then, since truthmakers necessitate, whenever that composition exists, it is true that *Socrates is white*. But now consider a world in which that nature is assumed. In such a world, it is false that *Socrates is white*, since, again, Socrates does not exist, and so is not colored at all. And so the composition of Socrates's human nature and his accidental form of whiteness is not the truthmaker for *Socrates is white* in the actual world. In brief: truthmakers necessitate; but given the Incarnation and the possibility of a divine person assuming the human nature Socrates actually has, that human nature and its inhering accidental form of whiteness does not necessitate the truth of *Socrates is white*. Thus, that human nature and its inhering accidental form of whiteness are not a truthmaker for *Socrates is white*, contra Aquinas's view.

This shows that, provided one grants that it is possible for one and the same nature to exist either assumed or unassumed, and one grants the doctrine of the Incarnation, then one needs to revise the standard and common account of truthmakers for predications.

It is true that we would not *call* the above-discussed nature "Socrates's human nature" in a creation in which it were assumed. But that's merely a difference in name, or how we refer to the nature in question. We could refer to it otherwise. We could name the nature itself. Or we could refer to the nature, not in terms of the person, but rather in terms of the substantial form, supposing that the composite nature requires the same substantial form in all situations. In either case, the mere fact that I have referred to the nature in question by the name of the person who "has" that nature is not a problem. I have used the term as a rigid designator, as one might use the term "the inventor of bifocals" in the phrase "the inventor of bifocals might have died in infancy" to borrow a common example. He wouldn't have been the inventor of bifocals had he died in infancy, but we can still use the term to refer to the same man in such a scenario. Likewise, it wouldn't have been Socrates's human nature had it been assumed at the first moment of its existence, but we can still use that term to refer to the same nature in such a scenario.

Another worry that one might have concerning the argument in this section is that I have used the name "Socrates" to refer to one thing, and "Socrates's human nature" to refer to another. But, the objection continues, those terms refer to the same thing. Socrates's human nature is Socrates (the person) when it fulfills certain conditions (chief among them, not being assumed). Alfred Freddoso says, for instance:

> Aquinas, Scotus and Ockham all believe that Christ's human nature is a substance composed of a body and an intellective soul. They further agree—very plausibly, it seems to me—that in every case other than the Incarnation, an individual human nature by itself constitutes or just is a human suppositum or human person. (Freddoso 1986, 30)

Here, Freddoso attributes to Aquinas, Scotus, and Ockham the view that Socrates's human nature constitutes or is identical to the human person, Socrates. Thomas Flint says similarly:

> What am I? I am an individual human nature—a body/soul composite, we have been supposing. *Those* are the parts that I have; *they're* what make me what I am. Am I a person? That depends. Depends upon what? It depends upon how I'm *related* to something *distinct from me*; it depends upon whether or not I've been assumed by a divine person. (Flint 2012, 204)

Though their views of the Incarnation diverge elsewhere (in particular, Freddoso denies but Flint is sympathetic to the contentious theological premise I've been discussing here, that natures are contingently assumable) they both are inclined to the view that Socrates's human nature constitutes or just is the person, when it fulfills certain conditions.[14]

Suppose that view were true. "Socrates," then, is the name of a nature, and that nature is a person when it fulfills certain conditions. But then, even when Socrates's human nature is assumed, the proposition *Socrates is white* can be true. It can be true because, under the assumption that "Socrates" names the nature, the thing named still exists and is still a certain way—it still has an inhering whiteness accident. It does not fulfill the conditions for being a person in such a scenario, since it is assumed, but it still fulfills the conditions for the proposition, *Socrates is white*, being true. And so, on the view described with reference to Flint and Freddoso, we needn't revise the truthmaker for *Socrates is white*, even given the contingent assumability of human natures.[15] Were Socrates's human nature to retain a whiteness accident and to be assumed, it would still be true that *Socrates is white*.

In response to this worry, I agree that were "Socrates" another name for what I've been calling "Socrates's human nature," then the nature and the inhering accident of whiteness can be a truthmaker for *Socrates is white*, as it is for *Socrates's human nature is white*. But I see two problems with this response to the argument I provide in this section.

First, this is an idiosyncratic understanding of the name "Socrates." We normally treat that to be a *personal* name. We take it to track the person. Now, it might be that this is a mistaken way of understanding the name "Socrates"; perhaps we always should have understood names not to track persons, but to track natures. But if so, that's a case that has to be made. (Since neither Freddoso nor Flint were considering this particular argument, or this application of their views, it is no fault of theirs that they do not make the case with respect to this argument.)

Second, even if "Socrates" does name a nature that is contingently a person (given the contingent assumability thesis), we can still provide a name explicitly and specifically for the person. And when we do that, we can substitute that name in to the arguments above, and yield the same result: supposing that predicative truths about persons have truthmakers, those truthmakers cannot be the thing we normally point to as truthmakers for predicated truths. They cannot be, for instance, the inherence of an accident in a substance. For that very same substance can exist with the very same sitting accident inhering in it, and yet *that person is sitting* be false, given the contingent assumability thesis.

Conclusion

In conclusion, I have argued that the doctrines of transubstantiation, divine causality and freedom, and the Incarnation preclude certain live possibilities in contemporary analytic truthmaker theory. Transubstantiation precludes the possibility, defended by Lowe and Rodriguez-Pereyra, that properties alone are truthmakers for truths of contingent predication. The doctrines of divine causality and divine freedom together preclude the truth of Truthmaker Maximalism. And the doctrine of the Incarnation, when conjoined with an admittedly contested theological claim, requires a vast and sweeping modification to the standard account of what makes truths of predication true.

It is my hope that the work of this article has fulfilled, at least in part, the obligation enjoined upon me by the good fathers at Lateran V: to explain and address how the conclusions of some philosophers in the contemporary, analytic truthmaker debate are contrary to the revealed truths of the Christian faith.[16]

University of St. Thomas (MN)

Notes

1. These being his *Ars Generalis Ultima* ([op. 128] pars: 8, linea: 474), *Liber Correlatiuorum Innatorum* ([op. 159] dist.: 4, linea: 440) *Liber de Ente Infinito* ([op. 158] dist.: 4, linea: 433) and *Liber de Memoria* ([op. 111] dist.: 2, linea: 192). I thank Dr. Jack Marler for these citations.

2. For much more on medieval discussions of truthmakers, see Doyle (1987; 1988; 1995) and Embry (2014; 2015).

3. See Pawl (2008, chap. 3; 2016b).

4. Aquinas's *Commentary on Aristotle's Metaphysics*, lib.9 l.11 n.4. This is my translation from the Latin available at http://www.corpusthomisticum.org/iopera.html.

5. *Commentary on the Metaphysics*, b.9 l.11 para. 1897. See also *QDP* q.1 a.17 ad.29.; (Aquinas 1954, q.1 a.2 ad.3).

6. For more on Aquinas's thought on the relation of truth to reality, see Frost (2010), Inman (2012), and Pawl (2008, chap. 3; 2016b).

7. To see discussions of necessitation as a necessary condition for a viable truthmaker theory, see, for instance, Armstrong (2004, 5–7); Merricks (2009, 5–11).

8. This translation is from the Fathers of the English Dominican Province (1981).

9. For more on Wyclif's interesting metaphysics of the Eucharist, see Levy (2015).

10. Brower discusses this case as well. See Brower (2014, 245–250).

11. I offer a similar argument elsewhere (2012b), though there my target is not to show that Lowe's view of truthmakers for predications is precluded by dogmatic statements.

12. For this argument, worked out in much finer detail, see my article (Pawl 2012a). For another argument which aims to show that Truthmaker Maximalism is inconsistent with a certain type of temporal change or modal difference across worlds, see Pawl (2014).

13. I go into these two reasons for thinking that the human nature of Christ is a concrete, not abstract and shareable, thing in Pawl (2016a, chapter 2, section b).

14. I discuss this view in depth in Pawl (2016, 65–70).

15. As noted above, Freddoso denies the contingent assumability of natures, and so he has yet another reason to reject the argument I have given in this section.

16. I thank Alexander Pruss, Katheryn Rogers, and the other audience members at the American Catholic Philosophical Association meeting where I presented this paper. I especially thank Andrew Jaeger for his helpful comments on the paper.

Bibliography

Aquinas, Thomas. 1953. *Quaestio Disputata de Unione Verbi Incarnati*. Taurini: Marietti.

Aquinas, Thomas. 1954. *The Disputed Questions on Truth (in Three Volumes)*. Translated by Robert Schmidt. Chicago: Henry Regnery Co.

Aquinas, Thomas. 1981. *The Summa Theologica of St. Thomas Aquinas*. Translated by Fathers of the English Dominican Province. Christian Classics.

Armstrong, David Malet. 2004. *Truth and Truthmakers*. Cambridge University Press. doi: https://doi.org/10.1017/CBO9780511487552

Brower, Jeffrey E. 2014. *Aquinas's Ontology of the Material World: Change, Hylomorphism, and Material Objects*. Oxford University Press. doi: https://doi.org/10.1093/acprof:oso/9780198714293.001.0001

Cameron, Ross P. 2008. "How to Be a Truthmaker Maximalist." *Noûs* 42.3: 410–421. doi: https://doi.org/10.1111/j.1468-0068.2008.00687.x

Doyle, John P. 1987. "Suarez on Beings of Reason and Truth: Part 1." *Vivarium* 25: 47–75. doi: https://doi.org/10.1163/156853487X00058

Doyle, John P. 1988. "Suarez on Beings of Reason and Truth: Part 2." *Vivarium* 26: 51–72. doi: https://doi.org/10.1163/156853488X00048

Doyle, John P. 1995. "Another God, Chimerae, Goat-Stags, and Man-Lions: A Seventeenth-Century Debate about Impossible Objects." *Review of Metaphysics* 48.4: 771–808.

Embry, Brian. 2014. "An Early Modern Scholastic Theory of Negative Entities: Thomas Compton Carleton on Lacks, Negations, and Privations." *British Journal for the History of Philosophy* 23.1: 22–45. doi: https://doi.org/10.1080/09608788.2014.976759

Embry, Brian. 2015. "Truth and Truthmakers in Early Modern Scholasticism." *Journal of the American Philosophical Association* 1.2: 196–216. doi: https://doi.org/10.1017/apa.2014.28

Flint, Thomas P. 2012. "Molinism and Incarnation." In *Molinism: The Contemporary Debate*, edited by Ken Perszyk, 187–207. Oxford: Oxford University Press.

Freddoso, Alfred. 1986. "Human Nature, Potency and the Incarnation." *Faith and Philosophy* 3.1: 27–53. doi: https://doi.org/10.5840/faithphil1986312

Frost, Gloria. 2010. "Thomas Aquinas on the Perpetual Truth of Essential Propositions." *History of Philosophy Quarterly* 27.3: 197–213.

Inman, Ross. 2012. "Essential Dependence, Truthmaking, and Mereology: Then and Now." In *Metaphysics: Aristotelian, Scholastic, Analytic*, edited by Lukas Novak, Daniel D. Novotny, Prokop Sousedik, and David Svoboda, 73–90. Ontos Verlag. doi: https://doi.org/10.1515/9783110322446.73

Jago, Mark. 2012. "The Truthmaker Non-Maximalist's Dilemma." *Mind* 121, no. 484: 903–918. doi: https://doi.org/10.1093/mind/fzs124

Levy, Ian Christopher. 2015. *John Wyclif's Theology of the Eucharist in Its Medieval Context. Revised and Expanded Edition of Scriptural Logic, Real Presence, and the Parameters of Orthodoxy.* Milwaukee, WI: Marquette Univ Press.

Lewis, David. 1992. "Critical Notice of David Armstrong, A Combinatorial Theory of Possibility." *Australasian Journal of Philosophy* 70.2: 211–224. doi: https://doi.org/10.1080/00048409212345101

Lowe, E. J. 2006. *The Four-Category Ontology: A Metaphysical Foundation for Natural Science.* Oxford/New York: Oxford University Press.

Lowe, E. J. 2012. "Essence and Ontology." In *Metaphysics: Aristotelian, Scholastic, Analytic,* edited by Lukas Novak, Daniel D. Novotny, Prokop Sousedik, and David Svoboda, 73–90. Ontos Verlag. doi: https://doi.org/10.1515/9783110322446.93

Merricks, Trenton. 2009. *Truth and Ontology.* New York: Oxford University Press.

Ott, Ludwig. 1960. *Fundamentals of Catholic Dogma,* 4th ed. Herder.

Pawl, Timothy. 2008. *A Thomistic Account of Truthmakers for Modal Truths.* Unpublished Dissertation.

Pawl, Timothy. 2012a. "Traditional Christian Theism and Truthmaker Maximalism." *European Journal for Philosophy of Religion* 4.1: 197–218.

Pawl, Timothy. 2012b. "Transubstantiation, Tropes and Truthmakers." *American Catholic Philosophical Quarterly* 86.1: 71–96. doi: https://doi.org/10.5840/acpq_2012_4

Pawl, Timothy. 2014. "Change, Difference, and Orthodox Truthmaker Theory." *Australasian Journal of Philosophy* 92.3: 539–550. doi: https://doi.org/10.1080/00048402.2013.839726

Pawl, Timothy. 2016a. *In Defense of Conciliar Christology: A Philosophical Essay.* Oxford University Press. doi: https://doi.org/10.1093/acprof:oso/9780198765929.001.0001

Pawl, Timothy. 2016b. "A Thomistic Truthmaker Principle." *Acta Philosophica* 25.1: 45–54.

Pohle, Joseph. 1911. *God: His Knowability, Essence, and Attributes: A Dogmatic Treatise Prefaced by a Brief General Introduction to the Study of Dogmatic Theology.* B. Herder.

Rodriguez-Pereyra, Gonzalo. 2006a. "Truthmaker Maximalism Defended." *Analysis* 66.3: 260–264. doi: https://doi.org/10.1093/analys/66.3.260

Rodriguez-Pereyra, Gonzalo. 2006b. "Truthmakers." *Philosophy Compass* 1.2: 186–200. doi: https://doi.org/10.1111/j.1747-9991.2006.00018.x

Tanner, Norman P. 1990. *Decrees of the Ecumenical Councils 2 Volume Set.* Washington, D.C.: Georgetown University Press.

Existential Thomist[1] Reflections on Kenny: The Incompatibility of the Phoenix and Subsistent Existence

John F. X. Knasas

Abstract: My target is Kenny's claim that if God can be thought not to be in the same manner as men or phoenixes, then God too is an essence/existence composite. I argue that our ignorance about the existence of the phoenix and our ignorance about God do not have the same bases and so they do not lead to the same conclusion, namely, a distinction between thing and existence in both cases. The notion of the phoenix is existence neutral because it is reflective of conceptual notes that have to be existence neutral in order to be in existential multiplicities. Our notion of subsistent existence is not existence neutral but it is composed of a formed intention of existence that gives it an independence from the context of the second operation in which it was formed. The first case leads to a situation involving a distinction between essence and existence. Knowledge of the existence of the phoenix adds something over and beyond the essence of the phoenix. In the second case, knowledge of the existence of subsistent existence does not do that because existence is what the formed intention here is of. What knowledge of subsistent existence adds does not belong to it. It belongs to us. It adds our second operation knowledge of the *esse* of sensible things and our reasoning from that to subsistent existence.

In the fourth chapter of the *De Ente et Essentia*, Aquinas states that one can know what a man or a phoenix is and yet not know if they have being in reality (*ignorare an esse habeant in rerum natura*). For Anthony Kenny "the *On Being and Essence* argument from phoenixes to the real distinction between essence and *esse*, can be seen to be fatally flawed."[2] Kenny's difficulty with the argument is not what rattles most Thomists, viz., whether the argument establishes the real distinction between essence and existence. Kenny says that it does.[3] Rather the difficulty is that the argument's conclusion is at odds with the context of the chapter. The context is one of distinguishing separate immaterial substances, called intelligences, from God. Aquinas will argue that though these substances lack a matter/form composition, they do not rival the simplicity of God. In them is still found a composition of essence and existence. But far from supporting that way of distinguishing separate substances and God, the phoenix argument leaves the two still conflated, for God also can be thought not to be in the same manner as men or phoenixes. As Kenny says, "Atheists, after all, have a concept of God; otherwise they wouldn't know what it was they were denying when they deny that God exists."[4] Hence, both intelligences and God would have to be essence/existence composites.

Importantly, Kenny concludes that the best way to understand Aquinas's notion of God as pure being is to realize that being does not mean existence. What does it mean? It means that God is something and that God is this something alone, whether God exists or not.[5] In the end, the phoenix argument is embraced by Kenny not for Aquinas's purposes of distinguishing essence from existence but for purposes of de-existentializing God's nature. Kenny thinks that he has Aquinas on his side because outside of his early writings, Aquinas never employs the phoenix argument again.[6]

What would remain of the real distinction between essence and existence? In his earlier book on the *quinque viae*, Kenny is happy to help Thomists attain clarity.[7] Kenny translates statements of individual existence, for example, "Socrates exists," into statements of essence. The guiding idea is taken from Aquinas, "Everything has existence through form: *Omnis res habet esse per formam.*" Hence, "Socrates exists" is retranslated into "Socrates is a human being."[8] The real distinction in Socrates can, then, be understood as the distinction between form considered by itself or as had by something.[9] So, since what God is is what God is alone, then God would lack this sense of real distinction. But at this point Kenny ceases any further collaboration with Thomistic metaphysicians. That God is understood to be some predicate alone, i.e., a subsistent form, has problems avoiding issues with Plato's ontology. In particular, back in *Aquinas on Being*, the issue is that of a predicate without a subject.[10]

Is the phoenix argument in opposition to Aquinas's understanding of God as subsistent existence? At first look, Kenny's claim that they are incompatible looks correct. If I can distinguish the phoenix from its existence because I can know what a phoenix is without knowing that it is, then I can do the same thing for God. So, whatever God is essentially, it is not existence.

A quick and simple reply to Kenny might appear to be the following. Whatever has the essence/existence distinction is caused. But God is the first cause. Therefore, God lacks the distinction. As neat as this reply looks, the reply fails to acknowledge that Kenny has *already* tagged God with the distinction, and so the conclusion seems to be, not that God lacks the distinction but, that God is caused. So the more fundamental challenge for the existential Thomist is to show that *from the beginning* of one's deliberations our existential ignorance of the phoenix is different from our existential ignorance of God. To meet that challenge I think that it is necessary to understand Aquinas's doctrine of "formed intentions."

Aquinas succinctly presents the doctrine in his *Summa Contra Gentiles* I, 53. Aquinas describes how having been informed by the species of the thing, the intellect goes on to form an intention of the thing understood.

> Now, since this understood intention is, as it were, a terminus of intelligible operation, it is distinct from the intelligible species that actualizes

the intellect, and that we must consider the principle of intellectual operation, though both are a likeness of the thing understood. For, by the fact that the intelligible species, which is the form of the intellect and the principle of understanding, is the likeness of the external thing, it follows that the intellect forms the intention like that thing, since such as a thing is, such are its works. And because the understood intention is like some thing, it follows that the intellect, by forming such an intention, knows that thing.[11]

This formed intention is distinct from the intelligible species that both actualizes the intellect and is the principle of intellectual operation. In the preceding paragraph Aquinas says that such a formed intention is necessary because the intellect, like the imagination, understands both a present and absent thing and also because the intellect "understands a thing as separated from material conditions, without which a thing does not exist in reality."[12]

This text suggests two contrasting views. One view is the more original. It follows the intellect's actualization by the species of the thing. With its talk of "an act of understanding," "the definition" which the notion signifies, and the comparison to the imagination, the preceding paragraph makes clear that Aquinas is referring to the first operation of the intellect that Aquinas describes in his commentary on Lombard's *Sentences*.[13] It is this first intellectual operation that Aquinas glosses in the *De Ente et Essentia* as the "absolute consideration of essence."[14] As has been explained elsewhere,[15] characteristic of absolute consideration is a penetrative movement of intellectual attention from some presented multiplicity of instances to the perception of a commonality, or essence.

Another view is subsequent and follows the intellect forming an intention of the essence. While absolutely considering the essence, we are aware that on the side of the considering we are fashioning a likeness of the essence. The latter results in a view of essence separated from material conditions of the instances in the mentioned multiplicity. Hence, the original view of essence should be a view of essence still immersed within the material data. And the second view should be of essence more independent from the data.

The importance of this distinction of views will become evident as I go along. Suffice it to say now that the distinction is valuable to understand a conundrum associated with Aquinas's claim in his *Questiones Disputatae de Veritate* that there can be falsity in the first operation insofar as the first operation can produce wild combinations, for instance, understanding a non-sensing animal or understanding the definition of a circle of a triangle.[16] Such crazy views could not result from the absolute consideration of essence insofar as it is understood to be controlled by the data. In other words, intellecting animal in the data of Tom and Fido would mean always coming back to those instances. Insomuch as Gibraltar is not among those original instances, then in that context animal would never be combined with it. One sees that for these exotically false combinations to be made the essence must be represented in a manner more independent of the data that first acquainted us with it. This more independent representation is what is achieved by what at *C.G.* I, 53 Aquinas calls the "intention formed within the intellect." As represented independently from the data set that originally acquainted us with the essence, the essence is free to be erroneously combined with other intentions.

So far the doctrine of formed intentions has been in terms of the first operation of the intellect. But the doctrine continues into the second operation. In sum,[17] the second operation is a rebound of intellectual attention from some commonality grasped in the first operation. The rebound brings the commonality back to the data in which it was spied. It also affords a distinct appreciation of the peculiarities of the data, for example, the differentiae of the species man and brute. Once the intellect knows the differentiae, then it can also form intentions of them that set the differentiae apart from the species in which they are found.

We now have a flurry of formed intentions of intelligible objects. They are found independent of the contexts in which the objects were originally delivered to intellectual awareness. As mentioned, this situation with formed intentions permits wild combinations that would be impossible if our attention stayed on what we were aware of before we formed the intentions. Noteworthy is that the original contexts in which the commonalities and peculiarities are originally spied are different. One is the first operation, the other is the second operation. The first context is a penetrative movement of attention into a data set; the second is a reflexive movement of attention back to that data set. This is the original life of the intellect. Formed intentions are independent expressions of the results of these mental movements.

Now among the formed intentions of the second operation can be the *esse* of the thing, i.e., the thing's existence understood as a distinctive *actus* had or possessed by the thing. Sometimes the commonalities that we know are individuals. Not only is a commonality like animal spread out in a multiplicity of its species, so too is Socrates spread out in a multiplicity of temperatures, complexions, postures, etc. In these cases it is the individual that is the commonality.[18] But an individual also is found in an existential multiplicity. In light of Aquinas's immediate sense realism, the real individual also cognitionally exists. This multiplicity allows the individual to be conceived as existence neutral by the first intellectual operation and its real existence to be grasped by the second intellectual operation as an *actus* of its own.

The relation of this act to the substance with which it is composed also bears mention. In respect to the substance rendered a being by composition with *esse*, *esse* is prior (*prius*), first (*primus*), most profound (*profundius*), and most intimate (*magis intimum*).[19] *Esse* is the core around which the thing revolves. We are so accustomed to conceiving acts of a thing as items subsequent and posterior to the thing that the notion of an act basic and fundamental to its thing is strange. But if one is to understand *esse* as provided by the intellect's second act, usual ways of thinking must be suspended.[20]

Presented with the *esse* of something, the intellect is in a position to form an intention of this *esse*.[21] Like any formed intention, the formed intention of the thing's *esse* acquires a certain independence from the context in which it was first grasped. This means that the intellect possesses an intention of existence that does not present it, as does happen in its second operation. Consequently, I can think not only of a vacation in Hawaii, knowing that it does not exist, but I can think of an *existing* vacation in Hawaii knowing that it does not exist. In the latter case, to know that the vacation does not exist does not mean that we are not thinking of it as existing. Also, thinking of it as existing does not mean knowing that it exists.

It is this formed intention sense of *esse* that is involved in the Latin predicate "*est*." Propositions, or enunciations, are also cases of formed intentions. In the commentary on Aristotle's *Peri Hermeneias*, Aquinas says that as employed in propositions '*est*' principally signifies "the actuality of every form commonly, whether substantial or accidental."[22] Two paragraphs earlier this actuality is the *esse* composed with the thing in what is meant by being, *ens*.[23] But since the *esse* is signified, it is clear that we are not dealing with *esse* as known in the second intellectual operation. That distinction is why it is always appropriate to ask whether a proposition is true or false. So, it is clear that the intellect goes on to form an intention that is a similitude of the *esse* of the thing that it grasps by the second operation. The formed intention is not so much a similitude that it presents the *esse* that it is a similitude of. Only when the formed intention of existence is spotlighting what is grasped by the second operation will the formed intention have implications for reality. Otherwise, the formed intention may express or mean existence, but it will not present existence, as happens in the second operation. In sum, the intellect is in possession of an existence neutral sense of existence.

So far this material promises to answer Kenny. If this formed concept of *esse* is what is used in our thinking about God, then obviously it will still make sense to ask if God exists. To accommodate that question, it is not necessary, as Kenny thinks, to deexistentialize our conception of God. But two issues loom up. First, as expressing what is grasped in the second operation, the formed intention of *esse* is highly individual and particular. Just as your tan is yours and mine is mine, so too are our *esses*. An understanding of the nature of *esse*, of *ipsum esse*, remains to be presented, for God, according to Aquinas, is the nature of *esse*. Second, as expressing what is grasped in the second operation, the formed intention of *esse* expresses *esse* as the act *of a thing*. It is a portion of a composite situation. But in God *esse* is the thing; in God *esse* is not something possessed. In Thomistic terms there is a difference in the mode of signification. As Aquinas says, we think the simple as that by which something is and we think the composite as what exists. To think God as *esse* we have to somehow think the simple act of *esse* as an existent. As Kenny said, we have to Platonize and to think a predicate without a subject.[24] In sum, these two issues indicate that for all our efforts so far, the formed intention of *esse* has nothing to do with God.

Both issues require telling more of Aquinas's metaphysics. So, to the first issue, Aquinas does not leave *esses* in disintegration. He reapplies the first intellectual operation to formed intentions of *esses*. Just as there is something the same in your tan and in mine, so too there is something the same in our *esses*. Aquinas variously refers to the sameness in *esses*. It is: *esse formale, esse commune*, the *ratio essendi, ipsum esse*.[25] But as a commonality, *esse* is unique. Even though it seems to be most general, it does not have a content in inverse relation to its extent. It is not as Kenny claims the "thinnest" predicate.[26] One can see this richness in Aquinas's description of the diversification of *esse formale* into individual *esse*s in his *Summa Contra Gentiles* I, 26. In the second argument, Aquinas speculates that *esse formale* could be diversified in two ways.[27] The first way is through added differences. The second way is through *esse formale* itself which diversifies itself in light of the different natures to be actuated. Aquinas eliminates the first on the basis that being (*ens*) is not a genus to which differences are added. In the just previous chapter, Aquinas noted that the differences added to a genus must be extrinsic to the genus under pain of placing the genus twice in the definition of the species. But, Aquinas insists, there is nothing outside of being. Hence, being cannot be a genus.

The appeal of *C.G.* I, 26 to chapter 25 obviously indicates a close connection between *esse* and *ens*. The basis for the connection lies in the role of *esse* if one is to have something that is more than existence neutral, in short, more than nothing. In other words, there is nothing outside being because apart from *esse* there is nothing. Hence, *esse inquantum est esse*, or *esse formale*, will not be diversified by differences coming from the outside. Rather, it will diversify itself in light of the thing it will actuate.

The formed intention of *esse formale*, then, is not pale and insipid but full and robust. And so, it is no surprise to see Aquinas transferring its richness to God as God is understood to be *ipsum esse subsistens*. For example, at *S.T.* I, 4, 2, Aquinas argues that because the perfections of all things pertain to the *perfectio essendi* and because God is *ipsum esse subsistens*, then God has the perfections of all things.[28] Elsewhere, Aquinas admits that God is a thing that is the "essence of goodness, of unity, and of existence (*ipsa essentia bonitatis et unitatis et esse*)."[29] But that brings us to the second issue. *Esse formale* is a portion of a larger picture. As mentioned, it expresses a commonality that is seen in individual *esse*s, each of which is an act *of a thing*. As such, *esse formale* is connected with the non-generic notion of being, the *ratio entis*. It will be understood to exist only as part of a being, just as running is understood to exist as part of a runner. Hence, Aquinas uses this observation about *esse formale* to deny adamantly the error of those who identify God and *esse formale*: "Their reason also failed because they did not observe that what is most simple in our understanding of things is not so much a complete thing as it is a part of a thing. But, simplicity is predicated of God as of some perfect subsisting thing."[30]

Aquinas is both using *esse formale* to think God and not using it. If this is not to be a contradiction, then Aquinas somehow is modifying *esse formale*, as originally apprehended, in order to make it appropriate for claims about God. From originally viewing it as a part, we come to view it as a subsistent. How can the mind look at *esse formale* so that it is less representative of a part of a being and more representative of a being itself? In short, how does Aquinas employ *esse formale* to think of God?

It should be noted that neither abstraction nor forming an intention have enabled *esse* to shed its status as a part. The abstraction of *esse formale* was formed from various acts of *esse* brought before the mind in its second operation. The relation of those acts to a subject is retained in the abstraction. That relation continues in the formed concept of *esse*, as, for example, it would continue in the formed concepts of differentiae. Is there another manner in which *esse* might be handled? Back in the question six of the commentary on Boethius's *De Trinitate*, Aquinas says that our confused cognition of the divine quiddity and of the quiddity of separate substance is attained "by negations; for example by understanding that they are immaterial, incorporeal, without shapes, and so on."[31] Earlier negating is identified with separating: "Nevertheless, we reach a knowledge of [God and separate substances] . . . by way of negation (as when we separate from such beings whatever sense or imagination apprehends)."[32] Finally, separation is explained as another capacity of the intellect's second act.[33] Not only can the second act compose in the reflective manner previously mentioned, but it can divide or separate in the sense of bringing negation to bear on some mental material.

Can negation be wielded on the formed intention of the *ratio entis* of which *esse formale* is a portion so that *esse formale* stands forth less as a portion and more as a reality? I believe so. By using negation to occlude, or to blot out, the non-*esse* portion of the ratio *entis*, called "*essentia*" by Aquinas,[34] Aquinas leaves *esse formale* standing less as a part and more as a whole unto itself. The unique nature of the negating permits this result. In this case negating is not and cannot be an erasure. *Esse formale* arises as a commonality in individual *esse*s that are acts of various things. To erase the things would be to lose the *esse*s and the commonality of *esse formale*. The things have to remain even while they are removed so that their *esse*s can present *esse formale*. This handling of the subjects is made possible by negation in the sense of an occluding or blotting out. Since the things are only covered over, their *esse*s remain to present *esse formale*, but now as *ipsum esse subsistens*.[35]

So, the original grasp of *esse* as the individual act of a thing does not preclude going on to form an intention of *esse* that expresses the metaphysical conclusion of subsistent *esse*. But because we are speaking of God in terms of a formed intention of existence, then by the intention itself we do not know if God exists. These thoughts explain how Aquinas can say a number of striking things. First, "God exists" is in itself a self-evident proposition because God is his existence, but it is not self-evident to us.[36] You would think that not being evident to us would mean that we could not know that the proposition is self-evident in itself. But the situation is clarified by realizing that the terms of the proposition are what this paper has been calling formed intentions of *esse*. Because God is his existence, the formed intention of the predicate "*est*" just repeats the formed intention of the subject "*esse subsistens*." So, we can see that the proposition is *per se notum quoad se*. But because we are dealing with formed intentions here, the proposition is not *per se notum quoad nos*. In other words, it is perfectly appropriate to ask if "God exists" is true.

Second, that question should bring us back to the original context in which we formed the intention of *esse*. That original context was the grasp of the *esse* of sensible things by the second operation. In his *De Ente et Essentia*, shortly after his remark about the phoenix, Aquinas shows how such *esse* leads to the conclusion of subsistent existence and underwrites the formed intention of the proposition "God exists." Where *esse* is had or possessed, it must be caused efficiently and not caused by the thing that possesses it.[37]

Third, the formed intention of *esse* would explain why Aquinas's *viae* to God proceed only with a nominal definition of God and yet one would understand this nominal definition to be God's most proper name of "*Ego sum qui sum*," as is argued by some Thomists like the Rev. Joseph Owens C.Ss.R. in a metaphysical interpretation of the *viae*.[38] Because we understand subsistent existence in terms of a formed intention of existence that does not present what we are conceiving, then for us the understanding of subsistent existence is just nominal and does not reveal the essence of God. For us "*Ipsum esse subsistens*" is *both* a nominal definition and the most proper name of God.

So what is my answer to Kenny's objection? Our ignorance about the existence of the phoenix and our ignorance about God do not have the same bases and so they do not lead to the same conclusion, namely, a distinction between thing and existence in both cases. The notion of the phoenix is existence neutral because it is reflective of conceptual notes that have to be existence neutral in order to be in existential multiplicities. Our notion of subsistent existence is not existence neutral in this way, but it is composed of a formed intention of existence that gives it an independence apart from the context of the second operation in which it was formed. The first case leads to a situation involving a distinction between essence and existence. Knowledge of the existence of the phoenix adds something over and beyond the essence of the phoenix. In the second cause, knowledge of the existence of subsistent existence does not do that because existence is what the formed intention here is of. What knowledge of subsistent existence adds does not belong to it. It belongs to us. It adds our second operation knowledge of the *esse* of sensible things and our reasoning from that to subsistent existence.

Center for Thomistic Studies
University of St. Thomas, Texas

Notes

1. Characteristic of Existential Thomism is the interpretive claim that Aquinas's idea of the act of being (*actus essendi*) is the central element in Aquinas's understanding of what it means to be a being (*ratio entis*). For a summary of the tenets of Existential Thomism, see Joseph Owens, *St. Thomas and the Future of Metaphysics* (Milwaukee: Marquette University Press, 1973), 36–49.

2. Anthony Kenny, *Aquinas on Being* (Oxford: Clarendon Press, 2002), 62. Given that the phoenix is a mythical bird, I understand our existential ignorance about it to consist in not knowing if it has cognitional existence in the mind of some imaginer.

3. Ibid., 36. But Kenny admits difficulty in formulating an understanding of the real distinction. His best shot is "a picture of two entities of a similar kind with a metaphysical fissure separating them" (6). With that understanding in mind, he mentions that the question

of a real distinction between essence and existence is as weird as asking if there is a real distinction between the threeness and the blindness in three blind mice. For another Kenny attempt to construe the real distinction, see infra in my text at nn. 7 and 8.

4. Kenny, *Aquinas on Being*, 37.

5. "Being enters into the quiddity of God as it does into the quiddity of phoenix, with this difference: that being is the only thing that enters into the quiddity of God, so that it can be said to be identical with it. But this being is something quite different from actual existence: it enters into the quiddity of God whether or not there is such a thing as God." Ibid., 62.

6. But it is certainly implied by Aquinas's first *Summa Theologiae* reasoning for the identity of essence and existence in God. See *S.T.* I, 3, 4. The first reasoning clearly reiterates the reasoning of the paragraphs following the phoenix argument in the *De Ente*. The phoenix argument is essential for the reasoning of those paragraphs.

7. Anthony Kenny, *The Five Ways: St. Thomas Aquinas' Proofs of God's Existence* (New York: Schocken Books, 1969), 88–90.

8. But this guiding idea should be understood in the light of the *Summa Contra Gentiles* II, 54 in which form is a "*principium essendi*" insofar as it is the "*complementum*" of the substance whose actualization is through *esse*. This thinking leaves *esse* a distinctive act from form and ruling over form which as part of a substance is still not a being (*ens*) until composed with *esse*. For the idea that the *esse* of a form is the form's being had or possessed by a subject, Kenny cites *S.T.* III, 17, 2: "If any form or nature does not pertain (*pertineat*) to the personal *esse* of a subsistent individual, that *esse* is not called the *esse* of that person without qualification." It seems an interpretive stretch to take the antecedent of this conditional proposition as: "If any form is not had or possessed by a subsistent individual."

9. "Goodness and humanity, he says, are not signified in actuality save insofar as we signify that they *are*. Only if John *is* good, not just if he will be, or can be, or is thought to be good, will John's goodness be actual and not merely potential. So the *esse album* of Socrates appears to be not simply the form, Socrates's whiteness, but the actual having of the form; but of course that form will itself only have real existence, or *esse*, if Socrates has *esse album*. It is in this sense that Aquinas says that *esse* is the actuality of every form and nature." Kenny, *The Five Ways*, 88–89.

10. "But it is hard to see how the notion of pure form can be explained by reference to predication. Forms are forms of the entity which is the subject of predication: Socrates's wisdom is what corresponds to the predicate in the sentence 'Socrates is wise', . . . In the same way, a pure form would be something that corresponded to a predicate in a sentence that had no subject: but this seems close to an absurdity." Kenny, *Aquinas on Being*, 30. Kenny's complaint seems similar to Aquinas's observation that our way of signifying the existent is in composite fashion; see *S.T.* I, 13, 1, ad 2m. Infra in my text at nn. 29–32, I attempt to explain how the "negation" capacity of the intellect's second operation can remove this mode of signifying for *esse subsistens*. In his "On Kenny on Aquinas on Being," *International Philosophical Quarterly* 44 (2004): 577–578, Gyula Klima defends the real distinction in another way. Using remarks of Geach, Klima uses the distinction between a creature and its vital activity to present the distinction. In God there is no such distinction; so God's essence is his existence. Klima is influenced by Geach's interpretation of Aquinas's use of Aristotle's remark (*De Anima* II, 4, 415b 13) that the life of living things is their being. But Joseph Owens shows that Aquinas identifies life with *esse*, not *esse* with life. *Esse* remains a distinct

actus of its own not glossed in other terms. See Joseph Owens, "The Accidental and Essential Character of Being in the Doctrine of St. Thomas Aquinas," in *St. Thomas Aquinas on the Existence of God: the Collected Papers of Joseph Owens*, John R. Catan, ed. (Albany: State University of New York Press, 1980), 243–244 n22.

11. *C.G.* I, 53; trans. Anton C. Pegis, *Summa Contra Gentiles* (Notre Dame: University of Notre Dame Press, 1975) I, 188–189. See also, Aquinas, *Questiones Quodlibetales*, V, 5, 2c. For a current discussion about the fundamental role of formal signs, see John O'Callaghan, "Concepts, Mirrors, and Signification: Response to Deely," *American Catholic Philosophical Quarterly* 84 (2010): 133–162.

12. Pegis, *Summa Contra Gentiles*, 188.

13. "There is a twofold operation of the intellect. One of these is called by some the '*imaginatio intellectus.*' In the third book of his *De Anima*, the Philosopher names it the understanding of indivisibles [*intelligentiam indivisibilium*]. It consists in the apprehension of the simple quiddity. By another this operation is called by the name "*formatio.*" The other of these [operations] is what they call "*fidem,*" which consists in the composition or division of the proposition [*propositionis*]. The first operation looks on the quiddity of the thing; the second looks upon its being [*esse*]. And because the notion (*ratio*) of truth is based on being [*esse*] and not on quiddity, . . . so truth and falsity are properly found in the second operation and in its sign which is the enunciation [*enuntiatio*], and not in the first or in its sign which is the definition" *In I Sent.*, d. 19, q. 5, a. 1, ad 7m; my translation.

14. For absolute consideration, see Aquinas, *On Being and Essence*, as translated by Armand Maurer (Toronto: Pontifical Institute of Mediaeval Studies, 1963), 46–47.

15. For example, John F. X. Knasas, *Being and Some Twentieth-Century Thomists* (New York: Fordham University Press, 2003), 182–188.

16. "For it may happen that a definition will be applied to something to which it does not belong, as when the definition of a circle is assigned to a triangle. Sometimes, too the parts of a definition cannot be reconciled, as happens when one defines a thing as 'an animal entirely without the power of sensing.'" Aquinas, *De Ver.* I, 3c; trans by Robert W. Mulligan, *Truth* (Chicago: Henry Regnery Company, 1952), I, 13–14. See also *In I Sent.*, d. 19, q. 5, a. 2, ad 7m.

17. Again, for the Thomistic texts, see Knasas, *Being and Some Twentieth-Century Thomists*, 189–191.

18. "Again by knowing the principles of which the essence of a thing is composed, we necessarily know that thing itself. Thus, by knowing a rational soul and a certain sort of body, we know man. Now, the singular essence [*singularis essentia*] is composed of designated matter and individuated form. Thus, the essence of Socrates is composed of this body and this soul, just as the universal essence [*essentia hominis universalis*] of man is composed of soul and body, as may be seen in *Metaphysics* VII. Hence, just as the latter principles fall within the definition of universal man, so the former principles would fall in the definition of Socrates if he could be defined. Hence, whoever has a knowledge of matter and of what designates matter, and also of form individuated in matter, must have a knowledge of the singular. But the knowledge of God extends to matter and to individuating accidents and forms. For, since His understanding is His essence, He must understand all things that in any way are in His essence. Now within His essence, as within the first source, there are virtually present all things that in any way have being [*esse*]. Matter and accidents are not absent from among these things, since matter is a being [*ens*] in potency and an accident is a being [*ens*]

in another. Therefore, the knowledge of singulars is not lacking to God." Trans. Anton C. Pegis, *Summa Contra Gentiles* I, 211–212. Also, in the *Questiones Disputatae de Potentia Dei*, "*Quaelibet autem forma signata non intelligitur in actu nisi per hoc quod esse ponitur.*" *De Pot.* VII, 2, ad 9m. To be noted is that the *De Ente*, ch. 1 speaks of essence as that by which a thing falls into a category. Hence, essence can stand for what a thing is and for its definition. This is the reason for also referring to essence as quiddity. Interestingly, then, the discussion of essence in the *De Ente* is not exhaustive. It omits the singular essence which does not have a definition. Lamentation about the *De Ente* not including much elaboration of *esse* should be coupled with lamentation about the *De Ente* not featuring the *singularis essentia*. Kenny's talk of the universal and individual essence, *Aquinas on Being*, 14, should not be equated with Aquinas's remarks at *C.G.* I, 65. For Aquinas the individual *is* the individual essence; for Kenny Socrates *has* an individual essence. Also, on p. 46, Kenny insists that there is "no individuation without actualization (only what actually exists can be identified, individuated, counted)." In the two following texts Aquinas also speaks of the individual substance considered in itself (*de se*), not considered in its essence (*de essentia*): "We find in the world, furthermore, certain beings, those namely that are subject to generation and corruption, which can be and not-be. But what can be has a cause because, since it is equally (*de se aequaliter*) related to two contraries, namely, being and non-being (*esse et non esse*)." *C.G.* I, 15, *Amplius*; Pegis trans., I, 98–99; "Again, everything that can be and non-be has a cause; for considered in itself (*in se consideratum*) it is indifferent to either, so that something else must exist which determines it to one." *C.G.* II, 15, *Praeterea*; Anderson trans., II, 48. Cf., "you will see that the notion of existence emerged with the question whether the particularized concept, *this thing*, was anything more than a mere object of thought." Bernard J. F. Lonergan, "*Insight*: Preface to a Discussion," *Proceedings of the American Catholic Philosophical Association* 32 (1958): 80.

19. "it follows that something is the cause of its own being [*causa essendi*]. This is impossible, because, in their notions the existence of the cause is prior [*prius*] to that of the effect. If, then, something were its own cause of being [*causa essendi*], it would be understood to be before it had being [*haberet esse*]—which is impossible." *C.G.* I, 22, *Amplius. Si*; Pegis trans., I, 119. Even though the cause is called "*prius*," clearly the *esse* is also. The thing cannot trump the priority of its own *esse* to be a cause of it. "Now the first [*primus*] of all effects is being [*ipsum esse*], which is presupposed to all other effects, and does not presuppose any other effect." *De Pot.* III, 4c; L. Shapcote trans., *On the Power of God* (London: Burns Oates and Washbourne, 1934) 1, 102. The primacy of *esse* is implied in further texts. For example, "From the very fact that being [*esse*] is ascribed to a quiddity, not only is the quiddity said to be but also to be created; since before it has being [*esse*] it was nothing, except perhaps in the intellect of the creator, where it is not a creature but the creation essence." *De Pot.* III, 5, ad 2m; Shapcote trans., ibid., 110; "God at the same time gives being [*esse*] and produces that which receives being [*esse*], so that it does not follow that his action requires something already in existence." *De Pot.* III, 1, ad 17m; ibid., 88. "But being [*esse*] is innermost [*magis intimum*] in each thing and most fundamentally present [*profundius*] within all things, since it is formal in respect of everything found in a thing" *S.T.* I, 8, 1c: Pegis ed., *Basic Writings*, I, 64.

20. Joseph Owens remarks, "The notion that there is an accident prior to substance in sensible things is repellent to the ingrained human way of thinking. Yet the effort has to be made for the metaphysical understanding of existence. Not substance, but an accident, being is absolutely basic in sensible things. This has to be understood, however, in a way

that does not make being function as the substance. Strictly, it is not the being that is there, but the substance that has the being. The nature cannot take on an adverbial relation to its being." *An Elementary Christian Metaphysics* (Houston: Center for Thomistic Studies, 1985), 75. Despite a microscopic analysis of the Thomistic texts that uncovers "twelve types of being," Kenny, *Aquinas on Being*, 189–192, nowhere mentions *esse* as an act of its own in a *sui generis* relation to its subject. The closest Kenny comes to the idea is on p. 46 when he mentions the possibility that Aquinas early on may have followed Avicenna in which "the relation of existence to essence as being exactly parallel to that of form to matter or accident to substance."

21. That the intellect forms intentions of the objects of its second operation was a truth Gilson was forced to clarify by F.-M Régis. This admission lead Gilson to reserve *conceptus* for formed intentions of the first operation, and *conceptio* for formed intentions of the second operation. For the discussion between Régis and Gilson, see Etienne Gilson, *Being and Some Philosophers* (Toronto: Pontifical Institute of Mediaeval Studies, 1952), "Appendix." As I will explain, this distinction between formed intentions is crucial for addressing Kenny's challenge.

22. *Aristotle: On Interpretation, Commentary by St. Thomas and Cajetan*, trans. Jean T. Oesterle (Milwaukee: Marquette University Press, 1962), Book I, lect. V, n. 22, p. 53.

23. "This is indeed most clearly seen in saying 'being' [*ens*], because *being* is nothing other than *that which is*. And thus we see that it signifies both a thing, when I say 'that which,' and existence [*esse*] when I say 'is' [*est*]." Ibid., 52. In *Aquinas on Being*, 56, Kenny disputes the existential sense of "*est*" "since existential statements are only a tiny fraction of the number of sentences that we compose and employ." It is true that for Aquinas not every assertion expresses *esse*. Armand Maurer, "St. Thomas and Eternal Truths," *Mediaeval Studies* 32 (197), 91–107, shows that the "is" in "eternal" truths corresponds to no *esse* proper to the truth itself. For Aquinas, just as essences considered in themselves abstract from every being, so too do truths when considered in themselves. Using terminology taken from John of St. Thomas, Maurer says (101) that at best these truths can be said to have a "negative" eternity in that in themselves they abstract from any subject in and through which they can come and go in being. As so entertained, the "eternal" truth is not being envisaged with any existence at all.

24. Kenny, *Aquinas on Being*, 102, hits the mark when he says that "Aquinas's approach makes it look as if he is not opposed to Platonic Ideas in general or logical grounds, but merely has qualms about particular examples of such Ideas." Consider the following from Aquinas's proem to his commentary on the *Divine Names*: "The Platonists considered by an abstraction of this kind not only the ultimate species of natural things but also the most common species, which are the good, the one, and being [*bonum, unum et ens*]. They maintained one first thing that is the essence itself of goodness and of unity and of being [*ipsa essentia bonitatis et unitatis et esse*], which we call God and which [we say] all others are called good or one or beings through derivation from this first thing. . . . Hence, this position of the Platonists is not agreeable to the faith or truth insofar as it contains separate natural species, but in respect to what they say about the first principle of things, their opinion is most true and consonant with the faith of Christians." (My trans.) Of course, this paper is an attempt to show the logical grounds upon which Aquinas can hold this distinction.

25. "*Esse commune*" and "*esse formale*" are used interchangeably at *C.G.* I, 26. There a key point is that *esse formale* is not diversified in and through additions from the outside, as happens when a difference is added to a genus. (See n28 below.) At *De Pot.* 7, 2, ad 9m,

Aquinas is again speaking of *esse commune* (see ad 6m), and he repeats this key point. But he goes on to say that *esse* is not determined as potency by an act but as an act by a potency. Then at *S. T.* I, 4, 1, ad 3m, Aquinas characterizes "*ipsum esse*" as received to receiver (*receptum ad recipiens*) rather than receiver to received (*recipiens ad receptum*). Finally, in the next article, God is characterized as *ipsum esse per se subsistens* and so has the entire "*perfectio essendi*" just like a subsistent heat would have heat "*secundum perfectam rationem*." In these spots the thinking about *esse* is the same, though the terminology is modulating from *esse commune* to *esse formale*, *ipsum esse*, *perfectio essendi*, *ratio essendi*. For further discussion, see Knasas, *Being and Some Twentieth-Century Thomists*, 208–210.

26. Kenny, *The Five Ways*, 92.

27. "Furthermore, things are not distinguished from one another in having being, for in this they agree. If, then, things differ from one another, either their being must be specified through certain added differences, so that diverse things have a diverse being according to their species, or things must differ in that the being itself is appropriate to the natures that are diverse in species. The first of these alternatives is impossible, since, as we have said, no addition can be made to a being in the manner in which a difference is added to a genus." Pegis trans., 129.

28. "Since there God is subsisting being itself [*ipsum esse subsistens*], nothing of the perfection of being [*de perfectione essendi*] can be wanting to Him. Now all the perfections of all things pertain to the perfection of being; for things are perfect precisely so far as they have being after some fashion [*aliquo modo esse habent*]. It follows therefore that the perfection of no thing is wanting to God. " Aquinas, *S. T.* I, 4, 2; as edited by Anton C. Pegis, *The Basic Writings of St. Thomas Aquinas* (New York: Random House, 1945), Vol. I, 39.

29. See supra n24.

30. *C.G.* I, 26. There are other issues: *esse formale* is open to addition, *esse subsistens* is not; *esse formale* is an abstraction existing only in the mind, *esse subsistens* is in reality.

31. Aquinas, *In de Trin.* VI, 3; as translated by Armand Maurer, *The Division and Methods of the Sciences* (Toronto: Pontifical Institute of Mediaeval Studies, 1963), 78.

32. *In de Trin.* VI, 2; ibid., 70.

33. "and another [intellectual operation] by which it joins and divides, that is to say, by forming affirmative and negative statements." *In de Trin.* V, 3; ibid., 28.

34. "essence must mean something common to all the natures through which different beings are placed in different genera and species, as for example humanity is the essence of man, and so with regard to other things." Aquinas, *On Being and Essence*, as trans. by Armand Maurer (Toronto: Pontifical Institute of Mediaeval Studies, 1968), ch. 1, 30.

35. This understanding of negation as blotting out also solves the other two difficulties with using *esse formale* to think *esse subsistens*. By occluding the things, negation dumbs down the *esses* in which *esse formale* is a commonality. Hence, *esse formale* is presented less as an abstraction. Likewise, its capacity for addition by its diversification into individual *esses* is removed because the things in the light of which *esse formale* diversifies itself are removed. For other presentations of this play of negation to craft, for metaphysical purposes, a representation of *esse subsistens*, see Knasas, *Being and Some Twentieth-Century Thomists*, 236–244; John F. X. Knasas, *Aquinas and the Cry of Rachel: Thomistic Reflections on the Problem of Evil* (The Catholic University Press of America, 2014), 270–275. In his "The Universality of the Sensible in the Aristotelian Noetic," ed. John R. Catan, *Aristotle: The Collected Papers of*

Joseph Owens (Albany: State University of New York Press, 1981), 69–71, Joseph Owens uses negation to attain concepts for the hylomorphic components of matter and form. Unlike my wielding of negation, in Owens's usage negation does not render the remainder as subsistent but still as a part. To accommodate these two uses of negation, I think that the "blotting out" character of the negation should be understood as able to be either heavy or less heavy. Some coverings allow what is covered to still appear. Also, in "Aquinas: 'Darkness of Ignorance' in the Most Refined Notion of God," *The Southwestern Journal of Philosophy* 5 (1974): 107, Joseph Owens further employs negation to produce the "*ignorantia*" and "*caligo*" in which Aquinas says, at *In I Sent.*, d. 8, q. 1, a. 1, ad 4m, that God is best known in this state of life. In my opinion, this point of application, that is still a natural state, is obviously outside of metaphysics. But those interested in seeing how I, in contrast to Owens, understand the application of negation at this point can see Knasas, *Being and Some Twentieth-Century Thomists*, 245n74.

36. *S.T.* I, 2, 1c.

37. For a description of the reasoning, see Knasas, *Being and Some Twentieth-Century Thomists*, 214–224.

38. See supra n10, the mentioned John Catan edition, *St. Thomas Aquinas on the Existence of God: the Collected Papers of Joseph Owens.*

A Thomist Re-consideration of the Subject Matter of Metaphysics: Chrysostom Iavelli on What is Included in Being as Being

Domenic D'Ettore

Abstract: Catholic Philosophy has long acknowledged the primary place of Metaphysics, and a primary question of metaphysicians is "what is Metaphysics about?" This paper engages this primary metaphysical question through the lens of Scholastic dispute over the adequate subject matter of Metaphysics. Chrysostom Iavelli defended the position that the subject of Metaphysics is real being common to God and creatures against the position of his predecessor Dominic Flandrensis who had argued that it is categorical being to the exclusion of uncreated being. I find Flandrensis's position represented in the writings of notable contemporary Thomists, but not Iavelli's. This paper, offers a sixteenth-century Thomist's position on the subject matter of Metaphysics as a challenge to current Thomist consensus. It attempts to prompt a re-investigation of the reasons behind the current consensus both as a philosophical position and as an interpretation of St. Thomas Aquinas.

Fr. Lawrence Dewan, O.P., concludes his essay "What does it mean to Study Being 'As Being'?" with the following warning to the metaphysician:

> as soon as the expression, 'created being' is introduced, we spontaneously tend to set up a *wider* universal which would "contain under it" both creator and creatures. Against this, the whole point of the above text is that creation is the sort of origin of things that, to be properly understood, requires a therapy against just that sort of grossly deceptive convenience.[1]

The text Fr. Dewan refers to is from St. Thomas Aquinas's *Commentary on the Divine Names*, wherein St. Thomas distinguishes Divine Being from created being on the grounds that created being participates in *esse commune* whereas Divine Being does not.[2] Dewan's warning is directed at the intellect's tendency to look for a more common universal where there is none to be found. In this case, he holds that the intellect which conceives "being" as a "wider" universal "containing under it" both created being and divine being betrays its owner. "Being" or "being as being" or "*ens commune*," the science of Metaphysics' subject matter, does not include within its scope divine being. To the extent divine being is treated within the science of Metaphysics, it is exclusively as a cause of *ens commune*, never as contained within it. Dewan's interpretation of Thomas Aquinas's position is supported by other celebrated twenty-first-century Thomists including Fr. John Wippel[3] and Fr. Benedict Ashley.[4]

The sixteenth-century Thomist Chrysostom Iavelli (a.k.a. Chrysostomus Iavellus), O.P. defended precisely the position which Dewan warns against.[5] "Being as being" signifies real being common to God and creatures. And it is this being which provides the subject matter of the science of Metaphysics. This paper considers Iavelli's arguments for his position, giving special attention to his efforts to refute the position held by his fifteenth-century predecessor Dominic of Flanders, O.P (a.k.a. Flandrensis).[6] Flandrensis takes a position similar to the twenty-first-century Thomists, offering much the same interpretation of the same set of texts from Thomas Aquinas. The subject matter of Metaphysics is being as being, limiting being to created being divided into the ten categories. Iavelli reconsiders these arguments and texts, and finds Flandrensis's position unconvincing. With this paper, then, I present for contemporary consideration a sixteenth-century Thomist's position on the subject matter of Metaphysics. I hope that this will prompt a re-investigation of the reasons behind the current Thomist consensus both as a philosophical position and as an interpretation of St. Thomas Aquinas.

Iavelli provides two treatments of the adequate[7] subject matter of Metaphysics in his *In Libros Metaphysicos Aristotelis*. The first appears in the *Praefatio*, and the main discussion occurs in Book 1, q. 1 where Iavelli opens the main body of the work with a lengthy treatment of the question "Whether being as being taken absolutely and universally is the subject of Metaphysics."[8] Over the course of several folio pages Iavelli engages what he takes to be the three main options put forth by the Aristotelian tradition, the differences between Thomist representatives of this tradition, and his own rationale for answering the question he began with affirmatively. The three opinions on the subject of Metaphysics are:

1. The genus of separated substances.

2. Real being divided into the ten categories.

3. Real being taken absolutely, common to finite and infinite, created and uncreated.

The focus of this paper will be Iavelli's defence of the "third opinion" against the "second opinion" in Book 1, question 1 and the supporting passages in Books 4 and 6.

The Second and Third Opinions

Iavelli identifies Flandrensis as the Thomist standard-bearer for the "second opinion," i.e., the opinion that the adequate subject of Metaphysics is real finite being divided into the ten categories. The principal argument from Flandrensis which Iavelli raises first and returns to repeatedly, runs as follows:

First, the subject in Metaphysics is that of which we seek the principles and causes. But in Metaphysics, we seek the principles and causes of categorical being alone, because being as being does not have principles and causes, otherwise every being would have a principle, and then one would not arrive at a first being, which is the opposite of what is demonstrated in [*Metaphysics*] Book 12.[9]

Flandrensis's argument appeals to the common Aristotelian understanding that a science's subject matter is that whose principles and causes the science seeks and demonstrates.[10] Now if *ens inquantum ens* without qualification is the subject of Metaphysics, and it has principles and causes, then anything whatsoever which is being has at least a principle and cause. In other words, whatever is being would have some principle or cause through which it is being rather than non-being. If this were true, however, Aristotle could not have done what he did in *Metaphysics* 12; namely, demonstrate the existence of a being which does not itself have any cause or principle. Flandrensis draws the inference that unqualified *ens inquantum ens* cannot be the subject of metaphysics. Instead, only the part of being which is divided into the ten categories—that is, the part which has principles and causes—is Metaphysics' subject matter.

On the face of it, Flandrensis seems to have a compelling argument. The subject matter of a science has principles and causes. The First Principle and Cause, by definition, does not have principles and causes. So the First Principle and Cause could not fall within the subject matter of a science. The subject matter of the science of being as being would then preclude uncaused being. Iavelli himself accepts the major premise of the argument; i.e., that only what has principles can be studied in a science. He challenges the minor premise; i.e., that attributing principles to the First Principle entails the denial of the First Principle. Indeed, Iavelli claims that the main mistake of Flandrensis and those holding the second opinion was their inability to see how the First Principle could have a principle.[11]

Iavelli says that the third opinion holds that "Real being *per se* common to the finite and the infinite, that is, to the created and uncreated, is the adequate subject in this science," and he attributes this opinion to Aristotle, Avicenna, Algazel, Albert, Thomas, and Scotus.[12] Iavelli offers two brief "proofs" for his position along with brief objections from and replies to Flandrensis.

For his first proof, Iavelli argues that real being common to God and creatures meets a primary condition for the adequate subject matter of any science. Every science demonstrates the first and *per se* properties of its subject genus. The properties of being which Metaphysics demonstrates include the transcendentals, act and potency, finite and infinite. These are demonstrated not only of real being as divided into the ten categories, but of real being in general. Consequently, the *ens commune* studied in metaphysics is broader than categorical being.[13]

Iavelli supports his argument by responding to an argument from Flandrensis to the contrary. According to Flandrensis, Aristotle's *Metaphysics* demonstrates the properties of categorical being alone. As evidence, Flandrensis points to *Metaphysics*

5 where Aristotle divides being into the ten categories after having identified the subject of the science as being in *Metaphysics* 4.[14] Iavelli's reply is dismissive. He writes "this answer [of Flandrensis] is for the unlearned (*rudis*)." Noting the same text from *Metaphysics* 4, Iavelli points out that Aristotle gives *unum* as his example of a *per se* property of being. But *unum* and the other transcendentals are *per se* properties and convertible with real being in general and not only with categorical being. To quote Iavelli, "For something is being, and one, and good, and true which, nevertheless, does not belong in a category; for example, the first cause." He adds that in *Metaphysics* 5, besides dividing being into the ten categories, Aristotle also divides being into act and potency.[15]

Iavelli's second argument appeals to Aristotle's divisions of the speculative sciences and the intelligibility of being. He writes:

> since being as being has demonstrable properties, as will be declared in
> Book 4, it is truly knowable. Therefore, being as being ought to be the
> subject in some science. But [it is not the subject] in physics or math-
> ematics, because, as Aristotle says in Book 4, text one, since they are
> particular sciences they consider a part of being. If therefore it is not the
> subject in this science, it is necessary to posit another universal science,
> distinct from this science. [But] that is false because then there would be
> four speculative philosophies, which is contrary to what Aristotle says in
> Book 4, text 2. And that fourth [science] would be the first and universal
> science because it would be about the first and most universal subject.
> Consequently, Aristotle would have attributed to this [fourth] science
> the name of "first philosophy" and the name of "wisdom." Therefore,
> since this [science treated in *Metaphysics*] is first philosophy according to
> Aristotle, it belongs to it to speculate about being as being and not only
> about categorical being.[16]

Since being as being has demonstrable properties, there should be some science whose subject matter is being as being. If Metaphysics does not study being as being, but only being as divided into the ten categories, then there should be some other science which considers being precisely as being. This would be a fourth speculative science in addition to Metaphysics, Physics, and Mathematics. And this fourth speculative science, not the science of categorical being, would be properly called "first philosophy" or "wisdom." Since Aristotle clearly takes the science he is engaging within the *Metaphysics* to be "first philosophy," Aristotle likewise intends for its subject to be being as being without limitation to categorical being.

On the face of it, this argument and the one which precedes it, have merit provided Iavelli can maintain that, in fact, there are demonstrable properties of being as being prior to its limitation to the categories. If real being as being prior to its limitation to the categories has demonstrable properties, then there ought to be a science which has real being as being without qualification for its subject, and that science would be rightly called "first philosophy." And if the First Principle and

Cause of being as being has demonstrable properties precisely as being, then the First Principle and Cause of being as being falls within the subject of that science. To sustain his position, Iavelli needs to show:

(a) the transcendental properties of being as being apply prior to the division of being into the categories.

(b) the First Principle and Cause of being has principles as being.

He attempts to establish the first of these points in Book 4, and the second in Book 6. To maintain that his position reflects the thought of St. Thomas Aquinas, he has to show at least:

(c) the third opinion is consistent with St. Thomas's texts on the subject matter of Metaphysics.

I think these points are most clearly addressed in reverse order. And that is how the paper will proceed.

Disputed Interpretations of Thomas Aquinas

Iavelli takes up two texts from Thomas Aquinas's writings on the subject matter of Metaphysics beginning with Thomas's *Super Boetium de Trinitate*, q. 5, a. 4. There Thomas divides Divine Science into Sacred Scripture and Metaphysics. He explains that the former science studies divine things—or things separate from matter and motion—as its subject matter and the latter science studies divine things as principles of its subject matter.[17] Flandrensis and others of the "second opinion" understand St. Thomas to be separating the principles of a science strictly from the subject matter of a science, such that the principles cannot belong within the subject matter. Since the divine things are principles of beings studied in Metaphysics, they would then necessarily fall outside its subject matter. And consequently, the subject matter of Metaphysics would not be real being taken universally, but real being limited to categorical being.[18]

Iavelli thinks this interpretation misses St. Thomas's intention: "Blessed Thomas does not intend to deny that separated things are contained under the subject of Metaphysics, but he is showing the mode by which they are known by it." Iavelli explains that Metaphysics considers all beings, but some in different ways or modes than others. It considers categorical beings first and through their essences, insofar as these are the beings proportioned to our intellects. It considers principles of such beings secondarily through their effects.[19] In effect, Iavelli claims that what a science reaches through the mode of demonstration *quia* and what a science reaches through mode of demonstration *propter quid* both fall within the science's subject genus despite the difference in the mode of demonstration achieved about the object known. Sacred Scripture then differs from Metaphysics not so much in whether separate substances fall within its subject matter, but in its mode of demonstration about them. Scripture considers the separate substances through what their cause has revealed about them; Metaphysics considers the separate substances through what their effects reveal about them.

The second text Iavelli considers is the proemium to St. Thomas's *In Libros Metaphysicorum*. There Thomas says that although metaphysical science considers the ultimate causes, the separate substances, and *ens commune* or being as being, only *ens commune* is the subject of the science as it is the causes and properties of *ens commune* which the science seeks to demonstrate.[20] Once again, St. Thomas appears to limit the subject matter of Metaphysics to a portion of real being which excludes the separate substances and ultimate causes.

Iavelli denies the conflict between this text and his own position by explaining that it is not mutually exclusive to be both a principle of the members of a genus and a member of that same genus. For the separate substances and ultimate causes to be principles of *ens commune*, Iavelli writes, "it suffices that some subjective part of being, for example, corruptible being, is caused by them." The separate substances then can be within *ens commune*, just not the part of which they are the causes.[21] Again, then, he thinks those who find the second opinion in St. Thomas's text have mistaken St. Thomas's intention. St. Thomas denies that the subject matter of the science is the ultimate causes or the separate substances. He does not deny (at least not out-right) that the ultimate causes and separate substances are included within the subject matter of the science, insofar as they too can be and are treated as being, and are demonstrated to possess the properties of being.[22] After these remarks, Iavelli concludes question 1 with a statement of what he takes to be his opponents' undoing: "Their trap was that they did not know how it is true that being as being has principles and yet God who is contained under being does not have a principle. That however we will resolve in Book 6 . . . to avoid useless repetition."[23]

Can the First Principle of Being as Being
Have a Principle as Being?

I turn now to Iavelli's defence of point "b" above, namely, that the First Principle and Cause of being has principles as being. In Book 6, q. 1, Iavelli begins the discussion with a consideration of the meaning of "principle" and "causes" in a science. He writes:

> consider that Aristotle through "principles and causes" intends all that can be truly a medium for demonstrating some passion about a subject. . . . For it is necessary that every conclusion is deduced from some principle from which, even if it does not always depend according to being, it depends according to cognition. . . . From which it follows that in every science those things from which we proceed to conclusions are the principles and causes in that science . . . , therefore, effects have the *ratio* of principle and cause in demonstrating their causes.[24]

Iavelli's argument here harkens back to his position in Book 1 that the subject matter of a science includes both the things whose properties are demonstrated *propter quid* and the things whose properties are demonstrated *quia*. Here he adds the explicit distinction between principles of being and principles of cognition or knowledge of a being.[25] All demonstrations, both *propter quid* and *quia*, are through principles of knowledge, and in every case the principle of knowledge is the being or beings which are more known to us. That is, the "more known to us" is the medium of demonstration. Since the effects of the first principles of being are more known to us than the principles of being themselves, the effects of the first principles serve as the principles of our knowledge of the first principles. Hence, the categorical beings whose first principles in the order of their being are sought in Metaphysics are the principles in the order of knowledge in Metaphysics' demonstrations *quia* about the ultimate principles of being. Iavelli repeats the point below saying, "the First Cause, as it falls under the consideration of Metaphysics, has formal causes and principles in our understanding, which are either concepts or effects of the first cause, from which we demonstrate some things about it, as will be more manifest in Book 12."[26]

Does it follow from what Iavelli has said that the first principles and causes of being as being fall within the subject of Metaphysics? It does only if what is demonstrated about the First Cause or causes through their effects is demonstrated about them precisely as being; that is, only if the concept of being is the medium of demonstration. If Iavelli can show that the concept of being, which is the medium of demonstration in Metaphysics proofs about being as being, is also the medium for demonstrating the properties of the First Cause, he will have proven point "a)" above; namely, that the transcendental properties of being apply prior to the division of being into the ten categories. Iavelli attempts this task in Book 4, question 1.

The Concept of Being as Being and the Transcendentals

Iavelli promised in Book 1 to show in Book 4 that the concept of being extends to both created and uncreated being, and, consequently, that demonstrations about created and uncreated being alike can employ this concept as a medium. Addressing the concept of being and its unity across the categories and between created and uncreated being leads him through the controversy over the analogous or univocal character of being. And he opens Book 4, q. 1 on this issue.[27]

Following the example of the fifteenth-century Thomists John Capreolus, Paul Soncinas, and Thomas di vio Cajetan,[28] Iavelli offers a threefold division of analogy derivative from Thomas Aquinas's *In 1 Sent.*, d. 19, q. 5, a. 2, ad 1. There St. Thomas distinguishes three modes in which "something is said according to analogy":

1. According to intention only and not according to being.

2. According to being and not according to intention.

3. According to intention and according to being.

As examples of the third mode, St. Thomas offers "being" said of substance and accident, as well as "truth," "goodness," and all such said of God and creatures.[29] Iavelli explains how "being" is said analogously in the third mode analogy as follows:

> Just as an accident is a being (*ens*), insofar as it has connection to substance, and not conversely, and a creature is a being (*ens*), not from itself, but as

it participates being (*esse*) from God, to whom first and *per se* being (*esse*) belongs, and in this third mode being (*ens*) is analogous, and this third mode asserts contradiction, and is an efficacious medium in a syllogism.[30]

Iavelli restates his understanding of being common to God and creatures shortly after saying, "But we say that being (*ens*), as it is common to created and uncreated, expresses one concept, nevertheless unequally participated, by which an analogue of the third mode is constituted."[31] Hence, it is Iavelli's position that there is one concept for the being which God possesses first and *per se*, and which creatures participate from God.

Now although Iavelli speaks of this one concept of being as analogous in the third mode, he *does not* regard the concept of being as, so to speak, intrinsically analogous. He writes,

> *ens* in itself considered precisely and absolutely . . . is not univocal, nor equivocal, nor analogous. For it is not univocal, nor equivocal, nor analogous unless it is compared to its contents. . . . But being so considered in that prior [concept] is not compared to its contents, for first I consider being as being, then being as substance, or accident. Therefore as such, it is not univocal, nor equivocal, nor analogous.[32]

Note the phrase "being precisely and absolutely" is the same as he used in Book 1 when treating being as the subject of Metaphysics. This concept of being is neither univocal, equivocal, nor analogous. It only takes on such features when it is compared as found in or "participated" by its contents, and it is predicable of all of them.

It is Iavelli's position, then, that the intellect has one concept of being which is absolute and prior to the concepts of created and uncreated being, finite and infinite, substance and accident. This one concept is said analogously of the different modes of being, insofar as the various modes are ordered to one another; created to uncreated, and accident to substance. So just as unity, goodness, etc. are demonstrable properties of categorical beings insofar as they are signified through the concept of being taken absolutely, these transcendentals are also demonstrable properties of Uncreated Being insofar as it too is signified through the absolute concept of being. That is, if being belongs to God, and unity, truth, goodness, etc. are properties of being, then, unity, etc. belong to God's being.

Flandrensis had considered and rejected the idea that the application of the transcendentals to God shows that God is included within the subject of metaphysics. Speaking in the person of an objector Flandrensis writes:

> The properties considered in this science are not convertable with being as it is divided into the ten categories. Therefore, it [i.e., categorical being] is not the subject [of the science]. The antecedent is shown from the fact that not all which is *unum* is a created being. For *unum* belongs most of all to God, and yet God is not a created being.

Flandrensis responds to the objection by pointing to what he explains as the analogous (or equivocal by design) predication of the name *unum* to God: "*unum* does not belong to God and to creatures except by equivocating the term '*unum*.' For in this science the *unum* which is predicated of divine things is not considered, but created *unum*."[33] So although Flandrensis grants that the transcendentals are predicated of God, he still limits the subject matter of Metaphysics to created being on the grounds that God and creature are both *unum* only by analogy. I do not find Flandrensis elaborating on his assertion (and hope someone can point me to where he does). At face value, however, his argument here is not convincing. It seems that by the same reasoning, the subject of Metaphysics would be categorical substance alone to the exclusion of accidents, since properties of being belong to the accidents analogously to how they belong to substance.

A more compelling objection would have to address directly Iavelli's claims about the "absolute concept of being." For his part, Flandrensis denies that there is any concept of being altogether separate from the concept of substance. The unequal participation in the concept of being between the different modes of being is simply different ways of relating to the concept of substance.[34] On this basis, a defender of Flandrensis might deny that anything is demonstrated of God as "being," explaining instead that all demonstrations are made of God as "principle or cause of substance." This too, however, strikes me as unsatisfactory, since it seems to conflict with St. Thomas's own claim that transcendentals, such as good, are predicated substantially and essentially rather than merely causally about God.[35] (Other approaches from Flandrensis's position or from other Thomist understandings of "being" and its unity might fare better than these initial attempts. I hope to learn them.)

Conclusion

This paper set out to reconsider a widely accepted Thomist understanding of the subject matter of Metaphysics and God's place as a principle and cause outside of being as being. Drawing on the arguments of Chrysostom Iavelli against the position of his predecessor Dominic Flandrensis, the paper showed,

(a) that texts commonly cited from the writings of St. Thomas on the subject of Metaphysics do not necessarily commit him to excluding the principles of being as being from being as being,

(b) that, although the First Principle lacks a principle in the order of being, it does have principles in the order of knowing its being, and through these principles it has demonstrable properties as being, and

(c) that if the intellect's concept of being is analogous only posterior to the comparison of one mode of being to another, then the properties which are convertible with being so conceived are not limited to categorical being, but to any being insofar as it is being.

I think that if Iavelli is mistaken, it would be due to missing the mark on the concept of being. My own further investigations of this question will begin there. For here,

I draw the conclusion that Thomists need a stronger reason for denying that God is included within the subject of Metaphysics than that God is the First Principle and Cause of being as being and Himself being analogously to the being He creates. I may require intellectual therapy, and I submit to it presently.

Marian University
Indianapolis, Indiana

Notes

1. Lawrence Dewan, O.P., *Form and Being*, Studies in Philosophy and History of Philosophy, vol. 45 (Washington, D.C.: The Catholic University of America Press, 2006), 34.

2. Dewan is citing *In librum beati Dionysii De divinis nominibus expositio*,5.2, ed. C. Pera, O.P., (Rome/Turin: Marietti, 1950), 660.

3. John F. Wippel, *The Metaphysical Thought of Thomas Aquinas: From Finite Being to Uncreated Being* (Washington, D.C.: The Catholic University of America Press, 2000), 18: "for Aquinas metaphysics is indeed divine science, but philosophical divine science. This does not mean that divine things are the subject of this science, or that they are included within its subject. . . . Divine things enter into the metaphysician's field of consideration only indirectly, as principles or causes of its subject, that is being as being." Pages 11–22 provide a very helpful summary of the main texts and points of dispute over the subject of Metaphysics in Aristotle's *Metaphysics*, the positions of Averroes and Avicenna, and especially Thomas Aquinas's own texts.

4. Benedict M. Ashley, O.P, *The Way Towards Wisdom: An Interdisciplinary and Intercultural Introduction to Metaphysics* (Notre Dame, IN: University of Notre Dame Press, 2006) 139: "Aquinas explicitly denies that God is included in Being as Being in the sense of *ens commune*, since he is the cause and principle of *ens commune*, not part of it. . . . Thus, it is better to say that to know the First Cause is the *aim* or *goal* of Metascience, but is not included in its subject."

5. All references to Iavelli will be taken from Chrysostom Iavellus, *In Libros Metaphysicos Aristotelis*, in *Quaestiones, In Metaphysicam Aristotelis: Ab innumeris mendis repurgatae & in gratiam Philosophiae studiosorum denuo editae Accessit in hac editione, Tractatus de natura Metaphysices ex Epitome Metaphysica eiusdem autoris huc translatus, & duplex Index . . .* (Witebergae: Selfischius, 1609) [hereafter Selfischius, 1609].

6. All references to Flandrensis will be taken from Dominicus de Flandria and Cosmas Morelles, *R.P.F. Dominici De Flandria Ordinis Praedicatorvm . . . In Dvodecim Libros Metaphysicae Aristotelis, Secvndvm Expositionem Eivsdem Angelici Doctoris, Lvcidissimae Atqve Vtilissimae Quaestiones* (Coloniae Agrippinae: Ordo, 1621) [hereafter, 1621].

7. Scholastics distinguished between the most common, the adequate, and the principal part of the subject matter of a science. The texts from Thomas Aquinas treating whether God and the separate substances are parts of or exclusively principles of the subject matter of Metaphysics are regarded as investigating specifically the "adequate subject" of metaphysical science. On this point, see Iavelli's predecessor and opponent Flandrensis, *In 1 Met.*, q. 1,

a. 6 (1621: 9b). It is Flandrensis's position that real being common to God and creatures is the most common subject of Metaphysics, but not its adequate subject.

8. Iavelli, *In 1 Met.*, q. 1 (Selfischius, 1609: 1): "An ens ut ens absolute et universalissime sumptum, sit subiectum Metaphysicae?"

9. Iavelli, *In 1 Met.*, q. 1 (Selfischius, 1609: 4): "Prima, subjectum in metaphysica, est illud cujus principia et causas quaerimus. Sed in ea quaerimus principia et causas solius entis praedicamentalis, eo quod ens ut ens, non habet principia et causas, aliter omne ens haberet principium, et sic non esset devenire ad primum ens, cujus oppositum demonstrabitur in lib. 12." See Flandrensis, *In 1 Met.*, q. 1, a. 7 (1621: 10b). Flandrensis's discussion of the issues is more detailed than Iavelli's, but from my own reading of Flandrensis's text, I think that Iavelli accurately identifies the main points of contention. A lesser but still important objection is that Iavelli's position would lose the distinction between the subject matter of Metaphysics and that of Logic. I pass over this objection in this paper for the sake of space, but on this point see Flandrensis, *In 1 Met.*, q. 1, a. 7 (1621: 10b) and Iavelli, *In 1 Met.*, q. 1 (Selfischius, 1609: 5).

10. Flandrensis himself identifies fourteen characteristics of a science's adequate subject matter. For the full list, see Flandrensis, *In 1 Met.*, q. 1, a. 7 (1621: 10b–11a).

11. See Iavelli, *In 1 Met.*, q. 1 (Selfischius, 1609: 4): "Respondeo, negatur minor, nam manifestabitur in li. 6. quomodo haec praepositio est vera, ens ut ens habent principia . . . et tu sustine donec in lib. 6. resolvamus, quae illic formabuntur quaesita."

12. See Iavelli, *In 1 Met.*, q. 1 (Selfischius, 1609: 5): "Tertia opinio, quam reputamus ad mentem Aristotelis et Commenatoris et Avicennae in 1 suae metaphysicae et Algazellis et domini Alberti et B. Thomae et Scoti est haec, *Ens reale per se commune finito et infinito, id est creato et increato, est subjectum adaequatum in hac scientia.*"

13. See Iavelli, *In 1 Met.*, q. 1 (Selfischius, 1609: 7): "primo sic, Illud est subjectum in metaphysica cujus passiones primo et per se convenientes ei considerantur in metaphysica. Haec patet, quoniam est conditio requisita in subjecto cujuslibet scientiae, sed entis realis per se passiones primo et per se ei convenientes considerantur in 4. lib. passiones primo et per se entis, sunt transcendentia, et actus et potentia, et finitum, et infinitum entitative et istae considerantur in Metaphysica ut patet in lib. 4. et 9. et 10. ergo etc."

14. See Iavelli, *In 1 Met.*, q. 1 (Selfischius, 1609: 7): "Sed adverte, quod Flandrensis conatur hanc rationem solvere: dicens, quod metaphysica non considerat passiones entis, nisi ut dividitur in x. praedicamenta similiter ipsum ens, cujus signum dicit esse, quod Philosophus in lib. 5 cap. de ente dividit ens quod posuerat in 4. lib. subiectum metaphysicae in 10. praedicamenta." See Flandrensis *In 1 Met.*, q. 1, a. 8 (1621: 12a).

15. Iavelli, *In 1 Met.*, q. 1 (Selfischius, 1609: 7): "Sed haec responsio rudis est, quoniam philosophus in lib. 4. tex. 1. dixit, quod est quaedam scientia, quae speculatur ens inquantum ens, et quae huic insunt secundum se, exemplificans autem in tex. 3. de his quae per se insunt enti, nominat unum, et infra nominat species unius, et dicit ad eandem scientiam pertinere considerare de ente et uno, sed unum et alia transcendentia non consequuntur per se, sumendo per se convertibiliter ens praedicamentale: imo ens reale. Aliquod enim est ens et unum et bonum, et verum quod tamen non est in praedicamento, puta prima causa, falsum est etiam, quod philosophus in 5 lib. cap. de ente, dividit ens solum in x. praedicamenta quoniam in eodem cap. dividat per potentiam et actum, et constat quod utramque divisionem prosequitur."

16. Iavelli, *In 1 Met.*, q. 1 (Selfischius, 1609: 7–8): "Secundo sic arguitur, cum ens inquantum ens habeat passiones de ipso demonstrabiles, ut declarabitur in 4 lib. est vere scibile: ergo in aliqua scientia debet esse subjectum, non in physica, nec mathematica, quoniam ut inquit Aristoteles in 4 lib. tex. 1. cum sint scientiae particulares, partem entis considerant. Si ergo non est subjectum in hac scientia: oportet dare aliam scientiam universalem, distinctam ab hac scientia, quod est falsum: quoniam tunc essent 4 philosophiae speculativae quod est contra Aristotelem in lib. 6. tex 2. et illa quarta esset prima universalis scientia: quoniam esset de primo et universalissimo subjecto, ex consequenti falso attribuisset Aristoteles huic scientiae nomen primae philosophiae, et nomen sapientiae, cum igitur haec sit apud Aristotelem prima philosophia, ejus est de ente in quantum ens speculari, et non solum de ente praedicamentali."

17. See Iavelli, *In 1 Met.*, q. 1 (Selfischius, 1609: 8): "Primum est super Boetium de trinitate in questione qua quaerit de distinctione scientiarum speculativarum, illic sic dicit, theologia sive scientia divina est duplex, una in qua considerantur res divinae non tanquam subjectum scientiae: sed tanquam principia subjecti, et talis est theologia, quam philosophi prosequuntur, quae alio nomine metaphysica dicitur: alia vero, quae res divinas considerat propter seipsas, ut subjectum scientiae, et haec est theologia, quae sacra scriptura dicitur. Theologia ergo philosophica determinat de separatis, sicut de principiis subjecti. Theologia vero sacrae scripturae considerat de separatis, ut de subjecto."

18. See Iavelli, *In 1 Met.*, q. 1 (Selfischius, 1609: 8): "Tunc isti sic arguunt. Principia subjecti non continentur sub subjecto, aliter causa contineretur sub suo effectu secundum B. Thomam substantiae separatae considerantur a metaphysico, ut principia entis: quod est subjectum in metaphysica. Ergo non continentur sub subjecto metaphysica. text. consequenti ens reale per se acceptum in sua maxima universalitate, non est subjectum in hac scientia."

19. See Iavelli, *In 1 Met.*, q. 1 (Selfischius, 1609: 9): "Ad primum dictum B. Tho. respondeo, et dico quod ex eo non intendit negare, quin separata contineantur sub subjecto metaphysicae, sed innuit modum, quo cognoscuntur ab ea, unde adverte, quod licet omnia entia realia per se considerantur a metaphysico, et ut sic contineantur sub suo subjecto, non tamen eodem modo omnia considerantur, sed quaedam a priori et per essentias suas, utpote proportionate intellectui nostro, quaedam a posteriori et per effectus, quorum sunt principia, ut entia separata et immaterialia, cum ergo dicit B. Tho. quod metaphysicus considerat separata, ut principia entium, dedit modum cognitionis, quasi dicat, per effectus, ex quibus ascendimus ad cognoscendum haec praedicata de illis, scilicet principia causae, primi motores, aeterni, immateriales, intellectuales, etc."

20. See Iavelli, *In 1 Met.*, q. 1 (Selfischius, 1609: 8): "quamvis ista scientia, praedicta tria consideret, non considerat quodlibet eorum ut subjectum, sed ipsum solum ens commune. Hoc enim est subjectum in scientia, cujus causas et passiones quaerimus" See also Flandrensis, *In 1 Met.*, q. 1, a. 8 (1621: 12a).

21. See Iavelli, *In 1 Met.*, q. 1 (Selfischius, 1609: 9–10): "ad argumentum nego minorem, ad probationem nego consequentiam, quoniam ista propositio, substantiae sunt causae entis communis, non est necesse quod verificatur universaliter, sed partialiter: sufficit enim quod aliqua pars entis subjective, puta ens corruptibile, sit causatum ab eis."

A challenge to Iavelli's position here would have to engage Thomas Aquinas's own position that the first in each genus is the one which is the cause and principle of the others in the genus. See especially Thomas Aquinas, *De substantiis separatis*, cap. 6, in *Opuscula Theologica et Philosophica Sancti Thomae Aquinatis*, Opusculum XIV, (Parma ed., vol, 16.1, 1864), 188a: "Suprema autem in entibus oportet esse maxime entia: nam et in unoquoque genere suprema quae sunt aliorum principia, esse maxime dicuntur, sicut ignis est calidus maxime."

22. Iavelli does not attempt to discuss all relevant passages from Thomas Aquinas, and neither does this paper.

23. See Iavelli, *In 1 Met.*, q. 1 (Selfischius, 1609: 10): "Es adverte laqueum eorum fuisse, quia nescierunt intelligere quomodo sit verum quod ens in quantum ens habet principia, et tamen Deus qui continetur sub ente, non habet principium. Id autem nos resolvamus in lib. 6 et tu sustine usque illic, ne inutilis fiat repetitio. Haec pro praesenti quaestione sufficiant."

24. Iavelli, *In 1 Met.*, q. 1 (Selfischius, 1609: 254–255): "Quantum ad primum advurte [*sic*], quod Arist. per principia et causas intendit omne quod potest esse vere medium ad demonstrandum aliquam passionem de subjecto, omne autem reale habet rationem principii formalis, saltem secundum nostrum modum cognoscendi, quod ideo dico, quoniam si est medium a priori, habet rationem principii formalis ex natura rei, ut quando per quod quid est trianguli, demonstro ipsum haberet tres angulos aequales duobus rectis, si autem est medium a posteriori, ut quando in naturalibus demonstro causam per effectum, habet rationem principii formalis secundum nostrum modum cognoscendi, necesse est enim omnem conclusionem ex aliquo principio deducere, a quo licet non semper pendeat secundum esse, pendet tamen secundum cognitionem, cum omnis demonstratio procedat a notiori ei cui fit demonstratio: ex quibus sequitur quod cum demonstro in naturalibus aliquid de causa per suum effectum, effectus ut sic est causa formalis secundum rationem suae causae in demonstrando, et id consonant doctrinae B. Tho. exponentis propositum textum in 6. metaphysic. ubi inquit, omnis scientia intellectualis, sive sit solum circa intelligibilia, ut scientia divina, sive circa imaginabilia, ut mathematica, sive circa sensibilia, ut naturalis, sive etiam ex universalibus principiis ad particularia procedat, in quibus est operatio, ut sunt scientia practicae, semper oportet quod talis scientia sit circa principia et causas, quae quidem principia aut sunt certiora quoad nos, sicut in naturalibus, quae sunt propinquiora sensibus, aut simpliciora et priora secundum naturam ut mathematicis, haec ille. Ex quibus constat, quod in omni scientia illa ex quibus procedimus ad conclusiones, sunt principia et causae in illa scientia, constat autem quod in naturalibus ex effectibus procedimus, effectus igitur habent rationem principii et causae in demonstrando causas suas."

25. Flandrensis also distinguishes principles of being and principles of knowing. See Flandrensis, *In 1 Met.*, q. 1, a. 7 (1621: 10b). See also Thomas Aquinas, *De Veritate* 3.3 ad 7, where St. Thomas distinguishes "principia essendi" from "principia cognoscendi" and says that all principles of being are also principles of knowing, but that not all principles of knowing are principles of being, since effects are principles of knowing their causes.

26. Iavelli, *In 1 Met.*, q. 1 (Selfischius, 1609: 256): "Ex hac conclusione sequitur corrollarie, primam causam, ut cadit sub consideratione metaphy. habere causas et principia formalia apud intellectum nostrum, quae sunt vel conceptus vel effectus primae causae, ex quibus aliqua de ea demonstramus ut magis manifestabitur in libro. 12."

See also Iavelli, *In 1 Met.*, q. 1 (Selfischius, 1609: 256): "Respondetur, licet primo principio totius entis repugnet habere principium in genere entis, quoniam ut sic esset aliquid prius eo, tamen comparando ipsum ad intellectum nostrum in ratione cognoscendi, non inconvenit assignare sibi principium et est illud a quo incipit nostra cognitio de prima causa, quod quidem secundum rem est posterius, utpote effectus illius, secundum cognitionem autem nostram est prius, quoniam prius cadit sub nostro intellectu, quam cognitio primae causae." "It is answered, although it is repugnant to the first principle of the whole of being to have a principle in the genus of being, because as such it [the principle] would be something prior to it [the first principle of the whole of being], nevertheless, by comparing it to our intellect in the *ratio* of knowing, it is not unfitting to assign to it a principle and it is that by which our knowledge of the first cause begins, which indeed according to thing is posterior, insofar as [it is] its effect, but according to our knowledge it is prior, because it falls under our intellect prior to the knowledge of the first cause."

27. The remaining questions of Book 4 treat the transcendentals as properties attending to and convertible with the *ratio* of being as explained in this first question.

28. Iavelli refers to each of these authors at the beginning of *In 4 Met.*, q. 1 (Selfischius, 1609: 95). Their three positions on the unity of the concept of being, including their use of Thomas's threefold division of analogy, are treated in Domenic D'Ettore, "The Fifteenth-Century Thomist Dispute Over Participation in an Analogous Concept: John Capreolus, Dominic of Flanders, and Paul Soncinas," *Mediaeval Studies* 76 (2014): 241–273.

29. See Thomas Aquinas, *In 1 Sent.*, d. 19, q. 5, a. 2, ad 1 (Mandonnet, vol. 1: 492). The tradition of diversely reading this is alive and well. See especially Ralph McInerny, *Aquinas and Analogy* (Washington, D.C.: The Catholic University of America Press, 1996), 6–14, especially 11 and Lawrence Dewan, "St. Thomas and Analogy: The Logician and the Metaphysician," in *Form and Being: Studies in Thomistic Metaphysics*, Studies in Philosophy and the History of Philosophy, vol. 45 (Washington, D.C.: The Catholic University of America Press, 2006), 89–94. This article by Dewan can also be found in *Laudemus Viros Gloriosos: Essays in Honor of Armand Maurer, CSB*, ed. R. H. Houser (Notre Dame: University of Notre Dame Press, 2007).

30. Iavelli, *In 4 Met.*, q. 1 (Selfischius, 1609: 102): "Tertia est quando analogum dicit tantum, unam rationem, in qua non parificantur analogata, nec in esse importato per illam rationem, eo quod in uno analogato reperitur illa ratio, et illius esse connexionem habet cum alio analogato. Sicut accidens est ens, ut habet connexionem ad substantiam, et non econverso, et creatura est ens, non ex se, sed ut participat esse a Deo, cui primo et per se competit esse, et hoc tertio modo ens est analogum, et hic tertius modus, ponit contradictionem, et est medium efficax in syllogismo."

31. Iavelli, *In 4 Met.*, q. 1 (Selfischius, 1609: 103): "Sed nos dicimus, quod ens, ut est commune creato et increato, dicit unum conceptum, inaequaliter tamen participatum, quo constituitur analogum tertii modi."

32. See Iavelli, *In 4 Met.*, q. 1 (Selfischius, 1609: 98): "ens in se praecise et absolute consideratum, dato quod haberet unum conceptum, qui possit convenire omnibus suis contentis non est univocum, nec aequivocum, nec analogum. Nam univocus non est, nec aequivocum, nec analogum: nisi ut comparatur suis contentis, secundum unum aut plures conceptus, ut diximus supra. Haec enim est prima conditio. Sed ens sic consideratum in illo priori, non comparatur suis contentis, prius enim considero ens ut ens, quam ens ut substantia, vel accidens, ergo ut sic, non est univocum, nec aequivocum nec analogum." Iavelli does not directly compare his position here to Flandrensis's own account of the concept of being. But his particular insistence that the being is not univocal, equivocal, or analogous prior to comparison to its modes suggests at least a contrast with Flandrensis's claim that being is analogous in its predication to its inferiors but univocal as a specific habit in the intellect (see Flandrensis, *In 1 Met.*, q. 1, a. 4, ad 1 et ad 5 (1621: 6b–7a). Iavelli seems to be denying Flandrensis's claim that the concept of being has univocal, equivocal, or analogous character as a specific habit in the intellect, but only acquires any of those features in its comparison to its inferiors (i.e., to its various modes).

33. See Flandrensis, *In 1 Met.*, q. 1, a. 8, ad 1 (1621: 12b): "Porphyrius vero accipit ibi aequiuoce, vt idem est quod analogice: analogum enim dicitur aequiuocum a consilio. Et si arguatur. Passiones consideratae in hac scientia, non conuertuntur cum ente, quod diuiditur in decem praedicamenta. Ergo non est subiectum. Probatur antecedens; quia non omne illud quod est vnum, est ens creatum: vnum enim potissime conuenit Deo, et tamen Deus non est ens creatum. Dicendum, quod vnum non conuenit Deo et creaturis, nisi aequiuocando hunc terminum vnum: in hac enim scientia non consideratur vnum, quod praedicatur in diuinis: sed vnum creatum."

34. See Flandrensis, *In 1 Met.*, q. 1, a. 4, ad 5 (1621: 7a); *In 4 Met.*, q. 2, a. 6 (1621: 160a–b); and *In 1 Met.*, q. 1, a. 8, ad 2 (1621: 12b).

35. See Thomas Aquinas, *Prima Pars* 13.2 and 6.

Created Persons are Subsistent Relations:
A Scholastic-Phenomenological Synthesis

Mark K. Spencer

Abstract: The recent Catholic philosophical tradition on the human person has tried to articulate the irreducibility of the human person to anything non-personal, and to synthesize all of the best of what has been said on the human person. Recently, a debate has arisen regarding the concrete existence and relationality of persons. I analyze these debates, and show how both sides of these debates can be synthesized into a view on which human persons are both subsistent beings and identical to certain relations. First, I examine those strands of recent Catholic tradition that defend the concreteness and relationality of the person, drawing on some Existential Thomists and phenomenologists; in connection with this, I consider the ideas of the beauty and *mysterium* of persons. Second, I examine the opposing view, drawing on some traditional Thomists and personalists. Finally, I show how the scholastic notion of transcendental relations can reconcile these views.

To understand the recent Catholic philosophical tradition on the human person (CT),[1] one must consider what is common to most members of that tradition. Here, I consider two such commonalities. First, nearly all members of CT have portrayed the human person as irreducible to anything non-personal (e.g., to matter).[2] This focus on irreducibility has led in some strands of recent CT (e.g., Existential Thomism and some phenomenology) to a focus on the concrete existence of persons to the point that they have abandoned much of traditional—that is, scholastic, Aristotelian, or Platonic—metaphysics for its apparent lack of attention to the concrete.[3] By "a focus on the concrete existence of persons," I mean a focus on the real existence of persons with their properties and in their actual historical situation, rather than a focus on the essence or accidents of persons in abstraction from their real existence or situation. Other strands of CT (e.g., some Personalism and traditional Thomism) have criticized this focus on the concrete for its reductionism regarding those features of human nature that can only be known abstractly. This controversy indicates the importance of the second commonality of members of CT, including the members of both strands of this debate: the desire to synthesize the best of what has had been said on this topic

©2016, *Proceedings of the ACPA*, Vol. 89
doi: 10.5840/acpaproc2016102149

from both within and outside of CT. Far from being an insoluble disagreement, CT has the resources to synthesize the concerns of both sides. I show this in this paper by examining a debate in CT in which the ramifications of the controversy over concreteness are apparent, that over whether human persons are fundamentally relational, or are substances whose relations are accidental.[4]

I have two goals in this paper: first, to analyze and tell the story of recent CT on the question of the right account of the concrete existence and relationality of the human person, and second, to show how a synthesis of the sides of the aforementioned controversy can be drawn out of that story. This synthesis yields a theory of human persons as both subsistent and identical to certain relations including a relation of dependence on God, and as including what were traditionally regarded as essence and accidents, including accidental relations, where both of these are crucially important for understanding the person. To accomplish these goals, I first present the views of those in recent CT who argue that relationality is a central, irreducible feature of the human person, and evidence for that view; I then present the opposing view. Finally, I show how both historical and recent CT have the resources to synthesize the main concerns of each side.

One strand of the controversy over persons' concreteness and relationality arose in the context of an even broader debate in scholasticism over the relationship between essence and existence in created beings. Essence (*essentia*) is that by which a being (*ens*) has its intelligible content; an act of existence (*esse, actus essendi*) is that in virtue of which a being actually exists. Traditional Thomism holds that these are distinct principles in creatures. They are distinguished, among other reasons, to account for the facts that no creaturely essence exists necessarily, that any creaturely essence can be considered apart from knowing whether it exists, and that no creaturely being expresses the full actuality of existence. Rather, beings have a structure in which an act of existence is the actuality of an essence; by being added to an essence, the act explains the contingent existence of a being with that essence, and the essence explains the limitation of each act of existence to being the existence of this being with this intelligible content.[5] This view was opposed by other scholastics, such as Francisco Suárez: on his view, essence and existence are distinguishable only mentally: essence is a being considered as capable of existing, with all its intelligible content, and existence is a being considered in its concrete reality.[6]

Both these views were challenged in twentieth-century CT by Existential Thomism (ET), which developed Aquinas's claim that the act of existence is the fundamental actuality and perfection in a being, by arguing that this act, not essence, is the foundation of the unity, intelligibility, appetibility, and dynamism of each being.[7] The most "radical" of this school[8] argued, against traditional Thomism and Suárezianism, that essence is not really distinct from existence, nor can essence be considered as prior to existence, as capable of existing. On ET, nothing can be without, prior to, or outside of existence. Beings just are acts of existence with an intrinsic limit, which we call essence; they are not limited by an essence different from the act of existence. The sciences and traditional metaphysics cognize these limits by abstraction and thereby attain truths about creatures; however, abstraction cannot attain knowledge about the fullness of the concrete existence that each creature is. The way in which we attain knowledge of concrete existence will be discussed below in a consideration of intuition and aesthetic experience. On ET, human persons are acts of existence first limited in a spiritual way, so that they are capable of giving rise to self-perfective intellectual and free acts, and second limited in a material way, so that they are capable of being modified by external forces, and tend to give rise to effects external to themselves. Aside from identifying persons with acts of existence, this is somewhat similar to traditional scholastic views, on which persons are composites of spiritual soul and matter, the former being the form of the latter.

On the basis of this version of ET, Norris Clarke argued that all created substances are both subsistent and relational. Each substance is a dynamic, self-diffusive act of existence. Following traditional Thomistic terminology, Clarke calls this act a "first act," which tends to cause and manifest itself in "second acts," such as acts of knowledge and love in human persons. Since second acts are beings, they too are intrinsically limited existences. Through these acts, the human substance is related to others, since these acts are intrinsically related to their objects. Because of his or her irreducible immateriality, a human person can perform acts by which he or she intends (and so is related to) all of Being and its transcendental properties: by the intellect, the human person can cognize any being, revealing that Being is intelligible or true; by the will, the human person can love any being, revealing that Being is attractive or good and self-giving. While on this view a human person's existence differs from his or her acts, and so is not a relation but something related, the human person cannot exist without acting, that is, without second acts. While second acts are accidental with respect to first act, they are, on Clarke's view and contrary to traditional scholasticism, principles that are just as important in persons as their first acts. Since all being is self-diffusive, Clarke argues that action or self-communication is a transcendental property of Being, and so, in order to understand a being fundamentally, one must understand its relational acts. Relationality and substantiality differ, but are equally important "poles" of human persons, and of created substances in general.[9]

Others influenced by ET, such as Kenneth Schmitz and David Schindler, extend these claims. Creaturely beings are, on this view, three kinds of created *esse*. First, to be a creaturely being is to be from (*esse ab*) God, dependent on Him for one's being. The relation of dependence cannot be ontologically posterior to a creaturely existence, as an accident or second act, since creaturely existence is constituted by it—that is, this relation is prior to a substance's subsistence and to any of its other relations. One exists and subsists only by being dependent on God. First act in itself contains this relationality apart from any second act, though there is some distinction between first act's substantiality and relationality; they are two "poles" or aspects of one act of existence. These considerations provide strong reason to go beyond Clarke's view in this direction. Second, to be a creaturely being is to be in (*esse in*) oneself, to possess one's being stably and subsistently, such that one is capable of further action as a certain kind of being. In persons, *esse in* appears as subjective interiority, self-presence, and self-consciousness.[10] Third, to be a creaturely existence is to be directed towards (*esse ad*) others. First acts are actualized by and tend to cause second acts, and so first acts are intrinsically related to second acts. To be a being is to be active and self-manifesting not just through second acts, but in oneself, that is, in first act. This point is sometimes further extended by some members of ET: what were traditionally called second acts or accidents are not numerically different beings from first act, but are intrinsic developments of first act—that is, when I perform acts, especially spiritual acts of loving, knowing, and accepting what I receive from God, these acts are reductions of the amount of limitation that my dynamic, changeable first act has. A person is not just an act of existence with an intrinsic limitation (i.e., human nature), but is an act of existence with a unique history of relational acts and receptivities, which are intrinsic modifications of the act that is the person.[11]

ET is a metaphysics that highlights the concrete reality of beings more than their abstractly-knowable essences and properties; understanding this concrete reality requires a focus on beings' relationality and what were traditionally called accidents. These ET claims can be defended and furthered with evidence from other strands of CT that consider the human person to be relational, most of which are in the phenomenological tradition. Seeing how those strands of CT connect to those rooted in scholasticism allows us to see better the interconnectedness of recent CT, and to see some ways in which its various strands can be synthesized. Phenomenology sets aside theorizing about real existence and causality to consider what is given or appears in experience. As Jean-Luc Marion puts it, to be given is not the same as being caused: to be caused is to receive definable, stable being;[12] to be given is to be allowed intentionally and lovingly to appear and to be revealed.[13] While some phenomenologists in CT reject metaphysics, most in CT who have considered the relation between these approaches either use phenomenologically-clarified experience as evidence for metaphysical claims (reasoning like Aquinas from experienced effects to their causes), or they see experience as directly revealing reality,[14] or they think phenomenological findings require grounding in and explanation by metaphysical principles.[15] In each of these approaches, phenomenology and metaphysics work together for a more complete understanding of the human person.

Experiential evidence for the claim that persons are intrinsically relational is presented by Marion, on whose view one is fundamentally given to oneself as a gift from an other, God. I do not experience myself fundamentally as a "self." A "self" has been described variously in CT as a pure ego that has experiences and acts but no content itself,[16] a subjective interiority experienced as both material and spiritual,[17] a stream of experience,[18] or a directedness towards others.[19] Rather, underlying these experiences is my experience of being given to myself; I am not a "self," but a "gifted one." I do not exist prior to or apart from this givenness. Here we find not only experiential evidence for the ET claim that I am fundamentally relational, but also evidence that we should take a step beyond ET: my relation of being given must be identified with myself, rather than being a distinct "pole" from my selfhood or subsistence, for even these appear only and entirely in their being given. At no point can I fully comprehend myself; rather than having an essence that exhaustively accounts for what I am, I am constantly given to myself, such that understanding myself requires attending to this fundamental givenness, and openness to new ways in which I am given, none of which are determined or excluded by essential limitations in me.[20] But being given is not purely passive. Rather, I am given to myself such that I am called to respond to the Giver and to others with acts of knowledge and love according to my vocation, though with freedom to assent or refuse.[21] Here again Marion goes beyond the claims of ET: for Marion, the relations of being from a giver and being oriented to others appear and are identical; they are not distinct "poles" in our existence, as ET claimed. To experience the givenness of a thing, we must perceive it as given in love and tending thereby to self-manifestation, as exceeding our comprehension, requiring infinitely many interpretive acts to be fully known—all of this, Marion sums up, is to perceive it as beautiful. This brings us to another central feature of recent CT on this topic. Many members of recent CT have argued that beauty is a transcendental property of all Being, but Marion suggests going further: Beauty is just what Being fundamentally is.[22]

For many members of recent CT, the notion of beauty expresses the self-manifesting relationality and mysterious, unconceptualizable concreteness of beings. We can begin to understand these ideas by turning to a source for some of the ideas of Marion and ET, Hans Urs Von Balthasar. We shall see in the next section that Balthasar critiques the focus on the concrete, but here I examine his contribution to that focus. He holds that our fundamental experience of ourselves is of receiving ourselves from a Giver, and of being oriented toward and fitting with the world as a whole person.[23] I fundamentally have a holistic cognitive-appetitive experience of the world, an experience of the "heart" whereby I "feel" the world as intelligible and valuable, that is, as beautiful. My experience of knowing and responding to the beautiful is shaped by the object, rather than by any of my concepts.[24] Cognitive or appetitive acts, including acts of abstraction, arise only on the basis of this original, holistic experience. Beings are given in experience as exceeding themselves in referring to a Source that expresses Himself in them—that is, as intrinsically related to that Source, and to others through action, receptivity, and self-manifestation.[25]

Many others in CT also take up these themes. On the view of these thinkers, no concept can fully capture the uniqueness, beauty, and richness—or *mysterium*—that we encounter in beings, especially persons, for example, in the experience of another whom one deeply loves or of one's own subjectivity.[26] Traditional metaphysics can be criticized for reducing the richness and uniqueness of beings to what can be known through concepts,[27] without denying that concepts allow us to know beings in a realist manner.[28] In agreement with Balthasar, many members of recent CT have argued that prior to all concept formation, we have a holistic intellectual, sensory, and appetitive encounter with concrete existences. We do not always experience in temporal order the causal sequence in our powers, as presented by the scholastics, from sensory reception and collation of forms, to intellectual abstraction of species, to concept formation and judgment, to appetitive response. Rather, some scholastics, like Jacques Maritain, contend that we have unconceptualizable "intuitions" of the sensible and intelligible beauty of the world or of our own subjectivity, which involve our senses, intellect, and affections together, without the concept-forming power of the intellect.[29] John Deely elaborates on Maritain's views: in causing a sign, that is, a form or species, of itself to come to be in my mind, a being manifests itself to me, and allows me to be intentionally united to it; underlying all concept formation is this basic orientation to self-manifestation in each being.[30] Similarly, Lublin Thomist Piotr Jaroszyński, with similarities to Balthasar, describes an experience that we constantly have of the "impact" of the being as beautiful upon our cognitive and appetitive powers together, which underlies and allows for all our separate cognitive or appetitive experiences. In such an experience, will, intellect, and sense "interpenetrate," appearing as mutually conditioning parts of one holistic experience of fitting with Being.[31] In their holistic, supra-conceptual, and mysterious concrete givenness beings appear as intrinsically related to us, and we to them.

The relationality (*esse ad*) of intelligibility, appetibility, and, most fundamentally, of beauty, thus appear as intrinsic to beings, as the self-manifesting relationality of each being. Traditional scholasticism interpreted such relations as relations of reason: to say that a being is intelligible is not to say that it is really related to others, but just that a mind could cognize it.[32] But members of recent CT, such as Balthasar and Edith Stein,[33] have argued that this is inadequate to how we experience beings giving themselves: beings appear as actively manifesting and signifying themselves holistically even when there is no other to perceive them, and to manifest God in Whom they participate and Who expresses Himself in each being. It is in part due to these expressive relations, especially the relation to God Who cannot be comprehended, that each being appears as mysterious and unconceptualizable.[34]

To encounter the *mysterium* is to encounter a being in its rich uniqueness, individuality, and incommunicability.[35] These features have tended to be explained in CT as having a minimum of intelligibility, by attributing them to prime or quantified matter, accidents, a formal "this-ness," a mode of incommunicability, or an act of existence, each understood as adding no content to the being beyond making it a 'this,' an incommunicable instance of some species, that is, unable to be received by or become part of another. Or, these features have been attributed to a static individual essence, albeit one with individual intelligible content.[36] I make no claim here as to which of these is correct, but while each of these theories would explain why a being is a "this," an instance of some kind, each fails to explain the dynamic uniqueness and *mysterium* with which it gives itself. ET and Lublin Thomism capture what is missing in these accounts with the idea that the acts and experiences a person undergoes, and especially the free acts he or she performs, are modifications to who he or she fundamentally is.[37] Similarly, some versions of personalism such as Edith Stein's present the idea of a changeable essence: through acts, one can change who one fundamentally is, even while some of one's essential features always remain the same.[38] Each of these is an attempt to articulate the claim that to be a unique individual, especially a unique person, is to be intrinsically, dynamically variable, not just to have unique matter, this-ness, or static individual essence. It is to have what poet Gerard Manley Hopkins called an "inscape," a style or pattern of acting and relating that manifests an intelligible content in spontaneously chosen ways, which manifest the being and the ways in which God gives it and Himself in it.[39] In these claims, the relationality of including accidents in the existence of the person is joined to the relationality of self-manifestation: having both is intrinsic to beings.

If all of the foregoing is correct, no person can be fully described conceptually or abstractly. Rather, a person can be described in a narrative or history of his or her acts, relations, virtues, and vices, or in a poetic account of the initial encounter with his or her beauty or *mysterium*, or by a theological or sacramental account of the infinite depth by which he or she reveals God.[40] For the metaphysician who focuses on concreteness and relationality, these aesthetic and interpretive approaches are as necessary for metaphysics as traditional abstract methods. Indeed, many in recent CT have turned to narrative and history as a proper approach to understanding the person, including phenomenologists (e.g., Richard Kearney), the Radical Orthodox (e.g., Catherine Pickstock), analytic Thomists (e.g., Eleonore Stump), and virtue ethicists (e.g., Alasdair MacIntyre).[41] While in traditional metaphysics these approaches would have been the study of accidents, on the view that focuses on concreteness and relationality, they are foundational to any account of the human person, due to the elevated status that these acts have in an understanding of the person as concrete, dynamic existence. Some relations, such as a person's givenness, are identical to or constitutive of the person's substance, that is, these relations do not inhere in the substance as accidents, but are "subsistent relations," relations identical to the subsisting substance. Other relations, such as relational acts of knowing and loving, are posterior to but intrinsically modifying of that substance. Considering the person to be intrinsically embedded in a narrative or history allows for further elaboration of ways in which the person is relational. Human persons are not just constituted by their relation to God, but are also intrinsically related to their ancestors,[42] and thereby to their whole historical and traditionary situation.[43] Through these considerations, a focus on the relationality of the human person allows a synthesis of many strands of CT, and a more complete account of the irreducibility and concreteness of the person.

I now turn to the other side of the debate, which objects to what it sees in the first side as a one-sided focus on the concrete and relational. These responses center around the claim that this focus fails to attend fully to all of our experience, and so are actually reductionistic of the fullness of human persons. As Personalist Josef Seifert, following Stein, argues, the intellectual experience of abstract and universal ideas, and of real essences, is no less a correct experience of the world than the experience of concrete existence.[44] We experience things as having stable natures, which explain the powers, acts, and teleological orientations they exhibit. Erich Przywara and Balthasar note that the development of a being is only understandable if it is guided by an underlying, identity-preserving essence, and essence is only understandable on the basis of the concrete existence from which knowledge of it was abstracted. If we are to have a metaphysics that is rooted in the fullness of our experience, as many in CT desire, then that metaphysics should include essences distinct from, but united to, existence.[45] Przywara expresses this by saying the two principles are proportional or analogical to one another, that is, they fit together, and are understandable only in relation to one another. Furthermore, as the analytic Thomistic hylomorphists emphasize, beings, including ourselves, are also given in experience as having material parts, and a form-matter structure. We understand beings, including ourselves, better when we know their material structure in itself, not as reduced to dynamic, concrete, relational existence.[46] Even beauty is experienced as analyzable, that is, not just as a single cognitive-appetitive whole, but as having a real intelligible and sensible structure. Metaphysics should account for the concrete holism of beings, but also for their abstractly analyzable structure.[47]

While the opponents of the focus on the concrete generally do not deny that relations are important to understanding the person, they resist any claim that the person is identical to relations, or has relations at the same metaphysical level as his or her subsistence. Against Balthasar and ET, Steven Long argues that created substances, including persons, are independently existing beings with natures that have relations as accidents. By His act of creation, God produces *ex nihilo* things other than Himself, with their own existence and causality. If these beings were relations to Him, then they would be insufficiently other than Himself, and it would not be clear how they could be causes in their own right, since all causality would just be a relation of givenness by God. To be beings different than God, to whom God can give further gifts, substances must have their own natures and ends, which result from God's free decision, but which are not identical to any relation to Him. Long follows Aquinas, who holds that, like all relations, the relations of dependence on and being created by God differ from the substance as accidents inhering in the substance, such that the substance is prior in being to the relation.[48]

Scholastics before the contemporary period but after Aquinas, however, moved to some extent in the direction of ET. Suárez argued that the relation of dependence on God, while not identical to a substance, is not an accident; rather it is a "mode," a feature of a being that is distinct from its parts, really inseparable from that being, and helps to constitute that being.[49] Suárez's view seems somewhat similar to that of Schindler, for whom this relation is a "pole" within the being, though distinct from its subsistence; on some versions of the modal view, the mode is not really distinct from the being, but rather is rather modally or formally distinct. Other scholastics, including some Thomists, have held that substances are identical to relations of a sort, transcendental relations, coming closer to Marion's view. The notion of transcendental relations in this context originates in John Duns Scotus,[50] who held that a relation of dependence on God is identical to each substance. This relation is a transcendental relation, which is a relation or ordering to another that is identical to its foundation, as matter is identical to its ordering to form.[51] Transcendental relations were posited to account for the observation that principles such as form and matter are in themselves ordered to correlative principles, and effects to their causes, and vice versa—sometimes even when the things to which they are ordered do not currently exist. For example, something that can be a final cause is of itself ordered to its possible effects, even if it has no actual effects. Relationality, and subsistence and causality, are not opposed; rather, subsistent things are relational because dependent on their causes, and ordered of themselves to possible effects—that is, intrinsic relationality is necessary to be and constitutive of what it is to be a created cause or effect. We tend to think and speak of these orderings as accidents, but on this view they belong to what it is to be a created being.

The seventeenth-century Thomist John of St. Thomas did some work to reconcile Aquinas and Scotus's positions, and thereby provides a basis for reconciling the two sides of the current debate over the concreteness and relationality of persons. On his view, the relation of dependence on God is accidental to the individualized essence—that is, the essence plus its principles of individuation and incommunicability—of a being. But as existing, a being is a transcendental relation of dependence on God, as every effect is a transcendental relation to its causes.[52] The claim here is not that an existing being is a relation but not subsistent, nor that it is a relation without a foundation; rather, the claim is that to be a subsisting, existing, created being just is to be related to God by dependence: the subsistent foundation is the relation. This claim is furthered by some in recent CT, including Przywara and the Lublin Thomists Mieczyław Krąpiec and Andrew Woznicki.[53] On their views, persons, and all created substances, are composed of real principles—essence and existence, form and matter—that are transcendental relations to one another. Persons are also transcendental relations to their causes. Likewise, persons and all created beings are transcendental relations to one another, inasmuch as all beings form a single order or community, with each related to the others by analogy, that is, by proportions of similarity and difference. This structure and depth of each being manifests itself in intuition, as described above.

Drawing upon this notion of transcendental relations as found in CT, we can reconcile the main claims of the two sides of the debate. A substance's act of existence, on Aquinas's view, actualizes not only its individualized essence, but also its accidents; a human person (or, more generally, a supposit, that is, a complete being of any sort) includes not only substantial form and matter, but also accidents. While accidents can rightly be regarded as beings different from a substance or individualized essence, a supposit or person includes both.[54] On many recent interpretations of Aquinas, a person is a person through the act of existence: by existing, one possesses one's individualized essence and accidents, and is a subjective, free person, irreducible to anything purely non-subjective.[55] Drawing on this interpretation and the phenomenological data given above, it should be said, first, that the dynamic act of existence confers concrete actuality and *mysterium*, and self-manifesting intelligibility, appetibility, and beauty, on the other principles of a being, and, second, that those principles limit the act of existence to being the actuality and self-manifestation of this one kind of being. We should distinguish: (1) the substantial being and unity of a person, composed of the individualized essence, and an act of existence as actualizing that essence, where the essence is unchanging, different from any relation, and knowable by abstraction; (2) the accidental being and unity of a person, composed of the substantial being plus accidents considered as separate beings from that substance; (3) the personal or concrete being of a person, composed of the substance and accidents as all actualized and united by the one substantial act of existence. As a personal being, I have an unchanging essence, but through my accidents, I change in who I fundamentally am; I include, but am not reducible to, my matter, form, their composite, my accidents, or anything that is not a person. God creates and gives concrete beings, that is, persons and other supposits, in themselves, and only causes (or "co-creates") substantial and accidental beings as constituents of concrete beings.[56] A person is both identical to some transcendental relations, and includes other relations, including relational acts, as intrinsic modifications, though they are accidental with respect to the person's substance. My acts are as important as my substance to who I am, considered in my personal being.

What ET said about existence and Marion about givenness can be said on this view of each concrete, composite being (*ens*), allowing a synthesis of both sides of the debate. In light of the claims regarding essence made by Seifert and Przywara, and contrary to ET, concrete beings are not identical to existence. Rather, they are wholes that have an essence and act of existence, that subsist or exist in (*esse in*) themselves, that include their accidental acts as intrinsic modifications of their personal being, and that are transcendental relations of being given and caused by (*esse ab*) God and other givers, and of being oriented toward (*esse ad*) others in active self-manifestation. The person is not just a system of relations, nor are all relations reducible to accidents, either in reality or in the way in which the person is experienced; the notion of transcendental relations avoids these extremes. One's orientation to self-manifestation, which one has just by being a person with an act of existence, leads to acts, which are intrinsic modifications of one's personal being. These acts manifest the person as dynamic, given, mysterious, and beautiful, with an analyzable structure.[57] For the metaphysician to give the best possible account of persons requires an abstract account of their internal structure and essence,[58] but also requires the use of narrative, poetic, phenomenological, and theological modes of discourse. Each mode of discourse is rooted in the self-manifesting reality of beings, though each also can only achieve, through interpretation of the encounter with the *mysterium* of each being, a partial account of the full concrete existence of each being.[59] Metaphysics is an endless task.

This synthesis expresses a more complete account of the irreducibility of the person to anything non-personal than either side of the debate on its own. It furthermore brings together the concerns of both sides of the debate over the concrete existence of persons in a way that uses all the strands of recent CT. In this way, we can see the genuine unity and synthetic power of recent CT on the human person.[60]

University of St. Thomas, St. Paul, MN

Notes

1. By CT, I mean the intellectual tradition that has been historically shaped by the appropriation of Aristotelian and Platonic philosophy in a Catholic context. I include in CT those participating in this tradition who are not members of the institutional Catholic Church, and also those influenced by this tradition who do not themselves use the methods

or categories of Greek philosophy. By 'recent' CT, I mean the CT of the last hundred years. This is a vast tradition, and I certainly make no claim to give an exhaustive treatment of it here. Rather, I only treat its main strands as they are centered around the problem of giving a philosophical account of concrete personhood.

2. For recent accounts in CT of the reasoning behind CT's focus on the irreducible in the human person, see Kenneth Schmitz, "Created Receptivity and the Philosophy of the Concrete," *The Thomist* 61 (1997): 339–372; Karol Wojtyła, "Thomistic Personalism" and "Subjectivity and the Irreducible in the Human Being," in *Person and Community*, trans. Theresa Sandok (New York: Peter Lang, 1993). But, in less articulated form, this attention to the irreducibility of the concrete is already found in the early sources of CT, such as in ancient Greek thinkers like Aristotle, as shown by my "Aristotelian Substance and Personalistic Subjectivity," *International Philosophical Quarterly* 55 (2015): 145–164, and in early Christian thinkers like Irenaeus, as shown by Hans Urs von Balthasar, *Glory of the Lord*, v. 2, *Studies in Theological Style: Clerical Styles*, ed. John Kenneth Riches, trans. Andrew Louth et al. (San Francisco: Ignatius, 1984), 31–94.

3. I distinguish between metaphysics as traditionally done, e.g., in scholasticism, where it largely employs causal reasoning, and metaphysics in a more expansive sense, as any philosophical reflection on the fundamental features of reality (this is the sense in which I mean it here). In this more expansive sense, modes of philosophical reflection like Jean-Luc Marion's phenomenology of givenness or John Caputo's radical hermeneutics would still count as metaphysics. For a good summary of Caputo's critique of metaphysics and of his radical hermeneutics, see Christopher Ben Simpson, *Religion, Metaphysics, and the Postmodern* (Bloomington: Indiana University Press, 2009), 7–13.

4. Other debates could, perhaps, have been chosen to discuss and synthesize the main lines of recent CT on the philosophy of the human person, e.g., debates over the principle of individuation. But, the debate over the relationality of the person contains and goes beyond those other debates.

5. On Aquinas's account of essence and existence, see *Expositio libri Boetii de hebdomadibus* lect 1; *De ente et essentia* c. 4; *Quaestiones disputatae de potentia* q. 7, a. 2; *Quaestiones disputatae de veritate* q. 1, a. 1; *Summa contra gentiles* II, c. 52; *Summa theologiae* (*ST*), I, q. 3, a. 4. See S. Thomae de Aquino Opera Omnia, ed. Enrique Alarcón, http://www.corpusthomisticum.org/ iopera.html. See also the summaries of the view given by recent members of CT e.g., my "The Personhood of the Separated Soul," *Nova et Vetera* 12 (2014): 863–912; John Wippel, *The Metaphysical Thought of Thomas Aquinas* (Washington, DC: CUA Press, 2000), chs. 5–6. To speak of God as each creature's efficient cause does not mean that God alone efficiently causes beings. Rather, God must bestow an act of existence immediately on each being, even when that being is also efficiently caused by some secondary, created being.

6. Francisco Suárez, *Disputationes metaphysicae* (*DM*), ed. Salvador Castellote and Michael Renemann, available at http://www.salvadorcastellote.com/investigacion.htm, d. 31, s. 1, n. 13. This view, as contemporary Suárezian José Pereira, *Suárez: Between Scholasticism and Modernity* (Milwaukee: Marquette University Press, 2007), 101ff., contends, is meant to express the concrete reality of beings more clearly than the Thomistic view: every being is its own concrete essence and existence, rather than only sharing in these as principles.

7. See, e.g., Etienne Gilson, *Being and Some Philosophers* (Toronto: PIMS, 1949); Joseph Owens, "Thomas Aquinas," in *Individuation in Scholasticism: The Later Middle Ages and the*

Counter-Reformation, 1150–1650, ed. Jorge J. E. Gracia (Albany, NY: New York University Press, 1994), 173–194.

8. Some of the original Existential Thomists, e.g., Gilson and Owens, maintain the distinction between essence and existence, though they attribute the fullness of intelligibility and unity in beings to the act of existence. For the more "radical" school, whose views are summarized in the rest of this paragraph, see, e.g., Gerard Phelan, "The Being of Creatures: St. Thomas's Solution of the Dilemma of Parmenides and Heraclitus," *Proceedings of the ACPA* 31 (1957): 118–127; Phelan, "The *Esse* of Accidents," *New Scholasticism* 43 (1969): 143–148; William Carlo, *The Ultimate Reducibility of Essence to Existence in Existential Metaphysics* (The Hague: Martinus Nijhoff, 1966), 99–145; Matthew Schaeffer, "Thick-*Esse*/Thin-Essence in Thomistic Personalism," *American Catholic Philosophical Quarterly* 89 (2015): 223–251; as well as the sources from Clarke, Connor, Schindler, and Schmitz cited in notes 9 and 11 below.

9. Clarke's views presented here are summarized from his *Person and Being* (Milwaukee: Marquette University Press, 1993); see also "Action as the Self-Revelation of Being," "To Be is to be Substance in Relation," and "Person, Being, and St. Thomas" in Clarke, *Explorations in Metaphysics: Being-God-Person* (Notre Dame: UND Press, 1994). The orientation of beings, especially persons, toward action, is drawn from others in recent Thomism, e.g., Joseph de Finance, *Être et agir dans la philosophie de Saint Thomas* (Rome: Presses de l'Université Grégorienne, 1965), especially 241–246, who expresses the unity and relationality of being and action. It is also a major theme of many in the Personalist school of CT, e.g., Karol Wojtyła, *The Acting Person*, trans. Andrzej Potocki (Dordrecht: Riedel, 1979); "The Personal Structure of Self-Determination," in *Person and Community*. Correlative to the transcendental property of self-communication, on Clarke's view, is the ability to receive the self-communication of beings in some way; receptivity, and openness to communion, are thus likewise transcendental properties of Being, and especially of persons as the highest form of created beings. This is a further way that beings are intrinsically relational. Clarke says much here in line with traditional scholasticism, on which substances in first act—whether the first essential act, which is the form or soul, or the first act of being, which is existence—give rise to powers, whereby they perform second acts, and so relate to others and can be fulfilled. Something analogous to what is said here of intellectual cognition and appetite can be said of sensible and natural apprehension and appetite. Our openness to all of Being is a major theme in much recent CT; see, e.g., Edith Stein, *Finite and Eternal Being*, trans. Kurt Reinhardt (Washington, DC: ICS Publications, 2002), 294–324; Fernand Van Steenberghen, *Thomas Aquinas and Radical Aristotelianism* (Washington, DC: CUA Press, 1980), 71; Jan Aertsen, *Medieval Philosophy as Transcendental Thought: From Philip the Chancellor (ca. 1225) to Francisco Suárez* (Leiden: Brill, 2012), 430–432; Alice Ramos, "Introduction" in *Dynamic Transcendentals: Truth, Goodness, and Beauty from a Thomistic Perspective* (Washington, DC: CUA Press, 2012), 1–6.

10. On the idea that subjectivity is what is irreducible in the human person, see Wojtyła, "Subjectivity and the Irreducible in the Human Being," 211. But see also Catherine Pickstock, *Repetition and Identity* (Oxford: Oxford University Press, 2014), 31–38, on how there is something analogously like subjectivity in other beings.

11. The views presented here are drawn from: Robert Connor, "Relational *Esse* and the Person," *Proceedings of the ACPA* 65 (1991): 253–267; Schmitz, "The First Principle of Personal Becoming," *The Review of Metaphysics* 47 (1994): 768–774; Schmitz, "Created Receptivity"; David L. Schindler, "Norris Clarke on Person, Being, and St. Thomas," *Communio* 20 (1993): 580–592; Schindler, *Heart of the World, Center of the Church:* Communio

Ecclesiology, Liberalism, and Liberation (Grand Rapids: Eerdmans, 1996), 275–311. Several of these thinkers draw parallels between the relationality of creatures and the Trinitarian relations; I make no such claims here. I shall examine Marion and Balthasar's elaboration of similar relations in the being of the person below, but some of the Personalists suggest similar things. For example, Emmanuel Mounier, *Personalism*, trans. Philip Mairet (London: Routledge, 1952), 33–50, argues that the person is fundamentally both a bodily-spiritual interiority and secret subjective life, and also a directedness towards others through vocation, and towards oneself in self-affirmation.

12. Since participation involves taking part or sharing in the attributes of another, and so is a formal or exemplary causal relationship, being given is not the same as participating either.

13. Marion, *Being Given: Toward a Phenomenology of Givenness*, trans. Jeffrey Kosky (Stanford: Stanford University Press, 2002), 73–74; Jean-Pierre Lafouge, *Givenness and Hermeneutics* (Milwaukee: Marquette University Press, 2012), 21–23. Givenness is in part an expressive or signifying relationship; it is also a sacramental relationship in which the giving or the giver can be seen in the given, as John Milbank, "Beauty and the Soul," in Milbank, Graham Ward, and Edith Wyschogrod, *Theological Perspectives on God and Beauty* (Harrisburg: Trinity Press International, 2003), 1–6, shows. Such a view is also found in Existential Thomism in the claim that creatures are constituted as participating beings by God's intentional acts of knowing and willing, rather than purely by an act of efficient causality, at Clarke, "What Cannot be Said in St. Thomas's Essence-Existence Doctrine," in *The Creative Retrieval of St. Thomas Aquinas* (New York: Fordham University Press, 2009), 127.

14. See, e.g., John Haldane, "The Breakdown of Contemporary Philosophy of Mind," in *Mind, Metaphysics, and Value in the Aristotelian Tradition*, ed. John Haldane (Notre Dame: UND Press, 2002), 57–58; "Insight, Inference and Intellection," *Proceedings of the ACPA* 73 (1999), 42; John Milbank, "The Soul of Reciprocity Part One: Reciprocity Refused," *Modern Theology* 17 (2001): 336–338; Milbank, "The Soul of Reciprocity Part Two: Reciprocity Regained," *Modern Theology* 17 (2001): 490–492, 495–501; Edith Stein, *Finite and Eternal Being*, 277–278; Karol Wojtyła, "Subjectivity"; John Crosby, *The Selfhood of the Human Person* (Washington, DC: CUA Press, 1996), 49–65.

15. Schmitz, "Created Receptivity."

16. cf. Stein, *Finite and Eternal Being*, 46–52; Max Scheler, *Formalism in Ethics and Non-Formal Ethics of Values*, trans. Manfred Frings and Roger Funk (Evanston: NWU Press, 1973), 390. This position is also found in the New Natural Law tradition, e.g., Germain Grisez, "Sketch of a Future Metaphysics," *New Scholasticism* 38 (1964): 310–340.

17. This position is especially well developed by the Lublin Thomist Mieczyław Krąpiec, *I-Man: An Outline of Philosophical Anthropology*, trans. Marie Lescoe, Andrew Woznicki, and Theresa Sandok, et al. (New Britain: Mariel Publications, 1983), 89–106. See also Stein, *Finite and Eternal Being*, 46–52; Mounier, *Personalism*, 3–6; Karol Wojtyła, *Acting Person*, part III; Crosby, *Selfhood*, chs. 3–4.

18. Michel Henry, *The Essence of Manifestation*, trans. Girard Etzkorn (The Hague: Martinus Nijhoff, 2008), 307–309; *Philosophy and Phenomenology of the Body*, trans. Etzkorn (The Hague: Martinus Nijhoff, 1975), 219; *Incarnation: Une philosophie de la chair* (Paris: Seuil, 2000), 318–320.

19. See, e.g., Michael Purcell, *Levinas and Theology* (Cambridge: Cambridge University Press, 2006), 135–154; Emmanuel Mounier, *Personalism*, 33.

20. Jean-Luc Marion, *In the Self's Place: The Approach of Saint Augustine*, trans. Jeffrey Kosky (Stanford: Stanford University Press, 2012), 65, 284–288. Similar claims are made by John Zizioulas, *Being as Communion* (Crestwood: St. Vladimir's Seminary Press, 1985), 42–49. These claims are linked to the great nature-grace debate: the claim is that I am given to myself as a person such that I do not have a closed nature with its own limited end, but that I am rather given to myself as an open-ended person, capable of ever higher fulfillment if it is given to me by God—that is, my given existence is of itself open to grace. I do not intend to make any claims regarding this debate, but the view I conclude to in this paper is meant to be able to provide a basis for a future resolution to the nature-grace debate on which I both have a stable nature with its own proximate natural limited end, and have an entirely open-ended given historical concrete existence that is oriented by its Giver to a vocation of receiving grace.

21. Marion, *Being Given*, 282–308; *In the Self's Place*, 43. Marion builds on the work of Jean-Louis Chretien and Hans Urs Von Balthasar.

22. Marion, *Being Given*, 210–211; *In the Self's Place*, 138–139. cf. Marion, *The Erotic Phenomenon*, trans. Stephen Lewis (Chicago: University of Chicago Press, 2007), 126–127. On needing the right attitude to experience the givenness and beauty of things: Marion, *Erotic Phenomenon*, 116–119; *In the Self's Place*, 138–144 (but also see Scheler, *Formalism*, 488). On Being as fundamentally knowable through love, see Balthasar, *Theo-Drama: Theological Dramatic Theory*, v. 2, *Truth of God*, trans. Adrian Walker (Ignatius: San Francisco, 2004), 135, 177. See Maritain, *Art and Scholasticism*, trans. Joseph Evans (Notre Dame: UND Press, 1962), http://www3.nd.edu/Departments/Maritain/jmworks.htm), ch. 5, n. 66, who contends that beauty is the radiance of all the transcendentals. For the history of CT on beauty see Umberto Eco, *The Aesthetics of Thomas Aquinas*, trans. Hugh Bredt (Cambridge: Harvard University Press, 1988); Piotr Jaroszyński, *Beauty and Being: Thomistic Perspectives*, trans. Hugh MacDonald (Toronto: PIMS, 2011); Balthasar, *The Glory of the Lord: A Theological Aesthetics*, v. 1, *Seeing the Form*, trans. Erasmo Leiva-Merikakis (San Francisco: Ignatius, 1982), 17–124.

23. The notion of fitting with the world is further elaborated by others; see the summary of Jacques Maritain's views in John Trapani, *Poetry, Beauty, and Contemplation: The Complete Aesthetics of Jacques Maritain* (Washington, DC: CUA Press, 2011), 45–49, and Alice Ramos, "Moral Beauty and Affective Knowledge in Aquinas," chap. 10 in *Dynamic Transcendentals*, 181–204.

24. Similar claims are made by Marion, *Being Given*, 215–219. See also personalist phenomenologist Dietrich Von Hildebrand, *The Sacred Heart* (Baltimore: Helicon, 1965), 110–114, on the notion of the heart as the true self, in which I feel and respond to value in the world, and accept or reject my self.

25. These ideas from Balthasar are summarized from: *The Glory of the Lord*, v. 1, *Seeing the Form*, 235–241, 380–389; v. 5, *The Realm of Metaphysics in the Modern Age*, trans. Oliver Davies (San Francisco: Ignatius, 1991), 613–628; *Theo-Logic: Theological Logical Theory*, v. 1, *Truth of the World*, trans. Adrian Walker (San Francisco: Ignatius, 2000), 67–78, 102–107, 216–225. Cf. Oleg V. Bychkov, *Aesthetic Revelation: Reading Ancient and Medieval Texts after Hans Urs Von Balthasar* (Washington, DC: CUA Press, 2010), 62–67.

26. For a definition of *mysterium* see especially Erich Przywara, *Analogia Entis*, trans. John Betz and David Bentley Hart (Grand Rapids: Eerdmans, 2014), 182–185. cf. Schindler, *Heart of the World*, 305; Stein, *Finite and Eternal Being*, 242, 442.

27. Following Husserl, Edith Stein, *Finite and Eternal Being*, 279–281, and Gabriel Marcel, "On the Ontological Mystery," in *The Philosophy of Existentialism* (New York: Citadel, 1984), 12, contend that ideas of essences, genera and species, and of act and potency, are "empty" schematic concepts, that needs to be "filled" with the rich contents found in concrete individuals.

28. There are exceptions to this realism within CT. Some within CT (e.g., John Caputo, Gianni Vattimo) hold to a radical hermeneutics, wherein everything is ultimately a matter of interpretation, and so concepts would not correspond to a reality outside the interpretive scheme. Others (e.g., Michel Henry) hold a view on which only subjectivities with their immanent contents or stream of consciousness really exist, and so concepts would not correspond to any extramental reality.

29. See the summary of Maritain's statements on this experience at Trapani, *Poetry*, 40–49. For other statements of this experience, e.g., that of the Transcendental Thomist Pierre Rousselot see Gerard McCool, *The Neo-Thomists* (Milwaukee: Marquette University Press, 1994), 107. Bernard Lonergan, *Insight* (Toronto: University of Toronto Press, 1992), 569–572 notes that even when we understand the being through concept, the mystery remains, for we always use concepts by turning to images, which have a richness that cannot be summed up in concepts, for we are "by nature oriented to mystery." Marcel, "On the Ontological Mystery," 12–22, likewise notes that attempts to comprehend the world conceptually, rising above experience, leads to "mystery," because we are located within and parts of the very thing we are trying to understand. See also Balthasar on Guardini and Siewerth at *Seeing the Form*, 380–389.

30. Jacques Maritain, *The Degrees of Knowledge*, trans. Gerard Phelan (Notre Dame: UND Press, 1995), 127–136, 414–421. John Deely's views are well summarized in his *Semiotic Animal* (South Bend: St. Augustine's Press, 2010). For the ways in which Deely builds on Maritain and others in this tradition, see "The Immateriality of the Intentional as Such," *New Scholasticism* 42 (1968): 302. These thinkers do not claim that everything is reducible to existence.

31. Jaroszyński, *Beauty and Being*, 171–188, following Krąpiec, *Metaphysics: An Outline of the History of Being*, trans. Theresa Sandok (New York: Peter Lang, 1991), 179–189.

32. See, e.g., Aquinas, *DV* q. 1, a. 1, and q. 24, a. 1.

33. Balthasar, *Truth of the World*, 62–67; Stein, *Finite and Eternal Being*, 292–300.

34. On participation see Wippel, *Metaphysical Thought*, ch. 4. On how participation points to primacy of relation over substance see Radical Orthodox philosopher Adrian Pabst, *Metaphysics: The Creation of Hierarchy* (Grand Rapids: Eerdmans, 2012), 44–47, and on how all phenomena are rooted in participation in God, leading to excess of meaning in every name see Pabst, *Metaphysics*, 143–144 (though he wrongly claims that Marion denies this). CT has the resources to overcome a debate in secular phenomenology between the followers of Levinas and the followers of Merleau-Ponty. The former claims that the human person is entirely constituted by encountering the other and being directed to serve the other; the latter claims that the person is always in a reciprocal relation with the world, affected by but also affecting the world. CT overcomes this: an individual being is simultaneously entirely given by God, and oriented to active, reciprocal, receptivity to the world, and response to God. cf. Ian Leask, *Being Reconfigured* (Newcastle: Cambridge Scholars, 2005), 100–105; Milbank, "Reciprocity, Part Two"; Caitlin Smith-Gilson, *The Metaphysical Presuppositions of Being in the World* (New York: Continuum, 2010), 74–82, 169.

35. cf. D. C. Schindler, *The Catholicity of Reason* (Grand Rapids: Eerdmans, 2013), 73. Stein, *Finite and Eternal Being*, section VIII, distinguishes the uniqueness of a being, i.e., the content that is particular to this being; its individuality, i.e., that it is a "this"; and its incommunicability, i.e., its belonging to itself and not to another.

36. On the idea of essential content unique to a person see Crosby, *Selfhood*, 64–65; Josef Seifert, *Essence and Existence*, in *Aletheia* 1 (1977): 62–67; Stein, *Finite and Eternal Being*, 343, 481. Stein explains the other theories of individuation, as does Gracia, *Individuation in Scholasticism*.

37. See, e.g., Krąpiec, *I-Man*, 322–325.

38. See, e.g., Seifert, *Essence and Existence*, 72–77; Stein, *Finite and Eternal Being*, 151–152.

39. See, e.g., Hopkins's poem "As Kingfishers Catch Fire" and his journal entries for March 1871 (Gerard Manley Hopkins, Catehrine Phillips, ed., *The Major Works* (Oxford: OUP, 2002), 129, 204–205). For a good explanation of Hopkins's metaphysics and epistemology see Dennis Sobolev, *The Split World of Gerard Manley Hopkins* (Washington, DC: CUA Press, 2011). Hopkins is an influence on thinkers on both sides of this debate, e.g., Balthasar, *Glory of the Lord*, v. 3, *Studies in Theological Style: Lay Styles*, trans. Andrew Louth et. al. (San Francisco: Ignatius, 1986), 353–399; Kearney, "Epiphanies of the Everyday: Toward a Micro-Eschatology," in John Panteleimon Manoussakis, *After God* (New York: Fordham University Press, 2006), 4; Long, "Personal Receptivity and Act: A Thomistic Critique" *The Thomist* 61 (1997): 1–31. See Stein, *Finite and Eternal Being*, 244, on the mystery of beings as their symbolism of the divine, linked to their interiority.

40. This latter could be seen as a liturgical or celebratory language, affirming the goodness and inexhaustible depths of every being; see Marion, Robyn Horner and Vincent Berraud, trans., *In Excess: Studies of Saturated Phenomena* (New York: Fordham University Press, 2002), 142–145; Pabst, *Metaphysics*, 39; Catherine Pickstock, *After Writing: On the Liturgical Consummation of Philosophy* (Oxford: Blackwell, 1998); Josef Pieper, "What is a Feast?," in *Josef Pieper: An Anthology* (San Francisco: Ignatius, 1989), 149–157; Simpson, *Religion*, 44, summarizing William Desmond's view.

41. Pickstock, *Repetition and Identity*, 92–98; Eleonore Stump, *Wandering In Darkness: Narrative and the Problem of Suffering* (Oxford: OUP, 2010), 58–61, 77–81; Alasdair MacIntyre, *After Virtue* (Notre Dame: UND Press, 2007); Richard Kearney, *The God Who May Be: A Hermeneutics of Religion* (Bloomington: Indiana University Press, 2001), 6–19; Kearney, "Epiphanies." Kearney follows Paul Ricoeur in part on the idea of personal identity as narrative, and Merleau-Ponty on every being having a unique incarnated style, similar to Hopkins's inscape.

42. Zizioulas, *Being as Communion*, 50–53. This claim incorporates the analytic notion of essentiality of origins into a Catholic metaphysics of the person.

43. There is a "humanist" or "conservative" strand in recent CT that provides evidence for this claim; see, e.g., the works of Russell Kirk and Marion Montgomery.

44. Seifert, *Essence and Existence*, 435–436, 450–455; Stein, *Finite and Eternal Being*, section III.

45. Some, like Seifert, *Essence and Existence*, 454, think that the Existential Thomist view is pantheistic, since everything is existence, and pure existence is God, but this seems to overlook the relation of efficient causality between God and creaturely existence on the

Existential Thomist view. But even Norris Clarke ("What Cannot be Said," 129–131) admits that the Existential Thomist account of essence as "thin," that is, as just an intrinsic limit within existence, renders it very difficult to know how to talk or think about such essence as a real limit, unlike on the traditional "thick" account of essence as really limiting the existence.

46. See, e.g., David Oderberg, *Real Essentialism* (London: Routledge, 2008); Stump, *Aquinas* (London: Routledge, 2005), for good accounts of analytic Thomist hylomorphism. Especially among those influenced by analytic and Laval Thomism, e.g., William Wallace, *The Modeling of Nature* (Washington, DC, DC: CUA Press, 1996), there is the recognition, rooted in a hylomorphic approach, that facts about material structures and events in the human body are crucial parts of the cause and explanation for human experiences; see, e.g., Eleonore Stump's account of motor neurons as part of the explanation for how we encounter other persons as persons, not just knowing facts about them (*Wandering in Darkness*, 67–73), or various explorations of quantum indeterminacy as part of the basis for free human action upon matter, though the human form or soul "selecting" among quantum states in event of quantum state reduction, e.g., Wolfgang Smith, *The Quantum Enigma* (Hillsdale, NY: Sophia Perennis, 2005). Milbank, *Beyond Secular Order: The Representation of Being and the Representation of the People* (Blackwell, 2014), 265 claims that realism about matter and its non-conceptualizability is required to avoid idealism.

47. cf. D.C. Schindler, *The Catholicity of Reason*, 70–71. Furthermore, as phenomenologist Richard Kearney notes, in encountering another person, I experience him or her not just as given, but as having unactualized potential that is currently unknowable by me: beings are not just what is currently being given in them, but include stable potentialities in themselves.

48. Aquinas, *ST*, I, q. 45, a. 3, ad 3. For these critiques, see Long, "Personal Receptivity and Act," "Divine and Creaturely Receptivity: The Search for a Middle Term." and "Reply," *The Thomist* Vol. 61 (1997): 373–376; *Natura Pura: On the Recovery of Nature in the Doctrine of Grace* (New York: Fordham University Press, 2010), 81–89. For similar critiques of Existential Thomism see George Blair, "On *Esse* and Relation," *Communio* 21 (1994): 162–164; Lawrence Dewan, "The Individual as a Mode of Being according to Thomas Aquinas," *The Thomist* 63 (1999): 403–424; "Etienne Gilson and the *Actus Essendi*," *Maritain Studies* 15 (1999): 70–96; Ralph McInerny, *Praeambula Fidei: Thomism and the God of the Philosophers* (Washington, DC: CUA Press, 2006), 126–158. Responses to some of these relevant to this paper can be found by Norris Clarke, "Response to Long's Comments," *Communio* 21 (1994): 162–164; David Liberto, "Person, Being, and Receptivity," in Paul van Geest et al., eds., *Aquinas as Authority* (Utrecht: Thomas Institut, 2000).

49. *DM* d. 20, s. 3, n. 14–16; d. 31, s. 6, n. 18.

50. A similar notion, *the relatio secundum dici*, often equated by Thomists with transcendental relations, is found in Aquinas, *ST* I q. 13, a. 7, ad 1. To predicate a *relatio secundum dici* of some subject is to signify that that subject that has an ordering to another. I make no claim here as to whether this and transcendental relations are equivalent notions.

51. John Duns Scotus, *Opera omnia*, bk. 11, *Quaestiones in secundum librum sententiarum* (Paris: Vives, 1893), d. 1, q. 4, n. 26. Scotus is explicitly opposed by some later Thomists, such as Thomas Cajetan, *In I ST*, q. 45, a.3 (Rome: Leonine ed., 1888), 467–468.

52. John of St. Thomas, *Cursus theologici in primam partem divi Thomae*, v. 2 (Lugundi: Petrus Prost, 1642), d. 18, q. 44, a. 2, n. 19–22. See *DV* q. 21, a. 1, ad1, where Aquinas says that essence of itself is absolute and non-relational, but as good, a being is intrinsically

participating in God. Good is really identical to being, and so this is a place where Aquinas seems to implicitly endorse that each created being is identical to a relation to God.

53. Przywara, *Analogia Entis*, 287–288, 463–379; Woznicki, *Being and Order: The Metaphysics of Thomas Aquinas in Historical Perspective* (New York: Peter Lang, 1990), 89–92, 105–106, 234–235; Woznicki, *Metaphysical Animal: Divine and Human in Man* (New York: Peter Lang, 1996), 65–68, 161–171; Krąpiec, *I-Man*, 239–251; Krąpiec, *Metaphysics*, 16–19, 379–388, 452–463. Similar views are expressed in Oliva Blanchette, *The Perfection of the Universe According to Aquinas* (College Station: Pennsylvania State University Press, 1992), and by Stephen Hipp, "Existential Relation as Principle of Individuation," *The Thomist* 78 (2008): 67–106, on whose view essences are transcendental relations to acts of existence, and thereby individuate beings. See also the phenomenologically inspired William Desmond, who articulates an analogical, or, in his words, "metaxological" or "in-between" account of Being on which we experience both immediacy and community with other beings, and the irreducible otherness of other beings, such that any attempt to articulate knowledge about these beings requires that knowledge to be mediated both by oneself and by the others; see Simpson, ed., *The William Desmond Reader* (Albany: SUNY Press, 2012), 33–46. cf. Pickstock, *Repetition and Identity*, 12–13, 48–63.

54. *ST* I, q. 45, a. 4; q. 90, a. 2; I-II, q. 110, a. 2; III, q. 2, a. 2; *In III Sent.*, d. 6, q. 2, a. 2. Cf. Wippel, *Metaphysical Thought*, 241, 255–265.

55. cf. Spencer, "Personhood"; Wippel, *Metaphysical Thought*, 252 A similar view is that of Jacques Maritain, *Degrees of Knowledge*, 455–457; *The Person and the Common Good*, trans. John Fitzgerald (Notre Dame: UND Press, 1966), 41, on whose view, personhood or subsistence is a mode of completion in an essence by which a substance has its own proper act of existence, and so is capable of acting and giving itself on its own. A mode is a property that cannot exist, even by divine power, apart from its subject.

56. On the creation/co-creation distinction see *ST* I q. 45, a. 4. Some in CT draw a distinction between the transcendental or ontological beauty of a being, and its accidental or aesthetic beauty, but both are equally contained in the personal or concrete being and its beauty, which is what we first encounter in a being.

57. The person self-manifests as a *Gestalt*, a single observable form, in himself, and together with his situation. cf. Balthasar, *Seeing the Form*, 17–33; Bychkov, *Aesthetic Revelation*, 94–97.

58. Only by encountering things in their full actuality, irreducible to all conceptual knowledge, can we encounter the genuine reality and newness of things: cf. John Milbank, "Only Theology Saves Metaphysics," in Peter Candler and Conor Cunningham, *Belief and Metaphysics* (London: SCM Press, 2007), 495–496, following G. K. Chesterton. Aquinas grants that we cannot fully know beings, even their essence, in his *Commentary on the Apostles' Creed*.

59. cf. Marion, *Givenness and Hermeneutics*, 41–63; Milbank, "Only Theology Saves Metaphysics," 473–474; Jaroszyński, *Metaphysics and Art*, trans. Hugh McDonald (New York: Peter Lang, 2002), 150. Realist metaphysics requires developing practices rooted in genuine love for and wonder at these others, so that these interpretations will be guided by the things themselves. The notion of practice, developed by MacIntyre, has taken on an important role in virtue ethics and philosophical anthropology in much recent CT. The idea of metaphysics as a practice that we engage in is developed, with attention to the links between traditional metaphysics and aesthetic genres like narrative, by Thomas Hibbs,

Aquinas, Ethics, and Philosophy of Religion: Metaphysics and Practice (Bloomington: Indiana University Press, 2007), which builds on many strands in recent CT, including the scholastic and phenomenological. The way in which each being is oriented to infinite interpretations allows an integration of the most radical hermeneutics into a realist, scholastically-based metaphysics.

60. I am grateful to all those who attended the session at the ACPA meeting at which this paper was presented, and especially to George Heffernan, who commented on the paper, and to John Cahalan, Turner Nevitt, Fr. Philip Neri Reese, OP, and Thomas Ward. I am also grateful to John Crosby, Billy Junker, and Mathew Lu, for reading and commenting on an earlier draft of this paper.

How Must We Be for the Resurrection to Be Good News?

Chad Engelland

Abstract: While the promise of the resurrection appears wonderful, it is also perplexing: How can the person raised be one and the same person as the one that dies? And if the raised person is not the same, why should any of us mortals regard the promise of the resurrection as good news? In this paper, I articulate the part-whole structure of human nature that supports belief in the sameness of the resurrected person's identity and the desirability of the resurrection: (1) the immaterial core of the person must survive the destruction of the body; (2) the person must nonetheless be incomplete apart from the body; and (3) the personal core must be the source for the personal identity of the resurrected body. In light of these criteria, I conclude by arguing that survivalism rather than corruptionism is the more compelling account of death and resurrection present in the thought of St. Thomas Aquinas.

Blaise Pascal memorably maintained that the fear of death motivates the diversions of mankind: "Being unable to cure death, wretchedness and ignorance, men have decided, in order to be happy, not to think about such things."[1] The possibility that we should cease to exist or, continuing to exist, should cease to have our bodily way of being, is naturally a terrifying possibility. St. Augustine thinks we have an "obvious natural revulsion to annihilation,"[2] St. Thomas Aquinas thinks that "everything that has an intellect naturally desires always to exist,"[3] St. John Paul II thinks that in us "there is an irrepressible longing to live forever,"[4] and Socrates says "I have good hope that some future awaits men after death."[5] Now, Christianity claims to have some good news on this score. We are not only promised immortality as hoped for by a philosopher such as Socrates; we are promised the resurrection of our flesh, a possibility unanticipated by any philosopher—not even by Heraclitus, who counsels us to expect "the unexpected."[6] Surely, if this is a credible promise, it is good news. We need only recall its original proclamation to philosophers. St. Paul came to Athens and engaged with Epicurean and Stoic philosophers, who, like all Athenians, always wanted to hear something new. St. Luke records their reaction to the resurrection as follows: "Now when they heard of the resurrection of the dead, some mocked; but others said, 'We will hear

©2016, *Proceedings of the ACPA*, Vol. 89
doi: 10.5840/acpaproc201610547

you again about this.'"[7] The promise that Jesus will make all things new is so unexpected that even those who only want to hear novelties wanted to hear of it again.

Beyond the question of credibility, which is an issue for faith and theology, I want to isolate a specifically philosophical concern. While the resurrected person may appear to others and to himself to be the same person as I am now, it is not immediately clear that it really could be me. Why wouldn't the resurrected person be merely a clone that thinks he is the same as me? I want to ask philosophically, to the extent that it is a philosophical question, whether hope in *my* resurrection makes sense. Is the prospect of the dead's resurrection good news or only apparently good news? I think it is good news provided we understand the human person in a very particular kind of way, and I want to spell out the basic features of that way here.

I offer the following as conditional: what part-whole structure of human nature is necessary *if* the resurrection of the dead is to be meaningful to each of us? My thesis is that the resurrection requires an intellective hylomorphism: a dependent part (the body) that ceases to be at death and is restored later, and an independent part (the soul) that persists through death, establishes my selfhood, and causes the body to be, thereby making the restored body one and the same body. According to hylomorphism, soul and body constitute a single substance; according to intellective hylomorphism, the human soul not only animates the body, it can also exist in an incomplete fashion apart from the body. Death does not corrupt the soul, which is the personal core. This paper weighs in on the contemporary debate between corruptionists and survivalists among Thomistically inspired hylomorphic accounts of mind. The corruptionists think that the dead person is no longer a person; the survivalists think that the dead person remains the same person. In this paper, I side with survivalism against corruptionism; on my view, for the resurrection to be good news for each of us now living, survivalism must obtain.

I.

Why No Proxy Will Do. The resurrection of the dead appears as good news contrasted with the two apparent alternatives: existing in a disembodied manner in some mythical land of the dead or the immediate annihilation of self with the possibility of existing through some kind of proxy. The possibility of disembodied personal existence is manifestly dissatisfying, especially when we consider our loved ones, whom we love as embodied; that they will rise again, body and all, is very good news indeed. Compared to the possibility of existing through some kind of proxy, the resurrection is extremely good news, for, in the last analysis, existence through proxy is not personally satisfying. I cannot say of the proxy, "I, *Chad Engelland*, will still be *Chad Engelland* in virtue of that item." Consider the various candidates for proxy: reincarnation, progeny, fame, works, or in the latest hope, a computer program.[8] For *reincarnation*, how am I the same as the person from a former or future life? Not in terms of the body, not in terms of memories and experience, but just in terms of the bare soul-substance; yet this continuity is akin to the anonymous self-identity of a rock; it is not a living or personal identity; I now cannot say, I,

Chad Engelland, will be the same person then as now. Saul Kripke seems right to say that the identities of one's parents are essential for personal identity: "How could a person originating from different parents, from a totally different sperm and egg, be *this very woman?* . . . It seems to me that anything coming from a different origin would not be this object."[9] Reincarnation maintains that the parents are incidental; this means that reincarnation does not grant the sort of personal immortality that we naturally long for. For *living through descendants*, I continue only as a fainter and fainter echo: a biological inheritance that didn't entirely belong to me, a generous link in a chain of generations, and a living memory forgotten after several generations; as for living through one's works, deeds, or a computer simulation, I do not live, but a limited appearance of me might; still this is not the same as me. I am no longer there to experience and be experienced "in person." Having a photograph of a loved one is no real substitute for having that loved one himself or herself. If what we really want is to continue to be as the person each of us is now and for loved ones to exist as they are now, the proxy provides little consolation. Consider the desire that motivated the Ted Williams family to resort to cryogenics: "This is what we want, to be able to be together in the future, even if it is only a chance."[10] We want to be together in the future, and that means that each of us must really be. The proxy falls prey to vanity, for it is not what we really want. Rather it is a pale and ultimately unsatisfying substitute for personal immortality. As Woody Allen puts it, "I don't want to achieve immortality through my work, I want to achieve immortality through not dying."[11]

Opposed to the impersonal immortality of the proxy, resurrection promises personal immortality: "I, *Chad Engelland*, will continue to be as *Chad Engelland* thanks to the resurrection of the dead." It is apparently great news. And yet the resurrection of the dead is puzzling. Can it really distinguish itself from impersonal immortality? Resurrection holds that at some unspecified future point, the dead will come back to life. How can this resurrected person be the same person as each of us is now? Might it not be another person? In such a case, the resurrected person would in effect be a proxy for the person that died.

What does human personal identity require? We are not angels. The story of our genesis is essential to our identities. To be the same person, I must be the son of the same parents who came together at a particular time.[12] But this is not enough, for the same could be said of an identical twin. Personal identity also requires the same agency of experience. As a newborn, I looked up into my parents' eyes and smiled. They saw my affectivity, the fact that experience happens *for me*, and I saw in their eyes their affectivity, the fact that experience happens *for each of them*.[13] To be the same person means that we remain the same dative and agent of experience. Metaphysically, this requires that the same subject persist, for the agency of experience is an expression of this being. Each of us takes in the world from our own vantage points thanks to the fact that each is a separate being. There are at least three interrelated factors for personal identity: the resurrected person must [a] have the same genesis, [b] have lived the same life, and [c] be the same subject as the person before he or she died.

Why think that sameness requires continuity of existence? Why cannot the sameness be realized on the side of the creator? Surely if God can create a being at one time, he can recreate the same one being at another time, outfitted with the same genealogy, the same experiences, and the same subject. Let me spell out why I do not think this is the case. First, the recreated person would have a different story of its origins; rather than coming to be through the secondary causality of particular parents at a particular time, the recreated person would come to be independent of secondary causes at another time. Second, while the recreated person would likely be outfitted with the same memories as the original person, those memories would not be the fruit of experience; they would be memories of a life lived by another being. Third, the recreated person would not be the same subject, for a subject is not just something with a certain intelligibility; it is something with a particular act of being. The particular act of being does not merely actualize a certain divine idea; the particular act of being constitutes the root and ground of personal identity, which makes real my particular essence and activities. I am my act of being. While the "idea" may be the same in the recreated being, the act of being could not be; therefore the being would not in fact be the same.

In view of the above, we can say that the sameness of the resurrected must be realized *in* the creature; it cannot be realized simply on the side of the creator. W. Norris Clarke, SJ, puts it this way:

> The recreated entity might be a clone, *like* me in many ways, but not the *same* unique personal *me*, because the new unity, the self—the "I"— organizing the similar body is not the same as me, for the simple reason that it never experienced the same personal life, the same *story* with all its challenges, successes and failures, that became an inseparable part of my identity before my death. That self is simply gone, and not even the omnipotence of God can do what is a metaphysical impossibility: recreate the identical being that existed before, with no bond of continuity on the personal level between the before and the after.[14]

I want to think how we must be in order for the resurrection to be in fact good news, not just apparently good news. What are the necessary principles of human nature?

II.

The Criteria for Resurrected Identity. Let us take death to be the end of bodily being and resurrection to be the beginning again of bodily being. I regard this understanding of death to be a basic fact, confirmed both by ordinary experience and by philosophical and scientific investigation. The living body not only undergoes metabolic activity, it not only evidently perceives, feels, and moves, but it also serves to express the specifically human life of the mind. The corpse, by contrast, undergoes no such vital, perceptual, or personal activities. Moreover, the unity it heretofore enjoyed appears to be irremediably compromised. It is therefore not the same thing. What is it? A naturally occurring likeness of the person's body that once was. The frightful absence that marks the corpse marks a radical change of being. My sense of the resurrection comes from Christian witness: the resurrection of Christ as firstborn from the dead and the bold proclamation that the restoration of our bodily selves, spiritualized, is a possibility that will be actualized for all.[15] It is a basic feature of orthodox Christian teaching.

In order for the hope in the resurrection not to be empty, I think the following three criteria must hold:

[1] *The Principle of Personal Persistence*: When Patches the rabbit is run over by a bus, it perishes. The act of violence compromises the unity of the whole with a total loss of being; what remains, the carcass, *was* but no longer *is* a rabbit. Patches as a whole and in all its parts has ceased to be. Could God resurrect Patches? God could create a being just like Patches down to the last detail but, without some principle of continuity in being, it would not be Patches but a clone of Patches. From the point of view of the pet owner, that might not be a big deal; Patches's own point of view is not relevant, for Patches is not a person, not a spiritual being with a desire for immortality. But for humans, our own point of view is not irrelevant regarding our own death and resurrection and the death and resurrection of our loved ones. It is not enough for clones of us to be restored. It must really be us for this possibility to be personally satisfying. What enables the resurrected self to be the same self? There must be a principle safeguarding personal continuity; unlike the case of Patches the rabbit, death must not be the end of the entire substance. Of course, it is a basic fact that death, whether for Patches or for me, must involve the destruction of the body. But though I am my body I am not only my body. If I lose my leg, I am still human even though I am not a complete human being. Similarly, if I lose all my limbs I am still human even though I am not a complete human being. Finally, if I lose my whole body in death, I am still human even though I am not a complete human being. Privation can extend not just to the body part but to the whole part of us that is the body. Now, this privation of a whole metaphysical part is an extreme form of privation. My personal core must survive this extreme privation so that Chad Engelland alive and Chad Engelland resurrected would be the same person. The principle of personal persistence identifies that, as a condition for maintaining the identity of a person there must be something more than the bodily being that manifestly ceases to be with the event of death. And this persisting principle must be personal. For example, it would not do for just the teeth of the person to persist; it must be that which somehow instantiates the person.

Can't our bodies constitute personal identity? Can't we say, with Peter van Inwagen and other materialists, that God could, despite the appearances, somehow preserve the bodily organism, that, in effect, we will only appear to die?[16] Such conjuring is metaphysically possible, but it questions one of the basic facts of the case, which is that we know people die and their bodies decompose.[17] It also serves to deny that there is such a thing as the resurrection. Rather, the resurrection on this view is not something that will happen in the future; it is rather a code name for something that God already always does: makes it appear that people die while carting their living bodies off to somewhere else. It's van Inwagen's materialism that leads him to question the basic fact of death and to reinterpret the resurrection. Instead, I want to think of a way to make sense of the possibility of the resurrection that preserves the reality of the appearances and leaves the resurrection as a hoped-for futural event. Like Augustine and Aquinas, I do not find materialism compelling, and I can therefore accept the fact of death as something that is not illusory.[18] Van Inwagen is right to insist on a principle of continuity, but the body, evidently demising, is not the most promising candidate in our metaphysical makeup for this feat.

If the body does not account for personal persistence, what part can? The soul must not be bodily; it must be able to persist apart from the decomposing body, and it must constitute the root of personal identity.[19] As Augustine puts it, we love the deceased Apostle, because "we believe that what we love in him lives even now, for we love his just rational soul [*animus*]."[20] If the body ceases to be and yet the person continues to exist, there must be some non-bodily dimension of the person that survives. Now, we might resist the thought that the person, a body-soul composite, could somehow be the same person even while missing an essential part, the body. But, granting that the soul can exist apart from the body, we can see that it can in fact exist as the same human person provided that it contains virtually the powers of the non-existent body. Consider some relatively uncontroversial analogues. When we are sleeping, we are generally not exercising our higher order linguistic capacities, but we retain those powers in potentiality. Even though speaking is essential to us as human beings, it does not have to be continually exercised for us to be the human beings that we are. When we were babies, we did not even have the developed capacity to speak. We could still be human, without this essential attribute's development, because our nature remained as it were primed for this development. In fact, in order for our natural ability to speak to develop, we had to be exposed to the speech of others; feral children, for example, develop neither semantics nor syntax; consequently, natural powers can rest on extrinsic factors for their realization.[21] Infants and feral children, despite this lack, are nonetheless essentially human. Similarly, the soul of the dead person, bereft of the body, retains the *human* capacity to animate a body; though it lacks an essential part, it retains its essential ordering to that part. The separated soul remains primed for an actuality it cannot realize on its own.

[2] *The Personal Relevance of the Absent Body*: Unlike the case of Patches the rabbit, the human soul must be able to survive the event of death in order for the resurrected person to be the same as he or she is now. That means that in the case of humans, death must not be a substantial change; the body ceases to be, while the person does not. But for the resurrection to be good news, our bodies, as inessential as they are for our bare existence must nonetheless be essential for the living out of our human lives. The demise of the body must remain something other than a mere accidental change. Otherwise there would be no serious reason for each of us to hope in the resurrection. Set free from the tomb of the body we could look upon the prospect of a resurrection with disinterest. If the resurrection of the dead is good news, substance dualism, whether of the sort advocated by Plato or by Descartes, must not obtain. For the resurrection to be anticipated, the body must be part of

what we are. Augustine expresses this twofold whatness with admirable precision: "Man is a rational substance consisting of soul and body."[22] While our personal core, *who* we are, might persist through the death of the body, we nonetheless would remain less than *what* we are—unless the resurrection of the dead should occur.

Our bodies are also essential to *how* we are. To be a human is to be a being that can experience, act, and show things to each other.[23] What would life without our bodies be like? Because we lack experience of it, we cannot say with confidence what will be natural to us then, but we can be confident that for human nature as we experience it now, our bodies are essential. Without our bodies as the instruments of experience we would presumably have total emptiness of experience. We could not speak or be spoken to, we could not see or be seen, and we could not give or receive. Nor, does it seem, could we relive our memories, lost as they would be with the death of the body and the loss of our brains. It seems possible that we might achieve self-awareness and other peculiarly intellective acts; but such acts would not constitute a full human life. Now, I have no doubt that God will grant all sorts of cognitive achievements to this disembodied soul, but considering its natural powers alone, the life of a disembodied soul would seem to be a dreamless sleep accompanied by dim self-awareness. The natural life of the disembodied human soul would appear to be a life longing for wakefulness, longing for the restoration of the flesh.

[3] *What Persists Must Make the Body Be.* If the resurrection is to be good news, the resurrected body must really be my body. The provincial council of Toledo formulated this requirement with admirable clarity: "And we do not believe that we shall rise in an ethereal body or in any other body, as some foolishly imagine, but in *this very body in which we live and are and move.*"[24] According to the basic fact of death, the body has ceased to be. How then can my body that exists now, cease to exist when I die, and yet be restored as the selfsame body in the resurrection? I think it can be the same body provided that it has the same being. But it can only have the same being if that being has been held in reserve, as it were, by the persisting soul. The soul that survives must be the animating form of the flesh; it must make the body be the body it is. This means that the soul can cause to be only its own body and none other.

The resurrected body would be the selfsame body in virtue of being animated by our soul. What about our bodily remains? Mustn't they be incorporated into the resurrected body for it to be the selfsame body? Remember that death is destruction of the body. The promised miracle is that our bodies will be restored not that we never will have died or will have only seemed to die. And evidently death involves the demise of the body as a whole. Even a corpse artificially kept from decaying, such as Lenin's in Red Square, no longer is the body that it once was. Rather, it is a vestige that harbors no possibility of life within it; its matter has returned to subpersonal being. And many of the dead will be in the position of Father Thomas Byles, the priest who heard confessions on the sinking *Titanic* and whose remains have been dissolved into the sea. If the hope of resurrection for them is not to be in vain, the corpse must not be necessary for establishing the identity of the body.

Am I really saying that God could have resurrected Lazarus while leaving his corpse in the tomb? Yes, I am: Lazarus in this scenario would have his selfsame body in virtue of having his selfsame soul animating a body; the remains in the tomb are inessential. Still, it would not be fitting for God to have resurrected Lazarus while his corpse is on hand.[25] He would seem like a ghost, because his corpse is a sign of his being dead. Resurrection, to present faithfully the restoration of bodily life to the one that died, should involve taking up and cancelling the sign of death. And of course, thinking of Lazarus is misleading; the hoped-for resurrection of the dead will not restore us to mortal life as with Lazarus; it will bring us to immortal life. The body raised will not be the body in the same condition as the one that died, but one in its prime and, according to Augustine, one that will be better looking than the one each of us has now.[26] Thus, I grant that it may be fitting for bodily remains to be reincorporated somehow (I know not how) into the resurrected body, but it is not necessary. One will have the selfsame body thanks to one's selfsame soul that animates the body. Nor should this conclusion seem strange. Even in this life, after all, it is the form, rather than the ever-changing matter, that makes my body be the same through time.[27] I have the same body I did ten years ago even though on the physical level I am constituted of different molecules. Even more so, soul-form, rather than material parts, establishes the identity of the body before death and after the resurrection. Any animated body would be the same body if it is animated by the same form.

What about our brains? It is worth noting, of course, that talk of "the brain" is an abstraction, for it is but part of the nervous system which is itself but part of the body as a whole; perception is an activity that puts into play the entire person.[28] Still, as far as bodily organs go, the brain seems to be a kind of privileged part, which therefore occasions some puzzles of its own. Can we really say that we will be the same person even though our original brains will have returned to nothingness? I think the resurrected brain will be outfitted with the same memories; it will not be a replica, however, but the same brain thanks to the identity of the immaterial animating soul. It will belong to the same one person. What, however, of our memories? These are in some sense stored neurologically whenever we undergo experiences. Certainly, these new brains have to have the same memories as the old ones. But how can they be the same memories when the old ones were formed as the fruit of experience and the new ones are, as it were, uploaded? The point, however, is not the causal origin of the memories as physically stored; the point is whether or not the numerically same person was the subject of those experiences. Consider a different situation. Say I forget where I bought a pair of shoes; on the level of my neurons, the memory of the location of that shoe-buying no longer exists. However, my wife reminds me; the fact that the memory was stored outside of me and comes to be stored in my brain through instruction rather than experience does not compromise the reality that I myself bought the shoes at that store. However, it would compromise the reality if in fact they had been bought by someone else and my wife was misremembering or misinforming. It is the identity of the person that establishes the identity of the brain as an organ of the body and its memories as stored personal experiences.[29]

III.

Kinds of Parts. Peter Geach recognizes the importance of bodily sameness without, however, adequately accounting for its possibility. He maintains that apart from the body the soul is no longer the self but "a mere remnant." Therefore, only granting the resurrection can we hope for personal immortality; the mere continued existence of this remnant would not be personal: "The existence of a disembodied soul would not be a survival of the person Peter Geach; and even in such a truncated form individual existence seems to require at least a persistent possibility of the soul's again entering into the make-up of a man who is identifiably Peter Geach."[30] He affirms against dualism the contribution of the body to personal identity; he also recognizes the role of the soul's persistence in establishing continuity between the self that is alive now and the self that was alive then. The problem comes in the way he construes the soul as but "a mere remnant." It cannot mean the body makes the person again be the person it was before, for it is the soul that establishes the continuity of substance and the personal identity of the body.

Now, remnant is an ambiguous term. It means "that which remains." But what makes it ambiguous is whether what remains still is or no longer is what was there before; and if it is, what kind of part it is, simply a piece or that which instantiates the whole. So, we can point to the dead rabbit and say, these are the remains of Patches. That *was* Patches although, as a matter of fact, it no longer is Patches. In a different scenario, we might point to a single slice of pie and identify it as the remains of the whole pie that once was. Unlike Patches's remains, the pie slice still is a slice of pie; the point is simply that the whole is no more and therefore this part is a remnant. If we bake a new pie around the remnant, we won't say it's the same pie as before. Neither of these senses of remnant fulfills the requirements for the sameness of the resurrected person. In accordance with the first criterion, we can posit the possibility of a persisting part that instantiates the whole. This is the case with the hydra, a half-inch aquatic creature, which lives for years and years by monthly regrowing its body from stem cells. Rob Steele, a hydrobiologist, described its feat as follows: "It doesn't have any cells that hang around long enough to get old and decrepit, and therefore the individual doesn't get old and decrepit."[31] Similarly, the world's oldest tree is 9,950 years old despite the fact that its trunk and branches have died every 600 years or so. Leif Kullman, an ecologist who discovered this conifer, says that "as soon as a stem dies, a new one emerges from the same root stock. So the tree has a very long life expectancy."[32] In this sense of remnant, the persisting stem cells or root stock instantiate the identity of the organism across the continual regeneration of the rest of its body.

Remnant, then, can mean (1) what's left as a result of the body's ceasing to be, which I call "residue," (2) some part of a whole that survives that demise intact, which I call "a persistent part," or (3) some part that survives that demise intact and that instantiates the identity of the whole, which I call "the persistent core."[33] What does Geach have in mind by referring to the soul as "a mere remnant"? He seems to regard both the soul and the dead body as persisting parts, albeit in different ways. He says that the disembodied soul cannot say of itself, "I am Socrates," just as the single slice of pie could not say (if it were to say) "I am the pie." Also, he thinks the corpse somehow contributes to the personal identity of the resurrected person. I think he is mistaken on both counts. First, the body is not a persisting part but a residue, and it can therefore no longer contribute to personal identity. Consider the difference between the corpse of Socrates and the body of Socrates before he died. While a disembodied soul is not a complete person, a corpse is not a person at all. The corpse is a naturally occurring likeness produced by the body's loss of being. It is closer in being to a portrait than to a person. It can no longer make a significant contribution to the personal identity of Socrates. Second, the soul is not simply a persisting part, for that is not enough to establish the sameness of the self then and now; the soul must rather be the persisting core that makes the body be; the sameness of the soul as animating principle and not the "using up" of the corpse is what makes the person the same. What is lacking in Geach's account is the specification that, while the disembodied soul is not the whole person, it is nonetheless the root and ground of the person and only therefore is the resurrected person's body the same body as before. The soul is not just a persistent part; it is the personal core.

IV.

Thomistic Hylomorphism and Survivalism. According to the first criterion, the principle of personal persistence, versions of materialism fail to maintain personal identity; for these accounts hope in the resurrection is vain. Versions of dualism fail regarding the second and third criteria concerning the importance of the body and the role of the soul-form in establishing the sameness of the resurrected body; for these accounts hope in the resurrection is vain. However, hylomorphism in the version set out by Thomas Aquinas seems to fulfill the criteria laid out above provided it is construed along survivalist rather than corruptionist lines. According to corruptionism, death is a substantial change and therefore the separated soul is neither a human being nor a person until it is reunited with its bodily residue. According to survivalism, the persistence of the soul is enough to account for the persistence of the human person, and the soul, rather than some bodily residue, will make the restored body be the same body. Thomas deploys both accounts throughout his career, but survivalism is the superior one.[34] Corruptionism undercuts hope in the resurrection, for unlike survivalism it cannot account for the sameness of the self now and then. Also, it in effect denies the full reality of death as the complete loss of my bodily being and instead holds that my body somehow persists through the continuous substantial changes it undergoes: my body somehow remains my body through death and decomposition, etc. so that in the future some bit of my body can be rescued and returned to me at the resurrection.[35] Survivalism, by contrast, faces the fact that the body is no longer the same, for it has lost its being.[36]

Let me retrace the outlines of Thomas's survivalism here. He says the souls of men "remain" (*remanent*) apart from their bodies even though, as the form of the body, it is contrary to the nature of the soul to be apart from the body.[37] In arguing that we can be perfectly happy in the beatific vision without our bodies, he makes clear that the human soul, being an intellective soul, is an odd kind of part: "The relation of the [human] soul to being is not the same as that of other parts."[38] Why not? In other animals, the part-whole structure is such that the being of the part depends on the being of the whole, so that if the whole ceases to be, the parts either cease to be or change in being: "for the being of the whole is not that of any individual part: wherefore, either the part ceases altogether to be, when the whole is destroyed, just as the parts of an animal, when the animal is destroyed; or, if they remain, they have another actual being, just as a part of a line has another being from that of the whole line." In the unique case of the animal endowed with an intellect, the soul can survive the destruction of the whole in such a way that it remains the same and retains the being of the whole:

> But the human soul retains the being of the composite after the destruction of the body: and this because the being of the form is the same as that of its matter, and this is the being of the composite. Now the soul subsists in its own being, as stated in the I, 75, 2. It follows, therefore, that after being separated from the body it has perfect being and that consequently it can have a perfect operation; although it has not the perfect specific nature.

Thomas calls this unique kind of subsistent part that retains the being of the whole, the "principal part." Commenting on the death of Christ in the *Summa Theologiae*, Thomas says that even though the subject ceases to be a complete man, it does not cease to be the same subject. Why not?

> Man is said to be his own intellect, not because the intellect is the entire man, but *because the intellect is the principal part of man, in which man's whole disposition lies virtually* [*quia intellectus est principalior pars hominis, in quo virtualiter existit tota dispositio hominis*]; just as the ruler of the city may be called the whole city, since its entire disposal is vested in him.[39]

Consequently, the being of the resurrected body can be the same as the being of the body now, because it will be animated by the same principal part. Despite this agreement with the three criteria, Thomas says some things that might appear puzzling and challenging for the view I have laid out:

"*My soul is not I.*"[40] Does this assertion undermine the criterion of personal continuity? This is in effect Geach's suggestion, and this is the view advocated by contemporary corruptionists. However, Thomas thinks the soul is not I in the sense that my soul is not the entirety of what I am as a human being. Nonetheless, my soul is what makes my body be and be mine; the soul is the root and ground of my bodily being. Therefore, the disembodied soul can indeed say "I *am* (the principal part of) Thomas Aquinas" or more simply "I am the dead Thomas Aquinas."[41] It is just not in a position to say "I am Thomas Aquinas whole and entire." It won't be able to say that until after the resurrection. The separated soul is identical in subject to Thomas Aquinas but not identical in totality to all that Thomas once was and will again be.[42]

"If the resurrection of the body is denied, it is not easy, yea it is difficult, to sustain the immortality of the soul."[43] Thomas thinks that apart from the resurrection, the immortality of the soul is hard to affirm; I, on the other hand, maintain that apart from the immortality of the soul, the resurrection of the dead is hard to maintain. Thomas's point, I take it, is in fact mine: the resurrection of the body and the immortality of the soul are conceptually interdependent. The problem is that while the latter, as a natural possibility, admits of a philosophical defense, the former, as a natural impossibility, does not.

"But which old woman nowadays would not know that the soul is immortal? Faith is capable of much more than philosophy is."[44] When it comes to the soul, Christian revelation bestows more light than the greatest of philosophical speculations. Thomas thinks the immortality of the soul is difficult to maintain according to natural principles alone. But a philosophy inspired by revelation, what John Paul II calls "Christian philosophy," might nonetheless dare to defend philosophically the natural possibility of human immortality. Doing so without reference to theology might leave it in an embarrassing situation: the naked soul, without the body, appears an awkward thing. Thomas's anthropology, seen in this light, is a kind of philosophical anthropology worked out in reference to the resurrection. In this way, it fulfills the exact meaning of "Christian philosophy" articulated by John Paul II. It is "a philosophical speculation conceived in dynamic union with faith" and "includes those important developments of philosophical thinking which would not have happened without the direct or indirect contribution of Christian faith."[45] Intellective hylomorphism, which maintains both the immortality of the soul and the need for the body, is just such a philosophical development.[46]

V.

Conclusion. For the resurrection to be good news, a very particular and peculiar understanding of human nature is required. What must we be if we can die and resurrect as the selfsame person? We must be hybrid beings, neither pure animals nor pure spirits. Like animals, we can really die, but unlike animals this does not involve a complete loss of substance, for our spiritual cores persist. Unlike pure spirits, our separated souls are essentially incomplete, for our bodies are not incidental to what and how we are. Our restored bodies can be our bodies in virtue of being formed by our persisting part, our personal core, which is our intellective soul. What is death if it is neither a substantial change (as with pure animals) nor merely an accidental change (as with pure spirits)? Death, for us humans, is a radical change that cuts deeper than an accident but not as deep as the substance. I suggest we call it a "change in property," so that the loss of bodily being modifies something essentially human without compromising the identity of the person. Just as the ability to speak is essential to us humans though we need not have it to exist as the same person we are, so our bodies are essential to us humans though we need not have them to exist as the same person each of us is. But just as the loss of language is a great personal loss that cuts us off from a whole domain of properly human activities, so it is with the loss of our bodies. Consider Helen Keller's account of learning to speak: "I was born again that day. I had been a little ghost in a *no-world*. Now I knew my name. I was a person. I could understand people and make them understand me."[47] Though she remained the selfsame personal substance in learning to speak through the initiative of her teacher, she nonetheless realized something essential to being human and to living a full human life. Similarly, though we can remain the selfsame person through death, the resurrection will restore something essential to being human and to living a full human life: our animate bodies.

Resurrection is a possibility that belongs to the agency of God the creator; I want to open up the logical space in human nature for God's effect. Unless I am mistaken, human nature must have the part-whole structure I have iterated for the hope in the resurrection not to be in vain, whatever God's power might be. To hope in the resurrection entails believing both that the body is part of me and that the root and ground of my selfhood subsists in the part of me that is not bodily. It requires survivalism rather than corruptionism. Hence, on the last day, when I, God willing, rise again, I will have the same body and fully be the same person thanks to that part of me that persists through death. Can philosophy go further than presenting the above view of human nature conditionally? Can it argue for the immortality of the soul and the soul as form of the body? I believe so, but these are extremely difficult topics for another day, another venue, and maybe even another philosopher.[48] My aim here has been more modest: simply to clarify what's implicit in our hope.[49]

University of Dallas

Notes

1. *Pensées*, trans. A. J. Krailsheimer (New York: Penguin Books, 1995), 37.

2. *City of God*, trans. Henry Bettenson (New York: Penguin Books, 1972), 11.27. To support this claim, he says that if people were given the choice of immediately ceasing to be or living a longer life of misery, they would choose the latter.

3. *Summa Theologiae*, trans. Fathers of the English Dominican Province (New York: Benzinger Brothers, 1948), I, q. 75, a. 6. The senses are rooted in the here and now but the intellect apprehends things without temporal limitation.

4. Pope St. John Paul II, Apostolic Letter *Tertio Millennio Adveniente*, November 10, 1994, no. 9.

5. Plato, *Phaedo*, in *Plato: Complete Works*, ed. John Cooper (Indianapolis, IN: Hackett, 1997), 63c.

6. *The Art and Thought of Heraclitus*, trans. Charles Kahn (Cambridge: Cambridge University Press, 1979), 31. For Heraclitus's provocative musings on the reversibility of death, akin to the alterations of the seasons or the interplay of waking and sleeping, see Kahn, 210–227.

7. Acts 17:32 (RSV).

8. Stephen Hawking, for example, said, "I think the brain is like a programme in the mind, which is like a computer, so it's theoretically possible to copy the brain on to a computer and so provide a form of life after death." *Dailymail.com*, 21 September 2013, accessed February 27, 2015.

9. *Naming and Necessity* (Malden, MA: Blackwell Publishing, 1981), 113.

10. Richard Sandomir, "Note Dated 2000 Says Williams Wanted His Remains Frozen," *New York Times*, July 16, 2002.

11. Quoted by Sam B. Girgus, "Afterword: The Abyss: Woody Allen on Love, Death, and God," in *A Companion to Woody Allen*, ed. Peter J. Baily and Sam B. Girgus (Malden, MA: Wiley-Blackwell, 2013), 559–572 at 570.

12. See Chad Engelland, "On the Personal Significance of Sexual Reproduction," *The Thomist* 79 (2015): 615–639.

13. See Chad Engelland, "Unmasking the Person," *International Philosophical Quarterly* 50 (2010): 447–460.

14. *The Creative Retrieval of St. Thomas Aquinas: Essays in Thomistic Philosophy, New and Old* (New York: Fordham University Press, 2009), 188.

15. See, for example, *The Catechism of the Catholic Church*, no. 997: "In death, the separation of the soul from the body, the human body decays and the soul goes to meet God, while awaiting its reunion with its glorified body. God, in his almighty power, will definitively grant incorruptible life to our bodies by reuniting [*coniungens*] them with our souls, through the power of Jesus' Resurrection." For a theological overview of the issue, see Joseph Ratzinger, *Eschatology: Death and Eternal Life*, trans. Michael Waldstein and Aidan Nichols, OP (Washington, DC: The Catholic University of America Press, 1988), 69–214. He writes, "How can there be an identity between the human being who existed at some point in the past and the counterpart that has to be re-created from nothing? The irritated refusal of such questions as 'philosophical' does not contribute to a more meaningful discussion" (p. 106).

16. "The Possibility of Resurrection," *International Journal for Philosophy of Religion* 9 (1978): 114–121.

17. Van Inwagen distinguishes between "suspension of life," in which the organism enters into a reversible metabolic rest, such as a frozen cat, which could in principle be resuscitated, and "disruption of life," in which the organism ceases to exist. At the human death, the person's life is suspended but there remains a possibility for reanimation. But to maintain that the dead has only died in the first sense and not in the second he has to resort to metaphysical conjuring, and say that what we see evidently decomposing is not really the remains of the body, for the body has been whisked away and been replaced with this imitation. See *Material Beings* (Ithaca, NY: Cornell University Press, 1990), 147, and "The Possibility of Resurrection," 119–121.

18. Among the many problems with materialism is its inability to account for the fact that we can show things to each other. See Chad Engelland, *Ostension: Word Learning and the Embodied Mind* (Cambridge, MA: MIT Press, 2014), chapters 8–10. Another problem is its inability to account for the normativity of truth. See Chad Engelland, "Heidegger and the Human Difference," *Journal of the American Philosophical Association* 1 (2015): 175–193.

19. See Clarke, *Creative Retrieval*, 189.

20. Augustine, *On the Trinity*, trans. Stephen McKenna (Washington, DC: The Catholic University of America Press, 1963), 8.6.9. On Augustine's non-dualistic philosophical anthropology, see Chad Engelland, "Perceiving Other Animate Minds in Augustine," *American Catholic Philosophical Quarterly* 90.1 (2016): 25–48.

21. Derek Bickerton, *Language and Species* (Chicago: University of Chicago Press, 1990), 115–118.

22. *On the Trinity*, 15.7.11.

23. For a classical treatment, see Maurice Merleau-Ponty, *Phenomenology of Perception*, trans. Colin Smith (London: Routledge Classics, 2002); for recent restatements, see Maxine Sheets-Johnstone, "Animation: The Fundamental, Essential, and Properly Descriptive Concept," *Continental Philosophy Review* 42 (2009): 375–400, and Chad Engelland, *Ostension: Word Learning and the Embodied Mind*.

24. Quoted in *The Christian Faith in the Doctrinal Documents of the Catholic Church*, 7th ed., ed. Jacques Dupuis (New York: Alba House, 2001), 1016.

25. I am thankful to Chris Malloy for this point.

26. *City of God*, 22.19.

27. For a contemporary defense of the role of living form in organic identity, see Hans Jonas, *The Phenomenon of Life* (New York: Harper & Row, 1966), 64–98.

28. See Alva Nöe, *Action in Perception* (Cambridge, MA: The MIT Press, 2004), 209–231, and *Out of Our Heads: Why You Are Not Your Brain, and Other Lessons from the Biology of Consciousness* (New York: Hill & Wang, 2009).

29. For a non-reductive way of relating the brain and nervous system to the person as a whole, see Robert Sokolowski's fascinating discussion of "lensing" in *Phenomenology of the Human Person* (Cambridge, MA: Cambridge University Press, 2008), 225–237.

30. "Immortality," in *God and the Soul* (New York: Schocken Books, 1969), 24.

31. Matt Simon, "Absurd Creature of the Week: This Amazing Little Critter Just Might Be Immortal," *Wired*, http://www.wired.com/2015/02/absurd-creature-of-the-week-hydra/.

32. James Owen, "Oldest Living Tree Found in Sweden," *National Geographic*, http://news.nationalgeographic.com/news/2008/04/080414-oldest-tree.html.

33. The term, "persistent core," is similar to John Haldane's notion of "residual substance." See "The Examined Death and the Hope of the Future," *Proceedings of the ACPA* 74 (2001): 254. "Persistent core" has the advantage of highlighting the causal properties that enable this part and none other to bear the full weight of personal identity.

34. Scholars typically argue for one over the other, but Silas Langley convincingly shows that Aquinas ambiguously used both accounts from his first to his last writings. "Aquinas, Resurrection, and Material Continuity," *Proceedings of the ACPA* 75 (2002): 135–147. For a recent presentation of survivalism, see Eleanore Stump, "Resurrection, Reassembly, and

Reconstitution: Aquinas on the Soul," in *Die Menschliche Seele: Brauchen wir den Dualismus?* ed. Bruno Niederbacher and Edmund Runggaldier (Heusenstamm: Ontos, 2006), 153–174, and of corruptionism, see Patrick Toner, "St. Thomas Aquinas on Death and the Separated Soul," *Pacific Philosophical Quarterly* 91 (2010): 587–599.

35. Langley tries to make sense of Thomas's corruptionist account as follows: "Throughout all the substantial changes that some particular matter goes through, it still keeps *some* dimensions, *some* location, and thus *some* division from all other matter. There is a spatio-temporal trajectory here, even if nothing whatsoever remains numerically identical throughout it." "Aquinas, Resurrection, and Material Continuity," 142.

36. Survivalism, better than corruptionism, fits with Christian faith and practices: "The Church affirms that a spiritual element survives and subsists after death, an element endowed with consciousness and will, so that the 'human self' subsists, though deprived for the present of the complement of its body." "Letter of the S. Congregation for the Doctrine of the Faith on Certain Questions Concerning Eschatology," May 17, 1979, no. 3.

37. *Summa Contra Gentiles*, trans. Charles O'Neil (Garden City, NY: Hanover House, 1957), IV, c. 79. He argues for the fittingness of the resurrection as follows: "But nothing contrary to nature can be perpetual. Perpetually, then, the soul will not be without the body. Since, then, it persists perpetually, it must once again be united to the body; and this is to rise again. Therefore the immortality of souls seems to demand a future resurrection of the body."

38. *Summa Theologiae*, I-II, q. 4, a. 5, ad 2.

39. *Summa Theologiae*, III, q. 50, a. 4, ad. 2. Translation modified. I am thankful to Catherine Nolan for calling my attention to this passage.

40. "Man naturally desires his own salvation; but the soul, since it is part of man's body, is not an entire man, and my soul is not I; hence, although the soul obtains salvation in another life, nevertheless, not I or any man." *Commentary on the First Epistle to the Corinthians*, trans. Fabian Larcher, O.P. and Daniel Keating (http://dhspriory.org/thomas/SS1Cor.htm), n. 924.

41. Aquinas thinks that a disembodied human soul is not a "man" but is instead a "dead man" (*homo mortuus*). See *Summa Theologiae*, III, q. 50, a. 4.

42. For the distinction between being identical in subject and being identical in totality, see *Summa Theologiae*, III, q. 50, a. 5, in which Aquinas is dealing with the special case of Christ's body.

43. "If the resurrection of the body is denied, it is not easy, yea it is difficult, to sustain the immortality of the soul. For it is clear that the soul is naturally united to the body and is departed from it, contrary to its nature and *per accidens*. Hence the soul devoid of its body is imperfect, as long as it is without the body. But it is impossible that what is natural and *per se* be finite and, as it were, nothing; and that which is against nature and *per accidens* be infinite, if the soul endures without the body. And so, the Platonists positing immortality, posited re-incorporation, although this is heretical. Therefore, if the dead do not rise, we will be confident only in this life." *Commentary on the First Epistle to the Corinthians*, n. 924.

44. "Sermon 14," *Academic Sermons*, trans. Mark-Robin Hoogland, C.P. (Washington, DC: The Catholic University of America Press, 2010), 203. He had already written, "Just one old woman knows more about these things that pertain to the faith than heretofore all philosophers." "Sermon 14," *Academic Sermons*, 202.

45. *Fides et Ratio*, n. 76.

46. In 1977, Ratzinger made this claim regarding Thomistic anthropology, which in his judgment joins "Plato and Aristotle precisely at the points where their doctrines were mutually opposed": "Compared with all the conceptions of the soul available in antiquity, this notion of the soul is quite novel. It is a product of Christian faith, and of the exigencies of faith for human thought. Only the downright ignorance of history could find this contestable." *Eschatology*, 148 and 149, respectively.

47. Helen Keller, quoted in Steward and Molly Anne Graff, *Hellen Keller: Crusader for the Blind and Deaf* (New York: Dell Publishing, 1991), 17.

48. For a start, see Kenneth Schmitz, "Purity of Soul and Immortality," in *Texture of Being: Essays in First Philosophy* (Washington, DC: The Catholic University of America Press, 2007); Robert Sokolowski, "Soul and the Transcendence of the Human Person," in *Christian Faith & Human Understanding: Studies on the Eucharist, Trinity, and the Human Person* (Washington, DC: The Catholic University of America Press, 2006); and Michael Sweeney, "Allan Bloom and Thomas Aquinas on Eros and Immortality," *Interpretation* 23 (1996): 445–456.

49. I am thankful to Catherine Nolan, Jonathan J. Sanford, Chris Malloy, Michael Bowler, Gary Michael Gurtler, S.J., Molly Flynn, Mark K. Spencer, Turner C. Nevitt, and Isela Engelland for their critical comments on earlier versions of this paper.

Violence and the Obligations of Charity

Shawn Floyd

Abstract: According to one interpretive strand of the Christian moral tradition, charity requires complete renunciation of violence in all its forms. One should not summarily dismiss this view as extreme or unrepresentative of Christian teaching. After all, sacred Scripture urges us to love our neighbors (including our enemies) and repudiate wanton aggression, hatred, and personal reprisals. Yet while charity would have us disavow all varieties of malicious acts and urges, it is not obvious that it forbids using potentially lethal force. Relying on insights from Aquinas, I argue that charity may not only permit but *require* such force in order to combat the cruelty and aggression directed at our beloved or those in our care.

In Act 3, scene 7, of Shakespeare's *King Lear*, we encounter a particularly grisly episode in which Regan and Cornwall (the king's daughter and son-in-law, respectively) apprehend Gloucester for alleged treason. After restraining him, Cornwall carves out his eye before the audience. An unnamed servant intervenes in an attempt to prevent Cornwall from gouging out Gloucester's remaining eye. From the servant's pleas we know his concern is not only for Gloucester; he also wishes to protect Cornwall from his *own* malice:

> Hold your hand, my lord:
> I have served you ever since I was a child;
> But better service have I never done you
> Than now to bid you hold.

The servant's interference enrages Cornwall and Regan. Swords are drawn, Gloucester is blinded, and both Cornwall and the servant are killed in the melee.

This scene is as compelling as it is bloody. That a servant would jeopardize his own welfare in an effort to prevent an act of cruelty provides us with a bracing image of mercy and charitable concern. Even in spite of the scene's outcome, one cannot help but admire the servant's solicitude. And his effort to resist Cornwall's brutality while risking his own life should garner high praise. One might reasonably

© 2016, *Proceedings of the ACPA*, Vol. 89
doi: 10.5840/acpaproc2016122856

view him as a moral hero precisely because he defies the constraints of his station in order to prevent harms his inaction would guarantee.

Yet there are those who would object to the use of lethal force even if its aim was to shield vulnerable persons from harm or suffering. Among them are those who view any form of violence not only as unnecessary but as incompatible with Christian love, or charity. According to one interpretative strand within the Christian moral tradition, Jesus' command to love others is an exacting precept requiring the complete renunciation of violence.[1] Such a view cannot be summarily dismissed as extreme or unrepresentative of Christian moral teaching. After all, sacred scripture is unambiguous in its instruction that we not only treat others—including our enemies—with kindness, but also put aside personal animosities, quell hateful urges, and abstain from violent reprisals. On this view, Christian charity not only prohibits actions inconsistent with what love ordinarily prescribes, it also condemns malicious and vengeful urges that give rise to those actions.[2] For some who take this view seriously, it is difficult to understand how one could affirm the centrality of Christian charity and *not* renounce violence, including the use of force in resisting others' evil.[3]

There is much to commend in the aforementioned view. Love of neighbor, or charity, directs us to extend to enemies the sort of care and concern usually reserved for friends and kindred. Moreover, one cannot deny there is a broad range of acts, attitudes, and desires that are inimical to charity. I suspect no moral doctrine that purports to be Christian would countenance (say) military strikes that endanger noncombatants, state sponsored-assassinations, strife between neighbors, vengeful desires, or any hostile disposition that produces inordinate aggression. Yet while charity would have us disavow malicious acts and urges, it is not obvious that it also forbids using potentially lethal force when resisting harms perpetrated against our beloved, family members, or anyone placed in our care. In cases of this sort, charity may *require* the use of such force, or so I will argue. While this claim may seem counterintuitive to some, I suggest its counterintuitive appearance is due not to any conceptual incompatibility between charity and violence but to an improper view of charity. A corrective to that view will obviously require further exploration of charity's nature and demands. Such an exploration would provide good reasons to think that forceful resistance to evil may not only be permissible but obligatory.[4]

While defending this view, I will look to Thomas Aquinas's account of charity and the duties associated with it. I appeal to Aquinas not because I find him to be an incontestable moral authority. Nor do I think one will find within his work *decisive* support for the position I wish to defend. Yet I am persuaded that insights culled from his treatment of charity can provide clarity in the matters addressed here. I also recognize that other writers have expended considerable effort addressing topics closely aligned with the subject of this paper—specifically, military conflict. Yet the question of violence's permissibility is not restricted to this subject. Malevolence and injustice are ubiquitous in everyday life. They pose frightening possibilities for parents, friends, ministers, caregivers, or anyone who has a special duty to preserve the welfare of his or her beloved. My discussion of forceful resistance to evil will therefore move beyond the subject of military force or intervention in order to argue for a more general conclusion: in the course of our daily lives, charity may require that we employ potentially lethal force when resisting others' cruelty and aggression, especially when it is directed at our beloved or those in our care.

I. Charity as Neighbor Love

The notion that love would permit or even obligate us to use violence arguably betrays a profound confusion about what love is. Surely the acknowledgement that we have an obligation to love our neighbors would—at the very least—be accompanied by the recognition that we ought to avoid behavior that might result in their injury or death. But are love and violence exclusive in the way this argument suggests? If so, then the notion that love—and particularly love of enemies—might require us to use potentially lethal force would seem strange, if not nonsensical. In order to bring clarity to these matters, I will sketch Aquinas's account of charity, including charity towards enemies. I will then consider whether those who abide by the dictates of charity could ever be obligated to use force against their enemies. Doing so will provide us with the conceptual background for resolving apparent tensions between love and certain instances of violence. It will also enable us to address objections brought forth by those inclined to protest actions similar to those of Cornwall's servant, a subject to which I return in the paper's conclusion.

There are two reasons for focusing on charity as opposed to a more general conception of love. First, charity is love's ideal and purest variant. Charity is a divinely infused virtue (hence its designation as a "theological" virtue) that renovates our sinful habits and directs us to God. Charity also gives the rest of the virtues their form by determining the end to which virtuous acts incline (*ST* IIaIIae 23.8).[5] This claim should not suggest that charity directs virtuous activity to an end different from what the virtues—unformed by charity—would otherwise seek. The virtues by their nature are dispositions for what is best for us *qua* human beings. Yet charity perfects and ennobles the virtues; it enlists them into the service of love so they might work cooperatively with grace in pursuit of our heavenly end which, as Thomas Williams explains, "fulfills our nature, though in a way beyond nature's power."[6] Seen this way, charity's formative influence does not result in changing the virtues' nature. Rather, it acts as an efficient cause by directing those virtues to a supernatural end (*ST* IIaIIae 23.8 *ad* 1).

Second (and more importantly for our purposes), charity is a virtue whose object includes not only God but our neighbors. And while we have yet to say anything about who our neighbors are, those standing within the Christian moral tradition affirm that we have an obligation to love our neighbors through concrete acts of mercy—or almsgiving—which is one of charity's paradigmatic expressions (*ST* IIaIIae, 32.5).[7] On this view, then, charity is not simply a matter of having a kindly disposition toward our neighbors. It involves sensitivity to their needs and a willingness to aid those who suffer under the weight of poverty, bereavement, fear, and injustice.

But how inclusive should our charitable practices be? In other words, what is the *range* of persons to whom we owe our charity? On the one hand, charity is universal in scope. Its precept "love thy neighbor" is not a special duty to care only for one's kindred; it is a comprehensive moral requirement that directs us to love all persons. As Joseph Sollier explains, when we view others as fellow persons bearing God's image, we cannot restrict charitable concern to our beloved only. It must extend "to all the units of the human kind, to social outcasts, and even to enemies."[8]

On the other hand, Aquinas recognizes that we have neither the ability nor the means to extend our love to all people. Determining who we ought to love through (say) targeted acts of beneficence requires us to consider (among other things) our relationship to the person(s) in need. Aquinas appeals to Augustine on this score when he writes that the practice of charity requires that we "consider those chiefly who by reason of place, time or any other circumstance, by a kind of chance, are more closely united to us" (IIaIIae 32.9). He also expresses high regard for St. Paul's admonition that those who ignore the needs of their household deny sacred teaching and prove themselves to be worse than infidels (*ST* IIaIIae 26.7).

Initially, this account of charity may seem puzzling. To whom, precisely, should we direct our charity? Does the scope of charitable concern extend to all persons, or to our closest relations? Aquinas's account supports both answers. Charity's scope is universal in the sense that it directs us to care about everyone's general welfare and to pray for their salvation. It also requires that we be "prepared in mind" to help anyone in need when the opportunity arises. With respect to charity's exercise, however, a fair amount of ordering is required lest it become "injudicious and inoperative."[9] Here preference is usually given to loved ones, family members, or those charged in our care. There are occasions, however, when one ought to deprive oneself or one's family of some material necessity, say when others' needs are especially urgent or when the needs of those closest to us are slight.

The aforementioned exceptions do not contradict the general view that our obligations are generally cast by our roles as parents, friends, and caregivers. Rather, they serve as a reminder that good judgments do not result from consulting and applying uniform principles in complicated matters. We need prudence when determining how to respond in cases where competing needs are in play (*ST* IIaIIae 31.3 *ad* 1). While our loved ones and dependents remain more or less the default subjects of our charitable concern, even the most relationally distant persons cannot be excluded from its scope. The same goes for those with whom our relations are hostile or strained. In fact, the love of such persons—our enemies—provides for us one of charity's paradigmatic expressions.

II. Love of Enemies

For Aquinas, that we should love our enemies is axiomatic. In spite of the conflicts that sometimes exist between us and others, our shared nature and common desire for happiness binds us in important ways. We should not, therefore, withhold from our enemies the same general charity we have for our neighbors (*ST* IIaIIae

25.8). That is, we should inwardly love our enemies by (for example) praying for their salvation and being prepared to care for them by means of almsgiving when their needs are particularly urgent. Outside of such cases, however, loving an enemy by means of almsgiving is not a matter of obligation but of *counsel*, a subject which requires brief consideration if we are to determine whether charity obligates us to endure the harms our enemies may inflict on us or our beloved.

Acts pertaining to counsel are often associated with specific religious callings or vocations. While counsels are not morally-binding, their performance provides a surer or more expeditious path toward salvation (*ST* IaIIae 108.4). As Servais Pinckaers explains, the counsels provide "invaluable indications of ways to advance more smoothly and speedily along the path to the perfection of charity and the promised beatitude."[10] Consider, for example, those who remain chaste or voluntarily forgo material wealth for the sake of God. Adopting a life of this sort is not required for salvation. Yet by renouncing these goods, one puts aside whatever might disrupt one's pursuit of his or her spiritual end, thereby hastening his sanctification.[11] In short, the purpose of the counsels is not to prohibit what is ostensibly forbidden but to illuminate paths that are efficacious in producing holiness.

We should observe here that the counsels are not reserved only for those who choose to abide by the strictures of religious vocation. The Church extols these practices as being good for all and thus recommends them to every Christian as exemplary means to charity's perfection.[12] Yet not everyone is disposed to undertake the exacting demands of, say, perpetual virginity or poverty (regardless of how beneficial these particular counsels are) (*ST* IaIIae 108.4 *ad* 1). Moreover, some people are burdened by responsibilities that prevent them from observing the counsels in an ongoing way.[13] Persons who are married cannot permanently forgo sexual intimacy without neglecting the goods inherent in marital union. Nevertheless, married persons can—without repudiating those goods—practice periodic chastity in order to direct themselves to God through prayer and contemplation. Similarly, one can perform all varieties of mercy through almsgiving without committing one's whole life to serving the poor. In doing so, one observes the counsels, but only during a fixed time and in particular cases (*ST* IaIIae 108.4; IaIIae 108.4 *ad* 2).

Aquinas thinks of extending charity to individual enemies in a similar way. While we are not (usually) obligated to do so, we may love our enemies through targeted acts of mercy even when their needs are not urgent. Such mercy may involve any number of corporeal alms; it may also involve extending forgiveness to an enemy or refusing to resist his aggression (*ST* IaIIae 108.3 *ad* 2; *ST* IIaIIae 40.1 *ad* 2). Though charitable acts of this sort are—generally—not matters of precept, they (like periodic chastity or individual acts of beneficence) nevertheless demonstrate extraordinary love for God and are helpful in contributing to one's spiritual perfection.

There is a potential worry associated with this view. By designating charitable acts toward enemies as matters of counsel, some may wonder whether Aquinas's account pushes the most admirable expressions of love beyond the sphere of morally serious activity. This worry may be intensified by describing the counsels as (to use a term favored by recent commentators) "supererogatory."[14] Depending on how one understands supererogation, using the term in this context may suggest that the counsels are acts whose normative weight is comparatively substandard. So conceived, the counsels may appear hardly expressive of the sort of sacrificial love required by charity. One might even worry that the counsels' supererogatory nature makes loving enemies by means of outward acts simply a matter of personal discretion. For it appears that only the direst circumstances can impose on us a duty to perform moral labor on our enemies' behalf.

Close attention to what Aquinas says about these matters should disabuse us of the idea that counsels are either morally gratuitous or reserved for those whose interests are purely ascetic. His writings on this subject suggest that we have profoundly good reasons for performing charitable acts that fall outside cases of urgent need—reasons that may be easy to overlook if we (without proper elucidation or qualification) characterize them strictly in terms of supererogation.[15] For example, when we offer special prayers for our enemies or go out of our way to treat them well, we not only guard ourselves against hatred but contribute to the cessation of conflict through acts that inspire reciprocated love (*ST* IIaIIae 25.9).[16] Acts of this sort hardly lack moral seriousness. In fact, we can appreciate their significance by considering that their end is no different from that established by the commandments themselves: "charity from a pure heart, and a good conscience, and an unfeigned faith" (*ST* IIaIIae 44.1). Yet charity's perfection is an end for which there are diverse means open to those seeking to achieve it. The non-compulsory nature of these acts does not diminish their moral significance; rather it underscores the extent to which the moral life permits a variety of practices that are conducive to, though not singularly required for, our spiritual perfection.

Moreover, Aquinas does not minimize charity's demands by claiming that its exercise is often a matter of counsel. He acknowledges that there are occasions when we *should* refrain from (say) resisting others' aggression (*ST* IIaIIae 40.1 *ad* 2) and even suffer harm if necessary rather than succumb to hatred (*ST* IaIIa 108.3 *ad* 2; *ST* IIaIIae 43.8 *ad* 4). As we noted previously, acts of this sort contribute to both our and our enemies' betterment. Thus it seems reasonable to suppose that genuine concern for our enemies' spiritual good would entail a readiness to love them in precisely these ways (*ST* IIaIIae 25. 9). In his own gloss on Aquinas's account, Gregory Reichberg says that "Christians should be inwardly prepared to desist from self-defense . . . thereby undergoing hardship and even death, if such would prove spiritually beneficial to the neighbor."[17] This account leaves open the possibility that attentiveness to our enemies' spiritual good would, under the right circumstances, require extraordinary sacrifice on our part. So while loving enemies by means of specific acts is often a matter of counsel, we may sometimes have an obligation to offer special prayers for them, to nurture them by way of corporeal alms, and even love them through the forfeiture of our physical well-being. In other words, there may be occasions in which "charitable concern for the assailant, wishing what is good for him, entails the voluntary assumption of harm upon oneself."[18] Whether we have an obligation to assume such harm, however, depends on whether there is some actual good that our charitable efforts are able to achieve on our enemies' behalf.

III. Resisting Evil

This last point is important for appraising the unqualified commitment to nonviolence. Aquinas does not commend the endurance of evil as inherently praiseworthy. Regardless of whether such endurance is a matter of precept or counsel, he extols it only to the extent that it is efficacious in contributing to our (or our enemy's) welfare. He expresses this point in his discussion of patience. There, he notes that we should not seek to endure sorrow and pain for their own sake. To endure such things is meritorious only if they aim at a desirable end (*ST* IIaIIae 136.3). In his commentary on I Corinthians, he insists that we should not look to suffer evil unless such suffering was directed to some good.[19] Thus it would be commendable to endure another person's mistreatment if such endurance served to curb aggressive habits or prevented us from being consumed by self-destructive hatred. It would also be praiseworthy to endure such harm if doing so provoked in the assailant remorse and a subsequent desire to reciprocate the love he has been shown. In either case, it is crucial to note here that the willingness to endure suffering or invite it on oneself has no intrinsic merit.

Since the endurance of evil is not intrinsically good, perhaps there could be instances of such endurance that would be impermissible. Aquinas advocates precisely this view when he explains the different ways we might tolerate evil. On the one hand, we can forgive others for harms they've inflicted when doing so contributes to their spiritual welfare. Endurance of this sort is salutary because it hastens charity's perfection. On the other hand, we might tolerate the wrongs committed wantonly against our neighbors. Enduring evil in these cases would be expressive not only of moral imperfection but, worse still, vice—especially when we are capable of resisting the wrongdoer by employing appropriate means of protection (*ST* IIaIIae 188.3 *ad* 1). There is nothing virtuous about tolerating the aggression of those who are incorrigibly vicious and intent on harm. Such toleration may only embolden them and exacerbate an already unjust situation by exposing victims to further suffering. While such cases may be rare, their occurrence begs us to consider that a nonviolent posture would (at least in these instances) breach charity's demands. By refusing to resist evil, we leave our beloved vulnerable to the very harms from which we ought to shield them.[20]

It may be useful to point out here that Aquinas's distinction between proper and improper ways of tolerating evil appears in a discussion about whether members of lay (not clerical) orders can participate in armed conflict.[21] For him, considerations of charity can impose a duty on even religious brothers to resist evil through force. So long as their aim is not some worldly good "but for the defense of divine worship and public safety, or also of the poor and oppressed," they may be required to defend those who are vulnerable to others' aggression (*ST* IIaIIae 188.3). Despite the context in which this investigation appears, the principle informing Aquinas's account—e.g., that it is improper to tolerate evils inflicted on others—is hardly restricted to lay orders. The principle at work here appears to have wide applicability; it functions as a general guide for determining how we ought to respond when those under our care are subjected to brutality and aggression. Thus in the same passage Aquinas approvingly cites Ambrose's praise of persons who express their love by resisting those who rob our friends or threaten weaker members of our household (ibid.).[22] To endure patiently wrongs done to such persons would presumably be just as vicious as a soldier who refuses to prevent civilians from being victimized by aggressors.

Aquinas's discussion of resisting evil as a matter of charity is particularly insightful for our purposes. For him, using force in order to (say) stay the hand of an assailant or to protect one's children from harm is not a tragic but necessary departure from love. On the contrary, such resistance may be love's proper expression, at least insofar as it aims to defend the material welfare of those who suffer unjustly. According to the view presented here, it is not unreasonable to suppose that forceful resistance to evil may be a kind of almsgiving that—under certain conditions—one has a duty to perform. If this notion is correct, then our refusal to provide our vulnerable neighbors with the proper measure of protection would constitute an egregious disregard of charity itself.[23] For, as we have learned, charity demands that we love our neighbors by doing what is necessary to care for them. Moreover, whatever means are necessary for loving our neighbors have as much obligatory force as love itself. Thus Aquinas insists that "as love of our neighbor is a matter of precept, whatever is a necessary condition to the love of our neighbor is a matter of precept also" (*ST* IIaIIae 32.5).

IV. Some Conclusions

We are now in a position to respond to the concern posed at the beginning of section I. There, we asked how we could behave violently toward those whom charity obligates us to love. I suspect one of the worries that may generate suspicion about this possibility is that violence is often a manifestation of desires that are contrary to charity. This worry is not unwarranted. Aquinas himself recognizes that responses to aggression can be disproportionately severe and mingled with hatred (*ST* IIaIIae 41.1 and IIaIIae 64.7). And private conflicts are often generated by animosity and an eagerness to harm those who have allegedly done wrong (*ST* IIaIIae 41.2). Yet if the claims in the preceding section are correct, then it seems reasonable to suppose that our efforts to resist aggression or injustice are not always products of hatred or an inordinate desire for reprisal. As Jeff Polet points out, love for others "can often express [itself] through care, solicitude, and a desire to preserve, even if such care and preservation requires morally dangerous actions."[24] While it is true that the use of force is sometimes driven by malice, to suppose that such force is *by itself* evidence of such a drive begs a host of questions about the sort of motives at work when presumably well-intentioned people attempt to defend themselves or those in their care. We cannot, therefore, argue that all efforts to resist evil are disordered, at least not without assuming the conclusion that advocates of absolute non-violence wish to draw.

Moreover, an unqualified commitment to nonviolence seems strangely detached from considerations of both justice and prudence. As we saw in the previous section, only through a careful appraisal of others' relationship to us and their depth of need can we understand who, precisely, has a greater claim on our love (*ST* IIaIIae 31.3 *ad* 1 and 3). Charity is never extended indiscriminately; its exercise is always coordinated with a proper sense of what we owe our beloved and whether our efforts to care for them will be availing. Charity, then, does not usurp the obligations integral to our roles as parents, spouses, and caregivers. It is true that we must sometimes extend beneficence to non-relatives, strangers, and even enemies. Yet the propriety and efficacy of such beneficence require that its expression be governed by considerations of not only need, but desert. For to treat the needs of our beloved as morally equivalent to those of an aggressor could potentially disrupt our ability to protect our beloved in a way both justice and charity require.

I imagine advocates of non-violence would resist the notion that preferential considerations play any role in determining what, exactly, charity requires of us. For them, the radical nature of Christian love obliterates the grounds upon which we make such distinctions, making the enemy—even the villainous aggressor—no less an object of our love than the person he attacks.[25] Yet I hope it is clear by now that this position is based on an objectionable understanding of love—one that ignores sacred teaching's special attention to the poor and oppressed as well as its admonishment not to ignore the welfare of one's closest relations.[26]

This brief account of the disproportionate nature of charity's exercise might help us understand how we might love an enemy while forcefully resisting his malice. Consider the example with which this paper began. The servant has a duty to love both Cornwall and Gloucester. Yet their needs hardly carry the same evaluative weight or call for comparable treatment. Gloucester's predicament demands forceful intervention lest he endure further brutality. Failure to intercede on his behalf would guarantee further maiming and constitute a grievous violation of one's duty to protect those victimized by aggression. One might understandably conclude from this scenario that Gloucester ought to be the primary object of the servant's charity. Yet the scene in question is a bit more complicated than what I've described thus far. Recall that the servant is not preoccupied only with Gloucester's needs, as he attempts to prevent Cornwall from committing a depraved act. From this perspective, the servant hardly fails to love Cornwall; he extends to Cornwall a considerable degree of charity by breaching the constraints of his station for the sake of something even more valuable than Gloucester's sight, namely, Cornwall's spiritual well-being.

Clearly, then, the charity extended by the servant to each party is different given the disparate nature of their needs. His charitable efforts also manifest some inequity, too, although it may be difficult to explain the nature of that inequity. Intuitively, we might think that Gloucester's physical wellbeing is more urgent and thus make a greater claim on the servant's love. On the other hand, Cornwall's action is a clear instance of mortal sin. The spiritual damnation he risks as a result of his actions makes *him* the more pressing subject of the servant's charity.[27] That the servant would risk himself in order to prevent Cornwall from sinning might suggest that, in fact, *Cornwall* is the primary recipient of the servant's love.

I raise these possibilities only to put them aside for now. My purpose in raising them is to reinforce—and hopefully to make compelling—the point that charity does not refrain from shielding our beloved from injustice and harm. Indeed, the welfare of our beloved may obligate us to resist and prevent evil by aggressive means. If this account of charity is correct, then we have good reason to reject the view that Christian love imposes on us an absolute obligation to abstain from potentially lethal forms of resistance.[28]

Malone University

Notes

1. For theological defenses of this position, one should consult the works of John Howard Yoder, Stanley Hauerwas, and James McClendon. Philosophical treatments of nonviolence that engage the Christian tradition include: G. E. M. Anscombe, "War and Murder," in *Nuclear Weapons: A Catholic Response*, ed. Walter Stein (London and New York, 1961), 44–52; Robert Brimlow, *What about Hitler?: Wrestling with Jesus's Call to Nonviolence in an Evil World* (Brazos Press, 2006); James Kellenberger, "A Defense of Pacifism," *Faith and Philosophy* 4 (April 1987): 129–148; Stanley Hauerwas, "Pacifism: Some Philosophical Considerations," *Faith and Philosophy* 2 (1985): 99–104; Nancy Murphy and George Ellis, *On The Moral Nature of the Universe* (Fortress Press, 1996); Myron Penner, "The Pacifist's Burden of Proof," *Philosophia Christi* 7 (2005): 107–123.

2. As James Kellenberger notes, Christ's teaching on neighbor love concerns both outward behavior as well as our attitudes and intentions towards others ("A Defense of Pacifism," 141). With respect to the subject under discussion, Christ's teaching compels us to forgo "all violence of thought and action" (ibid.). While Kellenberger's paper seeks to address only war's impermissibility, he also thinks that Christian neighbor love encourages a more comprehensive rejection of violence (130).

3. While most readers may recognize the position I am describing as *pacifism*, the sort of pacifism I have in mind here is not confined to a refusal to support state-sanctioned war. Rather, it denotes a general opposition to the use of force even in private life. One might call the position I am describing here "absolute pacifism" which, according to Andrew Fiala, connotes "a maximal and universal rejection of violence and war." See his "Pacifism," *The Stanford Encyclopedia of Philosophy* (Winter 2014 Edition), ed. Edward N. Zalta. http://plato.stanford.edu/archives/fall2010/entries/pacifism/. Still, the term "pacifism" as it is generally used is often associated with a rejection of war. Kellenberger is representative here, as he describes pacifism as "a moral repudiation of all war" (129–130). For him, pacifism (so described) is a specific extension of a more general "repudiation of violence in all human relations" (130). In order to avoid unnecessary confusion about this matter, I will simply use "violence" and "nonviolence" as my primary terms.

4. A colleague has called my attention to Paul Ramsey's defense of a similar view in his *Basic Christian Ethics* (Westminster: John Knox Press, 1950). Unlike my paper, however, Ramsey's account is focused largely on the subject of war and self-defensive killing. See especially chapter five, "Christian Vocation," 153–190.

5. *Summa Theologica* (*ST*), trans. Fathers of the English Dominican Province (Westminster, Maryland: Christian Classics, 1981).

6. See his "Introduction" to St. Thomas Aquinas's *Disputed Questions on the Virtues*. trans. E. M. Atkins, ed. E. M. Atkins and Thomas Williams (Cambridge: Cambridge University Press, 2005), xxii.

7. For a more extensive treatment of mercy, the acts associated with it, and its obligatory nature, see my paper "Aquinas and the Obligations of Mercy," *Journal of Religious Ethics* 37.3 (2009): 449–471.

8. Joseph Sollier, "Love (Theological Virtue)." *The Catholic Encyclopedia*, vol. 9 (New York: Robert Appleton Company, 1910). Accessed 1 Aug, 2011. http://www.newadvent.org/cathen/09397a.htm.

9. Ibid.

10. *The Sources of Christian Ethics*, trans. Sr. Mary Thomas Noble, O.P. (Washington DC: Catholic University of America Press, 1995), 187.

11 Ibid.

12. Ibid.

13. Ibid.

14. For a helpful discussion of supererogation as it relates to the evangelical counsels, see David Heyd, *Supererogation: Its Status in Ethical Theory* (Cambridge: Cambridge University Press, 1982), 20–26. See also Stanley Vodraska, "Works of Mercy and the Principle of Familial Preference," *Faith and Philosophy* 22.1 (January 2005): 21–41.

15. I do not wish to suggest here that supererogation connotes a realm of moral acts that are less than morally serious. I simply wish to anticipate and diffuse the notion that supererogatory acts (at least as Aquinas understands them) somehow lack normative weight.

16. Gregory Reichberg's remarks on Aquinas's view are helpful. Extending tangible signs of love to the enemy, he says, "promotes another's good, for in being shown love where he would expect hatred, the adversary is induced to respond in kind. Commenting on Romans 12:21, 'Do not be vanquished by evil,' Thomas observes that when a good man, on account of the evil done to him, is drawn to do evil in return, he will allow himself to be vanquished by evil (*bonus a malo vincitur*). This one should never do, and in this respect, St. Paul's statement articulates an obligation strictly binding on all Christians. But, in addition, should the good man treat his persecutor with benevolence, acting with love where he is met by hatred, his enemy will be encouraged away from evil (*a malo trahas*). In this way, the good man can vanquish over evil (*bonus malum vincit*) by drawing his enemy into the circle of love." See his "Thomas Aquinas between Just War and Pacifism," *Journal of Religious Ethics* 38.2 (June 2010): 232. I owe much to Reichberg's article, which not only provided important insights to Aquinas's treatment of these matters, but called attention to several passages (both in Aquinas's *Summa Theologica* and his biblical commentaries) I otherwise would not have found.

17. Ibid., 231.

18. Ibid.

19. *Super I Epistolam B. Pauli ad Corinthios lectura*, trans. Fabian Larcher. Html-edited by Joseph Kenny, O.P., 15.2.925. Accessed June 23, 2016 (http://www.dhspriory.org/thomas/english/SS1Cor.htm#152). I am indebted to Eleonore Stump's *Aquinas* (Routledge, 2003) for

calling my attention to this passage (470). Her discussion of conditional versus unconditional goods is also helpful (see 470–71).

20. Stanley Hauerwas acknowledges that this objection is important, yet he quickly dismisses it as a contrivance of philosophers more interested in conceptual clarity than Christian faithfulness. See his "Pacifism: Some Philosophical Considerations," *Faith and Philosophy*, 2.2 (April 1985): 100.

21. In his discussion of this same passage, Reichberg points out that the order Aquinas is discussing is the Knights' Templar—an order of un-ordained brothers whose duties were primarily secular. The prohibition against bloodshed applied primarily to members of clerical orders "precisely by reason of their formal role as Christ's spiritual representatives on earth" ("Thomas Aquinas between Just War and Pacifism," 235). This point underscores Aquinas's view that moral duties and expectations are, in part, relative to the obligations integral to our vocation or station in life. Thus one of the reasons clerics (as opposed to lay persons) are prohibited from participating in war as combatants is that such activity would contravene the goods they have been appointed to promote (*ST* IIaIIae 40.2 *ad* 3 and 4). As Reichberg explains: "the nonviolence expected of priests results from the special tasks pertaining to their profession, tasks that are inconsistent with those demanded of other professions (particularly the military), but where all of the said professions are needed for the good ordering of society" (237).

22. Aquinas makes no explicit reference to charity in *ST* IIaIIae 188.3. Yet we should keep in mind that the question to which he is responding concerns whether soldiering contravenes the aim toward which religious life is directed, namely, the perfection of charity. Also, the preceding article describes the activities of religious life as being uniformly directed to charity: "And just as out of charity we love our neighbor for God's sake, so the services we render our neighbor redound to God, according to Matthew 25:40 'What you have done to one of these My least brethren, you did it to Me' (*ST* IIaIIae 188.2)." The specific task addressed in article 3 (soldiering) is but an instance of such activity.

23. Reichberg draws a similar conclusion: "failing to aid these innocent victims of violence, when the capacity exists, would violate the mercy by which we are called on to succor the poor and oppressed in the hour of their need" ("Thomas Aquinas between Just War and Pacifism," 234–235).

24. "Being 'Other Cheeky': Moral Hazard and the Thought of Stanley Hauerwas" *Humanitas* 22.1–2 (2009): 119.

25. John Howard Yoder makes this precise argument. See his *The War of the Lamb: The Ethics of Nonviolence and Peacemaking*, ed. Mark Theissen Nation and Matt Hamsher (Grand Rapids: Brazos Press, 2009), especially 146–147.

26. Polet addresses this problem as it appears in Hauerwas's work, which, he says, is fixated on "one strain of the gospels: that Christ's presence disrupts families and alters our moral commitments. This emphasis in the gospels, however, is offset by other passages, as well as Pauline teachings, that stress the moral requirements of charity associated with our immediate obligations in the household. Any sensible interpretation of scripture would require taking account of these often unresolved tensions." ("Being 'Other Cheeky,'" 116–117).

27. Eleonore Stump's remarks on Aquinas's account suggest there is good reason to interpret the servant's actions in precisely this way. She says: "when we see someone suffer as a result of human injustice, then on Aquinas's view (other things being equal) we have a clear obligation to do what is in our power to stop the suffering, *ceteris paribus*. Injustice is

a mortal sin which separates a person from God; in intervening we help to rescue not only the victim of the injustice but also the perpetrator, whose condition on Aquinas's view is otherwise apparently terminal" (*Aquinas*, 472). Of course, it is unlikely this is the precise point Shakespeare wanted to convey, but the servant's entreaties are at least suggestive of Stump's point.

28. I am grateful to Dan Maher for his comments on this paper. I am also grateful to Sean Benson for encouraging me to consider the case of Cornwall and the servant as an illustration of the position defended in this paper.

A Thomistic Analysis of the Hart-Fuller Debate

Peter Karl Koritansky

Abstract: In 1958, the *Harvard Law Review* published a now-famous debate between H. L. A. Hart and Lon Fuller regarding the proposed connection between law and morality. Whereas Hart defended a broadly positivist conception of law, Fuller advanced a kind of natural law theory that has greatly influenced judicial interpretation in the United States. This paper examines the debate and provides a commentary in light of the natural law theory of Thomas Aquinas. Whereas it is not surprising that Aquinas would reject the central tenets of Hart's positivism, it also appears he would have deep misgivings about the position defended by Professor Fuller, and particularly Fuller's understanding of how laws should be interpreted in light of morality.

I

It is well known that Thomas Aquinas is, if not the original, at least one of the most important defenders of the natural law tradition. That tradition, in spite of its medieval roots, is very much alive in contemporary jurisprudence and political thought. One of the most striking contemporary appearances of natural law in the United States has been in the writings of Dr. Martin Luther King Jr. As a Christian, Dr. King was well aware of St. Paul's teaching in Romans 13 that Christians must respect the rightful political authorities, not merely for prudential reasons, but because those authorities, presumably whether they rule justly or unjustly, derive their authority from God. It was not a frivolous question, therefore, for his fellow pastors to ask Dr. King to provide a reason for his disobedience to the segregation laws of Alabama. In response, Dr. King writes the following well-known remarks:

> One may well ask: "How can you advocate breaking some laws and obeying others?" The answer lies in the fact that there are two types of laws: just and unjust. I would be the first to advocate obeying just laws. One has not only a legal but a moral responsibility to obey just laws. Conversely, one has a moral responsibility to disobey unjust laws. I would agree with St. Augustine that "an unjust law is no law at all." Now, what is

©2016, *Proceedings of the ACPA*, Vol. 89
doi: 10.5840/acpaproc2016112150

the difference between the two? How does one determine whether a law is just or unjust? A just law is a man made code that squares with the moral law or the law of God. An unjust law is a code that is out of harmony with the moral law. To put it in the terms of St. Thomas Aquinas: An unjust law is a human law that is not rooted in eternal law and natural law.[1]

What King highlights in Thomas's natural law theory is one of its most distinctive features. It is not just the claim that there exists a natural law, or that legislators have a moral obligation to legislate according to it, or even that we are absolved from obedience to human laws that contradict the natural law. It is, rather, the claim that laws that are out of accord with the natural law are *not actually laws*. Nearly every time Thomas reiterates this principle he is quoting Augustine, who spoke not of natural law but rather that of which Thomas later says the natural law is a part, namely, the eternal law.[2] As it turns out, the eternal law is nothing other than divine providence itself inclining all the things of creation toward their proper ends and in accordance with the particular natures they have.[3] As Thomas will say, therefore, the natural law is nothing other than the eternal law as it is applied to human beings.[4] Precisely because the natural law governs all human affairs, positive (or "human") laws must be made accordingly. In fact, one might say that positive laws must be seen within the context of a legal order that far transcends the political community. Hence Thomas can defend the paradoxical notion of "illegal laws" as one might explain the invalidity of a human statute that directly violates some higher statute in the same legal order.

For example, let us suppose that a traffic officer decides that the legal speed limit in a certain area is too high and that he prefers the speed limit to be 20 KPH less than what it is. Acting upon this, he begins stopping motorists and ticketing them for exceeding, not the posted speed limit, but his own new speed limit. One might say that the new traffic law imposed by the officer has no legal status because the standard he imposes is out of accord with a higher law that he has no authority to change. The speed limit he imposes is not a law, therefore, but simply rather an imposition of his will upon the motorists. Thomas Aquinas says something quite similar, even stronger, when it comes to human laws out of accordance with the natural law. Rather than laws, such measures are mere "acts of violence."[5]

II

That positive laws are based upon a higher law and depend upon that higher law for their legal character is, of course, exactly what legal positivism denies. Although this thesis has been stated and restated many times, its most articulate representative continues to be the great twentieth-century legal philosopher H. L. A. Hart. In his famous essay, "Positivism and the Separation of Law and Morals," Hart attacks precisely the proposition that immoral or unjust laws are not really laws. To be sure, Hart nowhere states the Hobbesian version of legal positivism that might makes right, or that there simply is no such thing as justice beyond or above the positive law. The claim is much more limited, namely, that immoral or unjust laws, in spite of being poorly designed, harmful, inequitable, or whatever else would make them bad laws, are laws nonetheless and entail a legal obligation to obedience just the same as good laws. Hence, when Hart says that law and morality should be kept separate, he does not mean that laws should not reflect moral principles or that legislators do not have a moral obligation to legislate in accordance with morality. Instead, he is arguing that the question of what the positive law *is* must not be confused with the question of what the law *ought to be*. In short, Hart denies the Thomistic/Augustinian principle that "an unjust law is no law at all."

Hart advances several arguments to support his position (not all of which we can consider here). As he concedes, the point at which law and morality are most easily, but wrongly, conflated occurs in the process of interpreting laws. As one argument goes, laws very often require an interpretation that necessitates a reliance upon some standard of reasonability that is not imbedded in the law itself. Take, for example, Hart's own example of a law prohibiting the use of "vehicles" in a public park. The purpose of such a law seems clear, namely, to provide for a safer environment for those using the park. What must be done, however, is to define that to which the word "vehicle" refers. Obviously it includes automobiles, but what about bicycles, unicycles, or roller skates? Are not even wheelchairs a kind of vehicle? As the argument might go, all laws that require interpretation require an appeal to some sort of "ought." As a judge interprets the law just mentioned, he cannot reasonably address what the law actually means without simultaneously addressing what it ought to mean. Is it not the case, therefore, that when it comes to the interpretation of the law, the *is* and the *ought* are inextricably linked?

As Hart responds, although the question of what the law actually says must often be answered with reference to what it ought to say, this simple fact is far from demonstrating an inseparable connection, as some natural lawyers would argue, between the law and morality. As he puts it,

> the word ought merely reflects the presence of some standard of criticism; one of these standards is a moral standard but not all standards are moral. We say to our neighbor, "You ought not to lie," and that may certainly be a moral judgment, but we remember that the baffled poisoner may say, "I ought to have given her a second dose." The point here is that intelligent decisions are not necessarily identical with decisions defensible on moral grounds.[6]

We may well apply this line of reasoning to immoral laws that natural lawyers may be tempted to deprive of legal status. For example, the segregation laws of the American south indicted by M. L. K. Jr. may be said to violate basic moral principles of justice and human dignity. But it would be a mistake, Hart would argue, to interpret the meaning of these laws as something less morally offensive simply because of a presumed connection between law and morality. The law simply says what it says. It may be just or it may be unjust, but it only confuses matters to assert that an unjust law must be interpreted to mean something that is more morally palatable or to carry on the charade that the unjust law is not really a law. According to Hart, we should simply call it what it is . . . an unjust law. One may disobey such a law for conscientious reasons, but for the conscientious objector to argue that he is actually *more* law abiding for disobeying the unjust law, more obedient, he might argue, to the true spirit of the law, is nothing beyond empty rhetoric.

Hart provides another example which helps us understand his position even better. If any laws can be accused of such moral turpitude that they lose their legal status it would be the laws of Nazi Germany. As one case unfolded, a woman living under the Third Reich was intent upon disposing of her husband from whom she had gone astray. In order to end her marriage, she denounced him to the Nazi authorities for having been openly critical of the regime and even of Hitler himself. The husband was promptly arrested and sentenced to death (though the sentence was later revoked in favor of sending him to the battlefield, where he later died). Although the husband's actions were technically in violation of the Nazi statute, a post-Nazi German court tried his wife five years later for having violated a pre-existing German law forbidding anyone from illegally depriving a person of his freedom. The woman's case was very straightforward: She had broken no law because her husband did in fact commit the crimes of which she accused him. Nevertheless, the German court found her guilty on the grounds that the Nazi law was so morally repugnant that it provided no legal justification for her actions. As the court stated it, the law under which her husband was prosecuted "was contrary to the sound conscience and sense of justice of all decent human beings."[7]

While recognizing the difficulty of the situation, Hart criticizes the German court for its ruling. The fact that the Nazi statute violated basic norms of morality is not enough to say that such a law was not really a law. This does not mean that the woman should have been simply released. Hart agrees that she deserves punishment, but to say that her actions were illegal cannot be maintained without the charade of appealing to a nineteenth-century statute that has little or no applicability to her situation (if anyone deprived her husband of his freedom, it was the Nazis themselves). As bad as it may seem, Hart argues that if the court insisted upon bringing this woman to justice, it should have at least had the candor to say what it was really doing, namely, punishing her retroactively for breaking a law that did not exist at the time she denounced her husband. As Hart argues, this "would have made plain that in punishing the woman a choice had been made between two evils, that of leaving her unpunished and that of sacrificing a very precious principle of morality endorsed by most legal systems."[8] He continues, "the vice of [using] the principle that, at certain limiting points, what is utterly immoral cannot be law or lawful is that it will serve to cloak the true nature of the problems with which we are faced and will encourage the romantic optimism that all values we cherish ultimately will fit into a single system, that no one of them has to be sacrificed or compromised to accommodate another."[9] For Hart the danger of such reasoning is clear: Whereas the German court was able to manipulate the law in this case to make the situation come out in a morally acceptable fashion, the permissibility of interpreting the law to suit one's moral preferences has just as much potential to infuse immorality into the legal system as preserving it from immorality. What's more, the rule of law is itself threatened, since the judges are given license to rewrite the law according to what, in their minds, it ought to mean, instead of what it actually means. The conflation of law and morality may serve us well when the laws are bad, but it will become disastrous when the otherwise good laws become vulnerable to the arbitrary, or even pernicious, intentions of judges.

In response to Hart's essay, Harvard's Lon Fuller argues that law and morality are, in fact, inextricably linked. If Hart's position represents legal positivism, then, Fuller advances what might be considered a kind of natural law theory that largely prefigures his later, and much more influential, contribution to legal philosophy, namely, his 1964 publication, *The Morality of Law*. For the purposes of his 1958 essay in the *Harvard law Review*, entitled "Positivism and Fidelity to Law: A Reply to Professor Hart," Fuller approaches the subjects of law and morality, like Hart himself, from the perspective of interpreting law. It is especially in the interpretation of laws, Fuller argues, that the necessary link between law and morality becomes evident. If the purpose of interpreting a law is to apply it to a current situation, one must recognize that this cannot be done without rendering the law in question more coherent. There exists a link between law and morality, therefore, inasmuch as there exists a link between morality and coherence. Realizing that he cannot demonstrate such a link within the parameters of his essay, Fuller provides the following assertion:

> Professor Hart seems to assume that evil aims may have as much coherence and inner logic as good ones. I, for one, refuse to accept that assumption. . . . I shall have to rest on the assertion of a belief that may seem naïve, namely, that coherence and goodness have more affinity than coherence and evil. Accepting this belief, I also believe that when men are compelled to explain and justify their decisions, the effect will generally be to pull those decisions toward goodness, by whatever standards of ultimate goodness there are. Accepting these beliefs, I find a considerable incongruity in any conception that envisages a possible future in which the common law would "work itself pure from case to case" toward a more perfect realization of iniquity.[10]

Not only, however, does Fuller deny Hart's sharp distinction between the rules of morality and the rules of positive law, he also denies Hart's claim that the conflation of law and morality is more dangerous. As Hart argued, judges who confuse what the law is with what it ought to be have the tendency (or at least the power) to reorient otherwise good laws for their own subjective ends, which may have been far from the intention of the lawgivers themselves. As Fuller responds, however, whatever danger may exist by the presumption of law's deep connection to morality, the far greater danger comes as a result of presuming, in the interpretation of law, the irrelevance of morality for understanding the true meaning of a law. As he explains,

> let us suppose a judge bent on realizing through his decisions an objective that most ordinary citizens would regard as mistaken or evil. Would such

a judge be likely to suspend the letter of the statute by openly invoking a "higher law"? Or would he be more likely to take refuge behind the maxim that "law is law" and explain his decision in such a way that it would appear to be demanded by the law itself?[11]

Returning to Hart's own example of the post-Nazi court's decision to convict the woman for informing on her husband, Fuller responds that this actually underscores his point. As he interprets that court's decision, the woman's defense that she was simply acting in accordance with the positive law is rightly rejected only on the assumption that the Nazi law in question had no legally binding force and that it was, therefore, *not really a law* in any meaningful sense.[12] Hart prefers simply to call the Nazi law what it is, a morally wicked law which we have a legal, but not a moral, obligation to obey. For Fuller, however, this results in allowing the intolerable possibility that subjects will find themselves with conflicting obligations, one moral and one legal. On the assumption that law and morality are truly distinct, unrelated, or incommensurable, there remains no foothold by which to solve such a dilemma and so any proposed solution will be, in the end, arbitrary.

III

At first blush, it appears that, in comparison with that of H. L. A. Hart, the position of Lon Fuller is far more consistent with the natural law theory of Aquinas. To be sure, Hart's primary target is a dictum very much at the center of Thomistic natural law, namely, the notion that unjust laws are "no laws at all." Furthermore, Thomas would flatly reject the parallel obligations placed upon citizens by the positive law, on the one hand, and morality, on the other. For Aquinas, the moment one speaks of obligation one is already immersed in the waters of morality, so much the case that any obligation to obey the positive law is intelligible only on the premise that the positive law is anchored in the moral, or natural, law. As he explains,

> in human affairs a thing is said to be just, from being right, according to the rule of reason. But the first rule of reason is the law of nature, as is clear from what has been stated above (Q. 91, A. 2, ad 2). Consequently every human law has just so much of the nature of law, as it is derived from the law of nature. But if in any point it deflects from the law of nature, it is no longer a law but a perversion of law.[13]

From there, Aquinas goes on to make the well-known distinction between positive (or human) laws that are derived from the natural law as "conclusions from premises" and those which are derived "by way of determination." The first would concern positive laws that forbid things expressly forbidden by the natural law as well, such as murder and theft. The second concern things about which the natural law does not specify, such as on which side of the road we are to drive, what specific punishment will be for specific crimes, or even the extent to which our regime will be ruled democratically. Although Thomas admits that these second types of laws "have no other force than that of human law,"[14] it is crucial to notice that Aquinas's distinction in no way implies that some positive laws are derived from the natural law more than others. Conclusions and determinations, he says, are derived differently, but it remains that they are both derived from the natural law. In fact, once the positive law determines the traffic rules, writes a criminal code, and establishes its governing institutions, those norms become equally binding on citizens as are the prohibitions against theft and murder.[15]

But what about the dispute between Hart and Fuller regarding the interpretation or application of the positive law? Here, things are more complex. We may first observe that Aquinas would be doubtful at best with Fuller's intuition that the passage of time and the multiplication of judicial interpretations would naturally lead any legal system in the direction of moral goodness. Not that humans necessarily gravitate in the direction of "iniquity" either, but Aquinas never gives any indication that historical progress even so much as influences moral progress, whether in the interpretation of law, the act of legislating itself, or in any other dimension of human affairs. As John Finnis puts it in explaining this aspect of Aquinas's thought, "there is no reason to predict the triumph of good or evil in this world, whether in the long run or the medium term. Social theory's generality is not to be found in charting overall human progress, decline, or eternal returns."[16]

Aquinas's understanding of a judge's role in relation to the positive law gives us even more reason to think he would have backed away from Fuller's position, and possibly that he would have even landed, in this particular debate, more on the side of H. L. A. Hart. Upon examination, it is indeed surprising the extent to which Aquinas considers the judge beholden to the positive law, and even though the judge ought to be aware of the natural law, his judgments rarely appeal to this higher standard. As opposed to a legislator who would presumably direct his constant attention to the natural law from which all positive laws are derived, the judge stands one more step removed. As Russell Hittinger points out in *The First Grace: Rediscovering the Natural Law in a Post-Christian World*, the judge's removal from the natural law is made apparent by examining three different, but related, cases.[17] First, take the difficult case of the judge who knows that the accused is the victim of a false testimony. Aquinas explains as follows:

> If the judge knows that a man who has been convicted by false witness, is innocent he must, like Daniel, examine the witnesses with great care, so as to find a motive for acquitting the innocent: but if he cannot do this he should remit him for judgment by a higher tribunal. If even this is impossible, he does not sin if he pronounce sentence in accordance with the evidence, for it is not he that puts the innocent man to death, but they that stated him to be guilty. He that carries out the sentence of the judge who has condemned an innocent man, if the sentence contains an inexcusable error, he should not obey, else there would be an excuse for the executions of the martyrs: if, however, it contain no manifest injustice, he does not sin by carrying out the sentence, because he has no right to

discuss the judgment of his superior; nor is it he who slays the innocent man, but the judge whose minister he is.[18]

Alarming as it may seem, Aquinas's discussion of this scenario illustrates the weighty authority of positive law. Why is it that the judge may order a man he knows to be innocent to be killed? Because the law which the accused is charged with breaking is itself just. Granted, if the law was purely arbitrary, say, a superstitious law that required all those born on Friday the thirteenth to be killed, the judge would be required to withhold judgment. However, the flaw in this case is not with the law, but with the circumstances of the trial. Once the judge has exhausted all the possible means of exposing the fraudulent testimony (as Daniel was successfully able to do in uncovering the plot against Suzanna), he must honor the law by sentencing the man to death. Even in cases where the positive law manifestly fails to reach the right outcome, therefore, it may not be cast aside even by an appeal to natural justice.

But what about the case in which following the positive law would have disastrous results, not simply for one person, but for the community as a whole? Aquinas examines this possibility in his discussion of judgments that occur, as he says, outside the letter of the law. The examples are familiar. First, a law which requires the city gates to be closed clearly falls short in the emergency situation whereby a group of citizens are being pursued by the enemy.[19] Secondly, a law that requires deposits to be returned upon request is likewise lacking when a madman demands the return of his weapons with the stated intention of harming someone.[20] As Aquinas argues that a judge may act outside the letter of the law, it appears that he allows for positive law to be set aside for the sake of honoring the natural law. This is, however, not the case. The judicial virtue in question is what Aristotle called *epikeia*, by which judges (and indeed, even private citizens) act outside the written positive law. But does doing so indicate a preference for natural law, or natural justice, over the positive law? According to Aquinas, the answer is no. As Hittinger again points out, the judge is not exercising a presumed authority to invalidate the positive law in favor of the natural law. The laws in question are not unjust, they are (as all laws must be at some level) general. It is an unavoidable fact, however, that the more generally a law is stated, and the more instances it is able to cover, the more likely it may fail in given situations. For this reason, Aquinas makes it clear that by exercising the virtue of *epikeia*, the judge does not render judgment contrary to the law, but simply outside the letter of the law. In doing so, moreover, the judge in no way implies that the law was not well made. Generality, it appears, belongs to the nature of positive law and cannot be avoided. In rendering judgment outside the letter of the law the judge's guiding principle is not the natural law, but *the intention of the lawgiver*, who relies on the judge, not to correct his mistakes, but to apply his intended purpose to concrete situations. As Aquinas approvingly quotes Justinian's *Codex* in a reply to an objection, "he transgresses the law who by adhering to the letter of the law strives to defeat the intention of the lawgiver."[21]

Finally, what about situations in which judges are confronted with laws themselves that are manifestly unjust? As Aquinas explains, this might happen in two ways:

first, by running counter to the human good. Secondly, by contradicting the divine good. Any law, therefore, which commands one to commit murder or adultery, or forbids one from receiving the sacraments would fall into this category. Concerning those laws that contradict the divine good, such as laws of pagans requiring idolatry, Aquinas states bluntly that they should never be obeyed. Of those laws which contradict the human good, on the other hand, Aquinas says they may fall into any of three categories. First, they may be unjust with respect to their end, that is, because they are issued for the sake of someone's private interest rather than for the common good. Secondly, they may be unjust in respect of their author, as when the law is issued by someone without proper authority. Lastly, the law may go wrong in respect of its form, as when, Aquinas explains, "burdens are imposed unequally on the community, although with a view to the common good."[22] Now although these three examples of unjust laws are all subject to Augustine's dictum that "an unjust law is no law at all," Aquinas makes it clear that private citizens oftentimes ought to comply with the so-called law "in order to avoid scandal or disturbance." So even though one may live in a country that imposes confiscatory taxation upon the poor, for example, it may be better to comply with the statute even though it really amounts to nothing more than an act of violence.

But what about the responsibilities of the judge? One might expect Aquinas to give the judge license to correct the wicked law, or even to command one to violate it depending on the situation. This is not, however, what one finds. When confronted with laws constituting travesties of justice, Aquinas simply states that the judge must not render judgment, and this for a simple reason. Judges are beholden to the positive law, and since such acts of violence have no legal status properly speaking, the judge cannot render judgment according to them.[23] It is for this same exact reason, however, that the judge is powerless to change the law or to interpret the law in some other way that was intended by the lawgiver. Precisely because he is a servant of the positive law, his responsibilities presuppose a prior act of legislation.[24] Of course, if the judge is able to appeal to some higher law (such as a constitution) that the law before him contradicts, he may strike down the lower statute. But he does this not through an appeal to natural law or natural justice, but simply through an appeal to the higher positive law. One must further observe that for the judge to assume the role of a legislator would always result in laws that fall short of natural justice. Recall that, for Aquinas, one way of considering a law unjust is that, however well-intentioned or reasonable it may be, it is not rendered by legitimate authority.[25]

However much Professor Fuller's general understanding of the connection between law and morality coheres with Aquinas's natural law theory, therefore, it appears that Aquinas would have serious misgivings about the conclusions that Fuller draws regarding the interpretation of law. What would Aquinas think about Hart's example of the woman convicted under the post Nazi German court? Between punishing her retroactively (which Hart recommends) and engaging in the charade of trying her for violating a law that had little application to her case, Aquinas may well have recommended simply letting her go. Hart and Fuller would have, perhaps, done well to remember that an essential mark of human law (not to mention one of the reasons we need divine law) is that "it cannot punish or forbid all evil deeds."[26]

The University of Prince Edward Island
Charlottetown, PE

Notes

1. Dr. Martin Luther King, "Letter from Birmingham City Jail."

2. See, for instance, *ST*, I-II, Q. 95, a. 2 (corpus).

3. *Summa Theologiae* (*ST*), I-II, Q. 91, A. 1.

4. *ST*, I-II, 91.2.

5. *ST*, I-II, Q. 93, a. 3, ad 2; *ST*, I-II, Q. 96, a. 4 (corpus).

6. Hart, H. L. A., "Positivism and the Separation of Law and Morals," *Harvard Law Review* 71.4 (1958), 613.

7. Ibid., 619.

8. Ibid.

9. Ibid., 620.

10. Fuller, Lon, "Positivism and Fidelity to Law: A Reply to Professor Hart," *Harvard Law Review* 71.4 (1958), 636.

11. Ibid., 637.

12. Ibid., 655.

13. Thomas Aquinas, *Summa Theologiae*, trans. the Fathers of the English Dominican Province (Westminster, MD: Christian Classics, 1981), I-II, Q. 95, A. 2 (corpus)

14. Ibid.

15. See *ST*, I-II, Q. 96, A. 4

16. Finnis, John, *Aquinas: Moral, Political, and Legal Theory* (Oxford, 1998), 40.

17. Hittinger, F. Russell, *The First Grace: Rediscovering the Natural Law in a Post-Christian World* (Wilmington, DE: ISI Books, 2003), 104–112

18. *ST*, II-II, 64.6 ad 3

19. *ST*, I-II, 96.6

20. *ST*, II-II, 120.1

21. *ST*, II-II, 120.1 ad 1

22. *ST*, I-II, 96.4

23. *ST*, II-II, 60.5, ad 1

24. *ST*, II-II, 60.5 (corpus)

25. See not only *ST*, I-II, 96.4, but also *ST*, I-II, 90.3

26. *ST*, I-II, Q. 91, A. 4 (corpus)

Descartes as Catholic Philosopher and Natural Philosopher

Steven Baldner

Abstract: A Catholic philosophy requires an account of God as the first cause of all being. Descartes provides this, but he does so at a high price, for his Creator of ontologically and causally independent moments of creaturely existence precludes all secondary causes. Descartes's philosophy thus results in occasionalism, which I try to show is the unhappy result of errors in natural philosophy concerning material forms and duration. Suarez provides a contrasting scholastic account of creation, showing how novel, and problematic, Descartes's position is.

I t is a fair assumption that any Catholic philosophy must recognize God as the first cause. For confirmation of this assumption, we need look no farther than the great proponent of Christian philosophy, Etienne Gilson, who always insisted that any such philosophy must affirm that God is the cause of being.[1] To say that God is the cause of being is to say that God creates everything in the universe out of nothing, and this is equivalent to saying, as Descartes also maintains,[2] that God is causing everything to exist now and always out of nothing. Or, in other words, creation and conservation are equivalent terms. God right now is causing me and everything else in the universe to exist, and he is doing so by the sheer exercise of his efficient causality: God uses no instrumental or material causes, and God causes the entirety of every creature's being.

A second assumption comes from natural philosophy, but it is controversial, for it would be denied by some Catholic philosophers. The assumption is that whatever we say about God's causality cannot remove the natural, secondary causality that creatures possess. To say that God causes all being cannot mean that creatures are not also fully causes in the natural realm, however this might be defined. This assumption is needed if we are to hold that the natural sciences give us real knowledge about the world, but it is also needed to account for the free will and causality of rational creatures.[3]

The problem for this paper, then, is to show why Descartes cannot accept both of these assumptions, and he cannot do so, as I hope to show, because of fundamental mistakes in natural philosophy. In fact, Descartes consistently maintains the first claim, that God is the ongoing creator of all being, but he cannot consistently

© 2016, *Proceedings of the ACPA*, Vol. 89
doi: 10.5840/acpaproc2016113051

maintain the second claim of creaturely, secondary causality, and his position can be characterized as occasionalist. The focus of this paper will be on the argument that Descartes gives in *Meditation* III for the existence of God based on the nature of duration and God's continual re-creation. I will first explain this argument; second, I will contrast this argument with a similar sounding but in fact radically different scholastic argument in Suarez; and third, I will try to show that this argument rests on mistakes in natural philosophy.

Descartes's Argument for God from Duration

After giving at great length his well-known argument in *Meditations* III (1641) that God must exist, for only God could be the cause of the clear and distinct idea that I have of God, Descartes asks the question, "From what source, then, do I derive my existence?"[4] Could the source of my existence, Descartes asks, be something less perfect than God, perhaps myself? That is, could I have brought myself into existence? No, says Descartes, I could not have made myself, for if I had been the source of my own existence I would have given myself all perfections possible. And since I, who have the idea of God innately in me, have the idea of infinite perfection, I would have made myself infinitely perfect, in accord with this idea. That is, if I were giving myself existence, I would have made myself God. Clearly this has not been the result, and hence I can conclude that I did not cause myself.

In this meditation, Descartes thinks that it is fair to ask whether he would have given himself God's perfections, because he is in fact considering whether he has the power to make himself out of nothing (*ex nihilo*). If he had such power, surely he would also have the power to have made himself perfect, for it would be no more difficult to give himself God's perfections than it would have been to make himself out of nothing. The question of where his existence comes from is clearly for Descartes the question of creation.

And this point is made even clearer in what follows.

> I do not escape the force of these arguments by supposing that I have always existed as I do now, as if it followed from this that there was no need to look for any author of my existence. For a lifespan can be divided into countless parts, each completely independent of the others, so that it does not follow from the fact that I existed a little while ago that I must exist now, unless there is some cause which as it were creates me afresh at this moment—that is, which conserves me. For it is quite clear to anyone who attentively considers the nature of time that the same power and action are needed to conserve anything at each individual moment of its duration as would be required to create that thing anew if it were not yet in existence. Hence the distinction between conservation [*conservationem*] and creation is only a conceptual one, and this is one of the things that are evident by the natural light.[5]

Descartes argues, further, that if he had created himself, he would surely be aware of the power to do this, but he is aware of no such power. Nor could some other finite creature have done this, for such a finite creature, or a collection of several such, would have to have been able to cause Descartes himself and also the idea that he has of God, and, as has already been shown, no finite thing could be the cause of that idea. Hence, God must have been the cause of Descartes's existence.

Pierre Gassendi objects to this line of argument on the grounds that Descartes has confused two types of causes: the *causa secundum fieri* and the *causa secundum esse*.[6] The architect or the father is the cause of the coming to be of the thing (*causa secundum fieri*) but not the ongoing cause of being. On the other hand, God is the cause of being (*causa secundum esse*) of all things.[7] As such, Gassendi argues, God must logically always conserve exactly the same effect and not be producing new ones from instant to instant.

In response to this, Descartes points out that Gassendi has not appreciated the importance of the independence of the parts of time;[8] Gassendi has wrongly tried to pretend that the parts of time have some necessary connection. If, however, we correctly analyze time or duration (*de tempore seu duratione rei durantis*), we will see, as even Gassendi has to admit, that the individual moments of time are separate, one from another. The import of this is that the existent thing, as Gassendi does not deny, ceases to exist at each moment of time (*[non negas] rem durantem singulis momentis desinere esse*). As Descartes makes clear in his response to Gassendi, this argument is precisely about the nature of duration and the causal independence of each moment of duration.

In the *Principles of Philosophy* (1644), Descartes gives the same argument. The title of the paragraph in which the argument is given makes the point clear: "The fact that our existence has duration is sufficient to demonstrate the existence of God." The argument is the same as that in the *Meditations*.

> It will not be possible for anything to obscure the clarity of this proof, if we attend to the nature of time or of the duration of things. For the nature of time is such that its parts are not mutually dependent, and never coexist. Thus, from the fact that we now exist, it does not follow that we shall exist a moment from now, unless there is some cause—the same cause which originally produced us—which continually reproduces us, as it were, that is to say, which keeps us in existence.[9]

Again, Descartes says that this cause cannot be a power in us and it must, therefore, be God.

Three things are noteworthy about this argument for the existence of God. First, it is an argument that is based on a consideration of the nature of duration or time. It is an argument to demonstrate the existence of God on the basis of an effect, and the effect is the successive moments of duration. This argument is fundamentally different from the argument based on the idea of an infinitely perfect being in the Third Meditation; that, too, is an argument from effect to cause, but the effect in that case is the idea, the objective reality of which could not possibly be caused by a finite being. In this case, however, the effect is successive duration, and this effect will be found in any temporally existing creature, not just in the *res cogitans*.[10]

Second, the crucial thing to notice about duration, as Descartes is describing it, is that the successive moments of existence have *no causal connection one with another*. Because I, as an existent *res cogitans*, cannot cause the next moment in my life, some other cause (God) must be inferred to do the causing that I cannot do. And this lack of causal power applies not only to me but to all creatures subject to temporal duration.

Third, this is a kind of general argument for God's creation. Descartes demonstrates here, not just that God is the cause of one innate idea, but that God is the cause of all beings that exist temporally from moment to moment. Of course, God is causing each moment *ex nihilo*, because each moment is causally disconnected from its predecessor and its successor.

Suarez on Creation and Conservation

To get an appreciation of the novelty of Descartes's position, it will be helpful to consider the immediate scholastic context of Descartes's thought, at least insofar as Francisco Suarez (1548–1617) may be considered representative of that context.[11] Suarez's understanding of creation and conservation is fundamentally different from that of Descartes, and this difference can be seen especially in problems about the relation of creation to time. Suarez discusses creation at length in his *Metaphysical Disputations* and in doing so raises a number of questions directly relevant to Descartes's position.

First, Suarez tells us that the action of creating *ex nihilo* indicates no order to time.[12] The phrase *ex nihilo* indicates an order of nature and not an order of duration; thus, there is no implication that something created must have been brought into existence *after* non-existence. Each of Descartes's temporal moments is created after non-existence, as we have seen, but this, Suarez tells us, is not the essential meaning of creation. To say that God creates *ex nihilo* is to say that God causes existence without any material cause; it says nothing about temporal order: "It does not belong to the nature of creation that nothingness should precede it within some real duration; rather it belongs to the nature of creation only that nothingness should precede it in the conceptual and causal orders."[13]

Second, Suarez tells us that the act of creation is the simple giving of being as a simultaneous whole and not successively. "Creation is not effected successively, but is instead effected as a simultaneous whole and indivisibly."[14] Some, Suarez notes, object to this by trying to make a distinction between creation and conservation, such that the act of creation is effected as a simultaneous whole but conservation is effected successively.[15] Suarez responds that this objection is based on a false notion that creatures necessarily exist in some successive mode of duration. This, Suarez notes, is obviously false in the case of immaterial substances, and hence cannot be taken to be an essential element of the meaning of conservation.

Third, Suarez explains that he follows the position of Thomas Aquinas in see-ing that there is really no difference between the act of creation and conservation.[16] A number of objections to Suarez's position seem to reflect exactly the position of Descartes: that conserving things in being amounts to re-creating them from instant to instant. Suarez, however, argues that, if one objects to the distinction of creation from conservation on the grounds that conservation is conserving things in *succes-sive* instants, the view of time involved in such an objection—that of successively distinct instants—is simply a mistaken view of time.[17] It is wrong, Suarez argues, to regard time as successively discrete, because it is by nature a continuous reality.

> I reply that one and the same continuous time is sufficient for a mo-tion's being the same and, consequently, for an action's being the same. But the present instant, at which the creation is effected, is conjoined continuously with the subsequent time during which the conservation endures—continuously, I mean, in the way in which an indivisible ter-minus can be joined immediately to something divisible. Therefore, this is sufficient for the actions' [creation and conservation] being the same.[18]

Since there is no succession in the terminus of God's act or in the acquisition of the terminus, there is no succession in the action. The terminus is "an indivisible substantival *esse*."[19] Suarez says that one could imagine God's creating, annihilating, and re-creating the same angel—in such a case, these would be distinct acts. This, however, is *not* like creation, because creation is not a successive series of actions but a single continuous action.[20] Interestingly, Suarez allows for the possibility that God could, if He wished, re-create the same effect by different acts.[21] For example, God could have re-created the same angel at a succession of different moments by successively different acts. The acts would be different, but the effect, taken as a collection of events, would be the same. Suarez mentions this as a false but logi-cally possible position; let us note that this false position is very similar to that of Descartes. Descartes imagines that God creates the same or very similar things by distinct acts of creation, successively throughout time.

Fourth, Suarez tells us that the necessity of recognizing conservation comes, not from the successively discrete moments of time, but from the fact that all creatures participate in *esse* and need a cause of *esse* as long as they exist.[22] Unlike Descartes, but like Thomas Aquinas, Suarez argues for the ongoing causality of God's giving of being. Since creatures only participate in being, their being must be caused as long as they exist. This fact has nothing to do with their temporal duration and everything to do with the fact that creatures do not have being from their very nature.

Fifth, and finally, Suarez develops his famous doctrine of concurrentism,[23] a doctrine that, for reasons I hope will become clear, is entirely absent in Descartes's philosophy. In addition to the conservation of creation, Suarez holds that God also concurs in all creaturely actions. Every time a creature acts, God also acts—concur-rently with the creature. It is not enough that God makes and continues to make the creature to be, for God must also cooperatively and separately cause every action performed by any creature. If I chop wood, God concurs in that action, which is to say that God and I jointly cause the action of chopping. The chopping is only *one* action, but it has two concurrent causes, God and me. Each is fully the cause of the effect in its own order, for the effect would not occur without both causes.

One of the crucial features of concurrentism, as understood by Suarez, is that each concurrent act is a separate act of God. "For God concurs with [secondary causes] in such a way as to accommodate himself to each according to its need. Thus, just as he grants numerically distinct concurrences for numerically diverse effects, so too he grants concurrences that are distinct in species for actions that are diverse in species."[24] This feature is what distinguishes God's concurrence from conservation. Conservation is not a series of repeated acts; as we have seen, it is one and the same act with God's creation. Concurrence, however, is a series of different divine acts. By one single act, God makes and conserves an entire universe; by innumerable distinct acts God concurs with each individual creaturely action. Suarez, thus, insists that God's series of acts is *not* a series of recreations, as in Descartes's account of God's creation. Suarez's concurrentism is a series of divine actions within the context of an already existing universe.

The point of this excursus into Suarez's doctrine of creation is to show how radically different Descartes's position is from that of his Scholastic forebears.[25] For Suarez, creation is essentially unrelated to time or a temporal beginning, but for Descartes, each re-creation of things is a temporal beginning; for Suarez, creation or conservation is one continuous act across all time, but for Descartes it is a series of different acts; for Suarez, ongoing creation is implied by creaturely contingence in being, but for Descartes it is required by the fact of successive duration; and for Suarez, the full causality of secondary causes is guaranteed by the doctrine of concurrence, which is notably absent in Descartes.

Descartes's Occasionalism

Clearly, from his argument for continual re-creation or conservation, Descartes has a doctrine of God's ongoing causality. God is the continual cause of the existence of creatures. The question is whether Descartes also can allow for creatures to be true, secondary causes. The answer to this question is "no" for two reasons we shall now explore.

First, Descartes has an exiguous ontology, especially so in the case of corporeal substances. Matter is *nothing* other than extended being in three dimensions that can be moved. There is nothing else to be said about matter. As Daniel Garber and other scholars have noted, in ridding matter of substantial and accidental forms, Descartes is left with matter that is, of itself, completely inert. It can be moved, but it cannot cause motion. When Descartes explains his Laws of Nature concerning motion, he says that God is both the initial cause of motion and also the "preserver of motion in matter." These Laws of Nature are derived, Descartes tell us, from God's immutability. The Second Law is especially relevant: "Every piece of matter, considered in itself, always tends to continue moving, not in any oblique path but only in a straight line." The reason is revealing:

> The reason for this second rule is . . . the immutability and simplicity of the operation by which God preserves motion in matter. For he always preserves the motion in the precise form in which it is occurring at the very moment when he preserves it, without taking any account of the motion which was occurring a while earlier.[26]

Garber's comment on this is instructive:

> God stands behind the world of bodies and is the direct cause of their motion. In the old Aristotelian philosophy, the characteristic behavior of bodies was explained through substantial forms; in Descartes's new, up-to-date mechanism, forms are out, and God is in; in Descartes's new philosophy, the characteristic behavior of bodies is explained in terms of an immutable God sustaining the motion of bodies.[27]

God, as Garber says, was brought in by Descartes to do what the substantial forms of Descartes's teachers were no longer available to do.

Second, Descartes's understanding of God's re-creating of creatures from moment to moment makes it impossible for any secondary causality to bridge from one moment to the next. The interpretation of Descartes's argument has been a matter of dispute among scholars, in large part because it has occasioned a debate over whether Descartes does or does not hold an atomistic view of time, but the essential point is this. Regardless of how Descartes understands the "moment" of time, whether it is an indivisible instant or whether it is a short period of duration, the argument from the nature of time to the existence of God depends upon the absolute causal separation between moments of duration in the actually existent thing. That is, no creaturely efficient cause is capable of exerting its causality from one moment to the next. It is precisely for this reason that God's causality is required, for only God can cause the next instant. Only God can do this, because the immediate context of the next moment is precisely non-being. For a creature to be able to operate on the second moment would require that the creature exist at the second moment, but the second moment, until created *ex nihilo* by God, does not exist.

Peter Machamer and J. E. McGuire have seen this point clearly in a recent important study of Descartes.

> If God conserves the existence of material substances by re-creating them successively in independent moments of time, by the same action he re-creates their natures independently of each of the prior moments in which they have already existed. Moreover, if, as Descartes holds, there is only a modal distinction between the particular modes of bodies and their principal attribute, God's act of re-creating them, together with their principal attribute, determines all their modes independently of all prior

> moments in which they exist. . . . Accordingly, in Descartes's material
> world . . . there is room neither for secondary efficient causes understood
> in the traditional Scholastic senses that involve substantial forms, nor for
> acts of transeunt causation between bodies acting across time.[28]

These two reasons, in turn, stand on two mistakes in natural philosophy. Briefly, I shall mention each mistake.

First, Descartes, like all of his followers in modern philosophy, rejects Aristotelian hylomorphism and what he takes to be the Scholastic doctrine of substantial and accidental forms. As I have indicated, these are replaced by a very simple material ontology, such that matter is extension in three dimensions, and all modes of matter, including motion, quantities, and qualities, are explained entirely in these simple, geometric terms. The result is a completely inert matter. But why did Descartes reject the doctrine of form and matter?

This is a much larger problem than we can deal with here, but the fundamental point is this. Descartes reduced all corporeal causality into one kind of cause: efficient causality. And the efficient cause of bodies is always, without exception, a cause of motion. This way of understanding causality always pervaded Descartes's thinking, even when, in his younger days, he was trying to understand the scholastic idea of form. Thus, when he was presented with the scholastic quality of "heaviness" (*gravitas*), he thought of it as an identifiable *thing* that could make a body fall down.[29] Heaviness, he used to think, was a kind of substance that could be affixed in various ways to a body, just as clothing is a kind of substance that can be worn in different ways. Heaviness was a thing that could be diffused throughout a body or could be concentrated in one point.[30] In either case, it operated as an efficient cause. And what Descartes thought about qualitative forms such as heaviness was also what he thought about his version of the substantial form of man: the soul or the mind. The human soul or mind is an efficient cause of the body. The problem for Descartes in thinking about such a form in the non-human case, is to think of an efficient cause for which there is no empirical evidence. If, in fact, as Descartes thought, the motion of all bodies can be explained entirely mechanistically in terms of the transfer of quantities of motion, the supposition of invisible efficient causes would be entirely gratuitous and have no explanatory value.

This mistake, I would argue, is that of thinking of forms as though they were efficient causes. Aristotelian forms, however, do not push or pull material bodies to their natural places; they are, rather, the various expressions of the body's nature. Because of form, it makes sense to think of matter as having tendencies, natural motions, and inherent activities. But these forms do not efficiently cause any motions. Heavy bodies tend to fall downward, but they are not being pushed or pulled by their accidental or substantial forms.

The second mistake concerns Descartes's thinking about duration and time. There has been a lively scholarly debate about whether Descartes has an atomistic or a discontinuous view of time, on the one hand, or whether, on the other, he regards time as continuous.[31] The intricacies of this debate need not concern us, but let me note three things. First, Descartes is accustomed to distinguishing time from duration.[32] Time is a mode of thought and, as such, might be understood variously: atomistic in some senses but continuous in others. As a mode of thought time may be considered in different ways. Duration, however, is objectively in corporeal things, and duration is a mode of existence for all creatures, whether corporeal or incorporeal. The import of the argument from re-creation concerns the real, successive duration of things. And the moments of this successive duration must, I maintain, be understood to be ontologically and causally separate one from another. If they are not so understood, the argument from re-creation would fail utterly in demonstrating the existence of a First Cause.

Second, some of the debate about time is a debate about whether or not Descartes regarded causes as temporally simultaneous with their effects. On this point, I agree with those who argue that Descartes does maintain, along with his Scholastic teachers, that causes and effects must be temporally simultaneous. In fact, I would say, it is this doctrine that gives the re-creation argument its force. Precisely because causes must be simultaneous with their effects, it is impossible for creatures to exercise any real causality from one moment of duration to the next. Because the moments are discrete, separate, or discontinuous, the cause in one moment is powerless to effect anything in the next moment. Only God can cause the second moment, and he must cause it entirely from nothing.

Third, because he thinks of duration as discontinuous, Descartes must regard duration, and hence motion, as only apparently but not really continuous. There should, however, be no great surprise about this. It is notoriously difficult to think about motion, for any clear and distinct ideas we might have will be static and fixed, but the reality of motion is of something flowing and continuous. Aristotle's attempt, which Descartes abominated, to grasp the reality of motion as the act of the potential insofar as it is potential is an attempt to define or explain motion without including the *definiendum* in the *definiens* and without explaining motion away.[33] Such an attempt, however, will always fail to gain entry into Cartesian metaphysics. For his part, Descartes understands that there can be no such thing as motion in an instant,[34] but there would be no reason why motion, from Descartes's point of view, could not be described as a series of moments. This mistaken, mathematical or metaphysical, view of time (and hence of motion) makes possible the sort of re-creationist argument that Descartes has been giving, and allows for an understanding of motion and duration in terms that are clear and distinct. And such a view of duration and motion surely is clear and distinct, but mistaken.

Conclusion

I have attempted to show that Descartes's re-creationist argument is a failure for a Catholic philosophy. If a Catholic philosophy requires both that God be the complete cause of being and also that creatures be true secondary causes, Descartes has succeeded in showing the first but failed in showing the second. But his way of understanding God's causality is faulty, and faulty because of mistakes in natural philosophy. It is a mistake to think that all causality can be reduced to efficient causes and that substantial and accidental forms are efficient causes; it is also a mistake to think of time, duration, and motion as composed of discrete parts. Philosophers are much less likely to make such mistakes if they settle important problems in natural philosophy before they attempt metaphysics.

St. Francis Xavier University
Antigonish, Nova Scotia, Canada

Notes

1. Etienne Gilson, *Christian Philosophy*, trans. Armand Maurer (Toronto: Pontifical Institute of Mediaeval Studies, 1993), 14–23.

2. René Descartes, *Meditations* III (AT 7:48–49). References to Descartes will be to the standard critical edition, *Oeuvres de Descartes*, ed. Charles Adam and Paul Tannery (Paris: Vrin, 1996). The standard abbreviation, AT, will be given, followed by volume number and, after a colon, page number. Whenever a translation is given, it will be taken from *The Philosophical Writings of Descartes*, Vols. I and II, trans. John Cottingham, Robert Stoothoff, and Dugald Murdoch (Cambridge: Cambridge University Press, 1985), cited as CSM, followed by volume and page number.

3. Briefly, if occasionalism is true, then the scientific knowledge that we gain about the world is not knowledge about any causality that really exists in the world. On such a view, the apparent causes we see in nature are merely reflections of God's causality. We could thus get no causal knowledge about the material world, if occasionalism were true. In the case of human will and action, the problem for Descartes is that the sort of occasionalism his position implies would make it impossible for rational agents to exert any causality at all, not on the material world and not even on the mental world. And Descartes does recognize that human sensation and action require interaction between mind and bodies (see, for example, *Meditations* IV and VI), but the burden of this paper will be to show that Descartes cannot consistently affirm creaturely causality, even in the case of mind-body interactions.

4. The argument I am considering is found in *Meditations* III (AT 7:48–49).

5. AT 7:48–49; CSM 2:33. Note, I have changed "preserves," "preserve," and "preservation" in this passage to "conserves," "conserve," and "conservation."

6. This is Descartes's report of Gassendi's objection (AT 7:369).

7. The sun, too, is the ongoing cause of the existence of living things—in this sense, it is also for Gassendi a cause of being rather than merely a cause of the coming to be of the thing.

8. AT 7:369–370.

9. *Principles of Philosophy* I.21 (AT 8:13; CSM 1:200).

10. It might be objected that purely immaterial beings, such as angels, are not temporal beings. This is true, but, in fact, Descartes regards duration as a mode of existence for all creatures, including angels and thinking things. The duration in things that move and do not move is essentially the same: *Principles* I.57 (AT 8:27; CSM 1:212).

11. Tad Schmaltz, *Descartes on Causation* (Oxford: Oxford University Press, 2008), 24–48, makes a convincing case for the consideration of Suarez as the scholastic background to Descartes's thought.

12. *DM* 20.5.11. All references to Suarez are to his *Disputationes Metaphysicae*, 2 vols. (Hildersheim: George Olms, 1965) reprint from *Opera Omnia*, ed. C. Berton, vol. 26 (Paris, 1866). English translations will be taken from *On Creation, Conservation, and Concurrence: Metaphysical Disputations 20–22*, trans. A. J. Freddoso (South Bend, IN: St. Augustine's Press, 2002), cited as "Freddoso." Suarez's analysis of the meaning of *ex nihilo* here is taken from Thomas Aquinas; see, for example, Thomas's *Commentary* on the *Sentences* of Peter Lombard, 2 *Sent.* 1.1.2.

13. *DM* 20.5.19 (Freddoso, 104)..

14. *DM* 20.5.12 (Freddoso, 100).

15. *DM* 20.5.13 (Freddoso, 100).

16. *DM* 21.2.2–3. There is only a conceptual distinction between these two terms: *DM* 21.2.7 (Freddoso, 125). For Thomas, see *Summa theologiae* 1.104.1.ad4; *De potentia Dei* 3.3.ad6; 5.1.ad2.

17. *DM* 21.2.3.

18. *DM* 21.2.4 (Freddoso, 123).

19. *DM* 21.2.4 (Freddoso, 123).

20. *DM* 21.2.6.

21. *DM* 21.2.6.

22. *DM* 21.1.6–15. For Thomas Aquinas's similar position, see 2 *Sent.* 1.2.2; *De potentia Dei*, 3.1.ad11, *Summa theologiae* 1.44.1.

23. *DM* 22. An entire Disputation is devoted to this important topic.

24. *DM* 22.4.8 (Freddoso, 220).

25. Again, I take the liberty of making Suarez the representative of this tradition. I am well aware that Suarez does not speak for late scholastic Thomists, with whom he disputed, nor for figures like Durandus. It is known that Descartes was influenced by Suarez, and the differences between Suarez and other scholastics is not relevant to the points at issue. Thomists, for example, would not think that a doctrine of concurrence would be needed, or they would express it differently, but they would insist, as much as Suarez, on the full role of creaturely secondary causes.

26. *Principles* II.40 (AT 8:63–64; CSM 1:242).

27. Daniel Garber, "Descartes and Occasionalism" in *Causation in Early Modern Philosophy*, ed. Steven Nadler (University Park: Pennsylvania State University Press, 1993), 14.

28. Peter Machamer and J. E. McGuire, *Descartes's Changing Mind* (Princeton: Princeton University Press, 2009), 116.

29. This is explained in Descartes's *Sixth Replies* (AT 7:441–442).

30. See Daniel Garber's discussion of this: *Descartes' Metaphysical Physics* (Chicago: University of Chicago Press, 1992, 95–103).

31. The commonly held view that Descartes has an atomistic theory of time can be found in Norman Kemp Smith, *Studies in Cartesian Philosophy* (NY: Russell & Russell,

1902), 72–74 and 128–132; and *New Studies in the Philosophy of Descartes* (London: Macmillan, 1952), 202–203. Against this view a number of recent studies have argued either that Descartes had no definite position on this topic or that he held a continuous view of time: Richard T. W. Arthur, "Continuous Creation, Continuous Time: A Refutation of the Alleged Discontinuity of Cartesian Time," *Journal of the History of Philosophy* 26 (1988): 349–375; J. E. K Secada, "Descartes on Time and Causality," *The Philosophical Review* 99 (1990): 45–72; Geoffrey Gorham, "Descartes on Time and Duration," *Early Science and Medicine* 12 (2007): 28–54. Machamer and McGuire, *Descartes's Changing Mind*, chap. 4, argue, as I do, that the moments of duration must be ontologically and causally discrete.

32. *Principles* 1.57 (AT 8:26–27).

33. *The World*, 7 (AT 11: 39); *Rules for the Direction of the Mind*, 12 (AT 10: 426).

34. *Principles* II.39 (AT 8:64).

Is Mandatory Autonomy Education in the Best Interests of Children?[1]

Melissa Moschella

Abstract: In this paper I argue that liberal proponents of mandatory autonomy education tend to overlook or underestimate the potential threats that such an education poses to the overall well-being of children (including, ironically, threats to the development of genuine autonomy). They do so by paying insufficient attention to the importance of moral virtue as a constitutive element of and pre-condition for genuine autonomy, and by failing to recognize how the development and consolidation of moral virtue may be undermined by the sort of autonomy education they recommend. I develop my argument through engagement with the work of Eamonn Callan and Ian MacMullen, drawing on Aristotelian ethics to highlight the shortcomings in their accounts.

Introduction

Many philosophers and political theorists have argued that due regard for the future well-being of children requires providing them with an education that promotes autonomy,[2] understood as "the capacity for and commitment to ongoing rational reflection on all of one's ethical commitments,"[3] as well as the capacity for reasonable adherence to those commitments.[4] Generally speaking, autonomy education includes elements like exposure to diverse worldviews, engagement with criticisms of one's own worldview, and the development of critical thinking skills. It is argued that autonomy education should be required in schools even (or perhaps particularly) when parents would prefer to shelter their children from competing conceptions of the good, given autonomy's instrumental (and on some accounts also intrinsic) importance for a good life. Here I challenge this view from a child-centered perspective. In this paper I do not question the soundness of liberal arguments regarding the importance of autonomy. Rather, my criticism of liberal arguments for mandatory autonomy education is that they tend to overlook or underestimate the potential dangers of such an education for the overall well-being of children (including, ironically, dangers to the development of genuine autonomy). They do so by paying insufficient attention to the importance

© 2016, *Proceedings of the ACPA*, Vol. 89
doi: 10.5840/acpaproc201713159

of moral virtue as a constitutive element of and precondition for genuine autonomy, and by failing to recognize how the development and consolidation of moral virtue may be undermined by autonomy education particularly when such an education leads children to question the values taught at home. I develop my argument through critical engagement with the work of Eamonn Callan and Ian MacMullen. I focus on Callan and MacMullen because they show greater awareness of the potential dangers of autonomy education than most liberal authors, but still, as I will argue below, fail to recognize the full extent of those dangers and thus the full weight of the child-centered arguments against mandatory autonomy education even during adolescence.

Callan and MacMullen as Moderate Defenders of Liberal Autonomy Education

While both Callan and MacMullen do ultimately argue that respect for the future well-being of children requires mandatory autonomy education, they do so more cautiously than most, and recognize that there may be good reasons for delaying at least some aspects of autonomy education until secondary school.[5] In *Creating Citizens*, Callan makes it clear that autonomy education should be mandatory at least at some stage, in order to ensure that children achieve a minimal threshold of autonomy that he believes is necessary for a good life.[6] Yet elsewhere Callan criticizes other liberal theorists for focusing on developing children's capacity for autonomous *revision* of their conception of the good, while largely overlooking the equally-important capacity for autonomous *adherence* to a conception of the good.[7] Callan goes on to argue that teaching children the steadfastness necessary for adherence to a conception of the good may require, "shielding children from experiences one believes would confuse or corrupt them, engaging them in activities whose presuppositions they do not yet grasp, instilling beliefs whose grounds remain for some time unexamined."[8] Education that aims at promoting autonomy may place so much emphasis on the need to be committed to remaining open to rational revision of one's conception of the good that it could end up encouraging children to drift from one conception of the good to another, leading them to develop the habit of abandoning an ideal the moment a more attractive option appears (perhaps more attractive simply because of its novelty).

Concerns along these lines also lead MacMullen to recognize that there is a positive case for sending a pre-adolescent child to schools that "harmonise with and reinforce the ethical messages she receives at home."[9] One of the reasons against sending children to schools that will undermine the values they are taught at home is that it can result in moral confusion and "disturb the young child's fragile sense of self."[10] MacMullen cites psychological evidence, based on the work of James Marcia, that supports this point. Liberals usually worry about the situation of children whom Marcia categorizes as "Foreclosures," those whose commitments have been chosen entirely by parents in a way that effectively forecloses a real possibility for revision, due to "strong parental pressure to conform to family values."[11] However, another group that scored equally low in terms of self-directedness was what Marcia called the "Identity Diffusions." Those in this group have a hard time maintaining any set of beliefs over time and are "'easily influenced by others,'" precisely because they have "not developed the ability to make personal commitments."[12] What this research shows, according to MacMullen, is that "our efforts to avoid Foreclosure must not disrupt the coherence of the child's primary culture to the extent that she develops into an Identity Diffusion, lacking an understanding of the nature and value of personal commitments."[13] MacMullen's argument thus echoes and supports Callan's point that we need to be equally concerned about children's development of the capacity for autonomous *adherence* as we are about their development of the capacity for autonomous *revision*. Yet they still believe that, given autonomy's importance for well-being, autonomy education should be required at least at some stage in a child's education.

MacMullen balances concerns about the disruption of a child's primary culture with concerns about the importance of enabling children to become autonomous by recommending that mandatory autonomy education should not involve a challenge to the values taught at home until secondary school. On the basis of Jean Piaget's theory of cognitive development, MacMullen argues that before the age of eleven or twelve "it would be futile to try to move children beyond the limited practice of reason-giving within a fixed ethical framework."[14] Further, when schools reinforce, rather than challenge, the values that young children are taught at home, this provides the "secure grounding in a coherent primary culture" that is important for helping children to grasp "the nature and value of personal commitment" and to avoid "the kind of listlessness that can all too easily inhibit autonomy just as much as lack of critical reflection."[15] In other words, sending children to primary schools in line with parents' values (and thus sheltering them to a considerable extent from competing conceptions of the good) can prevent them from developing into Identity Diffusions or, in Callan's terms, from failing to develop the capacity for autonomous adherence to a conception of the good. Once they have reached the age at which they are intellectually capable of abstract ethical reflection, however, MacMullen believes that respect for children's autonomy interests requires that they be sent to schools in which they will be confronted with competing conceptions of the good.

Though correct to recognize the potentially pernicious effects on children of premature exposure to conflicting conceptions of the good life, MacMullen is too quick to dismiss the persistence of those dangers even into the adolescent years. It is true that by early adolescence children typically begin to exhibit a capacity to engage in formal, abstract thought, and that this capacity is a prerequisite for autonomous ethical reflection.[16] Yet the prerequisites for autonomy (and for leading a good life) are not only cognitive, but also *moral*. Attentiveness to the importance of moral virtue and the conditions for its development can help us to see why, even in secondary school, many children may not be prepared to profit from autonomy education, despite their intellectual capacity for abstract thought.

An Aristotelian Account of the
Moral Prerequisites for Autonomy

An Aristotelian understanding of moral virtue, the conditions for its development, and its relationship to the capacity for sound ethical decision-making, helps to expose some important gaps in the accounts of Callan and MacMullen. In particular, it shows how they (1) fail to give due importance to the ways in which sub-rational desire can undermine the capacity for truly rational revision of and adherence to one's ethical commitments, and (2) do not seriously consider how mandatory autonomy education, even in secondary school, might hinder or undermine the development of a mature moral character in which sub-rational desire is governed by and in harmony with reason.

On Aristotle's view, moral virtue involves the education of sub-rational desire under the guidance of reason. The ability to desire, choose, and act in accordance with reason requires a mature moral character, developed over time through the repeated performance of virtuous actions. Initially, such virtuous actions are non-autonomous, motivated not by a rational grasp of the goodness of one's action, but often by fear of punishment, desire for a reward, or love of one's parents or other educators. Nonetheless, by becoming habituated to act in accordance with virtue "from our very youth,"[17] we train desire to obey reason, even to the extent that, in the fully virtuous person, "it speaks, on all matters, with the same voice as reason."[18] By contrast, Aristotle speaks of those without virtue as riddled with profound internal divisions, describing them as inwardly "rent by faction." Those who lack mastery over their sub-rational desires "choose, instead of the things they themselves think good, things that are pleasant but hurtful," and "shrink from doing what they think best for themselves."[19] Such persons are clearly not autonomous and lack the prerequisites for leading a good life. Even if they are capable of and committed to ongoing rational reflection about their conception of the good, and even if they are capable of (cognitive) adherence to their ethical commitments, they are not consistently able to act in accordance with those commitments. This is an aspect of autonomy that neither Callan nor MacMullen emphasizes, but it is essential, both as a constitutive aspect of autonomy, and, as I will argue, as a prerequisite for the cognitive aspects of autonomy.

Lack of moral virtue not only threatens one's ability to act in accordance with one's ethical commitments, but also threatens one's ability to make sound ethical judgments in the first place. Practical reason—reason as directed toward acting or making—is, like theoretical reason, a capacity that needs to be developed and perfected. The perfection of practical reason as directed toward acting (*praxis*) is what Aristotle calls *phronesis*, practical wisdom.[20] Yet practical wisdom is inseparable from moral virtue, because following the dictates of reason and even being able to reason correctly about ethical matters requires disciplining one's desires and appetites. According to Aristotle, "it is impossible to be practically wise without being good [i.e., morally virtuous]."[21] For, as Aristotle explains, practical reasoning presupposes a starting-point, a first principle indicating that which is worthy of pursuit, and such principles are "not evident except to the good man; for wickedness perverts us and causes us to be deceived about the starting-points of action."[22] For instance, a virtuous person's ethical deliberations will evaluate potential choices and actions with reference to goods that are inherently choiceworthy, such as friendship or knowledge, while someone who lacks virtue will evaluate choices and actions with reference to the gratification of sub-rational desires, and may not even be able to grasp the intrinsic goods that are at stake. Even when it is not a matter of deciding how to act in a particular circumstance, but of reasoning more broadly about one's values and commitments, sub-rational desires can play a powerful, if often sub-conscious, role. A fourteen-year-old, annoyed by what he perceives as exaggerated parental restrictions regarding, for instance, the movies he is allowed to watch, will be all too eager to criticize the value system that motivates his parents to enforce those restrictions, and to embrace a competing one, regardless of the genuine merits of each. Every worldview has at least apparent internal contradictions. If one has sub-rational motivations for dismissing that worldview (because, for instance, it condemns conduct in which one desires to engage), one can easily take the presence of such apparent contradictions to be a decisive reason against adhering to it, without undertaking the difficult task of exploring further to see whether or not those contradictions are real or merely apparent.

Unlike the virtue of practical wisdom, which has both moral and intellectual aspects, critical thinking skills are morally neutral, insofar as they can be used both to provide a rational defense of a genuinely good way of life, and to rationalize morally deficient ways of life. While there will objectively be a better argument in favor of the genuinely good way of life, we are all too familiar with the ways in which a person who lacks moral virtue—a person who is in the habit of acting based on sub-rational desires rather than on a reasoned understanding of what is actually good—can be highly skilled at providing rational justifications for actions that are in fact not fully reasonable. For reason to be an effective tool in distinguishing good from bad ways of life, moral virtue is necessary. Even adolescents who have the *cognitive* aspects of the capacity for ethical reflection and choice, therefore, may lack the *moral* aspects of that capacity, insofar as their judgments (as well as their choices and actions) are distorted by sub-rational desire.

Psychological and neurobiological studies likewise indicate that, while intellectually adolescents demonstrate a sophisticated capacity for rational reflection, their decision-making is marred by short-sightedness and a much higher tendency to impulsivity and immediate gratification than adults. In line with Aristotelian theory, this research indicates not simply that adolescents are prone to act against their better judgment, but that their judgment itself is skewed by these sub-rational factors. For instance, "adolescents, in weighing the costs and benefits involved in a decision, tend to weigh proximate benefits more highly and more distal costs lower than do most persons over the age of twenty-one."[23] Further, brain imaging has revealed that, in those under eighteen, decision-making predominantly engages the limbic structures (the neurological seat of emotion), while for those over twenty-one, activity of the pre-frontal cortex (involved in reasoning) predominates.[24] Overall, the neurobiological evidence indicates that "the areas of the brain involved in mature executive decisions, that is, those necessary for the realization of reasonable and responsible choices," are still underdeveloped in adolescents, and that this neurobiological immaturity can significantly undermine the reliability of their judgment.[25]

A complementary psychological explanation of the differences between adult and adolescent decision-making focuses not on the more emotional and impulsive nature of adolescents' decisions, but instead on their tendency to lack insight into the "gist" of a situation.[26] Studies show that adolescents tend to make decisions based on a more literal and piecemeal analysis of information, in which they may often miss the forest for the trees, while adults tend to decide based on a "gist representation," an "interpretation that extracts the important nub of information."[27] An adolescent undergoing chemotherapy, for instance, may accurately assess the risks and rewards of drinking at a party, and judge that, for her, the social benefits of drinking outweigh the cost of undermining the effectiveness of her treatment. A mature adult, by contrast, would not even enter into such a cost-benefit analysis, for even to consider a trade-off between minor social benefits and survival would reflect a "fundamental failure of insight," an inaccurate or absent gist representation.[28] This research dovetails nicely with Aristotle's emphasis on the need for experience and moral maturity in order to grasp and order correctly the relevant human goods that are at stake in a particular decision, as well as the idea that over time the virtuous person develops the ability simply to "see" what ought to be done without the need for deliberation.[29]

Application of the Aristotelian Account to the Issue of Autonomy Education

The Aristotelian account, backed by psychological and neurobiological research, gives us several reasons to be wary of the claim that most adolescents will benefit, on balance, from criticism of their family's values and exposure to competing points of view. First of all, a cafeteria-style offering of different conceptions of the good life, in which none is presented as inherently superior to any of the others, can simply be an invitation to pick and choose elements of different conceptions insofar as they enable one to justify the indulgence of sub-rational desires. This is, of course, a temptation for someone at any stage of life. For the person of mature moral character, however, the long-standing habits of self-governance in accordance with reason afford an ability to think critically about different conceptions of the good life, and to revise views in accordance with reason and moral experience, rather than having the reasoning process be distorted by sub-rational desire or lack of moral insight. A child who has not yet achieved a stable self-dominion with reference to some conception of the good, or an adolescent who is only beginning to achieve that dominion, does not have the inner moral resources—the moral virtues—that are prerequisites for the ability to make fully reasonable judgments about conceptions of the good life. It seems to be precisely for these reasons that Aristotle thinks that ethics can be taught only to people of mature moral character, with sufficient life experience, for only "those who desire and act in accordance with a rational principle" will benefit from the study of ethics.[30]

Secondly, the fact that adolescents' reasoning tends to be distorted by sub-rational factors and lack of moral insight—and that they themselves generally do not recognize this—implies that adolescents still need authoritative parental guidance, including clear and consistently-enforced rules of conduct. Yet autonomy education aims in part at undermining the influence and authority of parents. Since practical wisdom depends on the prior acquisition of moral virtue, but moral virtue is developed through the education of desire by habitually acting as the practically wise person would act, the development and consolidation of moral virtue involves obedience to authority—relying on the practical reason of others who are more practically wise than oneself. Of course adolescents should be given more freedom to make their own decisions than younger children, as this experience is necessary for the development of their own practical reasoning capacity, but clear boundaries are still necessary to protect them from the impulsivity, short-sightedness and inexperience that tend to cloud their judgment.

Studies on parenting styles corroborate this claim, indicating that authoritative parenting—characterized by a blend of responsiveness and demandingness, with clear and firm standards of behavior but also respect for their children's individuality and encouragement of dialogue—produces the best outcomes not only in early childhood but in adolescence as well. According to the typology that developed out of the work of Diana Baumrind, authoritative parenting is contrasted with three other parenting types: (1) authoritarian parenting, which is high on demandingness but low on warmth and responsiveness, imposing strict standards with little or no room for dialogue, (2) indulgent or permissive parenting, which is high on warmth and responsiveness but low on demandingness, allowing "children to regulate their own activities as much as possible," and not insisting that children "obey externally defined standards," and (3) neglectful or disengaged parenting, low on both responsiveness and demandingness.[31] Studies have found that adolescents from authoritative homes report "significantly higher academic competence, significantly lower levels of problem behavior, and significantly higher levels of psychosocial development than adolescents from authoritarian, indulgent, or neglectful households."[32] Further, while authoritarian parenting is less effective than authoritative parenting, and both authoritarian and indulgent parenting are better than neglectful parenting, authoritarian parenting tends to produce better outcomes overall than indulgent parenting. Adolescent children of authoritarian parents "report less school misconduct, less drug use, fewer somatic symptoms, and a more positive orientation toward school than their indulgently reared peers."[33] Adolescents with indulgent parents scored better than those with authoritarian parents only on measures related to positive self-perception.[34] It seems, therefore, that while the best parenting includes high levels of both discipline and responsiveness (including respect for children's autonomy), lack of discipline tends to be more harmful than lack of responsiveness even in the adolescent years.[35]

The second potential danger of autonomy education can therefore be summarized as follows: The firm and consistent exercise of parental authority is important for the well-being of children all the way until adulthood. Autonomy education, by its very nature, encourages children to be critical of ethical claims or standards based on authority, and to trust their own reasoning instead. Education for autonomy could therefore be detrimental even to adolescent children—who often lack moral insight and whose reasoning is often still coopted by the influence of sub-rational desire—to the extent that it undermines the moral authority of parents by encouraging children to criticize their parents' values and offering sympathetic portrayals of ways of life that the parents have taught their children to view as bad.

This brings me to my third concern about autonomy education, which is that the weakening of parental moral authority can also undermine parents' efforts to foster moral virtue in their children, to teach habits of self-mastery, courage, fairness, generosity, and so forth. To introduce children to the complexity of the moral life and to competing conceptions of the good life before they have learned any one coherent moral view and have developed a strong moral character by habitually governing their actions in accordance with that view may thwart the process of developing a rational dominion over sub-rational desire. Even in adolescence, children's habits of self-dominion are likely in many cases to be too fragile to survive a critique of the conception of the good that grounded them. Exposure to the merits of conflicting moral views and to criticisms of the moral views that parents are trying to inculcate endangers the morally immature person's still precarious dominion of reason over sub-rational desire. This is especially the case when such exposure occurs in school—as opposed to inevitable contact with other viewpoints in the larger culture through the Internet, television, billboards, magazines, social interactions, and so forth—given that children are taught to view school teachers as trustworthy authorities.[36]

Conclusion

Particularly in cases where it conflicts most starkly with the values children are learning at home, autonomy education may be more harmful than helpful to children (even in secondary school) by (1) tempting children to abandon a good way of life without sufficient reason under the sway of sub-rational desire (thus weakening their capacity for autonomous adherence to a conception of the good), (2) undermining the parental authority that even adolescent children need to guide their still-immature practical reasoning, and (3) threatening the consolidation of moral virtue in children by leading them to question the value system that grounds those virtues. Further, on the Aristotelian account one could argue that a person who is not autonomous in the liberal sense but who possesses moral virtue is better off than the person who possesses *only* the cognitive conditions of autonomy but whose actions are effectively ruled by sub-rational desire. We should be *more* concerned about dangers to the development and consolidation of the moral virtues than about dangers to the development of the cognitive conditions of autonomy, since the former are preconditions for the latter, and the former are more indispensable to overall human well-being. Thus while advocates of mandatory autonomy education rightfully note the value of autonomy for leading a good life, their arguments are insufficient to show that those who receive an explicitly autonomy-promoting education are, on balance, better prepared to lead a good life than those whose parents shelter them from competing conceptions of the good life.[37] For while the latter are more likely to end up without a commitment to ongoing rational revision of their values, and to lack sympathetic understanding of diverse ways of life, the former (particularly if the values taught in school conflict sharply with those taught at home), are more likely to end up morally confused, incapable of the steadfastness and commitment required for autonomous adherence to a conception of the good, lacking moral virtue more generally, or succumbing to the ever-present temptations to substance abuse, irresponsible sexual conduct, and other problem behaviors that can have long-lasting negative consequences. These neglected considerations should play a more prominent role in debates about whether or not mandatory autonomy education is truly in the best interests of children.

The Catholic University of America

Notes

1. This paper uses material that (subsequent to the 2015 ACPA meeting) was published in Chapter 3 of my book, *To Whom do Children Belong? Parental Rights, Civic Education and Children's Autonomy* (New York: Cambridge University Press, 2016). Reprinted with permission.

2   While some authors defend mandatory autonomy education on civic grounds, here I will focus exclusively on child-centered arguments for autonomy education. Child-centered arguments for autonomy education can be found in: "The Child's Right to an Open Future," in *Whose Child? Children's Rights, Parental Authority, and State Power*, ed. William Aiken and Hugh LaFollette (Totowa, NJ: Rowman & Littlefield, 1980); Bruce Ackerman, *Social Justice in the Liberal State* (Binghamton: Yale University Press, 1980); Eamonn Callan, *Creating Citizens* (New York: Clarendon Press, 1997); Harry Brighouse, *School Choice and Social Justice* (New York: Oxford University Press, 2000); James G. Dwyer, *Religious Schools v. Children's Rights* (Ithaca: Cornell University Press, 1998); Ian MacMullen, *Faith in Schools? Autonomy, Citizenship, and Religious Education in the Liberal State* (Princeton: Princeton University Press, 2007); Rob Reich, "Testing the Boundaries of Parental Authority Over Education: The Case of Homeschooling," in *Moral and Political Education*, ed. Stephen Macedo and Yael Tamir (New York: New York University Press, 2002), p.275–313. Those who defend autonomy education primarily on civic grounds include (in addition to many of the above-cited authors): Amy Gutmann, *Democratic Education* (Princeton: Princeton University Press, 1999); Stephen Macedo, *Diversity and Distrust* (Cambridge: Harvard University Press, 2000). These theorists differ from one another on many points. Ackerman, for instance, bases his view on what he considers to be a fundamental liberal commitment to neutrality, and on the belief that non-autonomous lives cannot be good, premises which Gutmann (in *Democratic Education* though not in her earlier work on this topic) and Macedo explicitly reject. Nonetheless, each of these authors would support making some form of education for autonomy mandatory

(sometimes as a foreseen and desired side-effect of civic education) even against the objections of parents. Matthew Clayton takes this line of concern even further, arguing that it is a violation of children's autonomy for parents to inculcate *any* comprehensive conception of the good life in their children, even if they also expose their children to alternative views at the same time (Matthew Clayton, *Justice and Legitimacy in Upbringing* [Oxford: Oxford University Press, 2006]). In this paper I focus on the more moderate liberal view according to which it is permissible for parents to teach their children a comprehensive conception of the good as long as they also expose them to alternative views, both because this is the dominant view among liberals, and also because I believe that my critique of this view applies *a fortiori* to Clayton's view.

3. MacMullen, *Faith in Schools?*, 67.

4. I add this element to MacMullen's definition following Eamonn Callan's suggestion, explained further below, that "if possessing an autonomous character enables and inclines one to make appropriate revision, it must also enable and incline one to resist the pull towards inappropriate revision" (Eamonn Callan, "Autonomy, Childrearing and Good Lives," in *The Moral and Political Status of Children*, ed. David Archard and Colin M. MacLeod [New York: Oxford University Press, 2002], 118–141, at 127).

5. Callan is not as clear as MacMullen about the specific policy implications of his view, but his arguments seem to be in line with such a conclusion. Here I discount the case that Callan makes in *Creating Citizens* for mandatory autonomy education as required for the formation of future citizens, since my focus in this paper is exclusively on child-centered arguments for autonomy education (Eamonn Callan, *Creating Citizens* [New York: Oxford University Press, 1997]).

6. Ibid., 152.

7. Callan, "Autonomy, Childrearing and Good Lives," 127.

8. Ibid., 134.

9. MacMullen, *Faith in Schools?*, 184.

10. Ibid., 186.

11. Ibid., 187.

12. Ibid.

13. Ibid.

14. Ibid., 191.

15. Ibid., 188.

16. Ibid., 191.

17. *Nicomachean Ethics* II.1, 1103b25

18. *Nicomachean Ethics* I.13, 1102b28

19. *Nicomachean Ethics* IX.4, 1166b5–28

20. Art is the perfection of practical reason as directed towards making. The difference between acting and making is a complex one that I cannot enter into here. For an interesting discussion, see Sarah Broadie, *Ethics With Aristotle* (Oxford University Press, 1993), 202ff.

21. *Nicomachean Ethics* VI.12, 1144a37.

22. *Nicomachean Ethics* VI.12, 1144a34–36.

23. Brian C. Partridge, "The Mature Minor: Some Critical Psychological Reflections on the Empirical Bases," *Journal of Medicine and Philosophy* 38 (2013): 283–299, at 292. One factor related to adolescents' tendency toward short-sighted decision-making is that, due to neurobiological changes, sensation seeking rises to a peak during adolescence, thus "heightening reward salience by making the experience of potentially rewarding stimuli more rewarding" (Evan Wilhelms and Valerie Reyna, "Fuzzy Trace Theory and Medicial Decisions by Minors: Differences in Reasoning between Adolescents and Adults," *Journal of Medicine and Philosophy* 38 [2013]: 268–282, at 271).

24. Ibid., 293.

25. Ibid.

26. Wilhelms and Reyna, "Fuzzy Trace Theory and Medicial Decisions by Minors," 272.

27. Ibid., 273–276.

28. Ibid., 273.

29. *Nicomachean Ethics* VI.11, 1143b8–13; Louis Groarke, *An Aristotelian Account of Induction: Creating Something from Nothing* (Canada: McGill-Queen's University Press, 2009), 243.

30. *Nicomachean Ethics* I.3, 1095a10.

31. Diana Baumrind, "Rearing Competent Children," in *Child Development Today and Tomorrow*, ed. William Damon (San Francisco: Jossey-Bass, Inc., 1989), 349–378, at 353–354; L. J. Crockett and R. Hayes, "Parenting Practices and Styles," *Encyclopedia of Adolescence*, Vol. 2 (Elsevier, 2011), 241–248. doi: 10.1016/B978-0-12-373915-5.00077-2.

32. Susie D. Lamborn et al., "Patterns of Competence and Adjustment among Adolescents from Authoritative, Authoritarian, Indulgent, and Neglectful Families," *Child Development* 62, no. 5 (Oct. 1991): 1049–1065, at 1057. See also Patrick C. L. Heaven and Joseph Ciarrochi, "Parental Styles, Conscientiousness, and Academic Performance in High School: A Three-Wave Longitudinal Study," *Personality and Social Psychology Bulletin* 34, no. 5 (April 2008): 451–461.

33. Lamborn et al., "Patterns of Competence and Adjustment among Adolescents," 1059. See also Sigrun Adalbjarnardottir and Leifur G. Hafsteinsson, "Adolescents' Perceived Parenting Styles and Their Substance Use: Concurrent and Longitudinal Analyses," *Journal of Research on Adolescence* 11(4) (2001): 401–423.

34. Ibid., 1059.

35. It is also interesting to note that among Asian and African American adolescents, authoritarian parenting produces outcomes almost as positive as authoritative parenting, and that some minority children may actually benefit from a more authoritarian parenting style. Crockett and Hayes, "Parenting Practices and Styles," 241–248; Laurence Steinberg et al., "Over-Time Changes in Adjustment and Competence among Adolescents from Authoritative, Authoritarian, Indulgent, and Neglectful Families," *Child Development* 65, no. 3 (June 1994): 754–770.

36. The renowned psychologist and sociologist Francis Ianni conducted some noteworthy empirical research that supports this concern. Ianni and his associates observed and interviewed thousands of adolescents in a variety of communities across the United States in order to understand the roots of both success and failure in the delicate transition from

adolescence to adulthood. Ianni's conclusion is that "the most important determinant of how adolescence will be experienced and with what results" is "how the various social contexts of a community are integrated in terms of the continuity and congruence of their values, norms and rules." In other words, Ianni found that adolescents fare best—in terms of outcomes like academic and professional achievement, avoidance of delinquency, substance abuse and other problem behaviors, and overall psychosocial development—when family, school, church and peer groups offer a coherent set of values and standards, rather than presenting conflicting messages. This research suggests that the construction of a mature and stable moral identity in adolescence relies heavily on the scaffolding of a harmonious external structure of values. (Francis Ianni, *The Search for Structure: A Report on American Youth Today* [New York: The Free Press, 1989], 15.)

37. However, my account does *not* imply that there is no place at all for autonomy education in schools. Indeed, the Aristotelian view that I have presented itself speaks in favor of teaching critical thinking skills and encouraging rational reflection on one's beliefs, in part by engaging with conflicting points of view. Yet this has to be done at the right times and in the right ways so as to avoid the dangers of undermining parental moral authority and/or producing moral confusion in those too immature to benefit from a critical approach to their own values and exposure to alternative worldviews. Thus my view would support, or at least be compatible with, *non*-mandatory autonomy education programs—programs with an "opt-out" option, or programs offered in situations where even poor parents have feasible alternatives to public schools. Such programs should be non-mandatory so that the potential harms of lack of coherence between the values taught in school and at home can be avoided as much as possible. Further, worries about the inability of standardized autonomy curricula to consider differences in the moral maturity of children at the same grade level, or about the possibly deleterious effects of exposing children to contradictory views too early or in the wrong way, would be mitigated if parents were more involved in designing and implementing such curricula, had the effective ability to choose a school in line with their values, and could exempt their children from classes that they judged to be potentially harmful.

American Catholic Philosophical Association
Eighty-Ninth Annual Meeting

Minutes of the 2015 Executive Council Meeting

Boston Park Plaza
8 October 2015, 6 pm to 11:30 pm

---

1. Dinner in Clarendon room, 6 to 7:15. Meeting in Hancock room, 7:30 to 11:30 pm.

2. *Present*: Jorge Garcia, President; Kevin Flannery, S.J., Vice President; Daniel Dahlstrom, Past President; Mirela Oliva, Secretary; Steven Jensen, Treasurer; Jean DeGroot; Alexander Eodice; John Greco; Theresa Tobin; Gregory Doolan; Jon McGinnis; Siobahn Nash-Marshall; Michael Rota; Jennifer Hart Weed; Therese Cory; Gloria Frost; W. Matthews Grant; Karen Stohr.

3. *Secretary's Report*: Presented by Mirela Oliva, with copies for members.
   Vote: No votes taken.

4. *Treasurer's Report*: Presented by Steven Jensen, with copies for members.
   Vote: No votes taken.

5. *Report of the Financial Affairs Committee:* The Committee has evaluated the investment proposal of Matthew O'Brien, ACPA member. O'Brien has raised concerns about investing in companies related to actions contrary to the Catholic teaching (abortion, contraception, forced labor) and has invited ACPA to transfer its investments to O'Brien and Green Company. The committee has recommended to retain all holdings with TIAA-CREEF. The council has made the friendly amendment that the committee enquire with TIAA-CREEF about the option of ethical funds.
   Vote: Approved, with one vote against and one abstention.

6. *ACPQ Report*: David Clemenson presented the report, with copies for members.
   Vote: The report has been approved.

© 2016, *Proceedings of the ACPA*, Vol. 89
doi: 10.5840/acpaproc20158964

7. Request of the ACPA Committee on Priestly Formation (David Foster) to apply for grants under the institutional affiliation to ACPA (501c3). Motion: Before the council is able to make a decision, the committee will answer the following questions for the next meeting in 2016: Whether the Committee is appointed by the president? Whether the committee follows ACPA by-laws? What is the internal structure of the committee? The number of members and the length of their terms? Whether the committee can submit a proposal under 501c3? Whether there should be a bishop on this committee?

Vote: approved, 1 abstention.

8. *Aquinas Medalist 2016*: About the merits of both candidates.

Vote: Prof. Adrian Peperzaak, Loyola University, Chicago.

9. *Future Annual Meetings*: The 2016 meeting will take place in San Francisco, host University of San Francisco. Local contact: Prof. Thomas Cavanaugh.

10. *Election of two Executive Council members to the Executive Committee*: Jon McGinnis and Michael Rota.

11. Pro-Forma Election of New Members to the ACPA.

Vote: All approved.

12. Proposal ACPA Local Chapters (Timothy Kearns). Motion: The Planning Committee will explore in consultation with Prof. Kearns the development of a pilot project of Local Chapters.

Vote: Approved, 5 abstentions.

13. Diversity Proposal (Jorge Garcia). Motion: The Planning Committee will analyze the possibility of sponsorship of a presentation at the Annual Summer Institute for Diversity at Rutgers University.

Vote: Approved.

14. Proposal to support recent PhDs (Siobhan Nash-Marshall). Motion: The Planning Committee will consider ways to provide financial subsidies to unaffiliated recent PhDs for 3 years after their terminal degree.

Vote: Approved, 3 opposed.

15. Proposal to have remote participation via SKYPE for Council members who can not attend the meeting (Sarah Byers).

Vote: Rejected, 1 abstention.

Mirela Oliva
ACPA Secretary

October 8, 2015

American Catholic Philosophical Association

Secretary's Report (2014–2015)

I. News from the National Office

A. 2015 Meeting

1. For this meeting we had 42 papers submitted. Of these papers, 18 submissions were submitted as eligible for the Young Scholars Award. The members of the program review committee were: Jeffrey Bloechl, Thomas Cavanaugh, Raymond Hain, Patrick Toner, and John Zeis.

2. The hotel room contingent sold out before the deadline; we asked for and obtained an increase in rooms and a change of the deadline from September 15 to September 22. For the next meeting, it will remain difficult to contract a higher number. The hotel is asking for a minimal occupancy. They count not only the number of booked rooms, but also the number of nights booked. Not all the members booked the full amount of nights in the past.

3. We had 38 satellite sessions, including 4 ACPA-sponsored satellite sessions. Many sessions have overlapped, so we might consider scheduling satellite sessions also during the 5–7 PM time slot.

B. 2016 Meeting

1. The meeting will take place in San Francisco, hosted by University of San Francisco. Local contact: Thomas Cavanaugh.

2. The President-Elect Kevin Flannery S.J. has proposed the topic "Justice: Then and Now." The full description of the topic and the guidelines for papers submission are posted on the ACPA website. The submission deadline is March 1, 2016.

C. 2017 Meeting

We do not have yet a clear offer for 2017. St Vincent College has expressed interest. Local contact: Christopher McMahon.

©2016, *Proceedings of the ACPA*, Vol. 89
doi: 10.5840/acpaproc20158965

pp. 313–317

D. ACPA Elections

1. The complete results of this year's ACPA election (concluded April 1, 2015) are as follows:

Vice-President/President-Elect:
Thomas Hibbs (Baylor University)

Executive Council Members:
Kevin White (Catholic University of America)
Eileen Sweeney (Boston College)
Catherine Jack Deavel (University of St. Thomas, Minnesota)
Mark Gossiaux (Loyola University New Orleans)
Michael O'Neill (Providence College)

On behalf of the ACPA, I would like to thank these newly-elected scholars, and to thank all who were willing to stand for election.

2. The new election ballot (2015-2016) is ready and will be mailed soon. The bios of the candidates are now posted online. The deadline is 1 April 2016.

II. ACPA Membership

Membership Category	For 2015 Meeting Active in 2014	For 2014 Meeting Active in 2013	For 2013 Meeting Active in 2012	For 2012 Meeting Active in 2011	For 2011 Meeting Active in 2010	For 2010 Meeting Active in 2009	For 2009 Meeting Active in 2008
Professor	142	140	125	133	153	159	176
Associate Professor	104	135	117	113	126	120	134
Assistant Professor	186	155	133	144	201	222	167
Instructor	0	0	0	0	0	0	41
Lecturer	0	0	0	0	0	0	36
Student	215	256	225	181	250	235	238
Emeritus	89	93	89	100	106	110	125
Associate	118	99	84	74	80	78	81
Institutional	66	67	63	59	78	76	14
Library	0	0	0	0	0	0	60
Index/Exchange	19	19	20	21	22	0	0
Life	73	73	73	71	68	77	79
Totals	1012	1037	929	896	1084	1077	1151

A clearer idea of trends perhaps can be gathered from the following chart, which tracks membership from the year the person first became a member of the ACPA. B4 counts dues paying members whose first membership year has not been able to be traced.

Old Members	2014	2013	2012	2011	2010	2009	2008
B4	95	105	105	113	118	135	141
1941	0	0	0	0	0	0	0
1942	0	0	0	0	0	0	0
1946	0	0	1	1	1	1	1
1948	0	0	0	0	1	1	1
1949	0	0	0	0	0	0	1
1950	1	1	1	1	1	1	2
1952	1	1	1	1	1	2	2
1953	0	0	0	0	0	1	1
1954	2	3	3	3	3	3	3
1955	0	0	0	0	1	3	3
1956	1	1	1	1	1	1	2
1957	3	3	3	3	3	3	3
1958	3	3	3	4	4	4	4
1959	1	1	1	2	1	3	3
1960	5	5	5	5	8	10	10
1961	1	1	1	2	3	3	3
1962	1	1	1	1	2	2	2
1963	5	5	5	5	5	6	6
1964	4	4	4	4	5	6	6
1965	3	3	3	4	4	4	4
1966	3	3	3	4	4	5	5
1967	3	3	3	5	6	6	6
1968	4	4	4	5	6	6	7
1969	4	4	4	4	6	6	6
1970	6	6	6	7	9	10	11
1971	2	2	2	2	2	2	2
1972	3	4	4	4	4	4	5
1973	2	2	2	2	2	2	2
1974	10	10	10	10	11	11	11
1975	6	7	7	8	8	8	9
1976	4	4	4	6	6	6	6
1977	5	5	5	5	5	5	7
1978	6	6	6	6	7	7	7
1979	1	1	1	1	1	2	3
1980	9	9	9	9	9	10	10
1981	1	2	2	2	2	1	1
1982	3	3	3	3	3	4	4
1983	4	4	3	3	3	3	3
1984	1	1	1	1	1	2	2
1985	5	5	5	5	5	5	5
1986	1	1	1	2	2	2	3
1987	9	8	8	8	7	7	8
1988	4	4	4	4	4	3	3
1989	6	6	6	6	6	6	6
1990	7	7	7	7	8	11	9
1991	6	6	5	7	9	11	13
1992	13	12	13	13	14	14	15

Old Members	2014	2013	2012	2011	2010	2009	2008
1993	40	44	44	46	61	63	65
1994	12	15	14	16	19	19	19
1995	10	13	12	13	13	13	13
1996	9	10	9	9	10	16	20
1997	15	15	15	19	22	25	28
1998	8	8	7	8	12	11	13
1999	26	27	28	33	37	42	50
2000	23	23	23	25	31	37	40
2001	31	30	27	32	40	46	50
2002	21	21	19	23	33	37	39
2003	16	18	18	20	22	25	28
2004	12	14	12	14	19	22	28
2005	24	26	24	28	40	45	57
2006	22	23	22	31	43	49	68
2007	32	33	30	35	47	61	96
2008	36	43	41	44	64	96	101
2009	32	40	36	44	85	92	90
2010	32	37	36	40	54	53	
2011	61	77	77	127	120		
2012	41	78	81	0			
2013	86	86	88				
2014	87	90					
2015	82						
Totals	**1012**	**1037**	**929**	**896**	**1084**	**1100**	**1172**

III. ACPA Publications

A. ACPQ

Distribution Type	2014	2013	2012	2011	2010	2009	2008	2007	2006	2005
ACPA Members	993	1048	909	875	1062	1077	1151	1161	1166	1182
Subscribers	409	470	438	456	452	485	487	453	488	531
Index/Exchange	29	30	33	34	36	36	37	34	49	49
Totals	**1434**	**1518**	**1380**	**1365**	**1550**	**1598**	**1675**	**1648**	**1703**	**1762**

B. Proceedings

Distribution Type	2014	2013	2012	2011	2010	2009	2008	2007	2006	2005
ACPA Members	993	1018	909	875	1062	1077	1151	1161	1166	1182
Subscribers	124	165	109	174	131	88	133	148	129	120
Exchanges	19	19	24	25	32	27	27	27	42	43
Totals	**1136**	**1202**	**1042**	**1074**	**1225**	**1192**	**1311**	**1336**	**1337**	**1345**

IV. Thanks and Acknowledgments

On behalf of the ACPA, I would first like to thank my graduate assistant Andrew Grimes for his hard work through the year 2014–2015. I would also like to thank Catherine Peters and Francisco Plaza for their work at the 2015 meeting. Finally, I would like to thank the University of St. Thomas (Houston, TX) for its financial and institutional support of the National Office of the ACPA.

Respectfully submitted,

Mirela Oliva
ACPA Secretary

Assistant Professor of Philosophy
Center for Thomistic Studies
University of St. Thomas, Houston

October 8, 2015

American Catholic Philosophical Association

Treasurer's Report (2014)

I. Financial Statement

The Financial Statement shows that 2014 was a positive year for the ACPA. In 2014, the ACPA's total net gain of revenues over losses was $34,356 (compared to 94,917 in 2013). The Financial Statement shows that at the end of 2014, the Association's total liabilities and net assets were $720,496 (compared to $688,603 in 2013). Of this amount,$717,948 represents net (unrestricted) assets (compared to $683,592 in unrestricted assets in 2013). In 2014, therefore, the ACPA's net assets increased by $34,356.

	2014	2013
Total Assets	$720,496	$688,603
Liabilities	−$2,548	−$5,011
Net Assets	$717,948	$683,592
Gain or Loss from Previous Year	$34,356	$94,917

II. Annual Revenues and Expenses

Between 2013 and 2014, total annual revenues decreased by $28,160 (total revenues in 2014 were $133,487, while in 2013 they were $161,647), and total annual expenses increased by 32,401 (total expenses in 2014 were $99,131, while in 2013 they were $66,730).

	2014	2013
Annual Revenues	$133,487	$161,647
Change in Revenues	−$28,160	$17,731
Annual Expenses	$99,131	$66,730
Change in Expenses	$32,401	$1,400

©2016, *Proceedings of the ACPA*, Vol. 89
doi: 10.5840/acpaproc20158966

III. Annual Meeting

A summary of revenues and expenses in connection with the 2014 Annual Meeting is attached. The Association is very grateful to the local host institution —The Catholic University of America—for its direct donations of $6,000 in connection with the meeting. The Association would also like to thank Boston University for its gift of $1800. The attached financial statements show that the 2014 Annual Meeting resulted in a $36,592 deficit of expenses over revenues (compared to a deficit of $9977 in 2013).

	2014	2013
Annual Meeting Earnings or Losses	−$36,592	−$9,977

IV. Assets and Investments—Total: $720,496

The Statement of Financial Position lists our assets on December 31, 2014, as follows:

A. Cash and Cash Equivalents: $67,283

On December 31, 2014, the Association held $67,283 in Chase Manhattan checking and savings accounts, a TIAA-CREF money market, and the University of St. Thomas accounts.

	2014
Chase accounts	$51,822
TIAA-CREF	$11,473
UST accounts	$3,988
Total Cash	$67,283

B. Inventory and Supplies: $534

C. Non-cash Investments: $640,543

On December 31, 2014, the Association's non-cash investment holdings with TIAA-CREF were valued at $640,543.

V. Liabilities—Total: $2,548

Account Payable: $2,548

The amount of $2,548 represents expenses incurred by the ACPA in 2014 (such as fees attributable to work performed in 2014), but not yet paid for until after December 31, 2014, i.e., after the closing date for 2014 statements from the ACPA's bank and investment manager. Accordingly, the ACPA carried these not-yet-paid expenses as a liability.

VI. Reminder

The Association depends for revenue on membership dues and subscription payments. Therefore, the National Office reminds members to be prompt in paying their dues and/or subscription charges.

VII. Donations

As always, the Association welcomes donations. Since the ACPA is a tax-exempt organization under section 501(c)(3) of the Internal Revenue Code, all donations to the Association are tax-deductible to the full extent allowed by law.

VIII. Acknowledgements

On the behalf of the Association, the Treasurer would like to thank the University of St. Thomas in Houston for its generous financial support of the Association throughout 2014. In 2014, the Association received $9,000 in cash donations and $13,000 in in-kind donations from the University of St. Thomas, for a total of $22,000.

American Catholic Philosophical Association
Financial Statements

Years Ended December 31, 2014 and 2013

© 2016, *Proceedings of the ACPA*, Vol. 89
doi: 10.5840/acpaproc20158967

American Catholic Philosophical Association
Accountants' Compilation Report

Years Ended December 31, 2014 and 2013

TABLE OF CONTENTS

American Catholic Philosophical Association
Independent Accountants' Compilation Report

Years Ended December 31, 2014 and 2013

To the Board of Directors
American Catholic Philosophical Association
Houston, Texas

We have compiled the accompanying statements of financial position of American Catholic Philosophical Association (the Association) as of December 31, 2014 and 2013, and the related statements of activities and changes in net assets and cash flows for the years then ended, and the accompanying supplementary information contained in Schedule I. We have not audited or reviewed the accompanying financial statements and supplementary information and, accordingly, do not express an opinion or provide any assurance about whether the financial statements and supplementary information are in accordance with accounting principles generally accepted in the United States of America.

Management is responsible for the preparation and fair presentation of the financial statements and supplementary information in accordance with accounting principles generally accepted in the United States of America and for designing, implementing and maintaining internal control relevant to the preparation and fair presentation of the financial statements and supplementary information.

Our responsibility is to conduct the compilation in accordance with Statements on Standards for Accounting and Review Services issued by the American Institute of Certified Public Accountants. The objective of a compilation is to assist management in presenting financial information in the form of financial statements and supplementary information without undertaking to obtain or provide any assurance that there are no material modifications that should be made to the financial statements and supplementary information.

Management has elected to omit substantially all of the disclosures required by accounting principles generally accepted in the United States of America. If the omitted disclosures were included in the financial statements and supplementary information, they might influence the user's conclusions about the Association's financial position, results of operations and cash flows. Accordingly, the financial statements and supplementary information are not designed for those who are not informed about such matters.

Hutchinson and Bloodgood LLP

May 8, 2015

American Catholic Philosophical Association
Statements of Financial Position

Years Ended December 31, 2014 and 2013

ASSETS	2014	2013
Current assets		
Cash—checking and savings	$ 67,283	$ 95,101
Accounts receivable	9,636	27,125
Prepaid expense	2,500	—
Inventory and supplies	534	572
Investments, at market value	640,543	565,805
Total assets	$ 720,496	$ 688,603
LIABILITIES AND NET ASSETS		
Current liabilities		
Accounts payable and accrued expenses	$ 2,548	$ 5,011
Unrestricted net assets	717,948	683,592
Total liabilities and net assets	$720,496	$ 688,603

See independent accountants' compilation report.

American Catholic Philosophical Association
Statements of Activities and Changes in Net Assets

Years Ended December 31, 2014 and 2013

SUPPORT AND REVENUES	2014	2013
Annual meeting	$ 30,936	$ 31,472
Royalties	31,290	29,203
Donations from University of St. Thomas	21,500	19,400
Interest and dividends	9,247	7,373
Net realized and unrealized gain in investments	40,514	74,199
Total support and revenues	133,487	161,647
EXPENSES		
Annual meeting	67,528	41,449
Salaries and wages	15,208	12,900
Insurance	1,474	1,312
Accounting services	3,900	3,800
Web service charges	113	250
Travel stipend	10,908	7,019
Total expenses	99,131	66,730
Increase in unrestricted net assets	34,356	94,917
NET ASSETS, BEGINNING OF YEAR	683,592	588,675
NET ASSETS, END OF YEAR	$ 717,948	$ 683,592

See independent accountants' compilation report.

American Catholic Philosophical Association
Statements of Cash Flows

Years Ended December 31, 2014 and 2013

CASH FLOWS FROM OPERATING ACTIVITIES	2014	2013
Increase in unrestricted net assets	$ 34,356	$ 94,917
Adjustments to reconcile increase in unrestricted net assets to net cash provided by operating activities		
Net realized and unrealized loss (gain) in investments	(40,514)	(74,199)
Net change in:		
Accounts receivable	17,489	(4,286)
Inventory and supplies	38	39
Prepaid expense	(2,500)	—
Accounts payable and accrued expenses	(2,463)	(243)
Net cash provided by operating activities	6,406	16,228
CASH FLOWS FROM INVESTING ACTIVITIES		
Net purchases in investments	(34,224)	(7,335)
Net increase (decrease) in cash	(27,818)	8,893
CASH, beginning of year	95,101	86,208
CASH, end of year	$ 67,283	$ 95,101

See independent accountants' compilation report.

American Catholic Philosophical Association
Supplementary Information

Years Ended December 31, 2014 and 2013

American Catholic Philosophical Association
Schedule I: Revenues and Expenses of Annual Meeting

Years Ended December 31, 2014 and 2013

REVENUES	2014	2013
Registration and banquet	$ 23,136	$ 17,472
Donations:		
The Catholic University of America	6,000	—
Boston University	1,800	—
Notre Dame University	—	6,000
Marian University	—	4,000
Indiana University - Purdue University Indianaplis	—	4,000
	30,936	31,472
EXPENSES		
Banquet expenses	55,669	26,868
Honorarium expenses	1,800	4,000
Young scholar award	1,000	500
Aquinas medal and engraving	68	63
Meeting registration services	976	3,320
Printing and duplicating expenses	3,309	3,128
Postage	509	800
Travel	4,197	2,770
	67,528	41,449
Shortage of revenues over expenses	$ (36,592)	$ (9,977)

See independent accountants' compilation report.

Necrology (2015–January 2017)

Dominic Balestra, Fordham University (2016)

Dr. Charles Lohr, Fordham University (2015)

John Deely, St Vincent Seminary & College (2017)

Dr. George F. McLean RVP, Catholic University of America (2016)

Dr. Robert Joyce, St John's University (2014)

His Eminence Francis George OMI, Archdiocese of Chicago (2016)

Rev. Joseph Zycinski, Pontifical Faculty of Theology (2011)

Requiescant in pace.

© 2016, *Proceedings of the ACPA*, Vol. 89
doi: 10.5840/acpaproc20158968

Available Back Issues of the *Proceedings*

Volumes

No.	Year	
68	1994	*Reason in History*
69	1995	*The Recovery of Form*
70	1996	*Philosophy of Technology*
74	2000	*Philosophical Theology*
75	2001	*Person, Soul, and Immortality*
76	2002	*Philosophy at the Boundary of Reason*
77	2003	*Philosophy and Intercultural Understanding*
78	2004	*Reckoning with the Tradition*
79	2005	*Social Justice: Its Theory and Practice*
80	2006	*Intelligence and the Philosophy of Mind*
81	2007	*Freedom, Will, and Nature*
82	2008	*Forgiveness*
83	2009	*Reason in Context*
84	2010	*Philosophy and Language*
85	2011	*Science, Reason, and Religion*
86	2012	*Philosophy in the Abrahamic Traditions*
87	2013	*Aristotle Now and Then*
88	2014	*Dispositions, Habits, and Virtues*

Please send orders to:

Philosophy Documentation Center
P.O. Box 7147
Charlottesville, VA 22906-7147
Web: www.pdcnet.org

800-444-2419 (U.S. & Canada) or
434-220-3300
Fax: 434-220-3301
E-mail: order@pdcnet.org

All back issues of the *Proceedings* are $50 each, plus shipping per volume outside the US. Make checks payable to the Philosophy Documentation Center. Please send checks in U.S. dollars only. Visa, MasterCard, American Express, and Discover are accepted for your convenience.

© 2016, *Proceedings of the ACPA*, Vol. 89
doi: 10.5840/acpaproc20158969